Chinese Television and National Identity Construction

This book examines music-entertainment programmes on China Central Television, China's only national-level television network, exploring how such programmes project a nuanced image of China's identity and position in the world, which is in step with China's Party-state nationalism, and at the same time flexible and open to change as China's circumstances change. It considers the background of the development of television in China, and the political struggles between provincial and national television. It discusses the portrayal of majority Chinese, and of ethnic minorities and their music, which, the author argues, are shown as fitting with the Party-state rhetoric of 'a unitary multiethnic state'. It outlines how the Chinese of Greater China – Hong Kong, Taiwan, Macao and the overseas Chinese – are incorporated into a mainland centred Chinese identity, and it shows how the performances of foreign personalities emphasize the personalities' attraction to China, the uniqueness of the Chinese nation and Chinese civilization, and the revitalized role of China in the world. Overall, the book demonstrates how the variations of Chinese identity fit with the prevailing political ideology in China and with the emerging theme of a China-centred world.

Lauren Gorfinkel is a Lecturer in the Department of Media, Music, Communication and Cultural Studies at Macquarie University, Australia.

Media, Culture and Social Change in Asia

Series Editor
Stephanie Hemelryk Donald, University of New South Wales

Editorial Board:
Gregory N. Evon, University of New South Wales
Devleena Ghosh, University of Technology, Sydney
Peter Horsfield, RMIT University, Melbourne
Michael Keane, Curtin University
Tania Lewis, RMIT University, Melbourne
Vera Mackie, University of Wollongong
Kama Maclean, University of New South Wales
Laikwan Pang, Chinese University of Hong Kong
Gary Rawnsley, Aberystwyth University
Ming-yeh Rawnsley, School of Oriental and African Studies, University of London
Jo Tacchi, Lancaster University
Adrian Vickers, University of Sydney
Jing Wang, MIT
Ying Zhu, City University of New York

The aim of this series is to publish original, high-quality work by both new and established scholars in the West and the East, on all aspects of media, culture and social change in Asia.

For a full list of available titles please visit: www.routledge.com/Media-Culture-and-Social-Change-in-Asia-Series/book-series/SE0797

50. Singapore Cinema – New Perspectives
Edited by Liew Kai Khiun and Stephen Teo

51. Taiwan Cinema
International Reception and Social Change
Edited by Kuei-fen Chiu, Ming-yeh T. Rawnsley and Gary D. Rawnsley

52. Chinese Television and National Identity Construction
The Cultural Politics of Music-Entertainment Programmes
Lauren Gorfinkel

Chinese Television and National Identity Construction
The Cultural Politics of Music-Entertainment Programmes

Lauren Gorfinkel

LONDON AND NEW YORK

First published 2018
by Routledge
2 Park Square, Milton Park, Abingdon, Oxon OX14 4RN

and by Routledge
711 Third Avenue, New York, NY 10017

Routledge is an imprint of the Taylor & Francis Group, an informa business

© 2018 Lauren Gorfinkel

The right of Lauren Gorfinkel to be identified as author of this work has been asserted by her in accordance with sections 77 and 78 of the Copyright, Designs and Patents Act 1988.

All rights reserved. No part of this book may be reprinted or reproduced or utilised in any form or by any electronic, mechanical, or other means, now known or hereafter invented, including photocopying and recording, or in any information storage or retrieval system, without permission in writing from the publishers.

Trademark notice: Product or corporate names may be trademarks or registered trademarks, and are used only for identification and explanation without intent to infringe.

British Library Cataloguing in Publication Data
A catalogue record for this book is available from the British Library

Library of Congress Cataloging in Publication Data
A catalogue record for this book has been requested.

ISBN: 978-1-138-78297-6 (hbk)
ISBN: 978-1-315-76888-5 (ebk)

Typeset in Times New Roman
by Out of House Publishing

Contents

Foreword	vi
Preface	ix
Note on Romanization and Chinese names	xiii
Acknowledgements	xiv
1 Introduction: national identity in the Chinese context	1
2 Music-entertainment culture under the Chinese Communist Party	26
3 Overview of music-entertainment television in China	50
4 Multiethnic China	84
5 Greater China	122
6 Foreign identities	171
7 Conclusion	213
8 Glossary	221
Index	242

Foreword

Stephanie Hemelryk Donald

The book series *Media Culture and Social Change in Asia* has been running for 16 years (2001–2017). In that period, we have published more than 50 books and we continue to attract new scholars and established researchers to our list. The journey of the series has been exciting in several aspects, not least of which has been to observe the establishment of our sub-disciplines – media and film studies in Asia – as staple elements of academic global discourse on culture and society. That was not the case when the series began (although we can only claim to be a small part in this progress). There were already many fine scholars working in the region, but their work was not always afforded the visibility it deserved. Now, it is difficult to imagine an informed conversation about the global media or about world cinema that will not turn to Asia. Asia is after all a massive and vibrant element of the world we share. India and Indonesia are the most populous democracies on earth and with that status they pose communications problematics associated with the socio-political responsibility of maintaining an informed public. China continues its rise as a political actor and major player in world trade as well as an ambitious creator of local and global media content. South Korea, Japan and all the nations, maritime and mainland, that make up Southeast Asia have media and film cultures that describe and define communication and social practice for millions of people.

The role of media in building social identity and fostering aspirational culture has been discussed in recent collections edited by Martin and Lewis (2016), and Tay and Turner (2015), both including contributions on Asia-wide instances of the role of television in everyday life. There is then plenty of evidence of the continuing ubiquity of television as a core medium of national consumption, notwithstanding the specificity of different audience tastes, aspirations and needs (see for instance Barendregt and Hudson (2016) on Islamic publics and new televisual articulations of modernity in Malaysia). In this current volume, Lauren Gorfinkel concentrates her attention on China. She uses a wide knowledge of both contemporary Chinese history and Chinese media studies to position her book as a convincing argument for keeping an eye on television in the Chinese context. It is a well-timed intervention as there is so much to talk about in the second decade of the twenty-first century. China's current leadership under Xi Jinping has strong ambitions for the country's internal stability (as have all Chinese premiers since the death of Mao Zedong and the introduction of Reform). There is also, however, a notably strong push to create not only a harmonized population but one that accepts a common dream of China's past, present and future. This central tenet of propaganda meshes with commercial, cultural and indeed diasporic objectives by introducing new forms of nostalgic affect into the relationship between television, the nation and the population of the People's Republic.

Gorfinkel's study situates that relationship in the role of entertainment and music, national iconographies, the deployment of foreigners in China as points of difference or legitimation, and the encroaching management of ethnic minority identities. The book complements the works of fellow Australians, (especially the estimable work of Wanning Sun) and it is a great pleasure to have it in the series and on the shelves.

March 14, 2017
Sydney

References

Barendregt, B. and Hudson, C. (2016) Islam's got talent: television, performance and the Islamic public sphere in Malaysia. In F. Martin and T. Lewis (eds.) *Lifestyle Media in Asia: Consumption, Aspiration and Identity*. New York: Routledge, pp. 176–90.

Martin, F. and Lewis, T. (2016) *Lifestyle Media in Asia: Consumption, Aspiration and Identity*. New York: Routledge.

Tay, J. and Turner, G. (eds.) (2015) *Television Histories in Asia: Issues and Contexts*. London: Routledge.

Preface

One afternoon in July 2009, I was backstage, dressed and ready to step onto the China Central Television (CCTV) stage in Beijing. The studio space was abuzz and recording for the *'My Chinese Life' Global Chinese Storytelling Competition Awards Gala* (*'Wo de Hanyu shenghuo' quanqiu Hanyu gushi dasai jiexiao wanhui*) began. Soon it was my turn. I ran excitedly, brushing past Li Guyi, acclaimed by some as mainland China's first pop singer in the post-1978 reform era, and stayed in the shadows until host Zhao Baole announced the arrival of Gao Rui from Australia!

Dressed in a bright red and yellow Yi nationality performance costume (the Yi being one of China's officially recognized 55 minority nationalities), and with much fanfare, I walked onto the stage, smiled, and waved. As I stepped down towards host Zhao, he expressed an interest in my costume. 'Look, Gao Rui is already wearing our national clothes!' he exclaimed in Chinese. 'Can you tell me whose nationality these clothes are?' I responded that they were the clothes of the Yi people, the registered nationality of my husband.

On reviewing the edited version, broadcast on 29 October 2009 on CCTV4, CCTV's Chinese-language international channel, I noticed that as Zhao started talking about the clothing, the camera panned from my shoes up to my hat as if slowly absorbing the detail of the colour, design and, presumably, the curiosity, of an external 'other' (me, a white foreigner) dressed up in the costume of an internal 'other' (the Yi, a minority nationality). The question and answer session continued until my complex ethnic, national and gendered identity had been fully detailed, and indeed applauded. Zhao concluded the introduction with a mock prize, exclaiming: 'Ah! The China Wife Award should be given to her! She married a young Yi nationality man! Please welcome her with a round of applause.'

Piano music tinkled in the background, creating a sentimental mood. Then Zhao led me through intermittent prompts to tell and sing my Chinese story. It was about the power of popular Chinese music to unite me with Chinese culture, my husband and China itself in 2008, its Olympic year.

I had agreed to participate in the competition, which at the time entailed a performance in a tiny tea-house in Sydney, Australia. A small team of visiting Beijing Radio workers came armed with digital cameras as part of their global search for foreign Chinese-speaking talents. The performance was uploaded onto a website associated with Beijing Radio with the expectation of attracting votes from online viewers. A month later I was awarded with a trip to Beijing to perform on CCTV stage, beamed to millions in China and across the world.

My performance was one of numerous performances on Chinese television that have highlighted contemporary engagement with diverse ethnic and national communities both within China and around the world on a daily basis. Music-entertainment shows on Chinese television range from studio productions to large-scale outdoor entertainment shows, and from music video shows to reality singing contests. As with all television, these song and dance shows are infused with ideology and reveal shifting ideas about Chinese identity as a result of a range of political, socio-cultural and economic forces. This book interrogates the construction of identity in the context of Chinese television, with a focus on music-entertainment programming primarily targeting Mainland Chinese audiences. It examines nuances in how performers and participants on the television screens are represented as Chinese, ethnic minorities, the Han majority, Hong Kongers, Taiwanese, Macanese, overseas Chinese and foreigners, and considers how the programmes reflect relatively 'hardened' ideological messages concerning Chinese national identity and the state under the Communist Party as well as 'softer' cultural engagements with modernity and globalization.

In an era of increased globalization, people of different ethnicities have moved to China to work, study and live. There has also been massive internal migration within the world's most populous country, which has resulted in greater cross-cultural interactions between people of different ethnic groups and of different regions who bring their own cultural habits and norms. As nations undergo change they absorb and reject cultural influences such as clothes, music, languages and political ideas from heritages within and from abroad. The question of what it means to be 'Chinese' is also tied to shifting national and state agendas, desires and fears to be both distinct and to belong to the global community, as well as issues of legitimacy and control and questions such as 'who has the right to govern 'us'?' Within this context, this book examines strategies that entertainment producers and directors use to highlight the place of multiethnic nationalities within China as well as China's place within the global community, including how it deals with a variety of local, foreign, national and ethnic influences. It seeks to understand patterns in the way people perform 'as Chinese' and what these patterns can tell us about the vision that people with the power to influence the content of television programmes have for Chinese society and for China's place in the world today.

With a focus on the popular genre of music-entertainment programming, this book fills a gap in the study of music, politics, television and propaganda in China in the twenty-first century. It delves into the variety of music and entertainment practices that have been employed for the purposes of nation-building within the relatively controlled medium of China's state television and provides answers to such questions as: How is Chinese identity constructed and what are the roles of words, images and music in creating a sense of the Chinese nation? Who counts as Chinese? And how are cultural and ethnic 'others' marked? The book also considers how hybrid identities – such as Uyghur Chinese, Chinese Americans and foreigners in China – are portrayed and what they signify culturally and politically for the Chinese state.

Chapter 1 explains the significant role that cultural performance and television play in establishing notions of national identity, highlighting the constructed and fluid nature of national and ethnic identity formation. It details some of the major framings of Chinese ethnic identity in the post-1949 era under the leadership of the Chinese Communist Party, namely a multiethnic China, a Greater China and a civilizational China that foregrounds the role of foreigners in relation to the Chinese self. It sets the historical and theoretical groundwork that underpins the discussion of Chinese identity in this book.

Chapter 2 provides historical contextualization for the discussion of music-entertainment shows in latter chapters. It shows how music-entertainment television built on the traditions of creating a national music and entertainment culture through blends of Chinese and Western music that can be traced back to the nationalist movements of the early twentieth century. It shows how television built on the successes of radio, and highlights the role it has played under the control of the Chinese Communist Party in educating the Chinese people about the Party, their society and place in the world.

Chapter 3 examines competition and collaboration between the national broadcaster CCTV and provincial satellite broadcasters as Chinese television stations push for increased audiences, market share, and national and global recognition. The chapter also introduces the key music-entertainment programmes discussed in the book. In addition, it canvasses the regulations set by the State Administration of Press, Publication, Radio, Film and Television of the People's Republic of China (formerly the State Administration of Radio, Film, and Television) that have impacted on music-entertainment programming over the years, as well as issues of self-censorship and propaganda.

The focus of Chapters 4–6 is an in-depth analysis of the music, lyrics, spoken discourse and visuals across a broad spectrum of state-sanctioned Chinese music-entertainment television programmes during the latter four years of President Hu Jintao's leadership (2008–12), starting with China's Olympic year – a year of heightened nationalistic fervour – and the first four years of leadership under President Xi Jinping (2012–16). Examining these two time periods allows for a consideration of how programming and representations of ethnic pluralism and ethnic integration may have been impacted by CCP-led government cultural policies under different leaders, including the rhetorical shift from a Harmonious Society and Harmonious World under President Hu towards that of the China Dream under President Xi. While the focus is on the national broadcaster CCTV, which has a particular mandate to create a national feeling, these chapters provide comparisons with provincial satellite channels that target a nationwide audience.

Chapter 4 examines how PRC music-entertainment programmes construct the notion of a multiethnic China as well as how they frame selected 'minority' ethnic groups and the 'majority' Han. It examines a rigid, political and 'orthodox' style based on ideas of transforming, developing and modernizing folk songs in line with the discourse of state development and modernization; *yuanshengtai* ('original ecology'), which reflects social concerns about the preservation of 'intangible cultural heritage'; and ethno-pop blends that appeal to urban youth markets. Each of these styles is shown to work within the ideology of the 'unitary multiethnic state' while also reflecting changing directions in Party-state policies.

Chapter 5 interrogates the Greater China frame, including the constructions of Hong Kong, Macau, Taiwan and overseas Chinese from a mainland Chinese perspective. It highlights how PRC music-entertainment programmes are attempting to re-centre the PRC mainland within the Greater China sphere and how they celebrate the returns of Hong Kong and Macau to the motherland, and present hopes for unification with Taiwan. The chapter includes an analysis of how Chinese stars from outside of mainland China can help to promote state-sanctioned messages about China's prosperity and development while building a sense of greater PRC-centred Chinese solidarity.

Chapter 6 focuses on the performances of foreign identities on PRC music-entertainment programmes, including an in-depth analysis of particular performers from Liberia/Nigeria, Sierra Leone, the USA, the UK, Russia, Korea and Japan. Through consistent images of foreigners singing Chinese songs, speaking Chinese and wearing traditional Chinese clothing, it highlights 'harder' moments where messages of foreigners' attraction to China and mainstream Chinese culture are overtly presented to demonstrate the uniqueness of the Chinese nation and help build national pride among national audiences. It also highlights 'softer', more cosmopolitan moments where foreign stars help to validate China's global outlook.

Chapter 7 reviews the important role of music-entertainment television in helping to construct a sense of the contemporary Chinese self. It summarizes the political, economic and cultural significance of the types of framings that televised musical performances offer across the range of shows, with a particular focus on how music-entertainment helps to construct a sense of a China-centred world and of its attractiveness to its own citizens and the world. It also identifies areas for further research.

While the focus of this book is an in-depth textual analysis of a broad range of television programs, insights from original interviews with nine television practitioners who have worked on music-entertainment programmes on CCTV and provincial channels, including local adaptations of global formats like *The Voice*, have been woven in where relevant.

Note on Romanization and Chinese names

Throughout this book, I have used the *pinyin* system of Romanization for the names of programmes and performers following the Mandarin names as used on mainland Chinese television screens. I have also provided commonly known names of non-mainland performers if different to the *pinyin*, but have generally persisted with using their Mandarin names as a way of keeping a focus on PRC television framings. I have also maintained the Chinese word order for names in which the family name comes first. For instance, for Hong Kong singer Xie Tingfeng (Nicholas Tse), Xie is his surname and Tingfeng is his given name. However, I have maintained the English convention for Chinese-background authors of texts originally published in English, placing the surname last (e.g., Yiu-Fai Chow). Simplified Chinese characters for translations of songs, singers, films and other key terms mentioned in this study are included in the Glossary. All translations are my own unless otherwise noted.

Acknowledgements

This project began as a PhD dissertation at the University of Technology, Sydney, which was funded by an Australian Postgraduate Award (2008–12). Subsequent research and publication funding was received from the Faculty of Arts at Macquarie University (2015). I would like to thank my PhD supervisors Professor Wanning Sun, Professor Louise Edwards and Professor David Goodman for their exceptional guidance throughout and well beyond the PhD journey. I also appreciate the detailed feedback and constructive comments from Jeroen de Kloet, Anthony Fung, Xiaoling Zhang, Johanna Hood, Wei Lei and the anonymous reviewer for Routledge. Tingting Hu provided extremely helpful and timely assistance with extra research, glossaries, and interviews with television professionals during the latter stages of the project. Thanks also to commissioning editor Peter Sowdon for supporting the project, Bernadette Hince for proofreading, Victoria Chow and Rebecca Willford for copy-editing, indexing, and typesetting assistance and other staff at Routledge/Taylor and Francis who assisted with the project, as well as to Macquarie University colleagues and my students for providing the inspiration to clarify my ideas.

I also express my gratitude to the friendly staff at Radio Beijing Corporation who organized the inaugural *Global Chinese Storytelling Competition* in which I participated, as well as CCTV and the *Happy Five Continents* (*Tongle Wuzhou*) production team for the opportunity to experience television production from the other side of the camera. Details of this competition are also discussed in my joint article with Andrew Chubb (Gorfinkel and Chubb, 2015).

I'd also like to express my gratitude to Steven and my parents who supported me throughout this project.

Excepts of this text first appeared in other publications, but have been revised with new examples and take into account more recent developments. Portions of Chapter 4 (on multiethnic identity) appeared in 'From transformation to preservation: music and multi-ethnic unity on television in China' (Gorfinkel, 2012). An earlier version of parts of Chapter 5 (on Hong Kong) was first published in the article 'Ideology and the performance of Chineseness: Hong Kong singers on the CCTV stage' (Gorfinkel, 2011).

Parts of Chapter 5 (on Macau) appeared in 'Multimodal constructions of the nation: how China's music-entertainment television has incorporated Macau into the national fold' (Gorfinkel, 2013). Ideas from Chapter 6 also appear here from my book chapter with Andrew Chubb 'When foreigners perform the Chinese nation: televised global Chinese language competitions' (Gorfinkel and Chubb, 2015).

This book is dedicated to Joey and Emily: may you appreciate and find great joy in the curious and creative connections that you encounter in life.

References

Chow, Y.F. (2009) Me and the dragon: a lyrical engagement with the politics of Chineseness. *Inter-Asia Cultural Studies* 10(4): 544–64.

Gorfinkel, L. (2011) Ideology and the performance of Chineseness: Hong Kong singers on the CCTV stage. *Perfect Beat: The Pacific Journal of Research into Contemporary Music and Popular Culture* 12(2): 107–28.

Gorfinkel, L. (2012) From transformation to preservation: music and multi-ethnic unity on television in China. In K. Howard (ed.) *Music as Intangible Cultural Heritage: Policy, Ideology, and Practice in the Preservation of East Asian Traditions*. Aldershot: Ashgate, pp. 99–112.

Gorfinkel, L. (2013) Multimodal constructions of the nation: how China's music-entertainment television has incorporated Macau into the national fold. In E. Djonov and S. Zhao (eds.) *Critical Multimodal Studies of Popular Culture*. New York: Routledge, pp. 93–108.

Gorfinkel, L. and Chubb, A. (2015) When foreigners perform the Chinese nation: televised global Chinese language competitions. In R. Bai and G. Song (eds.) *Chinese Television in the Twenty-First Century: Entertaining the Nation*. Routledge: New York, pp. 121–40.

It was obviously not enough for me to have black eyes, black hair and yellow skin, I must say it, sing it, perform it. Chineseness, I began to understand, is not merely a biological category, but a social performance.

(Yiu-Fai Chow, 2009: 545)

1 Introduction
National identity in the Chinese context

Media and the making of a nation

Defining a nation is not an easy or natural process. Like all identities, nations are malleable, unstable and internally contradictory concepts that are constantly 'in the process of being made' (Bhabha, 1990: 3; see also Chow, 1998: 24; Russell, 1999: 275–9; Nelson, 1999: 348; Hall in Lee and Huang, 2002: 106). The premise for this book is that Chinese national identity, like other identities, is created, articulated and sustained through daily performances, including through the use, repetition and revision of certain symbols and themes (e.g., Anderson, 2006; Barthes, 1976; Billig, 1995, 2009; Guo, 2004: 10). Just as no identity is an island, the Chinese nation absorbs multicultural influences from both within China and beyond the boundaries of the People's Republic of China (PRC) state. Choices have to be made on which elements to include as part of the definition of 'us' and which to exclude as representative of some 'other'. Yet, despite the fluidity in the notion of what it means to be Chinese with different individuals and groups having their own ideas, and contestations around the concept, over time certain stories and symbols come to represent the very existence of 'the Chinese people'. For instance, speaking a language that has come to be known as Chinese, waving a Chinese flag, wearing a cheongsam (*qipao*, a traditional close-fitting Chinese dress for women with short sleeves, a slit skirt and a high collar, worn since the Manchu ruled China in the seventeenth century), or playing an erhu (a two-stringed fiddle), are actions that have come to symbolize 'Chineseness', just as much as looking a certain way.

Along with other forms of cultural performance, the media, as cultural institutions with power and influence over society (Hall, 1992: 296–7), offer particularly significant spaces for the realization and maintenance of national and ethnic identities. In *Imagined Communities*, Benedict Anderson (2006: 36–8) famously outlined the importance of print-capitalism and the fixing of national languages in forming a national consciousness in the eighteenth and nineteenth centuries. By reading the same print materials in the same 'national' language on a regular basis, a large number of people who would never meet in person and who may have spoken mutually unintelligible dialects could feel as if they belonged to the same cultural community (Anderson, 2006: 6, 26, 44; Barker, 1999: 65). Print technology and capital thus provided readers with sense of 'synchronicity' in inhabiting the same space and time, and a sense of shared identity based on being part of the same reading community (Chua, 2006: 80). In China too, print media based on a shared understanding of Chinese characters enabled people who spoke mutually intelligible and unintelligible 'dialects' of Chinese to feel as if they were part of a shared nation (de Francis, 1984).

Similar interpretations of the importance of the media in cementing a collective national consciousness have been applied to television (Hall, 1992: 293). In China, television supported the promotion of a single standard spoken national language (*Putonghua*) that was first developed in the 1950s. In the PRC mainland subtitling in simplified Chinese characters, also developed to promote literacy across China in the 1950s and which have become widely institutionalized, can be seen on most programmes. Television offers audiences ongoing opportunities to recognize themselves as part of the nation through the everyday experience of relating to people with typically national features, based in locations that are emblematic of the nation, and through stories interwoven with national stereotypes (Lopez, 1995: 262–3; Barker, 1999: 67). As people routinely share the experience of watching the same programmes with others across the nation, they may begin to feel as if they share common values as well as a sense of being united as a 'family'. Those at the 'periphery' in remote areas or outside of the mainstream become linked to those at the 'centre' – the dominant or official culture – through their television screens (Morley, 2004: 312).

More recently, however, newer technologies have challenged this sense of 'co-presence' that came from many people watching the same limited television programmes at the same time. The proliferation of channel options, as well as time-shift options including online video on demand, have led to a greater fragmentation of audiences. Scholars have thus started to question television's role in maintaining a sense of national cohesion. Rather than connecting with a national (or geographically specific) audience, users are creating a variety of personalized micro-communities, often based around particular and shifting tastes or interests. These communities can be both more transnational and more localized than the national imagined communities projected by official state broadcasters (Hjorth, 2009: 117). For instance, transnational online youth communities have been created around the dialect, music and youth culture of Shanghai (see Liu, 2013: 71, 183). Such communities are 'relatively unrestrained by the state-run censorship apparatus' (Voci, 2010: xx)[1] and create symbols of national belonging that can challenge official ones (Hjorth, 2009: 119). Nonetheless, television has maintained a certain salience in this new media environment. It too has adapted to online spaces, while continuing to attract significant audiences via broadcast, cable and satellite forms. Certain genres of television are thriving in the online context – music-entertainment being a prime example.

The very notions of 'nation', 'national identity' and 'nationalism' in the Chinese context – in contrast to the notion of 'empire' – began to attract widespread attention in the late nineteenth century, and became an important issue of debate after the collapse of the Qing Dynasty, China's last empire, in 1911. Since then, these terms have been defined, contested and redefined by various forces with various social, cultural, political and commercial goals. The Chinese Communist Party (CCP) has been a major player in the construction of national identity since the Party emerged as a force in the 1920s, and in particular after taking control of the mainland in 1949. But it was from the late 1970s, when the Party turned away from socialism and the task of raising class consciousness, that the project of cultural nationalism became the most prominent political goal in the PRC (Guo, 2004: 133; Rofel, 1995: 303–15).

A nationalist focus in the CCP was further deepened following the Tiananmen Square protests in 1989, during which the Chinese military opened fire on protestors calling for freedom of the press and freedom of speech, as well as better government accountability and worker control over industry. The protest resulted in hundreds of deaths and thousands of injuries (Richelson and Evans, 1999). After this incident, Party leaders framed the widespread political dissent and internal chaos as being caused by a lack of a patriotic spirit and an over-worshipping of 'Western' ideas (Guo, 2004: 43, 141). Rather than encourage an excessive adoption of Western practices, cultural nationalists argued for the revival of a national culture through the study, preservation and rediscovery of China's traditions, including Confucianism, which was previously discredited by the Communist leadership for contributing to China's stagnation and backward culture. Increasingly influenced by cultural nationalists, the Party began to reinforce the need for Chinese citizens to rediscover their own 'national spirit', 'national essence' and 'national culture' (Guo, 2004: x–xi, 2; Song, 2003: 81–99). The old idea of 'the Middle Kingdom' (the direct translation of the Chinese word for China, *Zhongguo*) was revitalized as a source of national inspiration and a variety of social campaigns and programmes, including through television and other media, were deployed to express and share with Chinese citizens what it meant to be Chinese and to have a sense of pride in their national culture.

On the whole, it may be said that official PRC media and social education campaigns have been quite successful in reformulating the people's conceptions of their own identity and place in the world, while at the same time enabling the CCP to renew and maintain its widespread legitimacy (Brady, 2008: 200, 202). It is thus worth examining in finer detail, from both a political and cultural perspective, how this has been done.

Overall, there has been very little research into constructions of identity on Chinese television. Textual analyses of television more often consider the role of visuals and spoken dialogue in creating a sense of national identity, while music and sound effects are often overlooked. This study highlights the important role of musical symbols in contributing to the construction of national identity in China in combination with visuals and words (see also

Cook, 1998: v, 23). Music is a unique trigger of memories, emotions and sense of connection with others (Catalyst, 2016). As Martin Stokes notes:

> The musical event evokes and organises collective memories and presents experiences with an intensity, power and simplicity unmatched by any other social activity. The places constructed through music involve notions of difference and social boundary. They also organise hierarchies of a moral and political order.
>
> (cited in Harris, 2005: 394)

Traditional songs and instrumentation can be used to establish a sense of ethnic solidarity or difference as well as a feeling of connection to the past, while the performance of pop songs with global inspirations can help establish a nation as having a modern and futuristic outlook, as being open to the outside world, and as being positively engaged and entangled with it. Furthermore, as van Leeuwen (1999) explains (also see Gorfinkel, 2013: 100), a sense of social unity, solidarity and belonging can be created through music when, for instance, many people sing in unison, or when they sing in harmony, with 'chordal pillars' helping to 'prop up' a single, dominant voice. Orchestral and brass instrumentation can help construct a sense of national strength as they work together like military or industrial machines – indeed the orchestra emerged as a popular form of expression during the Industrial Revolution and as new nations began to form in the eighteenth century. Drums and rhythm can give a sense of marching forward together. As Harris (2005: 394) argues, the CCP 'has clearly understood this power of music to organize political and moral hierarchies' and television has played an important role in using music for ideological purposes.

In this chapter, I provide an overview of the history of the cultural politics of Chinese national identity construction under the CCP, explaining three key frames of reference of national identity in the PRC: multiethnic China, Greater China, and civilizational China. Substantive analysis of these frames as constructed in music-entertainment television are covered in Chapters 4–6 respectively.

The three frames can be conceptualized as concentric circles, each representing a more broadly geographically inclusive vision of the Chinese nation. The inner ring, or multiethnic frame, relates to the constitutional definition of the PRC as a multiethnic nation. Representing the geographic core of China, it includes China's officially recognized 56 nationalities located within the mainland. They are the Han majority (*Hanzu*), which are said to constitute 92 per cent of the population (about 1.3 billion people), and 55 minority nationalities (*shaoshu minzu*) (about 106 million people), also referred to as ethnic minorities, which together make up the remaining 8 per cent (Hoddie and Lou, 2009: 51; Mackerras, 2004a: 147). The Greater China ring expands the core to include people in the two Special Administrative Regions, Hong Kong and Macau, as well as in the Republic of China (Taiwan). The PRC refers to people in these regions as 'compatriots' (*tongbao*). The great imagined Chinese 'family' or 'pan-Chinese nation' (*Zhonghua minzu*) also includes ethnic Chinese overseas (*huaren, huaqiao*). The third ring expands the circle to consider foreigners (*waiguoren*) or citizens of other nations who are not from Chinese backgrounds, especially those who are shown to be friendly towards China and who are attracted to Chinese culture and society.

While this book focuses on national and ethnic identity construction, other frames of identity, such as class, gender, generational and artistic identities are also significant and intersect with constructs of ethnic and national identity in a range of ways. Class identity, for instance, forms the historical basis for the Chinese Communist Party. In the early years of Communist rule under Chairman Mao Zedong from 1949 to 1976, every Chinese citizen was assigned a particular class, and class identities were the dominant markers of identity. Class identity was most strongly emphasized during the Cultural Revolution (1966–76) when official discourse on ethnic differences lost significance and gender differences were largely reduced to a single, masculine state-defined identity (Yang, 1999). The task of propaganda in the reform era, however, has not been to agitate citizens based on class differences but to unite its vast population and, to draw on the words of Benedict Anderson (2006: 7), to create a sense of 'deep, horizontal comradeship'. This new stance was designed to create stability internally and position the Chinese state as a legitimate, stable and globally competitive entity in a post-Communist world (Guo, 2004). While class consciousness remains embedded in the discourse of the Chinese state, it is now subsumed into the role of national cohesion (Yang, 1999). While workers and peasants used to be presented as the vanguard of society, they are now increasingly portrayed as backward and struggling. In contrast, entrepreneurs are shown to be making the most of the market-based economy and are the new vanguards of Chinese society.

Multiethnic Chinese

The notion of China as consisting of 56 nationalities, including one majority nationality/ethnicity and 55 minority nationalities, arose out of historical and arbitrary circumstances of the mid-twentieth century. Many Chinese struggled in the chaos resulting from Western encroachment in the mid-nineteenth century, the downfall of the Qing Dynasty in 1911, years of warlordism and the Japanese invasion from 1937 to 1945. Like its rival Nationalist Party (the *Guomindang/Kuomintang*), the CCP was determined to establish a strong China to avoid future chaos. Forming a solid national identity, or *minzu*, was considered a vital part of the solution. Both parties pushed the concept of a unified China cemented through the construction of a majority 'Han nationality' (*Hanzu*) alongside a few assisting 'minority nationalities' (*shaoshu minzu*) who did not identify as Han and whose support was necessary for the state-building project (Gladney, 2000).

There was a period in the early 1930s when CCP leader Mao Zedong went so far as to offer the various non-Han 'barbarian' groups the possibility of self-determination and even the right to form independent states completely separate from China if the CCP won national power (Gladney, 2000).[2] However, after the Communist Party emerged victorious and established the PRC in 1949, promises of self-determination were rejected. Instead of offering national autonomy to these groups, the Party offered them some concessions and privileges, including the establishment of 'autonomous' areas. These autonomous regions include Inner Mongolia (est. 1947), the Xinjiang Uyghur Autonomous Region (est. 1955), the Guangxi Zhuang Autonomous Region (1958), Ningxia Hui Autonomous Region (1958), and the Xizang Tibetan Autonomous region (Tibet) (1965). These regions are titled after the minority group with the largest population in these areas, although the Han have dominant numbers in all areas except Tibet and Xinjiang. Numerous autonomous prefectures and counties with strong non-Han populations within provinces have also been established. All of these areas have, however, been firmly integrated within the context of a unitary 'multiethnic' (or 'multinational') state (*tongyi de duo minzu guojia*) (Constitution of the People's Republic of China, 1982/2004; Leibold, 2010: 24; Mackerras, 2004b: 303). In other words, the notion of 'self-determination' came to apply to China as a whole in relation to its suffering at the hands of foreign imperialists, but not to the groups who became internal minorities.

For most of China's history until the early 1950s, various constellations of the national make-up were imagined, but no state had intervened or had been concerned to clarify the exact number and nature of the groups (Mullaney, 2004a: 198). China's ambiguous and fluid approach to ethnic identity began to end when a new Election Law in early 1953 stipulated that one representative seat at the National People's Congress was to be given to each minority nationality regardless of the size of its population. This was largely instated to fulfil the promise of affording rights and privileges to minority groups. When a census was taken between July 1953 and May 1954 in China's southwestern Yunnan province, around 260 distinct ethnic names were found in this province alone. This number was deemed politically untenable and on 15 May 1954, Beijing established the Yunnan Ethnic Classification Research Team with around 50 researchers, cadres and students to determine 'once and for all' the number of ethnic groups in the area who would be officially recognized (Mullaney, 2004a: 198).

The classification of China's internal ethnic groups purportedly followed Joseph Stalin's definition of ethno-national identity, which was based on the sharing of a common language, territory, mode of economic production and psychology/culture. However, few groups in China met all these criteria, and the categorization was more closely based on linguistic criteria where language families were equated with ethnic group identity. The hasty nature of the investigations was driven by political pressures, unfamiliar and unstable local conditions, and included local Han Chinese interpretations of other ethnic groups (Mullaney, 2004b: 217, 226; Cooke, 2008: 42). At a national level, out of the more than 400 groups that applied to the new Communist government-supervised ethnic identification programme, a manageable number of 41 nationality groups were officially recognized, reaching a final total of 56 by 1982[3] (Mullaney, 2004b: 207, 224–6; Tapp, 2008: 468; also see Mackerras, 2004b: 303–5).

In what Mullaney (2004a: 197) calls 'the strange calculus of Chinese nationhood', the formula of PRC membership became '55 + 1 = 1', referring to 55 officially recognized minority nationalities plus the Han nationality adding up to a single 'Chinese' (state) nationality. While diversity and flexibility can be observed in the representation of specific nationalities, the categories of classified nationalities themselves are now relatively fixed and non-negotiable. The Party-state has ruled that there are 56 nationalities, no more and no less. Despite allowing some level of choice for those of parents with different ethnicities, citizens of China can only be identified as one of these nationalities, rather than being 'mixed' Yi and Han, or Miao and Uyghur – although performers with 'mixed' identities in fact play important roles in Chinese music-entertainment television productions, and are essential to the dynamics and vibrancy of many of the programmes. With this formula, not only are all people in the PRC classified as either Han or one of the minority nationalities, but they are also positively identified as part of a unified PRC 'Chinese nationality' (*Zhonghua minzu*) and they are all 'people of China' (*Zhongguo ren*).

Even if individuals and collectives within the state do not think of themselves as Chinese, and Chinese is nothing but an imposed ascription, so far as the official discourse of the Party-state is concerned, people of all officially recognized nationalities living within the borders of the PRC – including all Tibetans, Mongolians, Koreans, Uyghurs and Kazakhs – are 'Chinese' and part of the Chinese nation (Guo, 2004: 14). For some groups, there has been no discontinuity between their self-conceptualizations and the nationality conferred on them by the state, while for others naming has led to a disjuncture between how they see themselves and how the state labels them (Cooke, 2008: 35). Some groups, such as the Bai, had until 1958 considered themselves 'ethnic Chinese', i.e., indistinguishable from the Han, until a new label led to a change in perception of their culture (Wu, 1991: 170–1). In some cases, there is a mismatch between what a group calls themselves and what the state calls them, resulting in a sense of ambivalence about their state-assigned identities (Mackerras, 2004a: 150). For instance, one group call themselves 'Monguors', but the state classifies them as 'Tu', which some view as a less dignifying and less civilized label, literally translating to 'people of the earth' (Cooke, 2008: 36, 47). Some groups, such as the Naxi, have enthusiastically adopted their minority status (Rees, 2000: 18). Many Uyghurs in Xinjiang and Tibetans in Tibet have actively resisted CCP and Han-dominated rule, and therefore reject the idea of being 'minorities' in a Han-Chinese nation. Yet, despite challenges from time to time, Mackerras (2004a: 149) argues that 'minorities appear generally content to obey Beijing, and their loyalties, expectations and political activities are directed towards the Chinese nation-state just as much, if not more than, those of the dominant Han people.'

It is also important to emphasize that multiethnicity in the PRC was not based on any scientific analysis of 'existing' nationalities, but came through an application process that was open to 'latent ethnic potential' for developing national identity. Following their recognition, the state and people of China have been in a more or less continual process of 'realizing' the forecasted categories, of turning the descriptions into reality (Mullaney, 2004b: 228, 231). Since the beginning of China's reform and opening up, the salience of the state-defined multiethnic categories and the idea of a singular 'Chinese' national identity have, in a significant way, been made real to citizens through performances of ethnicity in tourism performances and on television, particularly through song and dance.[4]

When the CCP came to power, minority nationality folk artists were organized into professional, full-time troupes. The Central Nationalities Song and Dance Troupe (*Zhongyang minzu gewu tuan*), established on 1 September 1952, recruited folk artists from remote areas around the country. By enthusiastically sponsoring minority nationality troupes, the CCP has been able to choose the artists and ensure the ideological suitability of performance content and style (Mackerras, 1984: 213, 215). Minority and Han performers from various performing arts troupes, including the Central Nationalities Song and Dance Troupe as well as army, navy and air force performing arts troupes, continue to play important roles on Chinese television.

It is important to note, however, that performances of ethnic diversity have not always been readily encouraged or permitted. Expressions of internal difference have at times been equated with opposition, and state-sponsored differences have even been rendered obsolete (Baranovitch, 2001: 365). For instance, anti-ethnic homogenizing policies dominated the Campaign Against Local Nationalism (1958–60) during the Great Leap Forward, and during the Cultural Revolution (1966–76), during which some minorities, especially Tibetans and Uyghur Muslims with strong religious traditions, were subjected to persecution (Baranovitch, 2001: 365; Mackerras, 2004a). Ethnic difference was also downplayed during the 'spiritual pollution' campaigns of the late 1980s (Gladney, 2000). During these periods of political unpredictability, many artists faced persecution (Yang, 2006) and it was unclear how they could express individual and sub-national identities (Mackerras, 1984: 215).

Since the social and economic reforms were implemented in the late 1970s, there has, in general, been much greater creative freedom afforded to the representation of China's nationalities. New policies of ethnic pluralism, enshrined in the 1982 Constitution and the 1984 Law on Regional National Autonomy, have encouraged a number of minorities to take charge of their own cultural representations and assert their own identities more strongly (Harrell, 2000). While using the framework of the state-defined categories, individuals have had 'the opportunity and freedom to express who they are and what they choose to represent' (Bai, 2007: 254).

Different Chinese political leaders and scholars, however, have placed a different emphasis on the degree to which ethnic differences should be accommodated, leading to sometimes conflicting policies. President Hu Jintao (2002–12), for instance, strongly supported ethnic pluralism, while Xi Jinping (from 2012), unlike his father who promoted pluralistic reforms, has pushed for more assimilationist policies (Leibold, 2015). Xi's 'China Dream' (*Zhongguo meng*) slogan has been premised on the notion of national unity and collective belonging though mandating 'Mandarin-language instruction and patriotic education in frontier regions'. He has also promoted the 'blending of ethnicities' (*minzu jiaorong*), seen in the encouragement of intermarriage between Uyghurs and Hans through cash and housing subsidies in the Xinjiang Uyghur Autonomous Region (Jacobs, 2016) as well as joint schooling and increased interethnic migration and mobility (Leibold, 2015). Xi has also resurrected the 'four identifications' (*si ge rentong*), which stress 'the affinity of minorities with the motherland, the Chinese nation/race, Chinese culture and the socialist road with Chinese characteristics', while adding a fifth identification with the CCP (Leibold, 2015).

While China's nationalities may distinguish themselves ethnically to various degrees, their main duty is clearly still to the Party-state. They must work within state-constructed discursive parameters and participate in national development plans constructed in Beijing. The Party authorizes revised histories of minority groups and insists on a policy of inclusiveness where marginal groups are seen as vital parts of the national whole, working together towards the goals of unity, stability and economic development.

In the market era, cultural products and events associated with minority nationalities have become popular among mainstream Chinese urbanites. Rising disposable incomes have enabled 'ordinary' citizens to purchase recordings and travel to 'exotic' locations to experience the 'internal difference' for themselves (Baranovitch 2009: 195). Much of the current allure of minority nationality culture, including in television programming, is based on selling 'ethnic colour' to audiences. The colouring of minorities is mainly based on their colourful clothing rather than the colour of their skin, although mainstream stereotypes of minorities as having darker or 'blacker' skin are sometimes vocalized. 'Colour' also refers to the 'exotic' and 'fresh' cultural offerings minorities bring, which contrast with what some have seen as a drab, official, 'stilted and suffocating Han urban culture' (Schein, 2000: 112). After opening to the world in the late 1970s after a period of isolation, ethnic diversity became a major resource for marketing China's uniqueness to consumers and travellers (Schein, 2000: 114).

In such appeals, minority nationalities have been framed as mysterious, 'internal others' with innate talents in singing and dancing (*neng ge shan wu*). These positive stereotypes are underpinned by ongoing negative assumptions by the majority Han that frame minorities as more primitive, backward and peripheral, a patronizing attitude that Louisa Schein (1997: 70) refers to as 'internal orientalism'. As cultural belonging is measured by levels of modernization, most minority nationalities, who have come from the less developed border regions, continue to be seen as lagging behind the Han (Cooke, 2008: 46–55). During the first three decades of Communist rule, even though Han chauvinism was discredited, official rhetoric placed the Han above ethnic minorities on a 'teleological grid of historical progress', underpinning assumptions of Han superiority (Harrell 2000). Since the 1980s, although the minorities and Han have been consistently framed as 'brothers and sisters' and equals in the same 'Chinese national' family (Schein, 2000: 114), the Han group clearly remains exceptional as the majority group and emblematic of the Chinese mainstream norm.

The notion of minorities as being primitive, pure and innocent even continues in alternative, anti-centre and anti-Han movements where minorities have come to define the very essence of the contemporary Chinese self. For instance, Leo Ou-fan Lee (1991: 207–8) describes the root-seeking (*xungen*) movement that began in the 1980s, where young urban Chinese artists began reflecting on the meaning and origins of their own culture. Fighting against the central, official, Beijing-based Communist culture in which they had grown up, and feeling they had been cut off from their cultural roots, such fiction writers as Gao Xingjian and Han Shaogong, and filmmakers like Chen Kaige and Zhang Yimou sought inspiration from a range of remote, rural and minority cultures as a way of gaining insights into the mainstream culture. They were eager to uncover ancient myths and rituals of a range of native cultures they imagined to be imbued with more vitality than that of Han urbanites who had experienced more direct influence from the Communist leadership. In the music scene, waves of Han singers drew on minority influences for inspiration. The Northwest Wind (*Xibei feng*) genre, for instance, developed out of a sense of fascination by urban Han singers for the feelings associated with a remote 'homeland' in China's northwestern areas of Gansu, Shaanxi and Xinjiang (Qian, 2014).

Animosity towards official culture has been extended to the hegemonic Han culture, seen as having been suffocated by both feudal Confucian and Communist ideology. The *xungen* writers, who have mainly been strangers to the 'exotic peripheries', have attempted to uncover the unfamiliar, internal 'other' as the primordial source of Chinese culture and civilization in relatively remote regions like Tibet and Heilongjiang, as well as ancient sites of the Han or Chu cultures (Lee, 1991: 211). The real purpose of the search appears to be not so much to recover lost cultures or agitate for minority nationality rights, but a desire to '"decentre" the oppressive political culture of the Party' and to uncover and celebrate Chinese cultural pluralism and cosmopolitanism (Lee, 1991: 208, 224).

As Chapter 4 shows, the vision of modern Chinese culture as being revitalized by peripheral multiethnic groups has been incorporated into mainstream Chinese television productions. To bring pleasure to mainstream, predominantly Han audiences, PRC television draws on stereotypes of minorities as being good at singing and dancing, and as being colourful, fun, primitive and pure, and at the same time uses blends of traditional ethnic and modern elements to present China as revitalized, modern and unique. While the basic framework of multiethnic unity continues to be the dominant template for mainstream minority-Han nationality performances on music-entertainment television, within this frame, in different contexts, artists have incorporated a variety of styles that allow for the simultaneous expression of unique differences and unity among the ethnic groups.

Cultural China: re-centring the PRC

Coined in the early 1970s and popularized by USA-based Chinese scholar Tu Weiming, the term 'Cultural China' began its circulation in intellectual journals outside of mainland China (Tu, 1994: 25–6).[5] At a time when the CCP was still widely promoting class consciousness as a pivot for social solidarity, the Cultural China debate outside of the PRC interrogated the ethnic identity of Chinese people who no longer resided in their ancestral land, including Chinese in Taiwan, Hong Kong, Singapore, Malaysia and the USA. Tu critiqued the previously dominant assumption that the 'true' Chinese culture could only be found in China and argued that the centre of Chineseness in fact no longer resided in China. He argued that the idea of China as the 'Middle Kingdom' was threatened as a result of the penetration of Western powers and their ideas and systems in the nineteenth century, and – most significantly – China's own rejection of traditional and Confucian culture under the Communist Party. He argued that under the CCP, Chineseness had been displaced from China to the extent that being a citizen of the PRC would no longer guarantee one's Chineseness (Tu, 1994: 2–3, 25, 27, 34; also see Chua, 2001: 114). Famous for his advocacy of New Confucianism, Tu used the term 'Cultural China' to describe what he saw as the emergence of a 'common awareness' among a transnational Chinese intellectual community, which symbolized the material and spiritual 'accomplishments' of the Chinese people (Tu, 1994: 1).

Tu also argued that with the rise of the economies of Japan, South Korea, Hong Kong, Taiwan and Singapore in the 1990s, these peripheral locations would 'come to set the economic and cultural agenda for the centre' (Tu, 1994: 13), and the PRC would be displaced as the centre or core of Chinese culture. While Tu saw Chinese culture as disintegrating under the Communist regime, under which many traditions were destroyed, he argued that it would be revived and preserved from the periphery in ways that would powerfully challenge the centre (Tu, 1994: 12; Ma, 2003: 22). As a New Confucian scholar, he argued that Confucianism would become the force that would unite all Chinese around the world as well as people from other East Asian countries including Japan and South Korea with a Confucian heritage (Chua, 2001: 114). He imagined that a mutual belief in Confucianism was what drove the new economies and the successes of pan-overseas Chinese business networks. While Tu's thoughts gained considerable traction in the early 1990s, after the Asian financial crisis hit in 1997, more people started to question idea of a single, thriving culturally Chinese or East Asian solidarity based on Confucian belief (Chua, 2006: 76, 78).

Furthermore, as the building of national identity has become a key pursuit of the PRC government in the reform era, the PRC Party-state itself has actively attempted to re-centre mainland China within a global Cultural China frame. Since the 1980s, mainland Chinese scholars and the media have been active participants alongside their overseas Chinese counterparts in the discourse on Cultural China and on the significance of Confucian thought (Song, 2003: 84–8). In the twenty-first century, PRC authorities have also attempted to reclaim control over the uses of Confucius and Confucianism as national icons. The news media has actively reported on the importance of China's Confucian heritage. Confucius statues have been erected by PRC authorities all over China and around the world (Zhu, 2011; *China Daily*, 2011; Allen, 2010) and Confucius' image has been used to promote Chinese language and culture internationally, particularly with the global spread of the state-sponsored Confucius Institutes (*Kongzi xueyuan*), which has similarities to Alliance Française, the German Goethe Institute and the British Council, since 2004.

As Song (2003: 91, 97) notes, the state's re-sanctioning of Confucian culture is clearly part of a pragmatic attempt by the state to strengthen its legitimacy following the chaos of the Cultural Revolution and the subsequent disorder that resulted from rapid economic and social change in the reform era. Fundamental Confucian tenets of social harmony, respect for authorities, obedience to superiors, devotion to the state and protection of the family have been promoted at a time when there is a clear need to pacify the country, stabilize society and regulate the people (Song, 2003: 91, 97; Chen, 2011). Notions of moral civilization and humanist values have also been valuable in a context of high levels of official corruption and the collapse of moral order following the Cultural Revolution. Confucian ideas have also operated as significant markers of a Chinese cultural tradition and have been used to build a sense of national identity following the void left by the turn away from socialism (Song, 2003: 94–9).

Given the very different socio-political histories of Chinese communities in Taiwan, Macau, Hong Kong, and among overseas Chinese abroad, the idea that they all feel a shared culture sense of the past and culture cannot be taken for granted (e.g., Chua, 2006; Ang, 1998). However, Beng-Huat Chua (2001, 2006) does argue that a loose sense of Chineseness exists across nation-state borders, not because of any essential ethnic ties or Confucian beliefs, but rather based on a common cultural economy through which popular culture is produced, circulated, and consumed and in which the PRC has participated in an increasingly active way in the reform era. People across these regions are connected through shared tastes, 'flows' and the consumption of common cultural products, productions and celebrities (Chua, 2006: 79; Cunningham and Sinclair, 2000; Zhu, 2008: 19). In other words, the marketing of popular cultural products such as films, television series and music across the region has resulted in a much more successful realization of a transnational Chinese community across borders than has a shared sense of Confucian culture. Chua developed the term 'Pop Culture China' to specifically describe the 'dense flow' of 'pop culture products' and networks of 'cultural-economic exchanges' between populations of Chinese in globally dispersed locations (Chua, 2001: 114; 2006: 77, 80). However flimsy the sense of unity may be, satellite television (and now the internet) has played a vital role in creating a new basis for building a common sense of time and space (Zhu, 2008: 19).

While theories on 'Cultural China' developed by overseas Chinese scholars in the 1990s attempted to displace the PRC from the 'centre', other theories, generally articulated under the banner of 'Greater China', have insisted on the centrality of the PRC mainland. In such analyses, the PRC takes centre stage, while the other entities 'orbit around the mother country like planets around a star' (Taylor, 2004: 175). The idea of Greater China reaffirms the notion that all Chinese are believed to be bound to mainland China no matter what their circumstances. This outlook has been criticized for blurring significant social and political differences between different geographic contexts where ethnic Chinese live and for giving the impression of 'all peoples of ethnic Chinese descent within a single, homogenous cultural bloc' (Taylor, 2004: 175). Yet it is important to recognize that the creation of such an image appears to be an important aim of the Chinese state and its media as it attempts to promote a sense of ethnic unity and assert the importance of the PRC on a global level.

With the growing strength of the PRC economy, the PRC is becoming an increasingly significant player in the transborder flow of Chinese popular culture. Tay (2009: 106, 107-8, 113) argues that while China may not necessarily be 'leading the way in terms of content, style or influence', it is the most powerful and sizable participant, providing the cultural, economic and political bedrock on which the market depends. For instance, in order to access the lucrative mainland market, producers of cultural products in Hong Kong will reconfigure their products to suit the tastes of mainland audiences and to ensure they are in line with official PRC regulations (Tay, 2009: 107-8).

Furthermore, with a high level of cross-cultural interaction between Hong Kong, Macau, Taiwan, overseas Chinese and the PRC mainland, producers in Taiwan, Hong Kong and elsewhere are forming joint ventures and joint production units with mainland Chinese television stations and production houses to produce programmes for consumption in all three regions (Chan, 2008: 26; Hong, 1996: 98). The resulting television cultures represent the palatable cultural differences, in which elements from all three places – including artists, producers, formats and stories – are integrated (Jonathan Friedman in Chan, 2008: 33). In this context, the cultural uniqueness of each area is becoming increasingly blurred. The various ways in which mainland Chinese music-entertainment programming is framing dynamic contemporary interactions between artists from the mainland, Hong Kong, Taiwan and further abroad and what this suggests about mainstream PRC conceptions of the notion of 'Greater China' are explored in Chapter 5.

Civilizational China: the attraction of foreigners

As with the discourse of multiethnicity and Greater China, the discourse of China's relationship with foreigners is complex and has fluctuated with the ebb and flow of different political movements and priorities. At times in China's history, Chinese identity has been conceived in cultural and civilizational rather than ethnic or racial terms. This meant that it was possible for 'barbarians' (or anyone outside of China) to 'become Chinese' because being 'civilized' and being 'Chinese' basically meant the same thing (Sun, 1996: 35). During much of the first 30 years of the PRC few foreigners had access to China. However, as China reopened to the outside world and developed economically in the reform era, foreigners have had the opportunity to visit and live in China again, making it easier to adopt Chinese 'civilizational' practices including speaking Chinese wearing Chinese-style dress, adopting Chinese mannerisms, celebrating Chinese festivals, and playing and singing Chinese music.

The place of foreigners in China remains affected by the ongoing discourse of China's 'century of humiliation' that began when the 'barbaric' but technologically advanced, foreign colonial governments, including the United Kingdom, the United States, France, Germany and Japan, occupied territories within China following the Opium Wars of the nineteenth century (Gries, 2005: 847). Citizens of the foreign powers had the right to live in, travel to, and conduct trade and missionary work in these concessions. While Chinese people were initially forbidden to enter most concessions, when they were allowed to enter by the 1860s they were generally treated like second-class citizens. While feeling a sense of inferiority over China's evident weakness compared to the West and Japan, Chinese people have also retained a strong sense of pride in China's cultural and civilizational accomplishments. The story of foreigners in the construction of a twentieth- and twenty-first-century Chinese identity remains underpinned by a tension between the desire to be modern and technologically advanced like the West and the desire to maintain a deep, cultural and traditional essence while keeping out unnecessary Western influences.

Who precisely is classified as a 'foreigner' (*waiguoren*, lit: outside country person) has been a matter of political, racial and ethnic debate, with popular culture playing a major role in navigating a sense of the Chinese self vis-à-vis the foreign 'other'. Various terms have been used to refer to foreigners. *Laowai* (lit: old outsider), along with *bairen* (lit: white person), is often used in China to refer to Caucasian/white-skinned people, and often specifically refers to people with blond hair and blue eyes, who speak English. Stereotypes of foreigners as being more open-minded (*kaifang*), extroverted, individualistic, adventurous, romantic, sexually licentious, modern and wealthy than Chinese are abundant in Chinese popular discourse (Erwin, 1999: 245; Mao, 2015). The term *laowai* originally had the meaning of 'layman' or unprofessional person but is now taken as an expression of endearment by many Chinese who see themselves as treating foreigners as they would their close friends who they often refer to by placing 'lao' (lit: 'old') before their surnames (For instance, *lao Wang*). However, many non-Chinese themselves see it as a pejorative or irritating term, especially when Chinese continue to use it to refer to local populations when the Chinese people themselves are overseas (Mao, 2015). While *laowai* may also be used to refer to black-skinned people, they are often marked separately as *heiren* (lit: 'black people') or *feizhou ren* (Africans) – even if they are actually from America or elsewhere – and have their own associated stereotypes (Olander and van Staden, 2016).

Asians (*yazhou ren*) of non-Chinese ethnicity who are more 'culturally proximate' to the Chinese are also often separately marked by their nationality, sometimes with derogative terms that reflect past wars and invasions. For instance, Japanese people may be heard being referred to as *xiao riben* (tiny Japanese) or *riben guizi* (Japanese devil) in everyday speech both by older populations who experienced first-hand the occupation and atrocities committed by the Japanese during the War of Resistance Against Japan (during the Second World War) and younger populations who have been educated about the invasions through the media (Mao, 2015). Westerners have also been called by derogatory terms such as *yang guizi* (foreign devil) as a result of their associations with histories of Western imperialism in China. In music-entertainment television, terms like *waiguo pengyou* (foreign friends) are mostly used, reflecting a general shift to more positive terms as China has improved its international status and as Chinese people have had significant opportunities to socialize with people from abroad (Mao, 2015).

The discourse of 'foreign friends' has long been integral to China's foreign policy. Brady (2002: 307–8, 317) defines 'foreign friends' as those 'non-critical' foreigners, with the 'power and influence to assist China', and who stand in opposition to those who openly criticize China. Based on her research on internal foreign affairs documents related to procedures for 'correctly' dealing with foreigners, Brady (2000: 944; 2002: 307) argues that the use of the term 'foreign friends' is part of a strategy to control and manage foreigners' presence and activities in China. Rather than representing genuine intimate personal relations, 'foreign friends' are part of the construction of a 'strategic relationship', aimed at 'neutraliz[ing] opposition' and 're-order[ing] reality' (Brady, 2000: 944; 2002: 307). China specialist Geremie Barmé (2008) has also noted that the word 'friendship' (*youyi*) has been 'a cornerstone of China's post-1949 diplomacy' with Mao Zedong declaring: 'The first and foremost question of the revolution is who is our friend and who is our foe.' The media reinforce particular politically correct perspectives on how to understand foreigners and their place within China.

China's music-entertainment programmes, which are constructed as a friendly genre, focus on friendly foreigners and offer little, if any, space for irony or criticism of the ruling Party. Everyone who appears on music-entertainment programming (domestic or foreign) is framed as a 'friend' of the Chinese Party-state, whether they be 'foreign friends' (*waiguo pengyoumen*), 'overseas Chinese friends' (*huaren pengyoumen*),[6] friends of particular cities in China where a show may be based in for that episode (e.g., *Lishui pengyoumen*), or general 'audience friends in front of television sets' (*dianshiji qian de guangzhong pengyoumen*). Nonetheless, it is significant that foreigners are mostly framed as 'friends' whereas overseas Chinese (*huaren*) are often evoked through the metaphor of 'family'.

As Chapter 6 illustrates, it is not just 'friendship' that is called for, but also foreigners' expression of 'love' for China. This finding may have reflected a change in attitude towards foreign relations in the Hu–Wen era, and the focus on developing a 'Harmonious Society'. At a global level, especially in the lead-up to the Beijing 2008 Olympic Games, the domestic promotion of a 'Harmonious Society' was matched with the rhetoric of a 'Harmonious World' (Zhang, 2010: 50). In this frame, as I argue, foreigners and Chinese are imagined as part of the same 'global village' (*diqiu cun*), although the representation of this 'multi-country' village is largely located in mainland China, and most often in China's political centre, Beijing. A discourse of foreigners realizing their dreams in China has also been strongly emphasized and reinforced with the promotion of notion of 'China Dream' under President Xi.

Another label used to describe foreigners is *Zhongguo tong* – 'China expert'/ 'old China hand' – which refers to a Sinicized foreigner who is admired for having mastered Chinese customs and language (Erwin, 1999: 244–7). Writing in the 1990s, Erwin distinguished between the few foreigners who were labelled as *Zhongguo tong* and the 'authentic foreigner' who was unable to speak comprehensible Chinese. She argued that the *Zhongguo tong* validated essential aspects of Chinese culture in connection to the West by indicating foreigners' respect and appreciation for certain Chinese civilizational characteristics. They may never be perfect Chinese – that is, they may make cultural 'mistakes' in conduct or language – but they are likable and ideologically in line with the CCP. Exemplary diplomatic friends of China who may not have spoken Chinese have also been included among noted *Zhongguo tong*. For instance, former US president Henry Kissinger, who helped formalize diplomatic relations between the USA and China in the 1970s after 23 years of diplomatic isolation; former president of the International Olympic Committee Juan Antonio Samaranch, who announced Beijing as the host of the 2008 Olympic Games; former prime minister of Japan Yasuhiro Nakasone, who improved relations between Japan and China in the 1980s, and former Australian prime minister Bob Hawke, who developed a close personal relationship with Chinese leaders and helped integrate the Australian and Chinese iron and steel industries, featured (among others) in a 2010 documentary series called

Zhongguo tong. This program aired on the Shanghai International Channel (ICS) in line with the Shanghai Expo. Former Australian prime minister (2007–10, 2013) Kevin Rudd, unique for his ability as a foreign leader to speak Chinese, however, did not impress authorities. In 2008, Rudd attempted to cleverly appropriate the term *zhengyou* (true friend) to describe his wish to speak frankly with his Chinese colleagues and offer honest criticism about contentious matters such as China's human rights violations. Chinese leaders, however, associated the concept with opposition politics (Callick, 2010a, 2010b).

Zhongguo tong most commonly refer to 'ordinary foreigners' living in China who appreciate Chinese language and culture and have mastered it to a great extent. One of the most famous *Zhongguo tongs* in the entertainment scene is Mark Rowswell, a Caucasian Canadian who became an instant celebrity after his performance of the comic art of crosstalk (*xiangsheng*) during the 1988 *CCTV Spring Festival Gala*. In the guise of his alter ego Dashan (literally: big mountain – Rowswell was relatively tall), this was the first time many Chinese had seen a foreigner speak fluent Chinese. Rowswell frequently appeared on Chinese television after this debut. In his role as Dashan, rather than being not quite perfect, this *Zhongguo tong* was comically constructed as knowing too much about China. As Rowswell (2015) explained:

> The standard comedic set-up for these performances pitted Dashan, the foreign student, against XXX [sic], the senior Chinese master who was going to show Dashan 'the glories of Chinese civilization' and yet over the course of the skit the master was revealed to be a blustering buffoon who knew less about Chinese language and culture than his foreign student.
> (Rowswell, 2015)

Rowswell has argued that:

> Dashan represents a Westerner who appreciates and respects China, who has learned the language and understands the culture and has even become 'more Chinese than the Chinese'. It's a very powerful and reassuring image that appeals to very deep-rooted emotions.
> (Rowswell, 2015)

Rowswell saw Dashan as a symbol of 'East meets West in a friendly, harmonious kind of way', which links to official diplomatic discourse, and highlights the inescapability of political connection when performing in public in China (Simpson, 2010).

However, among foreigners the Dashan character appears to be much less appreciated. One reason is that after Dashan became popular and gained a 'reputation for being a master of all things Chinese', many foreigners in China found their Chinese language skills and looks being constantly and unfavourably compared to those of Dashan in their everyday life (Rowswell, 2015;

Hessler, 2006). Some foreigners have compared Dashan to a 'trained monkey', implying that he was just performing for the bemusement of mainstream Chinese audiences at the foreigners' expense and that his performances on CCTV positioned him as pandering excessively to the authorities. Rowswell has rejected this criticism, preferring instead to view the Dashan character as being limited by 'Chinese cultural norms – the limits of what is culturally acceptable to a Chinese audience'. He has argued:

> That doesn't necessarily mean you pander. You can challenge the norms and push limits here and there, and I believe I have done and continue to do that, but in large part you work within culturally acceptable limits.
> (Rowswell, 2015)

While claiming his artistic independence, Rowswell has stated that:

> There have been times where the Chinese [officials] have asked me to do something and I have refused and they are quite respectful of that… But they don't want me to be involved in politics, anyway, especially the issues they feel sensitive about. I have never been asked to give a propaganda speech about Tibet and Taiwan, or how wonderful human rights are in China. The Chinese just want me to talk about culture or comedy.
> (cited in Simpson, 2010)

Rowswell has also noted that he was asked to appear on the CCTV military channel, which sings the praises of the People's Liberation Army. However, he said he refused because 'the military has nothing to do with me'. He also explained that he rejected a script that praised the 'motherland' because, as he told the producers, 'it was not my motherland', adding that 'They don't realise they are crossing the line because they treat me as one of their own. But I have never pretended I am Chinese' (cited in Simpson, 2010).

Criticism of Rowswell relates to a discourse of discomfort typically used by foreigners to mock themselves for performing as exotic spectacles or 'token' foreigners (whites or blacks) to sell things in a highly commercialized Chinese market. The 'foreign monkey' or 'white monkey gig' refers to performances conducted during promotional events like real estate opening parties, where foreigners may be invited to set up fake bands, often at the last minute without any expectation for the need to rehearse. Even if they are actual musicians (and many are not), they are often only required to mime playing guitars, keyboards and drums and sing for the viewing pleasure of prospective customers. There is a small but heated online discussion among foreigners who engage in these acts on what their performances actually mean – whether they are demeaning themselves, making the most of the opportunities available to them, doing it as an alternative easy income source to the stereotypical profession of English teaching, acknowledging the absurdity of the situation and doing it for a laugh, or contributing to a culture in flux (*Chengdu Living*, 2011).

In the market-era, the glamour of the West and the white body has been used to sell an image of modernity in China, with foreign models frequently used in advertising aimed at Chinese consumers. Essentialized symbols of Westernness have also been appropriated to serve political goals. In contrast to Edward Said's noted contribution to scholarly research on orientalism, or the West's stereotyping of 'the Orient' or 'the East', Xiaomei Chen (2002) uses the term 'Occidentalism' to describe the Party-state's appropriation of foreign symbols to help reconcile differences among the Chinese people and define a united Chinese self in contrast to the foreign Other. This framing parallels the construction of a solidified Han Chinese self that comprises more than 92 per cent of the population and blurs differences within China in contrast to a scattering of diverse ethnic minorities who make up a small minority. These tactics help to make the massive Chinese population of 1.38 billion (as of August 2017), which may otherwise be seen as internally differentiated on clan, linguistic and cultural lines, seem like a natural family.

At times, an idealized West has also been used as part of arguments in campaigns against the government. Chen explains that intellectuals who made the popular 1988 television series *River Elegy* (*He Shang*) glamorized Western society in a way that enabled a critique of the Chinese political regime at the time (2002: 33–7). She argues that 'to a large extent the success of *He Shang* can be attributed to its fundamental challenge to the Chinese conventional value system and worldview in the People's Republic'. The fact that it was shown on television at all in a strictly censored system reflects the period of political instability in China and the power struggle within the ranks of the top leadership, which culminated in the mass rallies and dispersion of protestors in Tiananmen Square the following year. CCTV directors and ministries in charge of broadcasting could have vetoed the series or suggested changes to the script, but they themselves 'may have had their accounts to settle with the ruling ideology' or may have 'deliberately looked other way... because they wanted this counter-discourse to appear' (Chen, 2002: 37–8).

Other scholars, such as Yan and Santos (2009) and Chu (2008), have used the term 'self-orientalism' to describe methods used by the Chinese government, advertisers, tourist agencies and filmmakers whereby exotic Western 'orientalist' stereotypes of China's national image are reappropriated, particularly to appeal to foreign audiences for marketing purposes. The idea of self-orientalism also suggests that the gaze and participation of 'the other' is being used in part to validate China's own worth to its own population.

The dominant discourse of China in the state-controlled media reflects what Song and Sigley (2000) call a 'Middle Kingdom Mentality', which refers to the construction of a positive image of China's cultural essence and links to China's attempts at national revitalization. The Middle Kingdom Mentality describes the output of scholars and commentators who have been working to 'restore' the Chinese nation and its relevant cultural traditions to their rightful place on the global stage. Chapter 6 shows that China's cultural programmes have played an important role in reasserting the attractiveness of

China and Chinese traditional and modern culture to foreigners as part of its 'soft power' push.

Since the early 2000s, China's Confucius Institutes have played a major role in promoting Chinese culture and language around the world. As one 2012 CCTV report proudly announced:

> The learning craze for Chinese language is at a global high. The name Confucius Institute may not have rung a bell back in 2004. But now as China's economic influences spread globally, so are the branches of this Chinese learning Institute. Seems like more and more people want to know or to be part of the rising power.
>
> (CCTV.com, 2012)

While foreigners have been encouraged to learn Chinese language and cultural practices, there is more ambivalence about the idea that foreigners might actually 'become Chinese' and fully assimilate into Chinese culture. Discussions and stories around cross-cultural marriage provides salient insights into this question. In many television shows, foreign women are shown to be culturally malleable while Chinese men remain steadfastly Chinese. As Erwin (1999: 238–53) explains, the television drama *A Beijinger in New York* (*Beijing ren zai Niu Yue*), popular in the 1990s, highlighted transnational Chinese male dominance, while the foreign woman was shown to be drawn to China in pursuit of her strong and attractive Chinese male partner. In this programme, the Chinese partner somehow maintains his essential Chineseness despite having an American wife and overseas education, while the foreign wife is shown to be in the process of becoming Chinese. Even the child of the mixed race couple who grows up in America is shown to become completely 'Chinese', in effect transforming the future of America into one that suits China's aims. Erwin's study suggests that the threat of the loss of Chinese cultural identity through intercultural/international marriage is mitigated through television dramas produced by Han males by emphasizing that an essential Chineseness remains stoic and unchanged through a process of globalization, while weaker ethnicities, cultures, and genders are somehow absorbed by a powerful and superior male Han Chinese culture. Thus, the old cultural civilization notion is reinforced in that, while Chinese are never acculturated into other cultures, barbarians can become (or almost become) civilized/Chinese. In many ways, this notion is replicated in CCTV music-entertainment's playful toying with intercultural marriage (see Chapter 6).

Notes

1 For instance, see Voci (2010) for an analysis of videos produced and shared on small screens through DV cameras, computer monitors, the internet and mobile phones; Chio (2009) on the production of village videos in rural southwest China;

and de Kloet (2005, 2010) on rock music scenes since the mid-1990s in Beijing, which take on very different forms to that broadcast on mainstream media.
2 According to the 1931 CCP Constitution.
3 Members of unrecognized groups were either identified as Han or 'lumped together with other minorities with whom they shared some features for generally political reasons' (Gladney, 2000).
4 See Hartley (2004: 16) for a similar argument in relation to the Australian national identity, and the important role of national and international media in the construction of 'multination' states.
5 Particularly influential was Tu Weiming's 1991 special issue of *Daedalus: Annals of the American Academy of Arts and Science*, later published as an edited volume called *The Living Tree* in 1994.
6 For instance, when popular male mainland singer Liu Huan walked on stage in Vancouver for *The Same Song* programme, he was told by the host that all those cheering in the audience in front of him were his 'friends' (*pengyou*), and was asked by the host to give his New Year wishes to 'all the overseas Chinese friends' (*suoyou de huaren pengyoumen*).

References

Allen, C. (2010) Confucius connecting Canberra, China. *ABC News*, 24 September. Available at www.abc.net.au/news/2010-09-24/confucius-connecting-canberra-china/2272622?site=canberra&source=rss (accessed 18 May 2017).
Anderson, B. (2006) *Imagined Communities: Reflections on the Origin and Spread of Nationalism*. London: Verso.
Ang, I. (1998) Can one say no to Chineseness? Pushing the limits of the diasporic paradigm. *boundary 2* 25(3): 223–42.
Bai, Z. (2007) Ethnic identities under the tourist gaze. *Asian Ethnicity* 8(3): 245–59.
Baranovitch, N. (2001) Between alterity and identity: new voices of minority people in China. *Modern China* 27(3): 359–401.
Baranovitch, N. (2009) Representing Tibet in the global cultural market: the case of Chinese-Tibetan Musician Han Hong. In A.N. Weintraub and B. Yung (eds.) *Music and Cultural Rights*. Chicago and Urbana: University of Illinois Press, pp. 187–218.
Barker, C. (1999) *Television, Globalization and Cultural Identities*. Milton Keynes: Open University Press.
Barmé, G. (2008) Rudd rewrites the rules of engagement. *Sydney Morning Herald*, 12 April. Available at www.smh.com.au/news/opinion/rudd-rewrites-the-rules-of-engagement/2008/04/11/1207856825767.html (accessed 18 May 2017).
Barthes, R. [trans. S. Heath] (1976) Rhetoric of the image. In *Image, Music, Text*. New York: Hill and Wang.
Bhabha, H.K. (1990) Introduction: narrating the nation. In H.K. Bhabha (ed.) *Nation and Narration*. London: Routledge, pp. 1–7.
Billig, M. (1995) *Banal Nationalism*. London: Sage.
Billig, M. (2009) Reflecting on a critical engagement with banal nationalism – reply to Skey. *Sociological Review* 57(2): 347–52.
Brady, A.M. (2000) 'Treat insiders and outsiders differently': the use and control of foreigners in the PRC. *China Quarterly* 164: 943–64.
Brady, A.M. (2002) The political meaning of friendship: reviewing the life and times of two of China's American friends. *China Review International* 9(2): 307–19.

Brady, A.M. (2008) *Marketing Dictatorship: Propaganda and Thought Work in Contemporary China*. Maryland: Rowman and Littlefield.
Callick, R. (2010a) Rudd treats a 'true friend' carefully. *The Australian*, 28 April. Available at www.theaustralian.com.au/news/opinion/rudd-treats-a-true-friend-carefully/story-e6frg6zo-1225859033809 (accessed 18 May 2017).
Callick, R. (2010b) Rudd may come unstuck over China relations. *The Australian*, 7 December. Available at www.theaustralian.com.au/opinion/rudd-may-come-unstuck-over-china-relations/story-e6frg6zo-1225966571679 (accessed 18 May 2017).
Catalyst (2016) Music on the brain. *ABC TV*, 8 March. Available at www.abc.net.au/catalyst/stories/4421003.htm (accessed 18 May 2017).
CCTV.com (2012) Confucius going global. CCTV.com, 16 December. Available at http://english.cntv.cn/program/cultureexpress/20121216/103832.shtml (accessed 18 May 2017).
Chan, J.M. (2008) Toward television regionalization in Greater China and beyond. In Y. Zhu and C. Berry (eds.) *TV China*. Bloomington: Indiana University Press, pp. 15–39.
Chen, R. (2011) Dispute over Confucius statue. *Beijing Review*, 27 February. Available at www.bjreview.com.cn/special/2011-03/02/content_336808.htm (accessed 18 May 2017).
Chen, X. (2002) *Occidentalism: A Theory of Counter-Discourse in Post-Mao China* (2nd edn). Oxford: Rowman and Littlefield.
Chengdu Living (2011) Performing in China: confessions of a white monkey. *Chengdu Living*, 16 December. Available at www.chengduliving.com/performing-china-white-monkey (accessed 18 May 2017).
China Daily (2011) Confucius statue unveiled in Beijing. *China Daily*, 13 January. Available at http://usa.chinadaily.com.cn/culture/2011-01/13/content_11848407.htm (accessed 18 May 2017).
Chio, J. (2009) Village videos and visual mainstreaming of rural, ethnic identity. In *Provincial China Workshop Proceedings*, Anhui University, Hefei (PRC), 12–14 October.
Chow, R. (1998) Introduction: on Chineseness as a theoretical problem. *boundary 2* 25(3): 1–24.
Chu, Y.W. (2008) The importance of being Chinese: orientalism reconfigured in the age of global modernity. *boundary 2* 35(2): 183–206.
Chua, B.H. (2001) Pop culture China. *Singapore Journal of Tropical Geography* 22(2): 113–21.
Chua, B.H. (2006) Gossip about stars: newspapers and pop culture in China. In W. Sun (ed.) *Media and the Chinese Diaspora: Community, Communications and Commerce*. London: Routledge, pp. 75–90.
Constitution of the People's Republic of China (1982/2004) Available at http://en.people.cn/constitution/constitution.html (accessed 18 May 2017).
Cook, N. (1998) *Analysing Musical Multimedia*. Oxford: Clarendon Press.
Cooke, S. (2008) Becoming and unbecoming Tu: nation, nationality and exilic agency in the People's Republic of China. In P. Allatson and J. McCormack (eds.) *Exile Cultures, Misplaced Identities*. Amsterdam, NY: Rodopi, pp. 33–56.
Cunningham, S. and Sinclair, J. (2000) Diasporas and the media. In S. Cunningham and J. Sinclair (eds.) *Floating Lives: The Media and Asian Diasporas: Negotiating Cultural Identity through Media*. St. Lucia: University of Queensland Press, pp. 1–34.

de Francis, J. (1984) *The Chinese Language: Fact and Fantasy*. Honolulu: University of Hawaii Press.
de Kloet, J. (2005) Popular music and youth in urban China: The Dakou generation. M. Hockx and J. Strauss (eds.) *Culture in the Contemporary PRC: The China Quarterly Special Issues New Series*. Cambridge: Cambridge University Press, pp. 87–104.
de Kloet, J. (2010) *China with a Cut: Globalisation, Urban Youth and Popular Music*. Amsterdam: Amsterdam University Press.
Erwin, K. (1999) White women, male desires: a televisual fantasy of the transnational Chinese family. In M.M.H. Yang (ed.) *Spaces of their Own: Women's Public Sphere in Transnational China*. Minneapolis: University of Minnesota Press, pp. 232–60.
Gladney, D. (2000) China's national insecurity: old challenges at the dawn of the new millennium. *2000 Pacific Symposium, Asian Perspectives on The Challenges of China*, Sponsored by the National Defense University, 7–8 March, Fort Leslie J. McNair, Washington, DC. Available at file:///C:/Users/Gao/Downloads/gladney_inss02%20(1).pdf (accessed 18 May 2017).
Gorfinkel, L. (2013) Multimodal constructions of the nation: how China's music-entertainment television has incorporated Macau into the national fold. In E. Djonov and S. Zhao (eds.) *Critical Multimodal Studies of Popular Culture*. New York: Routledge, pp. 93–108.
Gries, P.H. (2005) China's 'new thinking' on Japan. *The China Quarterly* 184: 831–50.
Guo, Y. (2004) *Cultural Nationalism in Contemporary China*. London: Routledge Curzon.
Hall, S. (1992) The question of cultural identity. In S. Hall, D. Held and T. McGrew (eds.) *Modernity and its Futures*. Cambridge: Polity Press/Open University, pp. 273–325.
Harrell, S. (2000) *Yi Studies as a Social and Historical Field*. Paper presented at a Harvard Workshop, June. Available at http://faculty.washington.edu/stevehar/yis-tudies.html (accessed 18 May 2017).
Harris, R. (2005) Wang Luobin: folk song king of the northwest or song thief? Copyright, representation, and Chinese folk songs. *Modern China* 31(3): 381–408.
Hartley, J. (2004) Television, nation, and indigenous media. *Television and New Media* 5(7): 7–25.
Hessler, P. (2006) *River Town: Two Years on the Yangtze*. New York: HarperCollins.
Hjorth, L. (2009) Web U2: emerging online communities and gendered intimacy in the Asia-Pacific region. *Knowledge, Technology and Policy* 22(2): 117–24.
Hoddie, M. and Lou, D. (2009) From vice to virtue: changing portrayals of minorities in China's official media. *Asian Ethnicity* 10(1): 51–69.
Hong, J. (1996) Cultural relations of China and Taiwan: an examination of three stages of policy change. *Intercultural Communication Studies* 1(1): 89–109.
Jacobs, A. (2016) Xinjiang seethes under Chinese crackdown. *The New York Times*, 2 January. Available at www.nytimes.com/2016/01/03/world/asia/xinjiang-seethes-under-chinese-crackdown.html?_r=0 (accessed 18 May 2017).
Lee, L.O. (1991) On the margins of the Chinese discourse: some personal thoughts on the cultural meaning of the periphery. *Daedalus* 120(2): 207–26.
Lee, T.D. and Huang, Y. (2002) 'We are Chinese' – music and identity in 'cultural China'. In S.H. Donald, M. Keane and H. Yin (eds.) *Media in China: Consumption, Content and Crisis*. London: Routledge Curzon, pp. 105–15.

Leibold, J. (2010) The Beijing Olympics and China's conflicted national form. *The China Journal* 63: 1–24.
Leibold, J. (2015) China's ethnic policy under Xi Jinping. *China Brief* 15(20). Available at https://jamestown.org/program/chinas-ethnic-policy-under-xi-jinping/#.VrUtWY9OLIX (accessed 18 May 2017).
Liu, J. (2013) *Signifying the Local: Media Productions Rendered in Local Languages in Mainland China in the New Millennium*. Leiden: Brill.
Lopez, A.M. (1995) Our welcomed guests: telenovelas in Latin America. In R.C. Allen (ed.) *To Be Continued… Soap Operas Around the World*. London: Routledge, pp. 256–75.
Ma, L.J.C. (2003) Space, place, and transnationalism in the Chinese diaspora. In L.J.C. Ma and C. Cartier (eds.) *The Chinese Diaspora: Space, Place, Mobility, and Identity*. Lanham, MA: Rowman and Littlefield, pp. 1–49.
Mackerras, C. (1984) Folksongs and dances of China's minority nationalities: policy, tradition, and professionalization. *Modern China* 10(2): 187–226.
Mackerras, C. (2004a) China's minorities and national integration. In L.H. Liew and S. Wang (eds.) *Nationalism, Democracy and National Integration in China*. London: Routledge Curzon, pp. 147–69.
Mackerras, C. (2004b) Conclusion: some major issues in ethnic classification. *China Information* 18(2), pp. 303–13.
Mao, Y. (2015) Who is a *laowai*? Chinese interpretations of *laowai* as a referring expression for non-Chinese. *International Journal of Communication* 9: 2119–40.
Morley, D. (2004) At home with television. In L. Spigel and J. Olsson (eds.) *Television after TV*. Durham: Duke University Press, pp. 303–23.
Mullaney, T. (2004a) Introduction: 55 + 1 = 1 or the strange calculus of Chinese nationhood. *China Information* 18(2): 197–205.
Mullaney, T. (2004b) Ethnic classification writ large: the 1954 Yunnan Province Ethnic Classification Project and its foundations in Republican-era taxonomic thought. *China Information* 18(2): 207–41.
Nelson, L. (1999) Bodies (and spaces) do matter: the limits of performativity. *Gender, Place and Culture* 6(4): 331–53.
Olander, E. and van Staden, C. (2016) What it's like to be black in China. *Huffington Post*, 5 April. Available at www.huffingtonpost.com/eric-olander/black-china-life_b_9843602.html (accessed 18 May 2017).
Qian, R. (2014) Lun 'Xibeifeng' liuxing yinyue de minzuhua fazhan [Discussing the development of north wind popular music]. *Music Grand View (Yinyue Daguan)* 1: 317.
Rees, H. (2000) *Echoes of History: Naxi Music in Modern China*. Oxford: Oxford University Press.
Richelson, J.T. and Evans, M.L. (eds.) (1999) *Tiananmen Square, 1989: The Declassified History*. National Security Archive Electronic Briefing Book No. 16, 1 June. Available at http://nsarchive.gwu.edu/NSAEBB/NSAEBB16/ (accessed 18 May 2017).
Rofel, L. (1995) The melodrama of national identity in post-Tiananmen China. In R.C. Allen (ed.) *To Be Continued… Soap Operas Around the World*. London: Routledge, pp. 301–20.
Rowswell, M. (2015) Why do so many Chinese learners seem to hate Dashan (Mark Rowswell)? He seems like a nice guy. Does he secretly eat children or something? 11 April. Available at www.quora.com/Why-do-so-many-Chinese-learners-seem-to-hate-Dashan-Mark-Rowswell (accessed 18 May 2017).

Russell, C. (1999) *Experimental Ethnography: The Work of Film in the Age of Video*. Durham: Duke University Press.
Schein, L. (1997) Gender and internal orientalism in China. *Modern China* 23(1): 69–98.
Schein, L. (2000) *Minority Rules: The Miao and the Feminine in China's Cultural Politics*. Durham: Duke University Press.
Simpson, P. (2010) Acting the fool. *South China Morning Post*, 21 November. Available at www.scmp.com/article/731167/acting-fool (accessed 18 May 2017).
Song, X. (2003) Reconstructing the Confucian ideal in 1980s China: the 'Cultural Craze' and New Confucianism. In J Makeham (ed.) *New Confucianism: A Critical Examination*. New York: Palgrave Macmillan, pp. 81–104.
Song, X. and Sigley, G. (2000) Middle Kingdom Mentalities: Chinese visions of national characteristics in the 1990s. *Communal/Plural* 8(1): 47–64.
Sun, W. (1996) *Reading the Other: Narrative Constructions of Japan in the Australian and Chinese Press*. PhD thesis, University of Western Sydney, Nepean.
Tapp, N. (2008) Romanticism in China? Its implications for minority images and aspirations. *Asian Studies Review* 32(4): 457–74.
Tay, J. (2009) Television in Chinese geo-linguistic markets: deregulation, reregulation and market forces in the post-broadcast era. In G. Turner and J. Tay (eds.) *Television Studies After TV: Understanding Television in the Post-Broadcast Era*. London: Routledge, pp. 105–14.
Taylor, J.E. (2004) Pop music as postcolonial nostalgia in contemporary Taiwan. In N. Rossiter and A. Chun (eds.) *Refashioning Pop Music in Asia: Cosmopolitan Flows, Political Tempos and Aesthetic Industries*. London: Routledge Curzon, pp. 173–82.
van Leeuwen, T. (1999) *Speech, Music, Sound*. London: Macmillan.
Voci, P. (2010) *China on Video: Smaller-Screen Realities*. London: Routledge.
Wu, D.Y. (1991) The construction of Chinese and non-Chinese identities. *Daedalus* 120(2): 159–79.
Yan, G. and Santos, C.A. (2009) 'China forever': tourism discourse and self-orientalism. *Annals of Tourism Research* 36(2): 295–315.
Yang, H.L. (2006) People's music in the People's Republic of China: a semiotic reading of socialist musical culture from the mid to late 1950s. In E. Pekkilä, D. Neumeyer and R. Littlefield (eds.) *Music, Meaning and Media*. Helsinki: International Semiotics Institute, University of Helsinki.
Yang, M.M. (1999) From gender erasure to gender difference: state feminism, consumer sexuality, and women's public sphere in China. In M.M. Yang (ed.) *Spaces of Their Own: Women's Public Sphere in Transnational China*. Minneapolis: University of Minnesota Press, pp. 35–67.
Zhang, X. (2010) Chinese state media going global. *East Asian Policy* (Jan–Mar): 42–50.
Zhu, L. [with Guo, S.] (2011) Confucius stands tall near Tian'anmen. *China Daily/People's Daily*, 13 January. Available at http://en.people.cn/90001/90776/90882/7259160.html (accessed 18 May 2017).
Zhu, Y. (2008) *Television in Post-Reform China: Serial Dramas, Confucian Leadership and the Global Television Market*. London: Routledge.

2 Music-entertainment culture under the Chinese Communist Party

In media studies, a distinction is often made between 'hard' television formats, such as the news and current affairs, which focus on factual, political and 'serious' information, and 'soft' entertainment forms, such as music, dance and drama, which focus on art, performance, human interest stories and what some people may view as 'trivial' information. These distinctions are part of a range of popular dichotomies that separate fact from fiction, information from storytelling, and the political from the apolitical. Yet these are arbitrary distinctions created through social and cultural convention. Both news and entertainment formats carry stories and dramas of human life, educate people on what is right and wrong, draw boundaries of belonging, and reinforce notions of cultural identity.

While the different formats offer stories with different sets of symbols and metaphors, both entertainment and news formats are political in the sense that they attempt to tell us about our society, politics and culture, and often in ways that serve the interests of those who maintain power over their production (Sun, 1995a: 93–7; Carey, 2009: 23; Bird and Dardenne, 1988; see also Herman and Chomsky, 1988). Encapsulated in both news and entertainment genres are frameworks – or ideologies – for making sense of the social and political world (Donald and Hall, 1986: x). Such frameworks impose particular ways of looking at events and relationships (Donald and Hall, 1986: x). It is through the analysis of cultural discourse that we can learn about the kinds of 'politics' or 'ideologies' that are operating at particular moments in time, including party, state and broader public and intellectual debates on what the nation could or should be like (see Silverstone, 1999: 148). Both news and entertainment television programmes, as with other cultural forms, can assist in giving meaning and order to the chaotic world in which we live and can attempt to resolve dilemmas and anxieties over our identity. The kinds of images and sentiments that are being performed in music-entertainment programming, as with any other genre, reflect 'constantly evolving' cultural, economic and political ideologies in society more broadly (Donald and Hall, 1986: xi).

The types of art and culture promoted and sanctioned by the Chinese Communist Party (CCP) have varied over time. Before exploring music-entertainment television per se, this chapter provides a history of musical culture under the CCP and sets the context for the phenomenon of politically, commercially and artistically inspired music-entertainment television. In its early days, the CCP, which was formally established in 1921, drew on an established tradition of political mass singing, which began during the Taiping Rebellion (1850–64), a bloody conflict fought between the ruling Manchu-led Qing Dynasty and the Christian God-worshipping movement of the Heavenly Kingdom of Peace. The leader of the Heavenly Kingdom of Peace, Hong Xiuquan, drew inspiration from congregational hymn singing introduced to China by Protestant missionaries from the West in the nineteenth century (Wong, 1984: 113–14). In a context of ongoing chaos, revolutions and wars, activists in the socialist movement in China composed and promoted similarly styled mass songs to inspire mine and railroad workers to go on strike, to unite peasants to agitate for land reforms and to fight against the humiliating foreign occupations. CCP song collections aimed at fermenting the revolution were published as early as 1926 (Wong, 1984: 118–21).

The CCP, like the rival Nationalist Party (*Guomindang*), which eventually fled to Taiwan, inherited the cultural iconoclasm of what is referred to as the New Culture Movement (*Xin Wenhua Yundong*). This cultural movement of the mid-1910s and 1920s emerged out of a sense of disillusionment with traditional Chinese culture and with the Chinese Republic, founded in 1912, which failed to address China's problems. The May Fourth Movement, which began in Beijing on 4 May 1919, helped turn the cultural movement into a political one. Students and a broader national community protested against the weakness of the Chinese government, particularly its response to the Treaty of Versailles, which allowed Imperial Japan to take over Chinese territories in Shandong formerly occupied by Germany. They began to see Confucianism and superstition as causes for much of China's weakness and backwardness and called for a new Chinese culture based on global and Western standards. The scientific and democratic culture of the West, they argued, was urgently needed if the Chinese were to survive as a nation in the modern world (Holm, 1991: 15). In 1933, at a time when the CCP, the Nationalist Party and local warlords were trying to unite against the common enemy (the Empire of Japan) following a number of invasions and incidents, the Central Chinese Government Ministry of Education organized a Mass Education Specialists Conference calling for the need to heighten the spirit of hatred against the enemy, work up the courage of independence and self-reliance, and acquire the habit of fortitude and ability to withstand hardships. After the second Sino–Japanese War formally broke out in 1937, a further social education campaign was launched to awaken national consciousness, teach people about the War of Resistance and fight for the cause (Hong, 2009: 3). CCP cadres argued that a key method for educating the masses was to be through new international forms of mass agitation and propaganda art, especially Soviet *agitprop* as well as 'scientific' Western art forms (Holm, 1991: 35).

However, Mao Zedong and other leading figures in the CCP argued that they could only abolish the backward Chinese culture gradually, and only with the popular approval and participation of the masses. In other words, any appeal to the masses had to be localized in order for the new messages to be relevant and intelligible to them. CCP officials like Qu Qiubai, elected minister of education in the Soviet People's Government and director of the Art Bureau in 1931 (also creator of the official Chinese translation of 'The Internationale', which was used as the anthem of the CCP until 1949), advocated for integrating new ideological ideas with carefully selected existing styles and practices. Tactics like putting new lyrics to old Chinese folk-song melodies were thought to be more easily popularized among workers, peasants and soldiers, and thereby more likely to further accelerate revolutionary goals (Holm, 1991: 16–24).

In 1935, Mao and his comrades settled in Yan'an after the historic yearlong 'Long March', a military retreat taken by the CCP's Red Army to evade the pursuit of the Chinese Nationalist Party. There they set up training for cadres on how to use the arts as a weapon of propaganda (Wong, 1984: 126). As a way of expressing a strong national identity in the face of deteriorating Sino–Japanese relations, leading composers also found that fusing Western and Chinese elements helped to form new songs that had a modern yet distinctively Chinese national flavour. In 1935, composer Nie'er, who studied Russian contemporary music in propaganda films, composed the instantly popular 'March of the Volunteers' (*Yingxiong jinxing qu*) for the patriotic film *Children of the Storm* (*Fengyun ernv*) (Wong, 1984: 122–3). The song was provincially selected as the national anthem of the PRC in September 1949, replacing the Republican 'Three Principles of the People' and the Communist 'Internationale'. It was briefly and unofficially replaced by 'The East is Red' (*Dongfang hong*) when the lyricist, Tian Han, was imprisoned during the Cultural Revolution in the 1960s, and was played in a number of different versions before being officially recognized in 1982 and eventually included in China's Constitution in 2004. It also became the national anthem of Hong Kong and Macau when they were returned to the PRC in 1997 and 1999 respectively.

The famous 'Yellow River Cantata' (*Huanghe dahechang*) is an orchestral piece that was considered a milestone in the way that it combined Western and Chinese elements. It still occupies a special place in the hearts of many Chinese. It was composed by Xian Xinghai in 1939 following the Japanese invasion in 1937 during a period of great suffering, and it 'tapped into the Chinese people's deep yearning to become a strong nation, free from foreign exploitation' (Hong, 2009: 1). The piece draws on the symbolism of the Yellow River, which is often referred to as the 'mother River of the Chinese nation' and 'the cradle of the Chinese civilization'. The river is not only as vital to China's livelihood as the Nile is for Egypt, but also symbolically 'joins Chinese hearts everywhere to their homeland, history, and roots' and 'nurtures the spirit and strength of the Chinese people' (Hong, 2009: 1–2).

The 'Yellow River Cantata' was based on a long poem written by revolutionary poet Guang Weiran who was the leader of one of many touring artistic troupes that used music to share patriotic and revolutionary messages with the masses, and was based on the harrowing experience of trying to cross one of the most dangerous gorges at Hukou Waterfall on the Yellow River in November 1938 in Shanxi province. In the poem the boatmen face their difficulty with 'strength, determination, and a fighting spirit' (Hong, 2009: 4–7).

It was during the Yan'an period that many writers and artists from the city first came into serious contact with 'common' people. They began drawing on indigenous forms of art and culture popular from rural areas, including music, dance, drama, comics and cartoons, and mixing them with foreign forms such as Soviet *agitprop* to raise national consciousness and stimulate the populace to carry on the War of Resistance against Japan, and later to fight against the Nationalist Party (Holm, 1991: 15–24; Hong, 2009: 4). Many folk songs, particularly from the surrounding northwest region, including the uplifting *yangge* folk theatre style, were collected and revised for the revolutionary cause (Wong, 1984: 126). In his influential Yan'an Talks at the Conference on Literature and Art in 1942, Mao called for arts that represented the broad masses (Wong, 1984: 126). He explained that in order to create powerful works, artists in the new China were to draw on the most accomplished forms from both Chinese and foreign traditions (Mittler, 2010).

In the 1950s, after the CCP emerged victorious in the civil war and the PRC was founded, composers, music researchers and music instructors from the city were specifically exhorted by Chairman Mao to go to the countryside to work with peasants. They were to continue to collect folk songs from all ethnic groups for the purpose of transforming them into propaganda tools. By revising and enriching the tunes and adding new words with political lessons in Mandarin Chinese (the language of the Han majority), these national treasures would be preserved and improved in a 'scientific' and 'modern' way. A modern song involved, for instance, discarding vocal ornamentation and introducing Western style open-throat singing, or adding a Western-style orchestral accompaniment. Revised folk songs were particularly used to educate peasants about the need for agricultural collectivization (Wong, 1984: 131–3).

In 1964, just before the start of the Cultural Revolution, Mao reiterated the directive 'to use the old to create the new and use the foreign to create a Chinese national art' (*Gu wei jin yong, Yang wei Zhong yong*) (Mittler, 2010: 390). In the same year, the CCP organized and staged a song and dance epic called *The East is Red* (*Dong fang hong*), which premiered at the Great Hall of the People. In October 1965 it was turned into a wide-screen colour stage art film by the Beijing Film Studio (*Beijing dianying zhipian chang*), August First Film Studio (*Ba yi dianying zhipian chang*) and the Central Newsreel and Documentary Film Studio (*Zhongyang xinwen jilu dianying zhipian chang*). The original stage show, which involved more than 3,500 performers and was produced under the general directorship of Premier

Zhou Enlai, commemorates the period from the early twentieth century to 1949 when the PRC was established. Its songs contain strong revolutionary messages and praise for Chairman Mao and incorporated the Chinese people's favourite Chinese artistic traditions, including singing, dancing and poetry recitations as well as a full orchestra that blended ethnic and Western music.

Song titles from *The East is Red* paint the scene and the correct view of modern Chinese history from the CCP standpoint. They include 'Misery Era' (*Ku'nan de niandai*), 'Anyuan Miners Club Song' (*Anyuan lukuang gongren julebu zhi ge*), 'Friends of Agriculture Song' (*Nong you ge*), 'Workers, Famers, Soldiers Unite' (*Gong nong bing lianhe qilai*), 'Martyrdom Song' (*Jiuyi ge*), 'Taking Up Arms to Rebel' (*Naqi wuqi nao geming*), 'Fight Tyrants and Divide the Land' (*Da tuhao fen tiandi*), 'Qilü Long March' (*Qilü changzheng*), 'Anti-Japanese Military University Song' (*Kang ri junzheng daxue xiaoge*), 'Nanniwan', 'Unity is Strength' (*Tuanjie jiushi liliang*), 'People's Liberation Army March' (*Zhongguorenmin jiefangjun jinxingqu*), 'People's Liberation Army Occupies Nanjing' (*Renmin jiefangjun zhanling Nanjing*), 'National Anthem' (*Guo ge*), 'Great Holiday' (*Weida de jieri*), 'Without the Communist Party There Would Be No New China' (*Meiyou Gongchandang jiu meiyou xin Zhongguo*) and 'Chairman Mao's Brilliance' (*Mao Zhuxi de guanghui*). Multiethnic dances include 'Xinjiang Dance' (*Xinjiang wu*), 'Dai Garland Dance' (*Daizu huahuanwu*), 'Li Grass Dance' (*Lizu caoliwu*), 'Korean Long Drum Dance' (*Chaoxianzu changguwu*) and the 'Miao Lusheng Dance' (*Miaozu lushengwu*). The production ends with 'Ode to the Motherland' (*Ge chang zuguo*) and the audience singing 'The Internationale' (*Guojige*).

Several of these songs, including 'Without the Communist Party There Would Be No New China', 'Ode to the Motherland' (sung at the Opening Ceremony of the Beijing 2008 Olympic Games) and 'Nanniwan' are still performed in public today. 'Nanniwan', while not explicitly using the words of the Party, refers to the pioneering work of the CCP in the Nanniwan area in northern Shaanxi province, about 90 kilometres southeast of Yan'an, in the late 1930s and early 1940s. It eulogizes the work in which the people under the guidance of the Party and Chairman Mao turned the barren hills on which important CCP battles took place against both the Japanese and the Nationalist Party into a welcoming place with crops, cattle and sheep. Old and young people, celebrities and ordinary people, continue to sing various renditions of the catchy tune set to a traditional folk melody of northern Shaanxi in both formal concerts and reality singing competitions, bringing back and reconstructing memories of this important historical moment.[1]

As well as drawing on the work of established composers, as part of Mao's promotion of the 'mass line' – from the masses to the masses – the Party also encouraged workers, peasants, soldiers and students to create their own revolutionary songs through coaching and holding songwriting competitions.

Many winning songs were published, broadcast or sung in mass rallies. Work units were also encouraged to collectively create songs. During the Cultural Revolution (1966–76) this effort was intensified, with proper music upheld as the 'spontaneous, direct, and collectively created outgrowth of physical labour' (Wong, 1984: 131). For the most part, these songs were 'simple, plain and easy to memorize', with a predictable melody and rhythm (Wong, 1984: 137). The types of songs composed in the socialist era include songs in praise of Party leaders (especially Chairman Mao), the motherland, the Party, the People's Liberation Army and the CCP; songs for special groups such as peasants, workers and soldiers and for work units; songs that announced major policy decisions; songs about foreign affairs (imperialists and friends); as well as songs expressing solidarity with Taiwanese people and a determination for Taiwan to rejoin the motherland (Wong, 1984: 134–6).

It has also been widely argued that during the height of the Cultural Revolution, severe restrictions were placed on the type of music China's 800 million citizens could access, with the 'eight model operas' (*bage yangbanxi*) generally believed to be the only works available in China at the time (Mittler, 2010: 383, 390). Produced in the first three years of the Cultural Revolution, and advocated by Chairman Mao's last wife, Jiang Qing, the 'eight' revolutionary model operas (*geming jingju*) actually included six modern operas – The Legend of the Red Lantern (*Hong deng ji*), Shajiabang, Taking Tiger Mountain by Strategy (*Zhi qu wei hu shan*), Raid on the White Tiger Regiment (*Qi xi bai hu tuan*), Ode of the Dragon River (*Long jiang song*), On the Dock (*Hai gang*) and two ballets, the Red Detachment of Women (*Hongse niangzi jun*) and The White-Haired Girl (*Baimao nv*). The operas were designed to propagate Mao's revolutionary line and his central role in bringing socialism to China, glorifying the People's Liberation Army and its revolutionary struggles against foreign and class enemies. They also highlight the bravery of the ordinary people (Clark, 2008; Mittler, 2010: 383, 390). By the end of the decade, the number of official model works rose to eighteen (Mittler, 2010: 378). Given the sensitivity of the Cultural Revolution, which was officially condemned by the Party in 1981, these songs are rarely performed in public today.

One curious exception was a large-scale commercial symphonic concert on 2 May 2016 called *In the Fields of Hope*. Held in Beijing's Great Hall of the People, and staged around the sensitive time of the 50th anniversary of the start of the Cultural Revolution (an event that went virtually unmarked in China), the concert involved the performance of red songs (*hongse geyao*) celebrating the Party's glorious socialist past, and most controversially included the song 'Sailing the Seas Depends on the Helmsman' (*Dahai hangxing kao duoshou*), written in 1964 which praises Mao Zedong Thought, and which became the anthem of the Cultural Revolution. The song reflects the craze for studying Mao Zedong among the Red Guards, epitomized through the widespread carrying of little red books of Mao Zedong quotations (*Mao zhuxi yulu*). The performance of the song at a concert that featured huge socialist-style images of both Chairman Mao and President Xi Jinping attracted strong condemnation within China. There was confusion and speculation as to whether the show actually had official backing. Some media, such as the *South China Morning Post* in Hong Kong argued that an event held in such a politically sensitive location must have been carefully pre-screened and must have had the approval of authorities, while official mainland media sources like the *Global Times* argued that the authorities had been duped by the organizers and would not have knowingly approved such a controversial performance that represented an era officially classified as a 'serious mistake' (Denver, 2016). While the concert may have brought up painful memories of the Cultural Revolution for some, it also shows that the revolutionary fervour and idealism of the times continues to be romanticized by many Chinese people (Daniel Leese in Cook, 2016).

More recent scholarship has suggested that there was much more innovation in culture and the arts during the Cultural Revolution than was previously thought. First, as Mittler (2010) argues, rather than demolishing the music of foreign and Chinese heritage, the intense popularization of the model works actually enabled a vast number of Chinese peasants who had never known about Western-style classical music, including piano concertos, ballet or opera, a chance to connect with it, while urban youth learned about Beijing Opera and other local opera forms. Despite the seeming limitations, composers in song and dance troupes (*gewutuan*) were able to experiment with new and unorthodox combinations of styles and instruments including, for instance, ensembles made up of a saxophone, *pipa* (Chinese lute), *yueqin* (moon zither), accordion, *erhu* (a two-stringed fiddle) and cello. Mittler also found that access to foreign and folk forms was varied and uneven. Some musicians kept officially banned forms alive in secret or played them openly when audiences and officials were none the wiser about the origins and banned status. For instance, in her interviews Mittler found music lovers who still listened to their records of Mozart, Beethoven and the Beatles during this time.

Mao's guiding principle of taking the best from China and the West to create a new culture has had enduring salience in the post-socialist era. His 1964 directive to develop a new Chinese style based on a fusion of Western and Chinese elements was reprinted in 1979 after the Cultural Revolution as China began to refocus on modernization and economic development (Wong, 1984: 128). While certain foreign and Chinese traditional forms have been frowned upon, and concerns over the flow of foreign cultures into China are underpinned by residual fears of cultural imperialism and a moral corruption of the masses, many musical styles have found their way into common life and flourish in 'improved', 'modernized', hybridized forms that often serve political and ideological needs (see Harris, 2005: 391).

After the Cultural Revolution, state broadcasters began to experiment with allowing audiences to select their own songs which they saw as representative of the era. The first popular music charts programme on radio, the dominant medium in the late 1970s and early 1980s, called *Listeners' Favourite Broadcast Songs* (*Tingzhong xi'ai de guangbo gequ*), aired on China

Central People's Broadcasting Station/China National Radio (*Zhongyang renmin guangbo diantai*) in conjunction with *Songs* (*Gequ*), the magazine of the Chinese Music Association in early 1980. Listeners were invited to vote for their top 15 favourite songs for the first time. At this time the masses were used to singing and hearing 'hard, strong, high, loud' songs, and given the chance to decide, the listeners who were mainly youth overwhelmingly chose love ballads. Conservatives bemoaned the 'unhealthy' choices of the people, fearing it would detract into 'decadence'. At the end of the competition the popular show was aborted (cnwest.com, 2013).

Suggesting political interference in the actual competition, it was widely believed that according to the charts 'Little Sister Finds Brother With Tears Flowing' (*Meimei zhao ge lei hua liu*) should have been the top song, while 'Celebration Drinking Song' (*Zhu jiu ge*), sung by Li Guangxi, should have come second. However, 'Celebration Drinking Song' was announced as the top song after the organizers carefully considered how it would best reflect the times. The song reflected a feeling of energy and a joyful mood among the people after hearing that the 'Gang of Four' (*siren bang*)[2] had been crushed, the Cultural Revolution was over, and a new era full of wonderful expectations for life had arrived (cnwest.com, 2013). The song rapidly spread throughout China, reportedly 'intoxicating' hundreds of millions of Chinese people, and becoming the 'carol of a generation' (Zhu jiu ge, n.d.). Based on the custom of expressing good wishes and respect to others during festive occasions and toasting guests during welcome banquets, the lyrics call on 800 million Chinese to come together, raise their golden cups and drink the fragrant victory wine (10,000 cups and still not drunk! *qian bei wan zhan ye bu zui!*). It makes direct reference to the 'October Victory', 'the Jubilee' and a 'bright future [following] the Party guidelines' built around 'the four modernizations'. The 'four modernizations' were goals first established by Zhou Enlai in 1963 and enacted by Deng Xiaoping from 1978 to strengthen China's economy in the areas of agriculture, industry, national defence, and science and technology.

Written in 1978, composer Shi Guangnan reportedly chose a passionate, soul-stirring, dynamic Xinjiang dance rhythm and melody for the material. By integrating influences from multiple ethnicities, the song highlighted the shared passion of the people across the nation at that particular political and historical juncture. The song was played during the 1979 CCTV internal New Year's Eve event, with a performance that was considered bold and innovative for the time. Holding wine glasses, guests reportedly ballroom-danced around the room, led by a singer who exuded intense enthusiasm and high spirits, with rich artistic appeal (Zhu jiu ge, n.d.).

In 2008, 30 years later, 'Celebration Drinking Song' was included as the opening song of the first episode 'Spring Returns to the Great Land' (*Chun hui dadi*) of the *Song Voices Float Over 30 Years – 100 Golden Songs Gala* series (*Gesheng piaoguo 30 nian bai shou jinqu yanchanghui*), broadcast on CCTV3. The series ended with the theme 'Harmonious China' (*Hexie Zhongguo*), with the final song being 'Me and You' (*Wo he ni*), sung at the Beijing 2008 Olympic Games by Liu Huan and Sarah Brightman. The series thus took audiences on a journey through China's flourishing history over 30 years of reform, from the joy encountered as it began to open up and reform under Deng Xiaoping to the quiet satisfaction and excitement at becoming a key player on the world's stage and achieving its Olympic Dream under the leadership of Hu Jintao and Wen Jiabao.

While the open-door policy allowed for the flow of foreign capital and technology, it also let in Western ideas and culture. From October to December 1983, conservative factions in the CCP launched a spiritual pollution campaign to try and rid the country of undesirable influxes from the West, including rock music and disco, which were considered vulgar, decadent and excessively indulgent – and especially corruptive to China's malleable and impressionable youth. While there was a moral underpinning to this campaign, some also saw it as an attempt to purge artists and intellectuals who were reluctant to promote orthodox visions of the CCP (Gold, 1984; Iyer and Aikman, 1983). The first major Western rock group to perform a large-scale concert in China was the British hit group Wham! in 1985 (Toufexis and FlorCruz, 1985). The 1980s also saw 'decadent' music from Taiwan and Hong Kong smuggled into mainland China, most representative of which was the smooth, romantic love songs of female Taiwanese singer Deng Lijun. In the early 1980s, it was often said that China was ruled by the two Dengs: Deng Xiaoping by day and Deng Lijun by night (Hooper in Rees, 2000: 135).

During the democracy movement of the 1980s, which eventually led to the Tiananmen Square crackdown on 4 June 1989 where government troops fired at protesters and killed hundreds if not thousands of citizens, many protestors used nationalist anthems and pop songs to rally support. Protesters were calling for a range of things including putting a stop to political corruption and nepotism, and responding to the ills of economic reforms that had benefited some and disaffected many others. A major pop 'anthem' of the times was Hou Dejian's 'Descendants of the Dragon' (*Long de chuanren*, also translated as 'Heirs of the Dragon'). In 1983, Taiwanese singer Hou Dejian became an instant celebrity with this song after defecting to the mainland. The lyrics are about a dragon called China in the 'faraway East'; the people of this ancient land, with 'black eyes, black hair, and yellow skin' are described as descendants of the dragon. According to Linda Jaivin (2001), who has written at length about the life of Hou, he wrote the song when he was a student in Taiwan at a time when cross-Straits relations were extremely sensitive and Taiwanese people could not travel to the mainland. The song reflects his sadness about being unable to reconnect with his ancestral homeland. Hou had said that when he wrote the song he simply wanted to 'get off my chest all the feelings… that the word "China" has inspired in me from the time I was a little kid listening to my father telling me stories of life in Sichuan before the revolution'.

While Hou himself was adamantly against national chauvinism, the song ironically became an expression of Chinese glory. It became popular not only in the mainland but also in Hong Kong, Taiwan and among the Chinese diaspora. Hou actually argued that 'if people would reflect on recent Chinese history, they would see that being a descendant of the dragon was "nothing to shout about"' (quoted in Jaivin, 2001: 9, 52–4). However, the song was aggressively promoted in the PRC to highlight the Taiwanese people's yearning for reunification. It was popularized at a time when China's paramount leader Deng Xiaoping believed that reunification would happen in his lifetime. There was also popular support in Hong Kong and Taiwan for the idea that all of China might be reunited for the first time in a hundred years (Jaivin, 2001: 56; Gold, 1995: 269–70). His performance of the song was also a feature of the 1988 *CCTV Spring Festival Gala* in 1988. In 1989, with Hou's active involvement in the democracy movement, the song took on new meanings when it was sung by protesters during rallies and a hunger strike led by Hou on Tiananmen. In the morning of 4 June 1989, when the CCP's military were about to occupy Tiananmen Square, Hou was one of two leading protesters who bravely negotiated with the military and diverted the potential fatal killing of demonstrators on the Square (NTDTV, 2011).

While the song continues to be performed as an anthem for Chinese solidarity in mainland China, Hou himself was not viewed favourably by authorities. After the government crackdown, Hou took refuge in the Australian embassy in Beijing, and in 1990 the authorities reportedly abducted him and deported him back to Taiwan on a fishing boat. He then migrated to New Zealand where he began writing books and screenplays (Foreign Staff, 2011). According to New Tang Dynasty Television (a New York-based anti-CCP media outlet that is associated with the Falun Gong, outlawed in mainland China), he also appeared widely on Taiwanese television discussing *The Book of Changes* and fortune-telling. He reportedly reconnected with mainland China in 2006, doing some behind the scenes work after a RMB 2 million donation to a civic organization, the China Human Rights Development Foundation. According Human Rights Web, Hou was nominated to be a honourable vice-chairman to this foundation which is constituted by a group of CCP members. He surprisingly appeared in a concert at the Bird's Nest Stadium (Olympic Stadium) in Beijing in May 2011, where he sang 'Descendants of the Dragon' with Li Jianfu who originally popularized Hou's song. However, as a result of stringent media control, most contemporary youth in China would have known little about Hou, the significance of his 'return' and the 1989 incident (NTDTV, 2011).

After the 1989 Tiananmen Square crackdown, many artists tried to distance themselves from politics and sought refuge in wealth and pleasure within the growing entertainment industry. Ironically, in this highly consumerist, celebrity-driven context, revolutionary culture became a highly prized consumer commodity (Gong, 2015: 161). The 1990s saw a revival of the red songs of the socialist era, which typically praised Chairman Mao, socialism and the CCP. Known as the Mao Zedong Craze (*Mao Zedong re*), the CCP cashed in on the market-led fashion, releasing an album in 1992 called *Red Sun* (*Hong taiyang*) with disco karaoke versions of revolutionary folk songs, thus successfully exploiting the market for both commercial and propaganda purposes (Harris, 2005: 402; Barmé, 1999).

While the totalizing doctrines of Marxism, Leninism and Mao Zedong Thought tended to be much more totalizing in the socialist era, in the market era ideology may be understood as an active social practice, which is often unintentional, and operates on the level of everyday sense-making (Zhao, 1998: 4; see also Hartley, 1994: 140–1). Party symbols can be used commercially, and many seemingly non-political symbols have the potential to become politically potent (Sun, 1995b: 195). For instance, appropriation of popular concepts such as 'dream' and 'family', as well as popular songs about 'youth' and 'love', are widely used to appeal to everyday emotions and can become invested with political meanings through associations in certain performances. The Party continues to draw on popular songs as well as creating new songs to educate the public about the importance of the CCP and China's national identity.

Representative songs and albums have been produced that eulogize the themes under different political leaders, although since Mao there has been a notable absence of leader's names in the lyrics of songs, apart from revived songs that celebrate the Mao era. An extensive repertoire of representative songs that have marked important moments in Chinese history continues to be used to educate the public about the importance of the CCP and national solidarity, with old songs often revived and reiterated to serve new political developments and reinforce a collective imagination. As Wong (1984: 143) notes, political songs 'form a chronicle of the vicissitudes through which, over the past hundred years, China has struggled to become a modern nation'.

Many celebrated official songs from the reform and opening up era are in the 'national style' (*minzu changfa*), which in a major way can be attributed to the efforts of one master vocal teacher, Jin Tielin. According to his profile on Baidu (China's Wikipedia equivalent),[3] Jin is an ethnic Manchu from Harbin who has worked at the China Conservatory of Music since 1981 and was president of the Conservatory from 1996 to 2009. He has built a Chinese vocal music system around strong vocal projection, clear articulation, Western operatic elements and a focus on songs with national themes. His famous students who have had celebrated careers as national first-grade singers include Peng Liyuan (wife of President Xi Jinping), Li Guyi (Jin's first wife), Tang Can, Song Zuying, Zhang Ye, Yan Weiwen, Dai Yuqiang, Zu Hai and Chang Sisi. He has trained more than 400 students who have gone on to key positions in China's formal arts institutes as well as in political and cultural apparatuses. Jin himself has been a member of the Chinese People's Political Consultative Conference (CPPCC, *Zhongguo renmin zhengzhi xieshang huiyi*), vice-chairman of the Chinese Musicians' Association (*Zhongguo yinyuejia xiehui*), vice-president of the China Society of Vocal

Music (*Zhongguo shengyue xuehui*), preparatory president of the Chinese National Vocal Music Art Research Association (*Zhongguo minzu shengyue yishu yanjiuhui*) and vice-president of the China Society of Ethnic Minority Vocal Music (*Zhongguo shaoshu minzu shengyue xuehui*). He has been a commentator and judge in many singing competitions including the prestigious *CCTV Youth Singing Competition*.

Exemplary songs by Jin's students sung in the 'national style', composed by a variety of musicians and lyricists, include Peng Liyuan's representative piece 'In the Fields of Hope' (*Zai xiwang de tianye shang*), Song Zuying's 'Good Days' (*Hao rizi*) and 'I Love China' (*Ai wo Zhonghua*), Yan Weiwen's marching song, the 'One Two Three Four Song', Liu Bin's 'Soldier Man' (*Dang bing de ren*), Zhang Ye's 'Into a New Era' (*Zoujin xin shidai*) and Dong Wenhua's 'Full Moon' (*Shiwu de yueliang*), originally a theme song for a television drama, and 'Story of Spring' (*Chuntian de gushi*), which commemorates Deng Xiaoping's tour of southern China where he strongly proposed a further deepening of economic reforms.

Jin's dream has been to carve out an academically rigorous national singing style and popularize Chinese vocal music around the world. A major success in this respect has been the achievements of Song Zuying, who was the first Chinese singer to hold a solo concert at the Golden Hall in Vienna in 2003. She has also performed solo concerts or been a feature singer at the Sydney Opera House (2002), the John F. Kennedy Centre for the Performing Arts in Washington D.C. (2008) and at the Royal Albert Hall in London (2012), as well as during the Beijing 2008 Olympic Games and the Shanghai Expo (2010). Her 2006 CD *The Diva Goes to the Movies: A Centennial Celebration of Chinese Film Songs* was nominated for a Grammy Award in the category of Best Classical Crossover Album.

Under the leadership of Jiang Zemin in the 1990s and early 2000s, songs in the 'national style', such as the choral and orchestral marching song 'The Three Represents and One Flag' (*San ge daibiao yi mian qi*), were created to spread the message of Jiang's major theoretical contribution to Party thought. The 'Three Represents' promoted ongoing scientific and technological development, the enhancement of national power, the 'great rejuvenation of the Chinese nation', national cohesiveness, the education of citizens on 'lofty ideals', 'moral integrity' and 'a strong sense of discipline', and a popular culture 'geared towards the needs of modernization, the world and the future'. All this was intended to allow the Party to 'constantly inject new vitality into itself' (*People's Daily*, 2006).

Interestingly, in 2015 former president Jiang Zemin commissioned Comrade Li Lanqing (vice-premier of the State Council between 1998 and 2003, and a member of the Politburo Standing Committee between 1997 and 2002) to create a song compilation called '45 World Famous Songs', aimed at enhancing international exchanges, increasing respect for different cultures, and deepening global friendships. In his preface to the compilation, the former President explained that China's deepening reform and opening and national strength have significantly enhanced its international status. Increasing exchanges with the international community have become more frequent and cultural exchanges are a particularly important aspect of such exchanges. He notes that there are a variety of ways to tell a good Chinese story and share China's outstanding culture with the world, and that to promote exchanges and friendship between China and other global nations it is also important for Chinese people to learn about 'advanced' foreign culture as well. He gave the example of the Three Tenors' Luciano Pavarotti who sang a Chinese song on one of their world tours, which helped to narrow the distance between Chinese and foreign audiences. At the same time, more Chinese artists are travelling to foreign countries to promote and disseminate Chinese culture and art. The purpose is to engage in acts of mutual interpretation of each other's art, and thus enhance mutual respect for it.

An article about Jiang Zemin promoting the compilation explains that he was a music lover in his youth. Many literary and music societies were set up in colleges and universities in the Nationalist Party areas and in the liberated zones. In the liberated zones most students sang Chinese and foreign love songs, art songs and film songs as well as folk songs and revolutionary songs. The article reports that Comrade Jiang's memory was very strong and he could still accurately sing many of the songs from his youth. However, some of songs seemed to be lost from the records. In particular, for many years he struggled to find a recording or the sheet music for the version of one English song called 'Moonlight and Shadows'. He requested fellow politician Li Lanqing to try and find the right version and provided him with a recording of his own singing. Li's online search could not find the right song. He then asked people in the United States to help find sites about the music and found a 'Moonlight and Shadows' song sheet. It was the 1936 version by the American songwriters Leo Robin and Frederick Hollander, written as the soundtrack for the movie 'Jungle Princess'. But there were still discrepancies between this version and Jiang's rendition, with large sections missing. He then remembered the famous English professor Comrade Chen Lin, and asked him if he knew the song. He did and surprisingly, as they chatted on the phone, he went straight into an impromptu version of the song, which was fully consistent with Comrade Jiang Zemin's lyrics. After further joint research with Professor Chen Lin as well as the Central Conservatory of Music Professor Tang Jianping, vice-president of the Central Opera Huang Xiaoman, and Cheng Fangyuan, they were able to recover the lost version sung on campus 60 years earlier that accorded with Jiang's lyrics and melody, and which was included on the album (*People's Daily*, 2016; *Guangming Daily*, 2016).

Other songs in this album included songs from famous Italian operas (e.g., 'The Woman is Fickle' from *Rigoletto*, 'The Drinking Song' from *La Traviata*, 'Oh My Beloved Father' from *Gianni Schicchi*, 'One Beautiful Day' from *Madame Butterfly*, 'I Lived for Art' from *Tosca*, 'None Shall Sleep (Nessun dorma)' from *Turandot*, 'People Call Me Mimi' and 'What a Cold Little Hand' from *La Bohème*; French songs (Edith Piaf's signature song 'La vie en rose', 'Toreador Song' and 'Habanera' from the opera *Carmen*); German and Austrian songs (e.g., 'Waltz' from the operetta *The Merry Widow*); Russian songs ('Troika', 'Moscow Nights', 'Katyusha' and 'My Moscow'); Anglo-American songs, (mainly from musicals: 'The Sound of Music' from *The Sound of Music*, 'Memory' from *Cats*, 'Think of Me' from *Phantom of the Opera*, 'Tonight' from *West Side Story*, 'Bring Him Home!' and 'Stars' from *Les Misérables* and 'Summer Time' from *Porgy and Bess*, as well as pop classics 'Scarborough Fair' by Simon and Garfunkel, and 'My Heart Will Go On' from the film *Titanic*); as well as Spanish songs (*People's Daily*, 2016; *Guangming Daily*, 2016).

During the era of President Hu Jintao and Premier Wen Jiabao (2003–13), the notion of 'Harmonious Society' (*hexie shehui*) and 'Harmonious World' (*hexie shijie*) was vigorously promoted as China's leaders reflected on the massive social inequality and environmental degradation that had arisen as a result of rapid economic development in the 1980s and 1990s. Introduced in September 2004, the notion of Harmonious Society reached full maturity after President Hu's speech in 2006 (Report of the Sixth Plenum of the Sixteenth Central Committee of the CCP, 2006). The report called for the development of a society with democracy, rule of law, fairness and justice, integrity and fraternity, vitality, stability and order, and harmony between man and nature. Many songs were created to spread the message of a stable and harmonious China under the leadership of the CCP and the notion of China's 'peaceful rise' (Gorfinkel, 2012). Harmonious music was used to educate the population about the concept of a harmonious and stable society (Yin, 2012). Songs educating the Chinese people on the notion of Harmonious Society link to a wide range of official messages. For instance, 'Harmonious Society Cultivates a New Wind' (*Hexie shehui shu xin feng*), aimed primarily at Party cadres, educated audiences on a new set of moral codes distributed in March 2006 called the 'Eight Dos and Eight Don'ts' (also translated as the 'Eight Honours and Eight Disgraces'), which aims to combat issues such as rampant corruption and self-centredness within the Party (Gorfinkel, 2012: 77). The song communicated the official code of conduct directly in the lyrics:

> Love the country; do it no harm.
> Serve the people; never betray them.
> Follow science; discard superstition.
> Be diligent; not indolent.
> Be united, help each other; make no gains at others' expense.
> Be honest and trustworthy; do not sacrifice ethics for profit.
> Be disciplined and law-abiding; not chaotic and lawless.
> Live plainly, work hard; do not wallow in luxuries and pleasures.
> (Xinhua, 2007)[4]

Other songs on 'Harmonious Society' – such as a piece called 'Harmonious Society' (*Hexie Zhongguo*) sung by female military performing arts singer Zu

Hai and the sweet-sounding female vocal group Black Duck Trio (*Hei yazi zuhe*) during a televised concert celebrating the tenth anniversary of Hong Kong's return to China – were linked the notion of the One China principle (*yi ge Zhongguo zhengce*) and the desire to unite Taiwan as well as Hong Kong and Macau with the mainland. The lyrics also consider harmonious connections between man and nature, and with neighbours and friends from abroad.

The notion of 'Harmonious World' was also a strong message in the lead-up to and during the Beijing 2008 Olympic Games. For instance, the song 'Forever Friends' (*Yongyuan de pengyou*) featured foreign and Chinese 'friends' singing happily in harmony. Led by Hong Kong-born Chinese-American pop star Li Wen (Coco Lee) and popular PRC pop star Sun Nan, the song reflected a cosmopolitan view of China engaging with friends from abroad and welcoming them to China (Gorfinkel, 2012).

'Forever Friends' was one of the songs selected to be part of the 'Top 10 Hits of the 2008 Beijing Olympic Games' (*2008 nian Beijing aoyunhui dashi jinqu mingdan*), which were widely promoted on television, on the radio and in public spaces. The songs brought together singers from the great Chinese family, including minorities and Han Chinese, as well as singers from Taiwan and Hong Kong, and overseas Chinese. Apart from 'Forever Friends', two other songs involved a harmonious interchange among celebrities, namely 'Beijing Welcomes You' (*Beijing huanyin ni*) and 'We Are Ready' (bilingual), led by Hong Kong martial arts star Jackie Chan (Cheng Long), who is also well-known in the West. The compilation also included two songs specifically created for the Paralympics, including the Paralympics theme song 'Everyone Is No. 1', sung in Chinese and English by Hong Kong star Andy Liu (Liu Dehua) and 'Cheers to Life' (*Wei shengming hecai*), sung by Tibetan-Chinese pop star Han Hong and male duo Yu Quan. The music video for both these songs brings awareness to audiences about the hardships faced by people with a disability and about how encouragement and personal perseverance can help overcome any impediment.

Compilations of songs of national praise also continued in the Hu–Wen era. For instance, in 2009 an album named *A Hundred Songs in Praise of China* (*Baige song Zhonghua*), comprising ten CDs with 18 songs on each disc, was promoted to commemorate the 60th anniversary of the establishment of the PRC. The album presented itself as a record of social development and progress, allowing people to reflect on beautiful memories from their youth and gain inspiration for the future. Accompanying notes explain that the Chinese people have gone through historical periods that have been both bitter and joyful, but that every period has been accompanied by 'beautiful songs that beat with the pulse of the times', with every musical note representing a 'buried footprint in the grassland'. It states that 'standing at a new historical vantage point, these songs act as the witness of history 'and present', emotional expressions, and reflections of the style and spirit of the nation' (*Hundred Songs in Praise of China* CD, 2009, author's translation).

The first and last CDs in the *Hundred Songs* album place a heavy emphasis on praise for the nation, beginning with the 'National Anthem of the PRC' (*Zhonghua renmin gongheguo guoge*) (CD1) and ending with 'Ode to the Motherland' (*Ge chang zuguo*) (CD10), both of which were also sung during the Opening Ceremony of the Beijing Olympic Games the previous year. Other songs overtly in praise of the nation in the title include 'I Love You China' (*Wo ai ni Zhongguo*), 'My Chinese Heart' (*Wo de Zhongguo xin*), 'My Motherland' (*Wo de zuguo*), 'I Love My Motherland' (*Wo ai wo de zuguo*), 'Motherland is Forever My Home' (*Zuguo shi wo yongyuan de jia*), 'Forever Blessings for the Motherland' (*Zuguo yongyuan zhufu ni*) and 'Bless the Motherland' (*Zhufu zuguo*). The compilation also includes songs of blessings for the Chinese nation, including 'Wish You Peace' (*Zhu ni ping'an*), 'Peaceful China' (*Ping'an Zhongguo*), and 'Tomorrow Will Be Better' (*Mingtian hui geng hao*). It also included a small number of popular love songs that may have originally been written by songwriters as a dedication to a loved individual but have been reappropriated to infer feeling for the nation in the context of the volume, such as 'Lovebird' (*Aiqing niao*) and 'A Small Umbrella' (*Yi zhi xiao yusan*).

In the lead-up to celebrations for the 90th anniversary of the establishment of the Communist Party of China in July 2011, the Central Propaganda Department, China Central Television, Central People's Broadcasting Station, China Musicians Association and the China Art Research Institute jointly organized the 'Sing Towards China – the Masses' Favourite Newly Created Songs' contest. From a year prior to the event, a nationwide six-month effort was put into finding an extensive collection of 'new red songs'. Out of the 18,132 participating works, 36 finalists were selected, culminating in the selection of the top ten winning songs. The selection criteria included the requirement that works had a beautiful melody, embodied the main theme of the times, praised the Party, praised the motherland and presented a fresh vision for a better life. Selected songs included popular songs in praise of the nation and family and included 'Country' (*Guojia*), sung by Hong Kong's Chen Long (Jackie Chan) and 'Go China!', which praises Olympic diver Guo Jingjing, basketball star Yao Ming, and film director Zhang Yimou (*The Guardian*, 2011; *Chongqing Daily*, 2011).

Multiple media formats were used to facilitate mass learning of the new red songs to further enrich their spiritual and cultural life. An official website 'Sing for China' (*Chang xiang Zhongguo*) – which attracted commercial sponsorship from one of China's largest privately owned retailers, a major domestic appliances chain store (Suning Electronics) – published the top 36 'masses' favourite new songs'.[5] *Guangming Daily* published musical scores, which were republished in other newspapers across the country. There were also CD and DVD compilations. These were strongly promoted in April and May of 2011 (*Chongqing Daily*, 2011).

One of the most active regions to promote the new red song fever was southwest China's Chongqing. The unusually charismatic Chongqing Party chief Bo Xilai was trying to change the image of the rapidly developing city, which had been hit by a police crackdown in 2009 that exposed a thriving and greedy criminal underworld, and instead restore 'red morals' and 'mainstream social values'. Between 10 April and 20 May 2011, Chongqing's 30 million-strong population was ordered to partake in a 'chorus of praise for the ruling party', with the *Chongqing Daily* reporting: 'We must use every means to earnestly organise singing lessons for all cadres and people in order to enrich the masses with spiritual culture.' Its municipal television and radio stations relayed live and recorded broadcasts of the 36 songs, its citizens were urged to download the 36 tunes from state television websites, and local newspapers reprinted the daily notations originally published in the *Guangming Daily*. The city held its own community singing competitions and other activities to actively guide cadres and the masses to sing new and old red songs. Grand events such as one held in the Yuzhong District Stadium on 19 April 2011 saw thousands of people from the community jointly singing such songs as 'Without the Communist Party There Would Be No New China' and 'Into a New Era', while 100 pianists jointly played 'The East is Red' and 'Ode to the Motherland' in celebration of the 90th anniversary of the establishment of the CCP. Writers, artists and music educators were also instructed to go deep into the grassroots to teach the masses how to sing and to reignite a red song sung boom in the city (*Chongqing Daily*, 2011; *Sydney Morning Herald*, 2011).

Bo Xilai argued that red songs were popular 'because they depicted China's path in a simple, sincere and vivid way' and there was 'no need to be artsy-fartsy' with only 'dilettantes' preferring 'enigmatic works'. He referred to Mao Zedong in messages to his people, but used these to inspire national unity rather than invoke class differences (*The Guardian*, 2011). Addressing concerns over a revival of a Cultural Revolution-style culture, Xu Chao, the official leading the red song drive, told the *Global Times* that ' "Red" doesn't only represent revolution, communism or socialism. It also includes elements that represent happiness, harmony, being positive and healthy. The term is actually quite inclusive' (*The Guardian*, 2011). Less than a year after these events, Bo Xilai – the son of the late Communist revolutionary Bo Yibo – suffered a dramatic downfall from power when he was expelled from the CCP on corruption charges in a case that was linked to the murder of British businessman Neil Heywood, and was sentenced to life imprisonment in 2013. A staunch critic of Bo, Premier Wen Jiabao made a number of allusions to the damage brought by the Cultural Revolution, which were seen as an indirect rebuke of Bo's attempts to revive a 'red culture'.

Under President Xi Jinping, the notion of the 'China Dream' has been extensively promoted by the Propaganda Department of the Central Committee, the Ministry of Culture, and the State Administration of Press, Publication, Radio, Film and Television of the People's Republic of China (formerly the State Administration of Radio, Film and Television). At the Literature and Artwork Forum (*Wenyi gongzuo zuotan hui*) held on 15 October 2014, General

Secretary Xi Jinping strongly promoted the 80 newly created and released 'China Dream' theme songs from 2013, along with selected works in other art forms that represented the style and feeling of an era. He praised artists working across a range of forms including music, dance, drama, literature, acrobatics and fine art for creating messages that effectively embodied the emotional and spiritual meaning of the 'China Dream' and which were carefully crafted to represent the nation's creativity, wisdom and strength. He expressed hope that the 'true' feelings expressed by songwriters and singers in their songs would resonate with the hearts of the masses. Building on the Party's long-standing position on the use of art to serve politics, Xi's talk emphasized that the Chinese nation needed to see a revival of Chinese culture, that 'positive' artworks needed to be created as representative of this era, and that the CCP's role in creating and supervising artworks should be enhanced and improved (China Dream theme song exhibition official website; *People's Daily*, 2015, 2015; CCTV.com, 2015; Beach, 2015).

Highlighting the coordinated link between the media, music and politics, in December 2015, the *People's Daily* published an article explaining that the new 'China Dream' themed songs were being widely sung and enjoyed by people young and old of all backgrounds, and that the television programming around them had attracted almost 70 million people. It explicitly stated that art workers should take responsibility for promoting the 'China Dream' and contemporary Chinese culture. It also said that academics and experts supported the need for 'China Dream' for the betterment of society. It quotes artistic workers expressing their inspirations for 'China Dream' songs in helping to build a greater sense of love for China (*People's Daily*, 2015).

Official 'China Dream'-themed song CD compilations with dedicated websites including audiovisual clips of the songs have also been produced.[6] In a third such set of 30 songs in 2016, participating performers included 12 military singers, five pop singers, five popular actresses, three successful contestants from popular reality television singing contents and three minority singers. No lyrics specifically mention the CCP or the leader Xi Jinping as in earlier eras. However, key words give full expression to the themes of the times. For instance, 'China Dream, Our Dream' (*Zhongguo meng, women de meng*) sung by Wang Li, a military singer in the Song and Dance Troupe of the Political Department of the Chinese People's Liberation Army Airforce (*Zhongguo renmin jiefangjun kongzheng wengong tuan*) and Zhang Yingxi, a singer in the Opera Troupe of the Political Department of the Central Military Commission (*Junwei zhengzhibu gongzuo geju tuan*) who is also signed with the Washington National Opera, sing about the 'China Dream' as being 'our dream', which relates to family and national prosperity, peace and pride in the nation. In the song 'Rely on You, Me, Him/Her' (*Yao kao ni wo ta*), Qiao Jun, a celebrated tenor from the Second Artillery Song and Dance Troupe of the Chinese People's Liberation Army (*Zhongguo renmin jiefangjun dier paobing zhengzhibu wengongtuan*) links patriotism to hard work. He tells audiences to 'love the nation' (*ai guo*) and 'respect their careers' (*jingye*), and suggests that the 'China Dream' will be realized when everyone plays their part. The militaristic and majestic orchestral and choral song 'The Road to Prosperity and Strength' (*Fuqiang zhi lu*), led by soloists Wang Li and Xue Haoyin in the 'national style', positions China as 'heading to wealth and power' (*Zhongguo zhengzai zouxiang fuqiang*) and 'resplendence' (*huihuang*) and suggests that only if China is strong can the people's happiness be guaranteed (*Zuguo qiangda renmin de xingfu baozhang*). The implications are that Chinese people should not rest on their laurels and that gratification is something to be delayed and obtained in the future with ongoing hard work and belief in the nation under the leadership of the CCP. The music draws on a triumphant Western orchestral and choral style.

Ping An (Anson Ping), one of China's most famous contestants from reality television contests including the *Voice of China* Season 1 in 2012, where he was affectionately referred to as China's Freddie Mercury, based on the style in which he sang the popular rock song 'I Love You, China' (*Wo ai ni Zhonguo*), contributed with a song called 'Everyone Has a China Dream' (*Mei ge ren dou you yi ge Zhongguo meng*). The lyrics reflect a nation bravely looking forward to the future. During the 2016 *CCTV Spring Festival Gala*, Ping An also sang a 'China Dream'-themed song with Wang Zining, the 2015 winner of the CCTV3 reality contest *Star Avenue*. The song 'Big Dreams, Small Dreams' (*Da mengxiang, xiao mengxiang*) links people's individual dreams to the national family and even the universe. Like other winning songs, 'Everyone Has a China Dream' stresses that difficulties and dreams can be overcome with hard work.

Other 'China Dream'-themed events staged for television include the *Build the China Dream – New 'China Dream' Theme Song Gala* (*Gongzhu Zhongguo meng – 'Zhongguo meng' zhuti xin chuangzuo gequ yanchanhui*) sponsored by the Propaganda Department of the Central Committee and CCTV, which was broadcast on CCTV1, CCTV3, CCTV4 and CCTV15 in November 2015. The one-and-a-half-hour production began with an image of a smiling headshot of President Xi Jinping superimposed on an image of the ceiling of the Great Hall of the People, easily recognizable with its central red star, and a written quote, accompanied by majestic orchestral music that read:

> To fulfil the Chinese nation's great revival is the greatest dream of the Chinese nation in the modern era. The China Dream means to realise the country's strength, vigorously develop the nation and enhance the people's happiness.

It's not only official songs that are being performed on the topic of the 'China Dream'. A music video that went viral online in 2014 called 'Big Xi Loves Mama Peng' (*Xi dada aizhe Peng mama*) featured mash-ups of photos and cartoons of President Xi and his wife Peng Liyuan, a celebrated singer in China, showing affection for one another. The video received more than 20 million views after just five days online and was reported on in online news sites. Sung and composed by popular singers Yu Runze and Xu An, known for their quirky Henan dialect songs, the lyrics compare Uncle Xi to a fearless tiger who everyone dreams to see, and Mama Peng to a beautiful flower who is helping to make a happy home, country and world. It urges men to learn from Xi and women to learn from Peng, particularly on how to express their love for one another by smiling at each other and holding hands.

The lyricist, Song Zhigang, reportedly said that he felt inspiration to write the song after seeing snippets of Xi and Peng together in the news, most specifically during the Asia-Pacific Economic Cooperation (APEC) meeting held in Beijing in 2014 (*Bohai Morning Post* (Tianjin), 2014). He said the song expressed his true feelings about the warmth he felt for the couple. After composing the melody, the lead singers of the band known as Artists Five Hundred (*Yi ming wu bai*), Yu Runze and Xu An, recruited nine children aged 4 to 12 to rap along and collected images of Xi and Peng from the internet to accompany the song in a video. After the video went viral, Yu and Xu became instant online celebrities. It was then forwarded by the social media platforms of major television and news networks, including CCTV News and Phoenix. Song Zhigang said that the Chinese people had been very interested in the Xi–Peng love story, and respected their communication and behaviour when on public visits. Song said the piece resonated strongly with netizens because it was down to earth and contained timeless messages of love. They hoped that through this song people would be encouraged to love and respect themselves and their lives, for 'if you love yourself, your home, and your country, then your family will be satisfied, society will be harmonious, and the nation will be strong'. Taken aback by the support from the millions of netizens, the band vowed to make more 'positive energy songs' (*zhengnengliang gequ*) (*Zhengzhou Evening News*, 2014), making this grassroots song, which may to some seem like a spoof (given its Henan accent and comical tone), completely in line with an official call for art that expresses a 'positive energy'. It may be seen as an example of taking popular culture 'from the masses to the masses', where originally unofficial culture from popular culture is gradually appropriated for official means.

'Positive energy' is a term that was widely publicized in 2014 and which has 'become synonymous with government propaganda efforts' (Beach, 2015). Such songs (as with a television drama called *Liangjiahe* about the village where Xi grew up during the Cultural Revolution) can be seen as 'local initiatives designed to cash in on the president's story' and the fact that they have not be quashed indicates that such cultural products are seen as 'politically acceptable and perhaps even useful in bolstering the president's image'. President Xi raised his point about 'positive energy' in his speech at the Beijing Forum on Literature and Art, which was widely compared with Mao Zedong's famous Talks at the Yan'an Forum. In the talk, Xi argued for a return to art in the service of politics, but instead of promoting class struggle as in earlier days, the goal was national rejuvenation and patriotism (Beach, 2015).

As this chapter has shown, political messages have long been embedded in music-entertainment in China, particularly since the early days of the Chinese nationalist movement. Under the CCP, the use of music and art to serve political goals has been and continues to be a strong aspect of the Party's propaganda and method of communicating key – though shifting – messages to the populace. The type of music and entertainment that has been promoted and sanctioned has also shifted over time according to what elites have viewed as 'advanced' global/Western culture in combination with the types of music and art that have been enjoyed by the Chinese masses at a grassroots level. Even in the early days of the CCP, foreign and local forms of music and entertainment have been actively merged in the effort to create 'modern' Chinese forms of art, a trend that continues today. Modern blends of music with politically sanctioned themes have been actively promoted through a range of media, including television, especially after it became widely accessible among the masses in the 1980s. The next chapter provides an overview of the history of television in China and an introduction to the types of music-entertainment programmes that have appeared on PRC television.

Notes

1 For example, 'Nanniwan' has been covered in concerts by Hong Kong singer Zhou Huajian (Wakin Chau/Emil Chau). It has also been sung by a young girl Celine Tam in 2014 and by a boy Bao Weier in 2015 on Hunan Television's reality singing show *China New Sound Generation* (*Zhongguo xin sheng dai*).
2 The 'Gang of Four' was a CCP faction comprised of Jiang Qing (Chairman Mao's last wife, who played a leading role), Zhang Chunqiao, Yao Wenyuan and Wang Hongwen. They came to prominence during the Cultural Revolution and were later charged with a series of treasonous crimes and officially blamed by the Chinese government for the worst excesses of the social chaos during this time.
3 Baidu (n.d.) Jin Tielin. Available at http://baike.baidu.com/view/44582.htm (accessed 18 May 2017).
4 Full lyrics to the song 'Harmonious Society Cultivates a New Wind' (*Hexie shehui shu xin feng*) can be found at www.jungewang.com/Musicplay/5281.com.cn_6230dce921f31e4b_957.html (accessed 18 May 2017).
5 This website includes the top ten songs and top ten music videos, as well as interviews with some singers, http://ent.cntv.cn/program/changxiangzhongguo/xxzg (accessed 18 May 2017).
6 The official songs can also be accessed online at http://ent.cntv.cn/special/zgmgqz/ (accessed 18 May 2017).

References

Barmé, G.R. (1999) *In the Red: On Contemporary Chinese Culture*. New York: Columbia University Press, pp. 1–19.
Beach, S. (2015) Spotlight back on Xi's 'positive energy' in arts. *China Digital Times*. Available at http://chinadigitaltimes.net/2015/10/spotlight-back-on-xis-positive-energy-in-arts (accessed 18 May 2017).

Bird, S.E. and Dardenne, R.W. (1988) Myth, chronicle and story: exploring the narrative qualities of news. In J.W. Carey (ed.) *Media, Myths, and Narratives: Television and the Press*. Beverly Hills: Sage Publications, pp. 67–88.

Bohai Morning Post (Tianjin) (2014) Si ming yinyue ren jiehe shishi chuangzuo yinyue yin guanzhu – you shou 'qing ge' jiao 'Xi dada ai zhe Peng mama [Four Musicians unite to create first 'love song' called 'Uncle Xi and Mama Peng'], 26 November. Available at http://news.163.com/14/1126/08/ABVB8I4900014AED.html (accessed 18 May 2017).

Carey, J.W. (2009) *Communication as Culture: Essays on Media and Society* (revised edn). New York: Routledge.

CCTV.com (2015) 'Zhongguo meng' zhuti xin chuangzuo gequ chengguo fengshuo, guangfan chuanchang ['China Dream' themed newly created songs are rich and widely sung]. Available at http://news.cntv.cn/2015/12/27/ARTI1451173284270730.shtml (accessed 18 May 2017).

China Dream theme song exhibition official website (*Zhongguo meng zhuti chuangzuo gequ zhan*). Available at http://ent.cntv.cn/special/zgmgqz (accessed 18 May 2017).

Chongqing Daily (2011) Chongqing yaoqiu meiti xunhuan bofang 36 shou hongge, shi renren hui chang ai chang [Chongqing requires media to loop broadcasts of 36 red songs, to show the people how to sing and get them to love singing them], 20 April. Available at http://news.163.com/11/0420/05/722FPJF70001124J.html (accessed 18 May 2017).

Clark, P. (2008) *The Chinese Cultural Revolution: A History*. Cambridge: Cambridge University Press.

cnwest.com (2013) 80 niandai 'tingzhong xi'ai de guangbo gequ' chulu shimo [The story behind the 1980s 'Broadcast songs listeners love']. Shaanxi cnwest discussion board, 16 January. Available at http://bbs.cnwest.com/thread-1145552-1-1.html (accessed 18 May 2017).

Cook, A. (2016) The Cultural Revolution at 50: a Q&A with four specialists (part one). *Los Angeles Review of Books*, 24 February. Available at http://blog.lareviewofbooks.org/chinablog/cultural-revolution-50-qa-four-specialists-part-one (accessed 18 May 2017).

Denver, S. (2016) Controversial concert spoils China's plans to bury Cultural Revolution anniversary. *Washington Post*, 9 May. Available at www.washingtonpost.com/news/worldviews/wp/2016/05/09/controversial-concert-spoils-chinas-plans-to-bury-cultural-revolution-anniversary/?utm_term=.296bb6832939 (accessed 18 May 2017).

Donald, J. and Hall, S. (eds.) (1986) *Politics and Ideology: A Reader*. Milton Keynes: The Open University.

Foreign Staff (2011) Tiananmen Square protesters: where are they now? *The Telegraph*, 4 June. Available at www.telegraph.co.uk/news/worldnews/asia/china/8555037/Tiananmen-Square-protesters-where-are-they-now.html (accessed 18 May 2017).

Gold, T.B. (1984) Just in time! China battles spiritual pollution on the eve of 1984. *Asian Survey* 24(9): 947–74.

Gold, T.B. (1995) Go with your feelings: Hong Kong and Taiwan popular culture in Greater China. In D. Shambaugh (ed.) *Greater China: The Next Superpower?* New York: Clarendon, pp. 255–73.

Gong, Q. (2015) Remoulding heroes: the erasure of class discourse in the Red Classics television drama adaptations. In R. Bai and G. Song (eds.) *Chinese Television in the Twenty-First Century: Entertaining the Nation*. London: Routledge, pp. 158–74.

Gorfinkel, L. (2012) Promoting a harmonious China through popular music-entertainment television programming. In J.T.H. Lee, L. Nedilsky and S.K. Cheung (eds.) *China's Rise to Power: Conceptions of State Governance*. New York: Palgrave Macmillan, pp. 71–89.

Guangming Daily (2016) Jiang Zemin we 'Shijie zhuming gequ 45 shou' zuoxu [Jiang Zemin writes the preface for '45 World Famous Songs'], 28 March. Available at http://news.qq.com/a/20160328/013649.htm (accessed 18 May 2017).

The Guardian (2011) Red songs ring out in Chinese city's new cultural revolution, 25–26 April. Available at www.theguardian.com/world/2011/apr/22/red-songs-chinese-cultural-revolution (accessed 18 May 2017).

Harris, R. (2005) Wang Luobin: folk song king of the northwest or song thief? Copyright, representation, and Chinese folk songs. *Modern China* 31(3): 381–408.

Hartley, J. (1994) Ideology. In T. O'Sullivan, J. Hartley, D. Saunders, M. Montgomery and J. Fiske (eds.) *Key Concepts in Communication and Cultural Studies*. New York: Routledge, pp. 139–44.

Herman, E.S. and Chomsky, N. (1988) *Manufacturing Consent: The Political Economy of the Mass Media*. New York: Pantheon.

Holm, D.L. (1991) *Art and Ideology in Revolutionary China*. Oxford: Clarendon Press.

Hong, X. (2009) *Performing the Yellow River Cantata*. Unpublished PhD dissertation, University of Illinois at Urbana-Champaign.

Hundred Songs in Praise of China CD (Baige song Zhonghua) (2009). Available at https://book.douban.com/subject/3930963 (accessed 18 May 2017).

Iyer, P. and Aikman, D. (1983) Battling 'spiritual pollution'. *Time*, 28 November.

Jaivin, L. (2001) *The Monkey and the Dragon: A True Story about Friendship, Music, Politics and Life on the Edge*. Melbourne: Text Publishing.

Mittler, B. (2010) 'Eight stage works for 800 million people': the great Proletarian Cultural Revolution in music – a view from revolutionary opera. *The Opera Quarterly* 26: 377–401.

NTDTV (2011) Tiananmen protestor switches sides? *New Tang Dynasty Television*. Uploaded May 5. Available at www.youtube.com/watch?v=Iuh_C6vKyTA&feature=youtube_gdata_player (accessed 18 May 2017).

People's Daily (2006) The three represents: news of the Communist Party of China, 23 June. Available at http://english.cpc.people.com.cn/66739/4521344.html (accessed 18 May 2017).

People's Daily (2015) Ouge Zhongguo, Changxiang Zhongguo – 'Zhongguo meng' zhuti xin chuangzuo gequ chengguo fengshuo, guangfan chuanchang [Eulogize the China Dream, sing the China Dream – 'China Dream' themed songs fruitful and widely sung], 27 December. Available at http://politics.people.com.cn/n1/2015/1227/c1001-27980598.html (accessed 18 May 2017).

People's Daily (2016) Jiang Zemin qing Li Lanqing bian 'Shijie zhuming gequ 45 shou' bing zuoxu [Jiang Zemin requests Li Lanqing to compile an album called '45 World Famous Songs' and writes the forward], 28 March. Available at http://news.ifeng.com/a/20160328/48235105_0.shtml (accessed 18 May 2017).

Rees, H. (2000) *Echoes of History: Naxi Music in Modern China*. Oxford: Oxford University Press.

Report of the Sixth Plenum of the Sixteenth Central Committee of the CCP (2006) *Resolutions of the CCP Central Committee on Major Issues Regarding the Building of a Socialist Harmonious Society*, 11 October. Available at www.hnmeida.com.cn/glcs/ydzb/xctz/xctz-zywj-zdjd02.mht (accessed 18 May 2017).

Silverstone, R. (1999) *Why Study the Media*. London: Sage.
Sun, W. (1995a) Propaganda – a dirty word? Deconstructing the propaganda model via the Chinese media. In *OUT/POST New Perspectives in Contemporary Thought*. Sydney: Faculty of Humanities and Social Sciences, University of Western Sydney, Nepean, pp. 85–99.
Sun, W. (1995b) *People's Daily*, China and Japan: a narrative analysis. *International Communication Gazette* 54(3): 195–207.
Sydney Morning Herald (2011) Chinese city of 30m ordered to sing 'Red songs', 20 April. Available at www.smh.com.au/world/chinese-city-of-30m-ordered-to-sing-red-songs-20110420-1dohw.html#ixzz4AYKj8j35 (accessed 18 May 2017).
Toufexis, A. and FlorCruz, J.A. (1985) China Peking rock: a dose of spiritual pollution. *Time*, 22 April.
Wong, I.K.F. (1984) Geming Gequ: songs for the education of the masses. In B.S. McDougall (ed.) *Popular Chinese Literature and Performing Arts in the People's Republic of China 1949–1979*. Berkeley: University of California Press, pp. 112–43.
Xinhua (2007) Building of socialist morality called, 19 Sept. Available at www.china.org.cn/government/focus_news/2007-09/19/content_1224942.htm (accessed 18 May 2017)
Yin, Q. (2012) Lun yinyue wenhua yu shehui hexie [Discussing musical culture and the Harmonious Society]. *Musical Works (Yinyue Chuangzuo)* 4: 127–9.
Zhao, Y. (1998) *Media, Market and Democracy in China: Between the Party Line and the Bottom Line*. Urbana: University of Illinois Press.
Zhengzhou Evening News (2014) Zhengzhou yinyue ren chuangzuo gequ 'Xi dada aizhe Peng mama zouhong [Song composed by Zhengzhou musicians 'Uncle Xi Loves Mama Peng' goes viral]. *China.com*, 24 November. Available at http://news.china.com/domestic/945/20141124/18998217.html?hao123 (accessed 18 May 2017).
Zhu jiu ge [Celebration Drinking Song] (n.d.) Baike.com. Available at www.baike.com/wiki/%E3%80%8A%E7%A5%9D%E9%85%92%E6%AD%8C%E3%80%8B (accessed 18 May 2017).

3 Overview of music-entertainment television in China

History of Chinese television

From its inception in May 1958, television in China has been invested with political tasks. During the Cold War, with Soviet assistance, the Chinese Communist Party (CCP) sought to establish the first Chinese television station before the American-backed Nationalists built one in the Republic of China on Taiwan. China's first television station, Beijing Television, the forerunner to China Central Television, was set up as the political 'throat and tongue' (*hou she*) of the CCP. In the early years of television, it was largely used as an ideological weapon to fight imperialism, revisionism and capitalism, as well as for intra-party struggles (Hong, 1998: 133; Huang and Yu, 1997: 568). As with other forms of culture and broadcasting, its aim was to persuade audiences of the importance of building a socialist modernity with workers and peasants at the vanguard of social change (Huang and Yu, 1997: 565; Zhao, 1999: 292). In these early days, there were already tensions regarding how to represent this new culture. Blatant political propaganda had been used, but by 1960 Beijing Television staff were arguing against such a tactic, which audiences saw as 'dull', 'monotonous' and 'insipid', and instead argued for the need to entertain and cater to popular taste in order to attract audiences to core ideological messages (Huang and Yu, 1997: 566–72). To appeal to audience tastes in the early years, China's television stations transmitted theatrical, operatic and musical performances as well as premieres of films and sports events (Bai, 2014: 31).

During the first three years of the Cultural Revolution, which lasted from 1966 to 1976, television, as with many other institutions, came to a standstill (Chang, 1989: 213; Huang and Yu, 1997: 567). In 1969, when it resumed in a limited way (Zhao, 1999: 292; Chang, 1989: 213), approved 'entertainment', a 'dirty bourgeois word' at the time according to author Anchee Min (1994),[1] largely consisted of the eight model operas. 'News' consisted of rolling captions of Chairman Mao's Thoughts, which were accompanied by the song 'The East is Red' (Huang and Yu, 1997: 568; Chang, 1989: 213), the lyrics of which defined Mao as a 'liberating star' who freed the people and brought them fortune.

However, access to television was extremely limited prior to the 1980s. Less than one million television sets were produced between 1958 and 1976 (Zhu and Berry, 2008: 3)[2] when China's population reached 930 million.[3] It was not until the market reforms of the late 1970s that television began to play much more than a negligible role in both Party-state propaganda and in ordinary people's lives (Zhao, 1999: 292). In the 1980s, after the death of Mao in 1976, and when Deng Xiaoping took the Party and China into a new era away from militant socialism and towards economic reform (Hong, 1998: 2–3), China began to follow a broader global trend of neoliberalism, adopting policies of market deregulation, state decentralization and reduced state intervention (Jin, 2007: 180, 185). In this new 'socialist market economy', television stations, along with other enterprises, were allowed to open up to market forces and seek profits (Tay, 2009: 108; Curtin, 2010: 118). The Party-state allowed ever-increasing amounts of popular entertainment to air as long as it did not disturb the social and political stability of the nation on which the CCP's legitimacy was based (Zhao, 1999: 292).

There was a rapid expansion in the number of television stations across China in the 1980s, largely driven by the development of a four-tier broadcast system, comprising of central, provincial, prefectural/municipal and county levels. Before the formulation of the new system in 1983, television stations were mainly run by central and provincial governments, while governments at local levels were discouraged from creating their own television stations. Under the new system, municipal and county-level governments were encouraged to provide broadcast services within their own jurisdictions if they could raise sufficient funds from local businesses or their own budget. Once they had a licence, they had considerable autonomy over management and operational finances (Bai, 2014: 31). The popularity of provincial stations grew dramatically in the 1990s, particularly as they gained licences to air nationally via satellite (Hong, 1998: 139) and as they chose to air entertaining television dramas that focused on the lives of ordinary people (Bai, 2014: 38).

The new market reform policies led to significant increases in living standards, including increased prosperity in the countryside. In a system that allowed people to generate their own wealth, urban residents and farmers could now afford to buy their own television sets as well as some of the products they saw advertised on their screens (Zhu and Berry, 2008: 3; Lull, 1991). Another significant factor in the rise of television viewership was the official change from a six- to five-day working week, implemented in May 1995. By offering citizens more leisure time, this initiative aimed to encourage consumption and stimulate the service and tourism industries (Ma, 2000: 27; Hou, 2009). With the additional time, television viewing became an increasingly popular activity (Hong, 1998: 139; Rofel, 1995: 314). The speed of television development in the post-Mao era was dramatic. In 1978, there were about three million television sets for a population of 950 million, but by

2000, 380 million people out of a total population of 1.2 billion[4] owned television sets, including people in some of the most remote parts of the country. By 2000, it was estimated that 92 per cent of the population had access to television (Zhu and Berry, 2008) and, by 2012, there was a penetration rate of virtually 100 per cent (Zhu, 2012).

Since the 1980s, broadcast television has been the main source of news, entertainment, and national communication for most people in the PRC (Huang and Yu, 1997: 572; Zhu and Berry, 2008: 1–3). Television remains the most effective method of reaching the widest spectrum of audiences given its affordability, and its accessibility in urban and rural areas via a range of platforms including terrestrial broadcast, cable, satellite and the internet. As an audiovisual form it can also readily reach both literate and illiterate audiences.

In the 1980s, it was through television that many, if not most, mainland Chinese people saw foreigners for the first time. Television fulfilled a curiosity among ordinary Chinese to glimpse at the lives of outsiders (Lull, 1991). Foreign language learning programmes, quiz shows and other formats made with UK, American, German and Japanese producers introduced audiences to new styles of entertainment (CCTV.cn, 2012). Viewing imported programmes, programmes about other countries, shows that featured foreign guests and programmes with a foreign design gave people a sense of connection to the outside world. Shows with an international dimension began to appeal to Chinese citizens' sense of cosmopolitanism. As Song (2015: 110) notes, becoming cosmopolitan and transcending locality has, for elite Chinese, become symbolic of a stronger, rising China.

Advertising was allowed on Chinese television from 1978 and between 1983 and 1998, the authorities heavily reduced or terminated subsidies for television stations, meaning that most urban television stations had to rely exclusively on advertising and third-party investment to fund operations (Zhu, 2008: 10). Increased competition for audience share led to a push for programming with diverse themes, styles and formats (Hong, 1998: 139; Chan, 2008: 27; Keane, 2003: 90; 2004: 65; Fung, 2009: 182, 185). In 1986, CCTV became the first station to begin large-scale sampling of audiences across cities, towns and villages to understand audience interests and generate ratings. It joined with provincial and municipal stations to conduct a national survey of urban and rural audiences every five years.[5]

While operating as financially independent organizations, all of China's television stations continue to come under the supervision of the State Administration of Press, Publication, Radio, Film and Television of the People's Republic of China (SAPPRFT), a 2013 institutional restructure of the former State Administration of Radio, Film and Television (SARFT, *Guojia Guangbo Dianying Dianshi Zongju*) – previously known as the Ministry of Radio, Film and Television. SAPPRFT is an executive branch under the State Council of the PRC. It operates under the guidance of the Chinese Communist Party Propaganda Department (*Zhong Xuan Bu*), which in turn comes under the direction of the CCP Central Committee (Shambaugh, 2007: 28–30; Zhang and Cameron, 2004: 310). SAPPRFT 'directly controls state-owned enterprises at the national level', including CCTV, China National Radio, China Radio International, China Film Group Corporation, China Radio and Television Transmission Network Corporation Limited and the China Radio and Television Website (State Council, People's Republic of China, 2014).

Despite ongoing political control, there is nevertheless often a strong confluence between the central authorities and the market. For instance, the China Radio, Film and Television Group (*Guangbo yingshi jituan*), which comprises the above SAPPRFT-controlled organizations, is China's largest and most powerful amalgamated multimedia state-owned and state-run media group. It was formed after China's entry into the World Trade Organization in 2001 as part of China's attempt to face 'challenges from powerful overseas media groups' (China.org.cn, n.d.; *People's Daily*, 2001). Part of its purpose is to position China's media as modern and globally integrated. With more than 20,000 staff and fixed assets worth 21.4 billion yuan, the conglomerate was set up not only to provide broadcasting, film, website and print services, but also advertising, technology development and property management. Its commercial goals were to make more than ten billion yuan in revenue every year. In 2001, Xu Guangchun, the chairman of the group's board of management, who was also deputy head of the Department of Publicity/Propaganda of the CCP Central Committee and director of SARFT, explained that the aim of the group was to be 'a top player in China and Asia and [to] be at the forefront world-wide' (*People's Daily*, 2001).

The music-entertainment genre

After television dramas, the most popular and highly rated genre on Chinese television on weekends, and third most popular after television dramas and news on weekdays, is what is known in Chinese as *zongyi*, 'comprehensive arts and entertainment' or 'variety' shows (Si and Zhang, 2013). According to research by Si and Zhang (2013), television audiences in the PRC in 2013 watched an average of 10.7 minutes of comprehensive arts programming per day on weekdays (compared to 32.2 minutes of television dramas and 14.5 minutes of news) and 16.4 minutes of comprehensive arts programming per day on weekends (compared to 30.2 minutes of TV dramas and 13.9 minutes of news). This category, which has received much less attention than television dramas and news in academic circles, includes reality singing contests and singing-entertainment galas, as well as comical sketches and short TV plays, and aims to appeal to a mass audience.

I use the term 'music-entertainment television' to focus specifically on popular arts and entertainment television shows where songs and singing play a central role. They include reality singing contests and general entertainment programmes with established performers; global formats as well as 'in-house' productions; studio productions and outdoor extravaganzas; roaming shows that take their stage and key performers to cities across China and even across the world; shows with regular episodes and one-off specials; and commercially oriented shows as well as those explicitly set up to commemorate political events. The types of music that appear on these shows include contemporary popular music, folk music and odes to the motherland. They are mostly songs that are widely known and easy for the general population to sing and follow along with the performers on their television screens. The sheer quantity of music-entertainment programmes that target a general populace on state-sanctioned Chinese television at present indicates that they are playing a significant role in contemporary Chinese society and politics. Ordinary contestants on reality singing contests, which are particularly popular, provide inspiration to viewers and function as models for how to live and achieve one's dreams in the contemporary neoliberal market economy where the state no longer provides for the people's needs but where one must excel and prove themselves through their own hard work (Ma, 2015; Luo, 2009).

Chinese cultural programming often embeds a 'subtle' approach to indoctrination and tries to creatively package political lessons in order to make them more effective (Fung, 2009: 187). Lu (1995: 4) argues that Party-state media officials have promoted the 'unconscious' education of the people through entertainment as one of the main aims of contemporary broadcasting. The assumption is that 'Under the veil of entertainment... audiences are oblivious to their own indoctrination' (Eric Kit-Wai Ma in Fung, 2009: 181). Ying Zhu (2008) has shown how popular prime-time television 'dynasty dramas' integrate messages that attempt to justify the CCP's top-down, Confucian leadership style and neutralize public hostility towards the government in the face of increasing social inequality, political corruption and inadequate local government practices. Anthony Fung (2009: 186) has shown how the global *Survivor* television reality format franchise has been used as a basis for educating younger audiences about the Long March whereby 20 challengers retrace the same 6,000 kilometres that the CCP Red Army took to retreat from the Nationalist Party forces in the 1930s, aiming to reignite a patriotic spirit and a sense of loyalty to the Party. The same can be said of music-entertainment programmes. It must be emphasized that more entertainment does not necessarily imply an erosion of the political role of television in China. Nor does being political necessarily imply that a show cannot be entertaining. Rather, different entertainment formats and strategies are being used by producers to meet a range of political, ideological and commercial goals and requirements (see Sun, 2002).

Music-entertainment programmes on CCTV

On 1 May 1978, at the start of the economic reforms, Beijing Television changed its name to China Central Television. The new and the only centrally administered channel headquartered in the nation's capital quickly gained prominence and influence as China's national television network, while a new station, Beijing Television, was set up to cater for the Beijing area (Chang, 1989: 213). CCTV grew rapidly after 1978. As of June 2016, it operated 50 channels including 16 free-to-air channels, 21 digital pay channels, 13 foreign language channels and 64 overseas bureaus. It was accessible to more than a billion viewers worldwide.[6]

CCTV was specifically established to represent the views of China's top leaders on key policy and ideological issues (Pugsley and Gao, 2007: 452–3). With its specific mandate to operate as a 'mouthpiece of the Party' and 'weapon of the state', CCTV is more closely censored than other stations (Fung, 2009: 179; Hong, 1998: 134, 138; Ma, 2000: 22–3). It also plays a particularly vital role in China's 'proactive propaganda' (Shambaugh, 2007: 29), aiming to educate and inculcate in 'internal' and 'external' audiences ideas and visions for society that are in line with Party aims. A key component of its contemporary propaganda at both a national and international level is the management of the state's image by promoting a positive view of China and by strengthening national cohesion (Zhang and Cameron, 2004). CCTV remains the most prominent, authoritative, influential and far-reaching of all China's television broadcasters.

The most popular music-entertainment shows on CCTV appear on CCTV3, its 'comprehensive arts and entertainment/variety' (*zongyi*) channel, which began in November 1995. In December 2000, it was split into three channels: CCTV3, the variety channel; CCTV15, the music channel; and CCTV11, the traditional opera channel. In early 2016, CCTV3 listed 11 daily or weekly regular music-entertainment shows, with another seven listed as being on hold. Some of those on hold had transformed into the new programmes.

CCTV's programming is strongly imbued with 'main melody' (*zhu xuanlv*) themes that directly concern national unity. These themes accord with the values of the CCP, aim to enhance the control of the CCP and promote patriotic and national feelings as well as national unity and harmony between the different ethnic groups. While all music-entertainment programmes on CCTV meet the main melody values, the most popular programme to do so is the is the annual *CCTV Spring Festival Gala*, a four-hour production aired on the eve of every Chinese New Year, which integrates political cultivation with entertainment.[7] Publicly broadcast on television since 1983 and led by the Propaganda Department of the CCP Central Committee, four themes have dominated the Gala, namely love for one's hometown and family; love for the motherland/ancestral land (*zuguo*); the spirit of being progressive and generous; and friendship and love (Yao, 2012).

Watching the *CCTV Spring Festival Gala* at home with the family has become a New Year's Eve ritual for families across China as well as for many Chinese living abroad. The show actively attempts to appeal to audiences in Taiwan, Hong Kong and Macau, and to Chinese overseas through activities such as inviting popular singers from these regions. It also features many songs about the great Chinese family. Despite its political underpinnings, the *CCTV Spring Festival Gala* has consistently maintained the highest annual ratings of any PRC television production, except for 2005 when the grand final of *Super Girl*, Hunan Satellite Television's unofficial take on the UK's *Pop Idol*, topped the charts (Zhong, 2007).[8] To give an indication of the number of viewers the Gala receives, the 2009 *CCTV Spring Festival Gala* reportedly captured '96% of the Chinese television viewing audience on the mainland and had more than 700 million viewers worldwide, including large numbers of people watching the show live via the internet' (Barco, 2009). This makes it the most-watched and longest-running show in global television history (CNTV, 2016).

After 30 years on air, however, and facing competition from other broadcasters and online providers who have staged their own galas, the production team has had to work hard to continue to make the show attractive to audiences. In recent years, extensive efforts have gone into creating a high-tech *CCTV Spring Festival Gala* to demonstrate China's technological advancements and sophistication. The China Television Technology Development Company, a wholly owned subsidiary of China International Television Corporation, established in 1993, which helps to produce the Gala, has partnered with leading global technology partners like Barco to enhance the lighting and audio production for such major CCTV events. It has invested in multidimensional moving stages and special effects software for stage simulation and massive on-stage videos. It has aimed to maximize accessibility through various online platforms including YouTube (officially banned in mainland China) for international viewers. For the 2009 *CCTV Spring Festival Gala*, the CCTV production crew and Barco worked together to create a show that 'seamlessly' blended live performances with visual effects that allowed the audience to be 'fully absorbed in the fabulous imagery'. Promotional material on the Barco website explains that the 'visual scale and brilliant color effects presented the audience with a 3D encounter along the lines of that experienced with the Hollywood blockbuster movie "Avatar"' (Barco, 2009).

Along with the *Spring Festival Gala*, CCTV also hosts other annual seasonal specials, such as the Lantern Festival (*Yuanxiao jie*) (since 1985), the *Mid-Autumn Festival Gala* (*Zhongqiu wanhui*) (since 1991) and the *National Day Gala* (*Guoqing wanhui*) (since 1999). These large-scale entertainment events are often rebroadcast on CCTV1's Comprehensive Channel as well as CCTV's international channels, highlighting the social, political and ideological significance placed on the programmes aimed at reaching as wide an audience as possible.

As the television network specifically mandated to provide programming for the entire Chinese nation, CCTV plays the dominant role in creating a sense of national identity. It aims to reach a broad spectrum of national audiences, including rural and multiethnic populations, older audiences and children, which may be relatively neglected by provincial channels. For instance, CCTV has produced music-entertainment shows like the weekly *Passionate Square* (*Jiqing guangchang*) that took its stage across China, particularly to public squares in small and developing towns, and featured 'ordinary' people from the working classes, such as construction workers, nurses, and schoolchildren enjoying and participating in the singing with the popular singers on stage. *Folk Songs China* (*Min'ge Zhongguo*) is unique in its focus on folk songs from different ethnic minorities from across the nation.

The attempt to appeal to a wide spectrum of audiences is also reflected though the inclusion of a hodgepodge of musical and performance styles. For instance, one music-entertainment show and even one act may be made up of performances by children, a choir of older adults, military singers, minority nationality folk singers and dancers, and pop stars from the mainland, Taiwan, Hong Kong and around the world. Typical examples of such shows include the now suspended *The Same Song* (*Tongyi shou ge*) and *Happy in China* (*Huanle Zhongguo xing*), which were large-scale concerts that took their stages to various cities across China. The Beijing studio-based reality singing contest *Star Avenue* (*Xingguang dadao*) also features 'ordinary people' (*laobaixing*) performing in a wide range of styles.

CCTV4, CCTV's Chinese-language international channel, began in October 1992, was revamped in January 2006, and has played a special role in reaching out to overseas Chinese and attempting to penetrate into Hong Kong, Macau and Taiwan (Zhang, 2011a: 59). It runs a music-entertainment programme called *Our Chinese Heart* (*Zhonghua qing*) that features popular singers from the mainland, Hong Kong, Taiwan, and across the Chinese-speaking world. The programme has also been made available to jet-setting travellers on China Southern Airlines.

Of all networks, CCTV also most carefully considers the moral and ideological impacts of programming, aiming for an appropriate 'balance' between different programme formats, which are believed by media officials to foster a sense of social stability. It aims to balance programming that is morally or ideologically instructive with programming that is entertaining, programming that promulgates socialist core values with those meeting audience demands, as well as programming that meets corporate demands with programming that protects viewers from excessive consumerism (Bai, 2015: 80–3).

CCTV has made significant investments in music-entertainment programming. Some more commercially oriented shows embed political and moral messages in subtle ways, while other 'specials' (*tebie jiemu*) are specifically created to commemorate political events. For instance, in 2008, special episodes of CCTV's MTV-style music video show *China Music Television* (*Zhongguo yinyue dianshi*) were created to celebrate the annual plenary sessions of the two organizations that make political decisions for the nation, namely the National People's Congress (NPC) and Chinese People's Political Consultative Conference (CPPCC), also known collectively as the 'two meetings' (*lianghui*). On 1 October 2009, drawing on the latest technologies, and highlighting its commanding position at the pinnacle of the Chinese television system, CCTV provided a live broadcast of the 60th anniversary of the founding of the PRC that was simulcast on 13 CCTV channels, 35 satellite channels and 176 terrestrial channels, as well as on mobile phone TV, internet protocol TV, mobile TV on public buses and online at CCTV.com. Reaching 2.62 million viewers online, the event produced a global record for a live internet broadcast. It was also the first time the National Day celebrations were broadcast in six United Nations working languages and in HD.

Like other Chinese television stations, CCTV is also currently an entirely commercial operation. However, part of its profit is fed back to SAPPRFT to pay for its political oversight (Zhu, 2012: 4). CCTV, according to Zhu (2012: 265) 'is the very model of China's post-command economy, a media conglomerate that is financially profitable, operationally autonomous, and yet ideologically dependent'. CCTV's commercial engagements in music-entertainment programming include naming rights and sponsorships. For instance, in 2008 it awarded naming rights to its prestigious *Youth Singing Competition* to Longliqi, a shampoo brand. CCTV3's roaming shows have also secured commercial naming rights for companies headquartered in or near the various destinations to which the show travelled. For instance, the Guangzhou-based kitchen company Oupai (known as Oppein in English) sponsored a 2008 episode of the weekly large-scale song and dance show *Happy in China* (*Huanle Zhongguo xing*), called *Happy in China – Charming Oupai* when it aired from Guangzhou.

There is also often a confluence between commercial and political messages. One of the key aims for Oupai in sponsoring *Happy in China* was to assert itself as a strong, famous, modern and globally competitive Chinese brand, which correlates with China's image as a rising power. The goal of this company, which has more than 1,000 stores across China and exports to over 40 countries and regions including in Europe and North America, was to rebuild the brand after the global economic downturn and promote the corporate strength of the Oupai brand to Chinese consumers. During the show, the audience were shown videos of Oupai's modern production workshop, its fashionable products, its high-spirited team and detailed statistics about the strength of the brand. These were intermingled with a performance of the Oupai enterprise song based on the company slogan 'Have a Home, Have Love, and Have Oupai' (*You jia you ai you Oupai*). Famous performers such as Taiwan-based Singaporean singer Lin Junjie (JJ Lin), were involved in a percussion set that made use of pots, bowls, pots, cups and other kitchen items.

The journey of this brand epitomized China's 30 years of economic development, the growth of private enterprise and innovation, and a shift from 'Made in China' to 'Created in China'. Host Dong Qing explained that Oupai was the first company to introduce kitchen cabinets to China as China began to open up to ideas from abroad and people began to be able to afford to own, build and renovate their own kitchens. During the episode, the brand was also praised by Wu Yimin, the executive vice-mayor of Guangzhou, for its role in guiding the development of Guangzhou and helping it to transform into a modern, open, harmonious and civilized city, a key message in the lead-up to Guangzhou's hosting of the 2010 Asian Games (CCTV's *Happy in China*, 2008).

The entanglement between commerce, culture, politics and CCTV can also been seen in marketing and brand communication techniques used by Oupai. Comparisons were made between Oupai and leading international company Procter and Gamble who had earlier sponsored a similar CCTV3 large-scale song and dance show, *The Same Song*, highlighting China's ability to 'catch up with the West' in its ability to create reliable big international brands. In a highly considered cross-promotion at a time when the creative industries were gaining traction, the songs performed by famous artists during the show were also made into a CD, which was to be made available in Oupai stores nationwide for playback and for sale (CCTV's *Happy in China*, 2008).

Politics does, however, sometimes interfere with commercial ambitions. For instance, after 31 years of airing commercial advertisements, from 2013 all commercial advertising was banned from airing during the *CCTV Spring Festival Gala*, China's most lucrative show. While sponsorships, product placements and mentions in hosts' speeches were still allowed, this was part of a government 'Zero Commercial Spring Festival Gala' campaign that began in 2010 and was aimed at limiting the commercialization of traditional Chinese culture. Over the three years, CCTV lost 1.75 billion yuan (US$280 million) in potential advertising revenue. Instead of an advertisement for Midea group, a leading Chinese home appliance manufacturing and export company, which won the bid to air an advertisement during the 2010 countdown, generating roughly 50 million yuan for ten seconds, the 2013 countdown featured a public service advertisement emphasizing the significance of Chinese traditional culture, family reunion and Chinese values. However, this action should not be seen as an entirely top-down operation as it also appeared to respond to a considerable number of audience complaints about excessive advertising during television programming (Chen, 2013).

CCTV also runs local and imported reality singing contests. The most formal and prestigious has been the in-house *CCTV Youth Television Singing Competition* (*Qingnian geshou dianshi dajiangsai* or *Qingnian geshou dasai* in short), which first began in 1984. Over the years, contestants have competed in the 'national style' (*minzu changfa*), Western operatic/bel canto style (*meisheng changfa*), popular music (*liuxing changfa*), 'original ecology' folk songs (*yuanshengtai*) and choral group (*hechang*) categories. Many winners of this competition have gone on to develop careers as regular singers for CCTV's regular music programmes. Other popular in-house shows have included the light-hearted *Star Avenue* (*Xingguang dadao*), in which contestants joke with hosts, and *I Want to Enter the Spring Festival Gala* (*Wo yao shang chunwan*), for which winning contestants have the chance to perform on the *Spring Festival Gala*.

CCTV has also invested in foreign formats, such as *Rising Star*, known in China as *China is Listening* (*Zhongguo zhengzai ting*, in 2013). The format is owned by Israeli production company Keshet International, and has also been sold to more than 30 other countries and territories. CCTV collaborated with private Chinese media production company Enlight Media (*Guangxian chuanmei*) who bought the rights to the format and broadcast the technically sophisticated interactive show in 2014. Enlight Media was the first private Chinese company to import a big-name format, beating stiff competition from other bidders, including Hunan and Jiangsu satellite television stations and other private production companies.

Rising Star allowed audiences to vote via a mobile phone or tablet app in real time and leveraged on the second-screen viewing habits, particularly among youth, whereby many audiences are likely to be playing on their tablets or smartphones while watching television (Beaumont-Thomas, 2013). A progress bar on the screen tracked the percentage approval rating as votes came in, and audiences' social media profile pictures appeared on a big screen on the stage. When the deal between CCTV and Enlight Media was announced, CCTV3 programme director Wen Ha expressed excitement about the format 'because of its cross-platform and interactive features, which are things that have never been seen before in Chinese television' (Coonan, 2014). The programme was a success with the online rating of the first episode of the show ranking third across all variety shows in China, and it was the top reality singing contest at the time.[9]

With China's entry into the World Trade Organization in 2001 and hosting of the Olympic Games in 2008, there has been a strong focus on China's globalization and in establishing China as a strong player in international trade. Since China's opening up, the flow of cultural products including television series, films and music has, however, been much greater from Taiwan and Hong Kong and other overseas markets into mainland China than the other way round (Tay, 2009). Chinese producers have been eager to reverse this trend. Reality singing format *Sing My Song* (*Zhongguo hao gequ*, lit: 'China's good song'), which premiered on CCTV3 in January 2014, became the first original mainland Chinese talent format to be exported abroad.

In this adaptation of *The Voice*, aspiring singer-songwriters on *Sing My Song* perform their own original songs rather than covers of popular hits of already famous stars. The UK-based international television distribution company ITV Studios Global Entertainment bought the rights from rights-holders Star China (*Canxing*) at the MIPTV (Marché International des Programmes de Télévision), one of the world's largest global distribution markets and television and online content development events, in Cannes in 2014. ITV was reportedly impressed by the results of the show's debut in China, where it reached 480 million viewers over the series and gained a total audience share of 37 per cent, boosting CCTV3's slot ratings by 59 per cent. ITV announced a Vietnamese version (to be produced by Cattienda Media and aired on VTV3) and a British version, and has noted substantial global interest in the series, including from Universal Music Group who were interested in 'casting singer-songwriters as the show's producer-judges, providing prizes and releasing original music from the series' (Walsh, 2015; 'ITV Studios Global Entertainment to Collaborate', 2014).

Vivian Yin, chief representative of Star China, explained that while Star China has extensive experience in localizing imported formats owned by ITV such as *The Voice*, *X Factor*, *Take Me Out* and scripted shows like Fox's *Glee* for PRC audiences, she was 'ecstatic' to see the process go in the other direction. Mike Beale, director of International Formats for ITV Studios said the deal was a fantastic example of the benefits of a British–Chinese creative partnership (Rodrigue, 2014; Geng, 2014).

Apart from trade in programmes and formats, CCTV has also experimented with globalization strategies that involve physically taking their shows overseas. For instance, *The Same Song*, a roaming show on CCTV3 that moved across China from city to city each week, experimented between 2005 and 2008 with hosting episodes in various global locations like New York, Vancouver, London and Sydney, where large numbers of Chinese people live. A former employee of *The Same Song* noted in an interview conducted for this book that the main aims for going abroad were to attract Chinese viewers and sponsors abroad as well as to attract local PRC audiences who were becoming bored with the format that had been running since 2000. The show was eventually pulled from production, with interviewees suggesting that it could no longer compete with the vast number of music clips and engagement with pop stars that ordinary people could now obtain online.

While imported reality shows have been popular in China, they are mainly aired on provincial satellite networks. In general, CCTV has focused on creating its 'own' formats, which may draw on the best from around the world and from China. For instance, *Open the Door to Luck* (*Kaimen daji*) on CCTV, launched in 2013, proudly explains on its website that this new large-scale variety show combines the world's latest television elements, while fully taking into account the needs and aspirations of the Chinese audience to determine a unique programme form that does not imitate or follow suit and is completely different to other national television programmes.[10]

As of early 2016, CCTV15, the specialized music channel, aired 11 regular music shows, including a six-day a week music-video programme, *China Music Video* (*Zhongguo yinyue dianshi*), as well as a programme *Folk Songs China* (*Min'ge Zhongguo*). The underlying tone of these shows tends to be on educating audiences about different forms of traditional and classical music that make up the rich heritage of Chinese and Western culture. CCTV also offers a pay TV music channel called 'Wind-Cloud Music' (*Yunfeng yinyue*), which launched on 9 August 2004. This channel owns the exclusive copyright to certain foreign programmes such as *M! Countdown* and *Super Star K* from Mnet Media in Korea, *Running Man* from SBS in Japan, *Music Station* from TV Asahi Japan, *C and D: UK* from Independent TV in the UK. Given CCTV's particular remit to focus on 'the nation', its shows are the main subject of this book.

However, provincial satellite channels cannot be ignored as they also have national reach and are often more popular than CCTV shows.

Music-entertainment programmes on provincial satellite channels

Provincial satellite channels spearheaded the rise of popular entertainment programming that catered more effectively to audience interests. Hunan Provincial Satellite Television's reality show *Happy Camp* (*Kuaile Dabenying*), first aired in 1998, was the first in a series of innovations that gave the channel a reputation for being a leader in entertainment programming and set off an entertainment trend across mainland China's networks.

In 2015, 19 provincial satellite channels listed 43 regular music-entertainment programmes, with 21 running at the time. Of these, Hunan Satellite TV, Zhejiang TV and Shanghai's Dragon TV (*Dongfang weishi*) had the best rating entertainment shows. According to the list of the top 30 rating comprehensive arts and entertainment episodes on provincial channels between 2005 and 2015, 14 episodes were on Hunan Satellite TV. This included the number one ranking episode, the *Super Girl* (*Chaoji nvsheng*) finals in 2005, the first hit reality television singing contest in China. The 2009 and 2011 finals of *Super Girl* also made it to the top 30 list. Also on the list from Hunan Satellite Television were the 2013, 2014 and 2015 finals of *I am a Singer* (*Wo shi geshou*), a reality format imported from MBC Korea involving a competition between already-famous pop stars (ranked 14), and the 2007 finals of *Happy Boy* (*Kuaile nansheng*), a male version of *Super Girl* (ranked 24).

Nine episodes of the top 30 were from Zhejiang Satellite TV. This included the second most-watched episode during this period, *The Voice of China* (*Zhongguo hao shengyin*) Season 4 finals in 2015, which was an official version of the imported Dutch format. Also on the list was *Chinese Dream Show* (*Zhongguo menxiang xiu*) (ranked 28), which drew on elements from the BBC television show *Tonight's the Night* along with elements from Zhejiang Television's earlier variety show *Under the Happy Blue Sky* (*Kuaile lantian xia*). Four top-rating episodes were from Shanghai's Dragon TV, including the third highest rating episode, the 2010 finals of *China's Got Talent* (*Zhongguo darenxiu*), which was China's first official import of a foreign reality contest (from the UK) (tvtv.hk, 2015).

Other foreign formats that were bought by Chinese television stations include *Chinese Idol* (*Zhongguo meng zhi sheng*, lit: China Dream Voice), the official version of *Pop Idol*, the British reality TV format (in 2013), and *Super Diva* (*Mama miya*) from Korea, which were broadcast on Dragon TV, and the *X Factor* (*Zhongguo zui qiang yin*) from American Fox broadcast on Hunan Satellite Television. An official Uyghur language version of *The Voice*, known as *The Voice of the Silk Road* also aired on a channel of Xinjiang Provincial Television, which only has provincial broadcast reach, but was also available online. Given the language barrier, however, few non-Uyghur Chinese would have watched this show.

Such globally inspired reality contests have been attractive to provincial broadcasters for their commercial appeal. Their appeal to middle-class youth has been attractive to advertisers and sponsors including Chang'an Ford (a joint venture between the Chinese and American automobile manufacturers),[11] which acquired naming rights for *Chinese Idol*, Jiaduobao herbal tea soft drink company, which acquired naming rights for *The Voice of China*,[12] and Mongolian Cow Yoghurt (*Meng niu suan suan ru*), which acquired naming rights for *Super Girl*.

Provincial satellite channels who broadcast global formats like *The Voice* and *Idol* appeal to a sense of global cosmopolitanism in a major way through contestants' singing of 'big' English-language pop songs, which are rarely performed on CCTV. For instance, in Season 1 of *The Voice of China*, the contestants sang Michael Jackson's 'Black or White',[13] Adele's 'Rolling in the Deep'[14] and Beyoncé's 'Halo'.[15] However, provincial channels still strongly appeal to a sense of national identity to create and maintain connections with a nationwide audience. Thus, while many singers started with big English songs in the early rounds, they often shifted to Chinese-language songs in the latter rounds. As one former employee of *The Voice of China* interviewed for this book noted, the reason for this was that singing in Chinese would better help the contestants to connect with a Chinese audience base:

> I don't know if audiences like these big English songs. But I think… the most compelling songs that attracted and resonated with the audience were usually not in English because they can't connect with the lyrics. Mentors advise contestants to choose Chinese songs in the battle round, because if they want to touch the audiences' hearts and move them, this will not only come from their voice, but also from the lyrics. English songs can touch people, but not all audiences can understand the lyrics. Language is still an obstacle.

Another element of global formats on provincial channels that has appealed to youth is an emphasis on the individual agency of the contestants and the significance of 'their story', as opposed to an overemphasis on collective, national stories on CCTV. The contestants' stories were often constructed around how their developing talents in singing helped them to overcome negative perceptions of some kind of personal mental or physical impediment, and how it had helped them to 'own' these differences, which in turn led to a blossoming of their self-confidence. Such impediments included having a stutter, being overweight, having a voice that was abnormally high-pitched for a male or having skin that was darker than other Chinese. One can argue then that the language of the song played a key role in their stories, from starting off with English songs where they may have originally drawn inspiration (and perhaps found refuge in the language and music of 'the other') towards growing their own unique (Chinese) personality, which they could proudly announce in front of a national audience. However, according to a former employee of *The Voice of China* interviewed for this book, the choice of an English language song had 'nothing to do with language' per se, but was all about the music that allowed them to demonstrate their story and talents:

> Choosing the big powerful English songs was mainly the singers' choice… Some rock singers chose Western classics because a lot of Chinese rock songs are influenced by Western rock songs. Singers just want to find the original rock music that influenced them in order to express their feelings and emotions. Some popular songs, like Adele, [were chosen] just because they believe these songs are more suitable for showing their timbre or skills. It's about personality and personal preference.

While the focus on individual interest, agency and choice as well as that of personal salvation is strongly conveyed in the discourse of interviewees, the shift to Chinese songs over the course of the show ensured each season ended with a strong feeling of collective Chinese sentiment. Interestingly, none of the former employees of global formats in China interviewed for this book mentioned a broadcast regulation stipulating that at least 75 per cent of songs aired on variety and reality shows must be in Chinese. The final song of the winner of Season 1 of *The Voice of China*, Liang Bo, was the rock song 'I Love You China' (*Wo ai ni Zhongguo*), originally sung by coach Wang Feng, highlighting the ongoing appeal of patriotism even in a highly commercialized, globally inspired context.

Overtly pro-CCP songs are also embedded at strategic moments in provincial satellite television contexts. Even on the number one ranked reality singing contest, Hunan Satellite Television's 2005 *Super Girl*, the winner Li Yuchun sang an overtly pro-CCP song 'Party, Beloved Mother' (*Dang a, qin'ai de mama*), while fellow contestant Zhang Liangying sang 'Me and My Motherland' (*Wo he wo de zuguo*).[16] On 30 August 2015, Ping An sang 'Ode To Yanan' (*Yan'an song*) on episode 9 of Jiangxi Satellite Television's *The Playlist* (*Chaoji gedan*) during the 70th Anniversary of the Victory over Japan (VJ) Day Special, a political commemoration that was embedded into the show.

In general, international television programme formats like *The Voice*, *X Factor* and *Idol* have been welcomed by many media professionals, officials and scholars in China because they are able to actively represent China's globalization while allowing for a relatively strong degree of control of content through the use of local songs, contestants, hosts and mentors. Unlike trade in complete programmes from foreign countries, such programme 'blueprints' allow local producers to creatively localize the programme for national audiences. Traditional Chinese characteristics such as the costumes and folk music of minorities can also be woven into the shows (Liang, 2015; Zheng, 2013). A number of Chinese scholars are excited by the new and innovative Chinese brands being developed out of unique blends of foreign and Chinese elements (Sun, 2011; Li, 2014). Working with foreign television partners also helps practitioners to open their

Music-entertainment television in China 65

eyes to what their industry lacks (Yang, 2007), enables them to learn new and 'advanced' television management approaches, and forms a basis for attracting international investment (Liu, 2009). While there is a strong sense of optimism for Chinese-foreign blends among some Chinese scholars, others are still concerned with the risks of the format trade, including the blind worship and copying of foreign formats, which they feel may actually reduce innovation and creativity as well as a sense of national spirit (Yang, 2007). Some are also doubtful that Chinese broadcasters with their limited resources and low efficiency models are adequately equipped to deal with the administration of high-quality commercial programmes (Tian, 2009).

While foreign imported formats are generally the most popular music-entertainment shows, there are many other reality singing contests and music-entertainment programmes on provincial channels. A perusal of their titles highlights a solid attempt to continue reigning in popular music to serve Party-state priorities. For instance, from 2006 to 2013 Jiangxi Satellite Television broadcast the *China Red Songs Gala* (*Zhongguo hong ge hui*), in 2013 Guizhou Satellite Television ran *Sing for China* (*Wei Zhongguo ge chang*), in 2009 Liaoning Satellite Television had *Singing China* (*Changyou Zhongguo*), Shandong Satellite Television has aired *China Star Strength* (*Zhongguo xing liliang*) since 2013, Shanxi TV has broadcast *Songs From the Yellow River* (*Ge cong Huanghe lai*) since 2014, and Sichuan Satellite Television aired *China Love Big Gala* (*Zhongguo ai da ge hui*) from 2011 to 2012. Programmes featuring songs in minority languages can also be found, such as *China Tibetan Songs Gala* (*Zhongguo Zang ge hui*) on Sichuan Satellite Television since 2011 and *Zhaxixiu* on Tibet Satellite Television since 2015. The title itself firmly educates audiences on the fact that Tibetan culture is a part of China.

Provincial networks also produce more overt propaganda music-entertainment shows similar in tone to those seen on CCTV. For instance, in 2014 Guangdong Satellite Television aired the *100 Songs in Praise of the Chinese* (*Bai ge song Zhonghua*) made up of patriotic songs such as 'China Dream' (*Zhongguo zhi meng*), 'Red Flag Fluttering' (*Hongqi piaopiao*), 'Descendants of the Dragon' (*Long de chuanren*), 'Spring has Come' (*Chuntian laile*) and 'Sing a Folk Song/ Mountain Song for the Party' (*Chang zhi shange gei dang ting*). In the same year, Guangdong Satellite Television ran a competition called *Sing Towards China* (*Bai ge song Zhonghua*) in celebration of the 65th anniversary of the PRC. The show was sponsored by the CCP Guangdong Provincial Party Committee Propaganda Department (*Zhonggong Guangdong sheng wei xuanchuan bu*), the Guangdong Agency for Cultural Affairs (*Guangdong sheng wenhua ting*), the Guangdong Radio, Film and Television Bureau (*Guangdong sheng guangbo dianying dianshi ju*) and the Guangdong Musicians' Association (*Guangdong sheng yinyuejia xiehui*), and involved cooperation with local choirs of governmental departments, universities, state-owned companies and schools.

Overall, while provincial channels are well known for their popular and commercially driven reality singing contests imported from abroad, there are also many locally produced music-entertainment programmes that follow a political line in terms of fostering both a particular kind of national identity and a positive impression of the CCP. At key moments Party-state politics can also be readily embedded within global formats, which can be easily localized.

Music-entertainment programmes on city and county television

Apart from the provincial satellite channel that each provincial television network runs and which has national reach, within each province are many other 'lower-tiered' channels at provincial, city and county levels. According to the *Chinese Broadcasting and TV Yearbook* of 2011, at the end of 2010 there were 247 television stations and 3,985 broadcasting and TV channels nationwide, including 178 paid channels and 16 HD TV channels (Wang, 2011: 31). The presence and type of music-entertainment shows varies from station to station. Many city and county channels air variety programmes on special seasonal occasions such as Mid-autumn Day, National Day and the Spring Festival. For example, Shanghai Television as a city channel has many regular music-entertainment programmes particularly on its Music Art Humanities Channel. These include *Frontline Music* (*Yinyue qianxian*), a show that promotes popular music and stars; *Freely Classic* (*Zongheng jingdian*), which focuses on classical music and symphonies; and *Live House* (*Xingguang xianchang*, lit: Star Stage), which invites stars as guests to play games with hosts, including singing competitions. Beijing Satellite Television runs a programme called *Music Masterclass* (*Yinyue da shike*) where kids sing patriotic and revolutionary songs, which, for instance, may have been their grandparents' favourite songs, are taught about the history of the songs, and receive guidance from seasoned mentors who are famous singers in China.[17] Other city-level broadcasters, like Harbin Television, do not seem to have any regular music-entertainment programmes, although they may have produced some one-off special galas to celebrate such events as the Spring Festival and National Day, and sometimes rebroadcast CCTV's music programmes. While visiting small counties across China I have seen small provincial county TV channels (as well as live performances) that involve students from local kindergartens and schools as well as local celebrities singing and dancing in performances led by hosts following a format similar to that of CCTV's roaming entertainment shows like *Passionate Square* (*Jiqing guangchang*) and *Happy in China* (*Huanle Zhongguo xing*).

Music-entertainment on foreign-owned TV stations in China

There are also music-entertainment programmes on foreign-owned Chinese-language satellite TV stations operating in China. Foreign channels with landing rights in China focus heavily on light entertainment and financial news, which are considered less controversial than other formats and are strategic choices made to ensure maintenance of their licenses. Ruoyun Bai refers to this as 'market censorship' (Horesh, 2014: 84). These channels are not widely accessible to a general Chinese public and are generally restricted to three-star hotels and above and to people whose jobs require access to foreign media, such as journalists. Some channels are accessible to people in certain areas of mainland China, such as in Guangdong province just across the border from Hong Kong.

MTV Mandarin, owned by MTV Networks Asia Pacific, which comes under the parent company Viacom, is one such foreign-owned television channel that services Chinese communities across Asia in places including Singapore, Taiwan, Hong Kong, Indonesia and Malaysia, as well as mainland China. The 24-hour music channel, which combines Mandarin-language and international music, first entered China through Taiwan. Premiering in Taipei on 21 April 1995, it was broadcast across Asia including mainland China via satellite. Television viewers on the mainland have had to arrange a special paid package to watch it.[18] In 1999 it gained rights to broadcast in foreign compounds and hotels of three-stars and above (Jin, 2011). In April 2003, after approval from SARFT, MTV obtained landing rights in Guangdong province and became the first foreign-owned TV channel to launch in mainland China (mtvchina.com, n.d.). It set up an 'MTV China' hub in Beijing. Its programmes feature Chinese popular music, English-language popular music from Europe and America, J-pop (Japanese) and K-wave (Korean) pop music, as well as entertainment news and interviews with singers.

Cooperation between MTV and CCTV began before MTV officially entered mainland China, with the *CCTV–MTV Music Gala* (*Yinyue shengdian*), starting in 1999. The latest Gala was held in Beijing in 2012.[19] Another event, the grand *MTV Style Gala* (*Chaoji shengdian*), which first began in 2003, involved cooperation with Beijing Television (BTV) in 2011.[20]

Competition and collaboration in the music-entertainment industry

Many people are critical of CCTV for its favoured status by the SAPPRFT, which allows it to gain what is widely seen as an unfair advantage in the market. The general director of CCTV even sits in the Party Committee of SAPPRFT as one of its core members (Meng, 2009: 262). As Zhong (2001: 173) explains, while CCTV is 'nominally a non-profit organisation representing the national government... it has used its official monopoly status to engage in a wide range of official-profiteering activities'. Zhong (2007: 78) criticizes CCTV for being 'a conspicuous bully', citing the example of its 2004 labelling of Hunan Satellite Television's *Super Girl* (*Chaoji nvsheng*) as an 'evil and popular program', but months later producing a competing talent quest, *Dream China* (*Mengxiang Zhongguo*), which was promoted as a 'healthy' alternative.

Dream China imitated many elements from *Super Girl*, including SMS and real-time voting as it attempted to generate interest in the next 'China Idol' (*Zhongguo ouxiang*). Contests were held in 13 cities across China, including Hong Kong – more cities than *Super Girl*.[21] However, certain key elements were missing from *Dream China* because of the more morally and politically inflected production values underpinning CCTV. While provincial networks are often known for providing programming that allows ordinary contestants as well as audiences to participate in a spontaneous and unscripted way, improvisations on CCTV often come across as 'fake' or 'skin deep' (Zhong, 2007: 74; Lu, 2009: 124). CCTV's shows tend to be much more formal, serious and rehearsed in style (Lu, 2009: 124; Zhong, 2007: 74). Even when they try to present a more participatory and spontaneous atmosphere, studio audiences tend to be presented as 'passive, voiceless decorations' who are 'spoken to' by all-knowing hosts (Lu, 2009: 124) and audience participation in the form of voting for favourite artists often appears to be based around 'rigged ballots' (Zhong, 2007: 74) or involve ballots with excessive input from professional media or officials rather than ordinary viewers.

Meng (2009: 262) argues that this type of bullying of provincial satellite channels has incited a long-existing 'disgust and anger among the average Chinese audience toward the monopoly of CCTV', while Zhong (2007) suggests that more popular support for *Super Girl* than *Dream China* could be defined as 'a symbol of popular revolt against the state broadcaster'. With its mass voting system, the democratic potential of *Super Girl* on Hunan Satellite Television in 2006 excited many commentators. For some authors, the massive interest in the show that allowed audiences to voice their opinions and cultivate desires for personal freedom and liberation represented their 'resistance' not only to CCTV but also to the political status quo (Ma, 2000: 31; Lu, 2009: 123). The 'depoliticized' approach that downplayed CCP top-down-style politics offered the potential for imagining a new kind of democratic bottom-up politics. For others, however, the outlet for audiences to 'have a say' was no more than a commercial tactic that had limited political significance beyond the show itself (Yu, 2001: 200, 204, 215). Allowing such programmes to be broadcast may actually be seen as part of a broader effort by the CCP to 'de-politicize' itself as an 'ordinary' day-to-day administrator in order to better appeal to PRC citizen audiences (Lu, 2009; also see Wang, 2006: 688).

While it has been popular to pit CCTV against the provincial networks who have become powerful contesters for audience share, provincial satellite channels and CCTV must be seen as part of a broader system that is both competitive and cooperative. On the one hand, competition is encouraged because it promotes a national culture that leads to audiences choosing Chinese programmes as opposed to foreign ones (Lu, 2009: 119, 123; Hong, 1998). On the other hand, cooperation allows the channels to not only promote Party policies concerning China's market economy and various aspects of its national cohesiveness, but also to appear strong on a global scale.

There are many examples of cooperation between television channels. For the most part, cooperative activities typically place CCTV in a dominant position. For instance, in the first season of CCTV's *I Want to Enter the Spring Festival – Direct to the Spring Festival Gala* (*Zhitong Chunwan*) in 2012, leading contestants from Zhejiang Satellite Television's *The Voice of China*,

Jiangxi Satellite's *China Red Song Contest* (*Zhongguo Hong Ge Hui*), *The Voice* Hong Kong (*Chaoji Jusheng*, lit: *Super Giant Voice*) (TVB) and Taiwan's (TTV) *Super Idol* (*Chaoji Ouxiang*) participated, along with contestants who had already become well-known from competing in CCTV's *Star Avenue* and *Feichang 6+1*, and six other provincial and regional satellite reality television singing contests. Many of these contestants already had a strong national following based on their participation in shows on provincial networks, but were in the running for even more expansive national and international exposure if they won the opportunity to perform on the *CCTV Spring Festival Gala*.[22]

The Party-state's efforts to create a cohesive national television system may be epitomized by the creation of the China Network Television (CNTV) platform, which is a comprehensive conglomeration of all of China's major television channels in one online hub. The launch of CNTV on 28 December 2009 represented a serious attempt to tap into the increasingly sophisticated and interactive online market and to appeal to audiences who were moving away from traditional television sets. By the end of 2015, the estimated number of internet users had reached 668 million, with a rate of access of more than 50 per cent of the population; this number is rising rapidly (Lee, 2016). CNTV has described itself as 'a national web-based TV broadcaster' that 'provides users with a globalized, multilingual and multi-terminal public webcast service platform' and presents itself as an ambitious one-stop portal for China's major television broadcasters on the internet.[23] A range of formats have been offered, including live broadcasts, video on demand, file upload, and search and videocast services. It aims to be an 'authoritative' and 'world-class online TV broadcaster' (CNTV Profile, 2010). It includes CCTV channels in foreign languages, including English, French, Spanish, Russian and Arabic, which have rebroadcast major annual music-entertainment events with subtitles, as well as CCTV and provincial channels in minority languages, including Uyghur and Tibetan.

Most of the content has been a reproduction and reprocessing of programmes and fragments from terrestrial and satellite television programming resources. However, it has also produced new programmes specifically for the internet, and has claimed to prioritize user feedback and incorporate internet users in the process of production (CNTV Profile, 2010). It has been attempting to directly compete with its competitors with its own social media, microblogging and video-sharing platforms like Ai Xiyou, which looks similar to its commercial rival, iQiyi, with its green colour scheme. The Ai Xiyou platform, however, was not well-known and was notably underutilized as a social media platform, with hardly any comments listed at the time of analysis. The CNTV site was also rather clunky and slow, both in the mainland and overseas, and audiences preferred to go to other online platforms like Youku, Tudou, Letv or iQiyi (or YouTube), which officially or unofficially also carried programmes from CCTV and other channels. Audiences could also access programming directly from the provincial channels' own websites where exclusive shows were usually quickly added. Nonetheless, efforts to establish a comprehensive online television platform are instructive of the Party-state's attempt to attract audiences to officially approved content in the online space. The CNTV/CCTV.com online platform has also been used to promote China's television content globally. Similar to the Olympic slogan 'One World, One Dream', the English language slogan for CNTV.cn and CCTV.com, as posted on the homepage, is 'One Click, One World' (or *Shiting Zhongguo, Hudong shijie*, in Chinese, which literally translates as 'Audiovisual China, Interactive World'.

The use of a range of new platforms also helps promote an image of China as 'modern', on the cutting edge and dedicated to building its cultural and media industries. Chinese television's venture into online and mobile spaces, including the creation of iPhone and iPad applications, can also be seen as part of the CCP's attempt to reach out to citizens via Web 2.0 technology and, as Cunningham and Wasserstrom (2012: 43) word it, 'reboot itself for the new millennium'. However, while an effort has been made by Chinese television stations to make clips from televised shows and music videos easily accessible online, it is important to note that they are also competing with a vast array of music-entertainment online content not produced by official mainland television channels.

Regulations affecting music-entertainment programming

The core role of the media and cultural programming in China under the CCP is to 'promote stability' and a 'positive image for the CCP'. Therefore, programmes that could 'disrupt social order' are restricted (Bai, 2015: 70). Many of the regulations are retrospective reactions to entertainment that is perceived to be excessive, trashy and of low taste. Three recent regulations released by SARFT/SAPPRFT in 2009, 2011 and 2013 respectively have impacted directly on music-entertainment programmes and also apply to talk shows and non-musical reality television programmes.

Chapter 5 of the 2009 'Radio and TV Regulations' (SARFT, 2009) stipulates restrictions to theme and content. Programmes are not allowed to report on stars' private lives or scandals. No malicious commercial speculation or promotion of luxury lifestyles is allowed. No screen violence, porn or unhealthy information should be aired. Shows should not be excessively stimulating or use malicious approaches in their programming. Great historical figures should not be the brunt of jokes. There should be no sexual overtones in dress or conversations. All programmes must be in Mandarin. Only guests from Hong Kong, Macau, Taiwan or foreign guests who have been approved by SARFT (now SAPPRFT) may be invited. No racism or personal judgements should be aired. In interacting with audiences, no prizes of high value are to be used to attract audiences and no gambling is allowed. Furthermore, provincial channels are not allowed to hold competition programmes more than once annually. Each programme should not run for more than two months and ten competitions. Each episode should not run for more than 90 minutes. The performances on competitions should occupy more than 80 per cent of the total length of each episode (meaning that other content such as talking, participants' stories, etc., should occupy no more than 20 per cent of the show). No less than 75 per cent of songs performed in each competition should be Chinese songs. Participants should be positive role models and should not have been involved in any scandals. Reality television programmes in particular should not infringe on copyright, include anti-traditional ethical and moral values nor promote negative aspects of human nature, have any sexual overtones or contain content that relates to religious or ethnic customs. They should also be devoid of violence, blood, murder, gangsters, drug use, smoking, gambling, porn and alcoholism. In addition, they should avoid plastic surgery, transsexuality and should not involve challenging the limits of the human body.

A 2011 decree, 'Suggestions for Further Strengthening the Program Management of Comprehensive Arts/Variety Programming on Satellite Television' (*Guanyu jinyibu jiaqiang dianshi shangxing zonghe shipin jiemu guanli de yijian*), ruled that entertainment programmes on provincial television channels were not to be aired more than three times weekly during the 5pm to 10pm prime time after July 2011. On 1 January 2012, SARFT enforced the entertainment restriction order, based on the 2011 decree, claiming to respond to audience complaints about the vulgarity of certain shows. It vowed to enforce new government stipulations for China's 34 leading provincial satellite stations, which required them to avoid excessive entertainment like reality television and talent contests and limit the total number of entertainment shows between them to nine during the prime-time of 7.30–10pm, for a maximum of 90 minutes in total, with a limit of two of their own entertainment shows each week. The channels were instructed to promote 'healthier' programmes such as news, educational programmes and documentaries, as well as programmes that promote harmony, morality, sociability and traditional Chinese values. In 2013, SARFT released a 'Notice on How to Apply the 2014 Television Variety Channel and Programs Arrangement and Record' (*Guanyu zuohao 2014 nian dianshi jiemu shangxing zonghe pindao jiemu bianpai he bei'an gongzuo de tongzhi*), which together with the 2011 decree became known in short as the 'Limit Entertainment Order' (*Xian yu ling*). The decree ruled that each provincial television channel was only allowed to import one foreign format at a time, and only four singing programmes could be aired during prime time across all the networks (Baidu, 2015).

Super Girl, aired on Hunan Satellite Television, is an example of a show that has been affected by oscillating regulations. The show ran for three years from 2004 to 2006. In 2007, SARFT began to limit entertainment and talent show programmes on satellite television channels, and Hunan Satellite Television stopped the show. In 2009, Hunan Satellite Television restarted the programme with SARFT's approval and changed the title to *Happy Girl*. It also ran in 2011, but not in 2010. At the end of 2011, with the new regulations, SARFT suspended *Super Girl* from future production. While the official reason for such decisions purportedly relates to the show's exceeding the acceptable air time throughout the season as stipulated in the regulations, the show was also directly criticized by CCP officials on moral and ideological grounds. In response to the suspension, Hunan Television news spokesman Li Hao explained that the network would incorporate more 'positive' content in its 2012 programmes (Thinkingchinese.com, 2011). *Super Girl* and its associated suit of singing talent reality programmes like *Happy Boy* (*Kuaile Nansheng*) were replaced with new content in the name of *Happy Camp* (*Kaule dabenying*) and *Progress Everyday* (*Tiantian xiang shang*) ('Chinese regulators take out the trash', 2011; NTDTV, 2011).

The sensitivity around hosting entertainment and other programming can also be seen in the SAPPRFT's ruling in June 2015 that guests of television programmes, especially on reality shows that often feature celebrity actors and actresses, are not to be employed as presenters or supports to the host. A circular that was to officially take effect on 1 July 2015 called for hosts to have full responsibility for 'guiding the audience and controlling the pace of the live broadcast'. It also called for hosts' qualifications to be checked, and 'more training for hosts and guests' to be provided before going to air to ensure that 'improper remarks or mistakes' aren't made during live broadcasts (*Xinhua*, 2015).

The above ruling appears to have affected (or come in response to) a blunder made off-air by one of China's most popular hosts Bi Fujian, affectionately known as Lao Bi, host of the popular CCTV3 programme *Star Avenue*. On 10 April 2015, Bi was suspended from all CCTV programmes for remarks made at a private dinner party that were caught on a mobile phone and later uploaded to the internet. In the video, Bi was seen singing a popular revolutionary song from *Taking Tiger Mountain by Strategy* (*Zhiqu wei hu shan*), a 1970 film based on one of the eight model plays of the Cultural Revolution, a contemporary Beijing opera. He added a wry personal comment following each sentence of lyrics:[24]

LYRICS: We are soldiers.
BI'S ADDITIONAL COMMENTARY: Oh, soldiers.
LYRICS: Come to the mountain
BI: What are you doing on the mountain?
LYRICS: Wipe out the reactionaries.
BI: Can you beat them?
LYRICS: Change the world. Decades of revolution and war everywhere.
B: That's hard.
LYRICS: CCP Chairman Mao.
BI: Don't mention that bad guy/son of a bitch. He hung out us to dry/tormented us.
LYRICS: Leading us ahead. A red star on the head. The flags of revolution are on both sides.
BI: What kind of dress-up is this?

LYRICS: Dark clouds are gone wherever red flags come. People in the liberation zones beat landlords.
BI: How do landlords piss you off?
LYRICS: The People's soldiers go through thick and thin with people. They come here to wipe out the Tiger Mountain.
BI: Boasting.

Bi's comments were applauded by his fellows at the dinner party, but were criticized by others for showing disrespect to the Party and to an important historical figure in China's history, thus highlighting the small degree of official tolerance for political irony.

Another regulation highlights the complexity of allowing foreigners to perform on Chinese television, which in part explains why there are few big-name foreign pop stars on Chinese television. Section 9 of 'Some Provisional Regulations Concerning Local Foreign Affairs Work in Radio and Television' (*Guangbo yingshi xitong difang waishi gongzuo guanli guiding*), which first came into force in 1988 (and was upgraded in 2005 with a similar statement in clause 16), states:

> Where all provincial, autonomous region and municipal radio and television stations invite foreign, Hong Kong and Macau region actors to perform in programmes on local radio stations and television stations, after obtaining agreement from our consulates and embassies abroad of the Hong Kong office of Xinhua, it is to be reported to the provincial, autonomous region or municipal government for examination and approval, and reported to the Ministry of Radio, Film and Television for filing.
> (SAPPRFT, 2005; English translation in Creemers, 2013)

According to Chinese scholars, recent regulations to limit television entertainment were implemented for a number of reasons, including concerns over an 'imbalance' over programming types on provincial channels. They were particularly concerned that provincial channels were shirking their responsibility to provide news to their constituencies (Xiao, 2012). The 'homogenization' and consistent copying of 'low quality' reality shows across channels was also thought to reflect a lack of creativity and fuel a sense of vulgar addiction that impacted negatively on Chinese social morality (Xiao, 2012; Yang, 2012). There was also a concern over audiences' 'blind worship' of celebrities, and the idea that many entertainment programmes pandered excessively to audiences' interests while failing to foster new interests (Xiao, 2012). Such imbalances were said to be caused by the blind pursuit of profit, weak management and lack of top-down control of the television industry (Yang, 2012).

Highlighting the close ties between academia and politics in China, Chinese scholars have argued that the solutions to this problem require enhancing the leading position and supervision of the government and CCP and for

Marxism to be drawn upon to support the core values of socialism, pass on Chinese traditional culture, and promote the spirit of endeavour (Yang, 2012; He, 2014). They have also argued that the behaviour and actions of television channels and practitioners need to be better regulated (Yang, 2012). They needed to raise the ideological level of entertainment programmes and promote artistry rather than 'vulgar' styles. They also called for provincial stations to take responsibility for producing programmes that perform a social service, especially news (Xie, 2011; Xiao, 2012: 42–3). Some scholars felt that if entertainment shows were broadly cut from programming, more television dramas would be broadcast instead (Xie, 2011), with the potential to threaten the music-entertainment television genre itself.

After the implementation of the 'Limit Entertainment Order', Bai (2015: 80–1) argued that many reality programmes that had become too popular disappeared in 2012 and 2013. Interrogating the nuances of the effects of these regulations, Cheng et al. (2013: 64–5) found that the diversity of genres increased on 19 channels but decreased on 13 channels. Channels with 'low diversity' continued to air a large number of television dramas and variety shows. Overall, the number of competition and reality shows actually increased and they continue to play an important role. After the regulations, Cheng et al. argue, many provincial channels still lacked 'creative' content, but in general the 'quality' of programmes during prime time improved.

As Bai explains (2015: 81–2, drawing on Magder, 2004, and Jian and Liu, 2009), given the structural underpinnings of China's television industry, state crackdowns on provincial satellite stations are somewhat unfair. Satellite networks were forced to adopt reality television formats in the 2000s precisely because they had few other options. The state maintained tight control over news production and CCTV dominated this space, so provincial channels had to concentrate on entertainment to differentiate themselves and attract the attention of national audiences. Reality television has been particularly attractive to networks because of their lucrative potential, with product placements, merchandising tie-ins and interactive elements.

Apart from needing to adjust content to meet specified television regulations, self-censorship is also widely applied by professionals working in the Chinese media industry. In news reporting (which is generally believed to be more stringently controlled than entertainment programming), Chinese journalists tend to self-censor by avoiding content that is going to be edited out anyway, or avoid taking risks that could lead to expulsion, termination or jail terms for broadcasting unacceptable material (Yu, 2001: 211). Self-censorship occurs in the music-entertainment television industry too, with, as noted earlier, political irony a rare occurrence. The internet is the place where songs and video clips embedded with political irony are most likely to be found.

However, as with the cultural and music industries more broadly, there is continued discussion by Party leaders, intellectuals and the public on what types of popular art are more or less appropriate for state development on television. There remains a strong investment in the political value of entertainment genres. Liu Zhongde, a delegate and director of the Science, Education, Culture, Health and Sport Commission of the CPPCC, and staunch critic of *Super Girl*, for instance, argued in 2006 that 'Popular art is an inevitable product of particular laws and social development and has a use that cannot be replaced' but there needed be appropriate 'direction' in the choice and 'level' of art that should be supported. In the context of television, he argued that market forces were leading to the production of shows that pandered excessively to 'low' tastes and risked creating a generation with an unhealthy mentality. Similar elements of concern to those raised during the 1983 Spiritual Pollution Campaign continue to surface: fear of cultural invasion, suspicion of market forces, concern for the spiritual health of the nation, preservation of national culture, fear that popular entertainment will corrupt the youth and the need to promote socialist morality (Martinsen, 2006). Yet, significantly, as de Kloet (2006) and Fung and Zhang (2011: 272) remind us, it is also worth noting that the biggest censor is often not the ideological arm of the Party-state but the media and music industries themselves, which tend to produce material that they think will be commercially successful and that will not offend the conservative morals of mainstream Chinese consumers.

With murkily defined and inconsistently imposed boundaries between the acceptable and unacceptable, musicians, industry professionals, producers, state-owned publishers and audiences are constantly testing out and challenging the formerly accepted boundaries (de Kloet, 2003: 182). Programme producers, directors, editors and performers develop a sense of what styles of cultural performance are acceptable in the various contexts in which they work. In the television industry, expressions that are allowed in one place may not be permitted or encouraged in another. There are a few types of performances, however, that are generally unwelcome across the board, including unauthorized political comments on separatist and independence movements such as Free Tibet; sexual innuendo, such as through dirty lyrics and the wearing of overly revealing clothes; and the gathering of large, uncontrolled crowds (de Kloet, 2006).

Conclusion

In China, given that all television in China is still ultimately under the control of the Party-state, which insists that its primary aim is to mould people's attitudes and beliefs (Hong, 1998: 138), entertainment and Party-state politics are inevitably linked in some way. However, while the Chinese Party-state still monopolizes political power and maintains control over cultural domains, including music and television, they are not constantly implementing power in a rigid, top-down totalitarian fashion. The totalizing effect of the state has faded (Hong, 1998: 134, 136; Tay, 2009: 108) and we need to move beyond the impression of the CCP as being driven by a 'single-minded will to power' or of China's media system as being 'static and one-dimensional' (Zhao,

2008: 352). Rather, as this chapter has demonstrated, the media reflects shifting Party priorities, 'competing bureaucratic interests', various responses to domestic and international developments, and 'different visions of Chinese modernity' (Zhao, 2008: 11, 25).

While CCP representatives continue to closely monitor content on all television channels, since the 1990s control has been maintained through negotiation between state propaganda and policy makers, media organizations, cultural workers, commercial enterprises, intellectuals and audiences (Huang, 2007: 405–6; Zhang in Chu, 2008: 184). As Zhang (2011b) explains, since the 2000s, the model of control may be one of hegemony. As both the state and media system adapt to political, social and technological shifts, the media are being used to build consensus and persuade audiences of the Party-state's ongoing legitimacy. The more empowered and autonomous the media are perceived to be from the Party-state's political apparatus, the more convincing they will be in justifying the political legitimacy of the CCP and its associated messages of a prosperous society. In other words, commerce and politics are working together in a relatively cosy partnership to produce cultural products that will satisfy the censors, attract audiences, and maximize profits (e.g., Huang 2007: 405; Tay, 2009: 111; Zhao, 1999: 303; Zhao, 1998: 2; Zhong, 2001: 168). The following chapters examine in depth how a range of televised singing events have been marshalled to create a variety of politically sanctioned impressions of the Chinese nation under the leadership of the CCP.

Notes

1 Anchee Min wrote in her memoir *Red Azalea* that she became a fan of the model operas as there were few other forms of diversion. Liking the revolutionary operas was also a way of stating that you were a revolutionary.
2 The privileged few who were able to watch television generally did so in public spaces and very rarely in private settings (Zhu and Berry, 2008: 3; Lull, 1991).
3 Population figures from Google population data (sourced from the World Bank), www.google.com.au/publicdata/explore?ds=d5bncppjof8f9_&met_y=sp_pop_totl&idim=country:CHN&dl=en&hl=en&q=china%27s+population (accessed 18 May 2017).
4 Population figures from Google population data (sourced from the World Bank) (as per above note).
5 Baidu, "Shoushilü" [Ratings]. Available at http://baike.baidu.com/view/1135.htm#4 (accessed Dec 20, 2016). CMS media research, a cooperation with the former Central Television Research and a French media group, Sofres Group, was the most authoritative media research group in China, see www.csm.com.cn.
6 Baidu, "Zhongyang dianshi tai" (CCTV). Available at http://baike.baidu.com/subview/9242/5245915.htm (accessed Dec 20, 2016). Also refer to the introduction to CCTV on its official website, www.cctv.com/profile/intro.html (accessed 18 May 2017).
7 The idea for the show appears to have been derived from a documentary in 1956 called 'Spring Festival Big Gala' (*Chunjie da lian huan*), which was produced by the Central Studio of News Reels Production, as well as a 1979 internal gala for CCTV staff called 'Welcoming the New Spring Arts and Entertainment Gala' (*Ying xin chun wenyi wanhui*) (QQ, 2009; *Chongqing Evening News*, 2010).

8 *Super Girl* obtained a recordbreaking rating of almost 12 per cent of the national audience, corresponding to an audience of 400 million.
9 Baidu, Zhongguo zheng zai ting [*China is Listening*] profile. Available at http://baike.baidu.com/view/15154291.htm (accessed 18 May 2017).
10 Kaimen da ji [Open the Door to Luck] website, http://tv.cctv.com/lm/kmdj/index.shtml (accessed 18 May 2017).
11 Adam Lambert, an American singer who was one of the finalists of *American Idol* Season 9 in 2009, appeared on the *Chinese Idol* auditions as a guest judge in 2013.
12 Jiaduobao reportedly received a great return on their investments in *The Voice of China* over the first three seasons. It saw surging offline sales. Brand recognition in third and fourth tier cities increased considerably through association with a programme that was a hot topic of conversation among millions of netizens. After two years of cooperation, Jiaduobao became the number one herbal tea soft drink brand in China and occupied around 80 per cent of the market share of herbal tea brands in China. However, their cooperation stopped after Season 4, reportedly because of copyright conflicts between Star TV, Zhejiang TV and Talpa in Holland (*Beijing News*, 2013; Jiemian.com, 2016).
13 Michael Jackson's 'Black or White' was sung by contestant Zhang Wei.
14 Adele's 'Rolling in the Deep' was sung by contestant Huang He.
15 Beyoncé's 'Halo' was sung by Yi-Chinese contestant Jike Junyi.
16 Zhang Liangying sang 'Me and My Motherland' in the finals of the 2005 *Super Girl* contest on Hunan TV.
17 One episode of *Music Masterclass* (*Yinyue da shike*) on Beijing Satellite Television from 2015, for example, began with a ten-year-old boy, Zhu Zhenming learning the song 'The Sun is the Reddest, Chairman Mao is the Closest' (*Taiyang zui hong, Mao zhuxi zui qin*). Audiences were first introduced to the song via a black and white clip of the original singer of the song, with the boy sitting and watching studiously with Chinese pop star Han Lei, before the original singer, Bian Xiaozhen, from an army performing arts troupe, now 69 years old, walked onto the stage. The boy explained that he chose this song because it was his grandfather's favourite song. Bian explained that it was written immediately after Chairman Mao died and shared how it felt like the sky had fallen in and as if her family had lost a parent. She suggested to the boy that singing this song would be a way of showing love for his grandfather. She taught him to perform it with spirit and dedication: with a smile, looking ahead, arms outstretched. After that the boy is seen on stage, wearing a red Olympic tracksuit with the characters for 'China' emblazoned across it. His grandfather also appeared on stage and explained he was also in the army in 1968. The original singer and lyricist could be seen sitting in the audience. The studio had an atmosphere of considerable respect for the older generations that played a significant role in the building of modern China. The boy started by singing the song solo in a very slow and moving way before shifting to an upbeat modern version, accompanied by a live band. Everyone expressed their pleasure at seeing this song being passed down the generations and that it was still being sung 39 years later. The boy and teacher Bian then sang the song together in the modern version and the audience stood up, clapped, danced and sang along.
18 Baidu, MTV Zhongwen pindao [MTV Mandarin channel] profile. Available at http://baike.baidu.com/view/1120768.htm (accessed 18 May 2017).
19 See *CCTV-MTV Music Gala* profile at http://baike.baidu.com/view/497658.htm (accessed 18 May 2017).
20 Baidu, MTV Chaoji shengdian [*MTV Style Gala*]. Available at http://baike.baidu.com/view/5539482.htm (accessed 18 May 2017).
21 Baidu, Mengxiang Zhongguo [*Dream China*]. Available at http://baike.baidu.com/view/10128.htm#reference-[4]-10128-wrap (accessed 18 May 2017).

22 *Direct to the Spring Festival Gala* website (2013). Available at http://ent.cntv.cn/special/2013ztcw/index.shtml#tz (accessed 18 May 2017).
23 See live channels on the CCTV official website at http://tv.cntv.cn/pindao/#jump_w (accessed 18 May 2017).
24 *Taking Tiger Mountain by Strategy* was based on the novel *Tracks in the Snowy Forest* (*Lin hai xue yuan*) written by Qu Bo and published by the People's Literature Publishing House in 1957. The story was set in 1946 during the Chinese Civil War and was a thriller about a group of soldiers who went into the snowy mountains to search for and fight hidden bandits and brigands. 1,560,000 copies of the book were printed between 1957 and 1964 in three editions. The book was translated into English, Russian, Japanese, Korean, Vietnamese, Mongolian, Norwegian and Arabic. The 1970 film (directed by Xie Tieli) is arguably one of the most watched films of all time, having received 7.3 billion views by 1974 according to official Chinese government statistics, suggesting that all Chinese citizens at the time had seen it seven times (Clark, 1987: 145) This is not because it was particularly popular but largely because it was one of only a few films produced and permitted for public viewing during the Cultural Revolution. It was shown an average of ten times a year in most villages and failure to attend was construed as a sign of political deviation (Robertson, 2001: 229). A Chinese-Hong Kong 3D epic action film, *The Taking of Tiger Mountain 3D* (directed by Tsui Hark), also based on the book and opera, was released in 2014. This film topped the Chinese box office for two weeks after opening, and is one of the highest-grossing films of all time in China.

References

Bai, R (2014) *Staging Corruption: Chinese Television and Politics*. Vancouver: UBC Press.
Bai, R (2015) 'Clean up the screen': regulating television entertainment in the 2000s. In R. Bai and G. Song (eds.) *Chinese Television in the Twenty-First Century: Entertaining the Nation*. London: Routledge, pp. 69–86.
Baidu (2015) Xian ling yu [Limit Entertainment Order]. Available at http://baike.baidu.com/view/6326054.htm (accessed 18 May 2017).
Barco (2009) Barco LED backdrop lights up annual *CCTV Chinese Spring Festival Gala*. Media release, 23 February. Available at www.barco.com/en/News/Press-releases/Barco-LED-backdrop-lights-up-annual-CCTV-Chinese-Spring-Festival-Gala.aspx (accessed 18 May 2017).
Beaumont-Thomas, B. (2013) Could *Rising Star* be the new *X Factor* for ITV? *The Guardian*, 29 Nov. Available at www.theguardian.com/tv-and-radio/2013/nov/28/rising-star-new-x-factor-itv (accessed 18 May 2017).
Beijing News (2013) Jiaduobao yuanhe san du guan ming Zhongguo hao shengyin [Why Jiaduobao is three times *Voice of China* brand], 12 November. Available at www.bjnews.com.cn/health/2013/11/12/292157.html (accessed 18 May 2017).
Brady, A.M. (2006) Guiding hand: the role of the CCP Central Propaganda Department in the current era. *Westminster Papers in Communication and Culture* 3(1): 58–77.
CCTV.cn (2012) Phenomena of the 1980s – *Follow Me*. Posted 4 May. Available at http://english.cntv.cn/program/documentary/20120405/101300.shtml (accessed 18 May 2017).
CCTV's *Happy in China* (2008) CCTV Huanle Zhongguo xing – meili oupai qing yangcheng [CCTV's *Happy in China – Charming Oupai –* pouring love on Guangzhou], Oct 16. Available at http://finance.qq.com/a/20081016/002747.htm (accessed 18 May 2017).

Chan, J.M. (2008) Toward television regionalization in Greater China and beyond. In Y. Zhu and C. Berry (eds.) *TV China*. Bloomington: Indiana University Press, pp. 15–39.

Chang, W.H. (1989) *Mass Media in China: The History and the Future*. Ames: Iowa State Press.

Chen, J. (2013) *Spring Festival Gala* and *Super Bowl* difference: advertising. *US-China Today*, 21 February. Available at www.uschina.usc.edu/(X(1)A(C-XTQnO Q0gEkAAAAODQ3MDljODItYzZjZi00ZWYzLWE1ZGUtMTJjOWRkOT BiZjg58-bgb7Rtb_yIma-NJek7Hh-Z5PI1))/w_usct/showarticle.aspx?articleID=18 710&AspxAutoDetectCookieSupport=1 (accessed 18 May 2017).

Cheng, J., Jin, X. and Pan, M. (2013) 'Xian yu ling' qianhou shengji weishe jiemu duoyang xing cedu [Measurement of the program diversity of China's provincial satellite TV Station before and after the 'Limit Entertainment Order']. *Chongqing Social Sciences (Chongqing Shehui Kexue)* 11: 61–6.

China.org.cn (n.d.) The media. Available at www.china.org.cn/english/features/ China2004/107177.htm (accessed 18 May 2017).

Chinese regulators take out the trash (2011) *World TV PC blog*, 28 October. Available at www.worldtvpc.com/blog/chinese-tv-regulators-trash (accessed 18 May 2017).

Chongqing Evening News (2010) Chunjie de jiaobu [Steps towards the *Spring Festival Gala*], 12 February. Available at http://news.163.com/10/0212/02/ 5V9PAM1K000120GR.html (accessed 18 May 2017).

Chu, Y.W. (2008) The importance of being Chinese: orientalism reconfigured in the age of global modernity. *boundary 2* 35(2): 183–206.

CNTV (2016) 'A backstage visit to CCTV's *Spring Festival Gala*', 7 February. Available at http://news.xinhuanet.com/english/video/2016-02/07/c_135082750.htm (accessed 18 May 2017)

CNTV Profile (2010), 9 June. Available at http://english.cntv.cn/20100609/102812. shtml (accessed 18 May 2017).

Coonan, C. (2014) Hot reality format *Rising Star* to show on China's CCTV-3. *Hollywood Reporter*, 11 September. Available at www.hollywoodreporter.com/news/ hot-reality-format-rising-star-732185 (accessed 18 May 2017).

Creemers, R. (ed.) (2013) Some provisional regulations concerning local foreign affairs work in radio and television. *China Copyright and Media – the Law and Policy of Media in China* blog, 5 Nov 1988, updated 28 January 2013. Available at https://chinacopyrightandmedia.wordpress.com/1988/11/05/some-provisional-regulations-concerning-local-foreign-affairs-work-in-radio-and-television/ (accessed 18 May 2017).

Cunningham, M.E. and Wasserstrom, J.N. (2012) Authoritarianism: there's an app for that. *Chinese Journal of Communication* 5(1): 43–8.

Curtin, M. (2010) Introduction. *Cinema Journal* 49(3): 117–20.

de Kloet, J. (2003) Confusing Confucius: rock in contemporary China. In M. Cloonan and R. Garofalo (eds.) *Policing Pop*. Philadelphia: Temple University Press, pp. 166–85.

de Kloet, J. (2006) Online video recorded interview. *World Conference on Music and Censorship*, 25–26 November. Available at http://freemuse.org/archives/832 (accessed 18 May 2017).

Fung, A. (2009) Globalizing televised culture: the case of China. In G. Turner and J. Tay (eds) *Television Studies After TV: Understanding Television in the Post-Broadcast Era*. London: Routledge, pp. 178–88.

Fung, A. and Zhang, X. (2011) The Chinese *Ugly Betty*: TV cloning and local modernity. *International Journal of Cultural Studies* 14(3): 265–76.

Geng, Q. (2014) Zhongguo zongyi 'zou chu qu' – Yingguo ITV yinjin 'haogequ' [Chinese variety 'goes out' – British ITV introduces *Sing My Song*]. *Chinanews.com*, 11 April. Available at www.chinanews.com/yl/2014/04-11/6055976.shtml (accessed 18 May 2017).

He, B. (2014) 'Ruhe tigao xin xingshi xia guangbo dianshi jiemu jianguan shuiping' sheng bing shijie [How to improve radio and TV regulations in the current context]. *Voice and Screen World*, 9: 11–13.

Hong, J. (1998) *The Internationalization of Television in China: The Evolution of Ideology, Society, and Media Since the Reform*. Westport: Praeger.

Horesh, N. (2014) *Shanghai, Past and Present: A Concise Socio-Economic History, 1842–2012*. Eastbourne: Sussex Academic Press.

Hou, L. (2009) 4.5-day workweek system proposed. *China Daily*, 3 March. Available at www.chinadaily.com.cn/china/2009-03/03/content_7531709.htm (accessed 18 May 2017).

Huang, C. (2007) Editorial: from control to negotiation: Chinese media in the 2000s. *International Communication Gazette* 69: 402–12.

Huang, Y. and Yu, X. (1997) Broadcasting and politics: Chinese television in the Mao era, 1958–1976. *Historical Journal of Film, Radio and Television* 17(4): 563–74.

ITV Studios Global Entertainment to Collaborate with Universal Music Group on Sing My Song TV Format (2014), 22 October. Available at https://itvstudios.com/global-entertainment-news/itv-studios-global-entertainment-to-collaborate-with-universal-music-group-on-sing-my-song-tv-format (accessed 18 May 2017).

Jian, M. and Liu, C. (2009) 'Democratic entertainment' commodity and unpaid labor of reality TV: a preliminary analysis of China's *Supergirl. Inter-Asia Cultural Studies* 10(4): 4–14.

Jiemian.com (2016) Jiaduobao wei shenme fangqi 'Zhongguo hao shengyin?' [Why did Jiaoduobao let *The Voice of China* go?], 18 April. Available at www.jiemian.com/article/614755.html (accessed 18 May 2017).

Jin, D.Y. (2007) Transformation of the world television system under neoliberal globalization, 1983–2003. *Television and New Media* 8(3): 179–96.

Jin, S. (2011) Weiyakangmu Zhongguo shichang de kuozhang yu jingying zhanlüe [Viacom's expansion and management strategy in China], 28 February. Available at http://211.71.215.185/ChuanMeiJingJi/content/2011-02/28/content_20606_4.htm (accessed 18 May 2017).

Keane, M. (2003) A revolution in television and a great leap forward for innovation? China in the global television format business. In A. Moran and M. Keane (eds.) *Television across Asia: TV Industries, Program Formats, and Globalisation*. London: Routledge Curzon.

Keane, M. (2004) It's all in a game: television formats in the People's Republic of China. In K. Iwabuchi, S. Muecke and M. Thomas (eds.) *Rogue Flows: Trans-Asian Cultural Traffic*. Hong Kong: Hong Kong University Press, pp. 53–72.

Lee, M. (2016) China's nearly 700 million internet users are hot for online finance, *Forbes*, 25 January. Available at www.forbes.com/sites/melanieleest/2016/01/25/chinas-nearly-700-million-internet-users-are-hot-for-online-finance/#4d8c77f11391 (accessed 18 May 2017).

Li, L. (2014) Quanqiuhua beijing xia Zhongguo dianshi wenyi de minzuhua 'tanxi' [Analysis of the nationalization of Chinese television in the context of globalization]. *Press Circles* (*Xinwenjie*) 13: 21–6.

Liang, J. (2015) Quanqiuhua shiye xia Zhongguo dianshi ye de fazhan lujing [The development of Chinese television in the context of globalization]. *Sichuan Drama* 3: 85–8.

Liu, X. (2009) Dui quanqiuhua shiye xia dianshi wenhua bentu sikao [Reflections on the localization of Chinese TV from the perspective of globalization]. *China Television (Zhongguo Dianshi)* 1: 43–6.

Lu, X. (1995) *Zhuchuren jiemu xue jiancheng [A Course for Programme Anchors]*. Beijing: Chinese Broadcasting Press.

Lu, X. (2009) Ritual, television, and state ideology: rereading CCTV's 2006 *Spring Festival Gala*. In Y. Zhu and C. Berry (eds.) *TV China*. Indianapolis: Indiana University Press: 111–25.

Luo, M. (2009) Cong shouzhong xinli tanxi dianshi xuanxiu jiemu de chuangzuo [An analysis of audience feelings about talent shows]. *Oriental Art* S2: 45–7.

Lull, J. (1991) *China Turned On: TV Reform and Resistance*. London: Routledge.

Ma, E. (2000) Rethinking media studies: the case of China. In J. Curran and M.J. Park (eds.) *De-Westernizing Media Studies*. London: Routledge, pp. 21–34.

Ma, J. (2015) Zhong Mei yinyue xuanxiu jiemu de chayixing duibi – yi 'Zhongguo hao shengyin', 'Meiguo zhi sheng' wei lie [Comparison between Chinese and American Talent TV Shows: Taking *The Voice of China* and *The Voice of America* as case studies]. *Radio & TV Journal (Shi ting)* 8: 28–30.

Magder, T. (2004) The end of TV 101: reality programs and the new business of television. In S. Murray and L. Ouellette (eds.) *Reality TV: Remaking Television Culture*. New York: New York University Press, pp. 137–56.

Martinsen, J. (2006) CPPCC: exterminate the super girls. *Danwei.org*, 26 April. www.danwei.org/trends_and_buzz/cppcc_exterminate_the_super_girls.php (accessed 18 May 2017).

Meng, B. (2009) Who needs democracy if we can pick our favourite girl? *Super Girl* as media spectacle. *Chinese Journal of Communication* 2(3): 257–72.

Min, A. (1994) *Red Azalea*. New York: Pantheon.

mtvchina.com (n.d.) Guanyu MTV Zhongguo [About MTV China]. Available at www.mtvchina.com/home/aboutus.php (accessed 18 May 2017).

NTDTV (2011) SARFT to regulate national TV talent shows. *New Tang Dynasty Television China Forbidden News*, 28 October. Available at www.youtube.com/watch?feature=player_embedded&v=0zJVOKAFmDQ (accessed 18 May 2017).

People's Daily (2001) State radio, film and television conglomerate established, 7 December. Available at http://en.people.cn/200112/06/eng20011206_86070.shtml (accessed 18 May 2017).

Pugsley, P.C. and Gao, J. (2007) Emerging powers of influence: the rise of the anchor in Chinese television. *International Communication Gazette* 69(5): 451–66.

QQ (2009) Ni keneng bu zhidao de Chunwan muhou gushi [The behind the scenes story of the *Spring Festival Gala* you probably didn't know], 26 January. Available at http://news.qq.com/a/20091012/000636.htm (accessed 18 May 2017)

Rodrigue, M. (2014) Britain's ITV nabs rights to *Sing My Song*. *Hollywood Reporter*, 7 April. Available at www.hollywoodreporter.com/news/miptv-china-scores-first-talent-694166 (accessed 18 May 2017).

Rofel, L. (1995) The melodrama of national identity in post-Tiananmen China. In R.C. Allen (ed.) *To Be Continued… Soap Operas Around the World*. London: Routledge, pp. 301–20.

SAPPRFT (State Administration of Press, Publication, Radio, Film and Television) (2005) Guangbo yingshi xitong difang waishi gongzuo guanli guiding' de tongzhi [Notice on some provisional regulations concerning local foreign affairs work in radio and television], 12 July. Available at www.sarft.gov.cn/art/2005/7/12/art_106_4563.html (accessed 18 May 2017).

SARFT (State Administration of Radio, Film and Television) (2009) Radio and TV regulations. Available at http://vdisk.weibo.com/s/yYOtj0eYAu5e1 (accessed 18 May 2017).

Shambaugh, D. (2007) China's propaganda system: institutions, processes and efficacy. *The China Journal* 57: 25–58.

Si, S. and Zhang, H. (2013) Zhongguo chuantong yuyue lei dianshi jiemu xianzhuang yu fazhan zhanwang – yi Zhongyan dianshitai yinyue dianshi jiemu wei li [The status quo and the development of Chinese traditional music TV programmes: the case of music TV programmes on CCTV]. *China Radio and Television Academic Journal (Zhongguo Guangbo Dianshi Xuekan)* 2: 54–7.

Song, G. (2015) Imagining the other: foreigners on the Chinese TV screen. In R. Bai and G. Song (eds.) *Chinese Television in the Twenty-First Century: Entertaining the Nation.* London: Routledge, pp. 107–20.

State Council, People's Republic of China (2014) State Administration of Press, Publication, Radio, Film and Television of the People's Republic of China, 4 September. Available at http://english.gov.cn/state_council/2014/09/09/content_281474986284063.htm (accessed 18 May 2017).

Sun, W. (2002) *Leaving China: Media, Migration, and Transnational Imagination.* Lanham: Rowman and Littlefield.

Sun, X. (2011) Quanqiuhua yu jing xia Zhongguo dianshi jiemu moshi de tuwei [Breakthroughs in Chinese television programme formats in the context of globalization]. *Movie Review (Dianying Pingjie)* 20: 74–6.

Tay, J. (2009) Television in Chinese geo-linguistic markets: deregulation, reregulation and market forces in the post-broadcast era. In G. Turner and J. Tay (eds.) *Television Studies After TV: Understanding Television in the Post-Broadcast Era.* Routledge: London, pp. 105–14.

Thinkingchinese.com (2011), Duan Linxi is the last *Super Girl* winner, 20 September. Available at www.thinkingchinese.com/duan-linxi-is-the-last-super-girl-winner (accessed 18 May 2017).

Tian, S. (2009) Jingji quanqiuhua yu Zhongguo dianshi chanye [Economic globalization and China's television industry]. *Modern Television Technology (Xiandai Dianshi Jishu)* 1: 133–5.

tvtv.hk (2015) 2005–2015 shengji weishi zongyi jiemu shoushilü fengzhi TOP30 Hao Shengyin 4 bu di Chaoji Nüsheng 2005 [2005–2015 provincial satellite variety show ratings top 30: *Voice of China 4* beaten by *Super Girl* 2005], 25 December. Available at www.tvtv.hk/archives/2767.html (accessed 18 May 2017).

Walsh, B. (2015) *Sing My Song* sells into Vietnam. *Real Screen*, 2 March. Available at http://realscreen.com/2015/03/02/sing-my-song-sells-into-vietnam/ (accessed 18 May 2017).

Wang, H. [trans. C Connery] (2006) Depoliticized politics, multiple components of hegemony, and the eclipse of the sixties. *Inter-Asia Cultural Studies* 7(4): 683–700.

Wang, L. (ed.) (2011) *Zhongguo dianshi shoushi nianjian [China TV Rating Yearbook 2010].* Beijing: Communication University of China Press.

Xiao, Y. (2012) Fan yulehua jing xia de 'xian yu ling' de xueli fenxi [A theoretical analysis of the 'Limit Entertainment Order' in the context of widespread entertainment]. *Media Times (Meiti Shidai)* 1: 39–43.

Xie, P. (2011) 'Xian yu ling' beijing xia dui shengji weishi fazhan de ji dian sikao xinwen jie [Rethinking the impact of the 'Limit Entertainment Order' on provincial channels]. *The Press (Xinwen Jie)* 8: 112–15.

Xinhua (2015) China to ban guest host in TV shows. *Xinhua*, 22 June. Available at www.china.org.cn/arts/2015-06/22/content_35878727.htm (accessed 18 May 2017).

Yang, C. (2007) Tan quanqiuhua dachao xia Zhongguo dianshi jiemu de bentuhua [Discussion of the localization of Chinese television programmes under the tide of globalization]. *Legal System and Society (Fazhi yu shehui)* 2: 771–.

Yang, H. (2012) 'Xian yu ling hou dianshi meijie shengtai huanjing de weiji yu chongjian' de dangdai chuanbo [Crisis and rebuilding of the ecological environment of television media after the 'Limit Entertainment Order']. *Contemporary Communication (Dangdai Guangbo)* 2: 49–51.

Yao, D. (2012) 1983 nian Zhongyang dianshitai 'Chunjie lianhuan wanhui' yu Zhongguo chengshi yinyue de xin zouxiang [1983 *CCTV Spring Festival Gala* and new trends in Chinese urban music]. *Movie Review (Dianying Pingjie)* 18: 87–9.

Yu, Y. (2001) Can the news media meet the challenges in China's post-Deng reform? In X. Hu and G. Lin (eds.) *Transition Towards Post-Deng China*. Singapore: Singapore University Press, pp. 195–218.

Zhang, J. and Cameron, G.T. (2004) The structural transformation of China's propaganda: an Ellulian perspective. *Journal of Communication Management* 8(3): 307–21.

Zhang, X. (2011a) China's International broadcasting: a case study of CCTV international. In J. Wang (ed.) *Soft Power in China*. New York: Palgrave Macmillan, pp. 57–71.

Zhang, X. (2011b) *The Transformation of Political Communication in China: From Propaganda to Hegemony*. Singapore: World Scientific Publishing.

Zhao, B. (1999) Mouthpiece or money-spinner? The double life of Chinese television in the late 1990s. *International Journal of Cultural Studies* 2(3): 291–305.

Zhao, Y. (1998) *Media, Market and Democracy in China: Between the Party Line and the Bottom Line*. Urbana: University of Illinois Press.

Zhao, Y. (2008) *Communication in China: Political Economy, Power, and Conflict*. Lanham: Rowman and Littlefield.

Zheng, T. (2013) Shilun quanqiuhua yu jing xia Zhongguo dianshi jiemu bentuhua de tuwei celüe. [Discussing the strategies of localization of Chinese television in the context of globalization]. *Journalism & Communication (Xinwen Chuanbo)* 7: 175–6.

Zhong, Y. (2001) The other edge of commercialisation: enhancing CCTV's propaganda. *Media International Australia incorporating Culture and Policy*, 100 (Aug): 167–79.

Zhong, Y. (2007) Competition is getting real in Chinese TV: a moment of confrontation between CCTV and HSTV. *Media International Australia* 124: 68–81.

Zhu, Y. (2008) *Television in Post-Reform China: Serial Dramas, Confucian Leadership and the Global Television Market*. London: Routledge.

Zhu, Y. (2012) *Two Billion Eyes: The Story of China Central Television*. New York: The New Press.

Zhu, Y. and Berry, C. (2008) Introduction. In Y. Zhu and C. Berry (eds.) *TV China*. Bloomington and Indianapolis: Indiana University Press, pp. 1–14.

4 Multiethnic China

In this chapter I consider three main styles in which China as a multiethnic state is constructed through music-entertainment programming. I begin with a discussion of the more 'hardened' styles, which I also refer to as 'orthodox'. These are moments that are heavily imbued with Party-political symbolism and where the 'fact' that China is made up of exactly 56 nationalities, with the 55 minorities and the Han majority united and living happily together, is made utterly clear. The 'national style' (*minzu changfa*) is often used in this form, which is a hybrid of Chinese folk influences and Western operatic singing and orchestral backing, with tunes sung in the national language (Mandarin/Putonghua), and themes relating to national glory and development. The style is based on the discourse of transforming, developing and modernizing folk song performances in ways that mirror the discourse of 'state development' (*guojia fazhan*) and 'modernization' (*xiandaihua*) more broadly. Through reinforcing visuals, language and music, this style overtly asserts the united multiethnic nature of the Chinese nation and a message that all Chinese, no matter what their ethnicity, are striving together under the leadership of the Chinese Communist Party (CCP) towards an even brighter future.

A second style, *yuanshengtai* ('original ecology'), offers a 'softer' view of multiethnic harmony by drawing more heavily on linguistic and cultural differences within the People's Republic of China (PRC). The meaning of *yuanshengtai* in song and dance performances has shifted over the years. It began to be strongly articulated in the form of authentic folk songs at a time of heightened social and state concerns regarding environmental preservation and the need to protect China's 'intangible cultural heritage'. In its more academic presentations (with the influence of ethnomusicologists) this style stresses the need to respect and preserve the folk music of minority nationalities and their related languages, musical instruments and clothing. These minority forms are then appropriated to represent the treasury of China's collective multiethnic history and culture. Once derided for being un-modern and 'primitive' (Jones, 2001: 103), under the *yuanshengtai* frame the 'colourful' and 'exotic' folk traditions have been reimagined as essential to saving the essence of Chinese culture and identity as a whole in the face of globalization and rapid domestic development. As time has gone on, televised performances of *yuanshengtai* have shifted away from an emphasis on primitiveness and purity towards creativity and cultural dynamism particularly through blending ethnic folk styles with popular music, linking to a more recent promotion of China's creative and cultural industries.

The third style, which I term ethno-pop, actively fuses various musical or visual elements of minority and Han Chinese folk music with Western-style popular music. This style reflects an appeal to youth and features stars from multiethnic backgrounds. Ethno-pop celebrates the rich and colourful diversity of China in a more commercially oriented and less dogmatic or academic way, and is designed to attract mainstream Chinese audiences. There is an overlap between all three styles, particularly with the shift in definition of *yuanshengtai* over the years.

All of the styles help to uphold the overarching Chinese Party-state ideology of the 'unitary multiethnic state'. However, the styles of presenting a unified multiethnic China reflect different political, commercial and artistic concerns. Different styles may be interwoven within the same programmes and even the same act to appeal to different audiences, while certain styles may be salient in particular contexts. For instance, hardened politicized orthodox forms, which offer strong messages, are most often seen during official national celebrations in shows that are directly sponsored by the state propaganda department. At other times, messages about the nature of the Chinese nation and state can be much more open. Overall, there is significant variety in the ways that the Han majority and 55 minority nationalities are performed musically, linguistically and visually on Chinese television. The various styles also suggest multiple influences on how to best present China's multiethnic identity, with the 'harder' nationalistic and 'softer' cosmopolitan sides being two extremes within a range of representations.

The orthodox style: a CCP-led multiethnic China

As noted in the Introduction, from 1949 (and earlier), the primary concern for official performances under Communist rule was to develop and modernize traditional styles of music, culture and art to fit the new socialist cause (Jones, 2001),[1] while from the 1980s, the development and modernization of these cultural forms has been used to pursue the goal of building a national identity. Traditional styles from both minority nationalities and Han have been incorporated into these causes.

A singing style that has been widely promoted on Chinese television and through China's conservatoriums is the 'national style' (*minzu changfa*, lit: national singing style). Chinese scholars describe it as more 'scientific' (*kexue*) than other styles, and it is created through refining traditional folk songs (or new songs that sound like folk songs) by combining them with elements of Western operatic or choral vocalization and Western orchestral accompaniments that are perceived to be more modern and sophisticated (see Li, 2004a).² The language of spoken and sung discourse in this style is always in the standard national language, *Putonghua*, rather than any local dialect or minority language. Also, if lyrics are adapted from older songs that may have earlier expressed personal or local sentiments, in official televised performances lyrics are often composed anew to promote ideological and pro-CCP messages, such as gratitude to the Party for ensuring national stability, development, happiness and peace. For example, 'The Red Sun Shines on the Border Regions' (*Hong taiyang zhao bianjiang*), created in 1966, draws on ethnic Korean culture in Jilin province, northeast China. The lyrics contain the words 'The CCP leads us towards victory, towards the future' (*Gongchang dang lingdao women shengli xiang qian fang*) (discussed further in Chapter 7).

This 'national style' plays an important role in signifying a sense of a unified socio-political entity. While 'national' songs have been derived from a rich source of Han and minority nationality folk melodies, merging these with Western operatic and orchestral elements has allowed the old to be both preserved and changed in a way that they became identified as the inherited property of all modern Chinese (Zou Wenqin, cited in Li, 2004b).³ In other words, while 'national' songs might draw influence from *any* minority nationality, the resulting composition represents *all* Chinese ethnicities. While each minority nationality contributes to the ongoing task of maintaining the rich diversity of Chinese music (Li, 2004b), the 'national style' of singing, accompanied by other similarly revitalized components such as dance, costume and language, continues to be upheld as the epitome of Chinese advancement and modernity in many Chinese music-entertainment programmes, especially on CCTV. The significance of this style has been highlighted by their prominent placement at the opening and closing of programmes. There are a number of variants in hardened, orthodox, 'national style' performances, as discussed below.

Fifty-six colourful peripheries, one central red China

The most obvious form of an orthodox style performance, typically associated with CCTV productions, is the spectacle of a large troupe of dancers wearing different ethnic minority-inspired colourful costumes dancing happily together. Typically they dance around a singer who, if female, is dressed in red. Male singers will often wear black, 'modern' Western-style suits with red ties or have red handkerchiefs in their jacket pockets. This style where voiceless dancers in minority nationality costumes dance happily around a singer in red in support of a core state message is emblematic of what other observers associate with the 'well-worn clichés of the representation of minorities of China' (Harris, 2012: 450).

Red is the major colour of the CCP and the PRC flag, allowing for conflation between the Communist Party and the Chinese nation. During the socialist era it was the colour of the revolution and revolutionary classes (the blood of the martyrs) and has an established history of reverence in PRC music and film through songs like 'The East is Red' (*Dongfang hong*), which was the de facto national anthem during the Cultural Revolution (Lee, 1995: 95) (see Chapter 2). In the reform years, the colour red has been associated with notions of national strength, prosperity, progress, ambition and love. Red is also conveniently the traditional symbol of good luck in China and thus has widespread appeal. Chinese music-entertainment television productions have continued to ensure that red remains the central colour of both the Party-state and Chinese national identity.

The CCTV special *Love My China: Nationalities' United Special Evening of Entertainment* (*Ai wo Zhonghua: Minzu tuanjie zhuanti wanhui*) is one of many examples where 56 colourful dancers dance around a central singer in celebration of national unity. This programme was broadcast on multiple channels two days before the celebration of the 60th anniversary of the PRC in September 2009. The programme was noted directly by one of the hosts as being sponsored by the Propaganda Department of the CCP Central Committee (*Zhongyang xuanchuan bu*), the United Front Work Department of the CCP Central Committee (*Zhongyang tongzhan bu*) and the State Ethnic Affairs Commission of the PRC (*Guojia minzu shiwu weiyuanhui*). The message of multiethnic unity was pushed strongly throughout the programme through the verbal discourse of hosts, on-stage interviews with minority nationality performers and various song and dance performances.

The television special emphatically concluded with a song and dance performance of the famous song, 'Love My China' (*Ai wo Zhonghua*), after which the entire programme was named. It served to leave viewers with a final patriotic thought that without doubt China is a happy and united multiethnic Chinese family. Through poetic metaphor, the song's lyrics reminded audiences that the '56 constellations, 56 flowers, and the 56 nationalities' brothers and sisters make one family'. High-pitched notes in Mandarin tugged at emotional heartstrings suggesting that the official language itself operates as a unifying force, particularly with the climactic phrase, 'the 56 languages converge into one sentence: Love My China'.

The song, as was often the case on CCTV around this time, was sung by the female first grade national singer and state artist Song Zuying, who has been a household name in China since 1990 when she sang 'Small Back Baskets' (*Xiao bei lou*) at the *CCTV Spring Festival*.[4] Song later gained significant international exposure through her duet with Plácido Domingo during the Closing Ceremony of the Beijing 2008 Olympic Games as well as through an 'East meets West' concert with popular internationally acclaimed Chinese pianist Lang Lang and Italian tenor Andrea Bocelli at the Royal Albert Hall in London's Olympic Year in 2012, where she sang the 2008 Beijing Olympic Theme Song 'You and Me' as well as ethnic Miao songs and Italian classics. She has also toured the United States of America, which included a performance with the New York Philharmonic at the Lincoln Centre in 2014 where she wore Miao traditional costumes. Her presence at the New York

Philharmonic Orchestra's Third Chinese New Year Concert represented the first time she had been absent from the *CCTV Spring Festival Gala* after appearing in it for 24 consecutive years. Given Song's important roles in unifying the state, promoting China on an international stage and as a Miao person, she embodies a proud, unified multiethnic, Chinese position that fits perfectly with Party-state messages.[5]

In this special, the lyrics of 'Love My China' were given visual emphasis through 56 dancers in 56 different multicoloured costumes dancing around her. Unusually, in this case, Song Zuying wore an elaborate silver (rather than red) dress, apparently the same one she wore at the Olympic Games, with a wide red belt around her waist. The dress seemed to allow for reflection on China's pride and achievement in hosting the major international event, linking the themes of national unity with national development and modernization.

As Song sang the final note, the dancers threw their red pom-poms into the air, which were then graphically 'captured' and transformed into the words 'Love My China' (*Ai wo Zhonghua*) on the screen. There was then a cut back to an image of the stage, with the same words written at the pinnacle of a rainbow in the set design that framed the whole stage. In case it was still not clear enough to audiences, the four hosts summarized again the main message of multiethnic state unity while an instrumental version of 'Love My China' continued to be played softly in the background. Standing upright in a straight line, each host, all well-known CCTV music-entertainment personalities, gave their concluding thoughts, mirroring the programme's beginning, and rounding off the production. First to step forward was female host Wang Xiaoya, dressed in red:

> Tonight we have used stories to describe the feeling of unity among the nationalities in the Chinese national family. So many moving things have happened that we cannot possibly describe each one, one at a time.

Then came male host Sa Beining, wearing a modernized, chic grey Tang-style suit (*Tang zhuang*), representing a proud Chinese nation where modern and traditional elements are merged to create a new strong culture:

> The 56 nationalities are bound by fraternal love, and have stood together through thick and thin. Joined by blood, the 'Chinese nationality' (*Zhonghua minzu*) are united with one heart, and will forever be an indestructible cohesive force.

Female host Dong Qing summarized lessons about China's history and its future, and emphasized the necessity of the CCP for the country's stability:

> In the Republic's 60 years under the leadership of the [Communist] Party, each of the nationalities have united and struggled together. Throughout these sixty years [they] have flourished and developed together. We

whole-heartedly wish the 56 nationalities a life in harmony, working together in times of difficulty [towards] harmonious development.

Finally, in an even gender balance, male host Bai Yansong, known for hosting music-entertainment programmes as well as more 'serious' news and current affairs programmes, concluded the programme by affirming that:

> In two days' time, we will together see in the new China's 60th anniversary celebrations. This is a magnificent moment. Indeed a completely new and historic starting point. The different nationalities' brothers and sisters, hand in hand and side by side, have walked together in the past, and must even more intimately walk (together) towards the future, to fulfil all our dreams. Tonight we bless the motherland. Tonight we bless the future.

These are among the most authoritative hosts of CCTV music-entertainment programmes and speak with trained certainty, eloquence and professionalism. Hosts, who are also Party members (as declared on their websites), are the most obvious embodiment of the 'mouthpieces' of the Party-state on music-entertainment television because they literally have the power and skills to guide interpretations and link disparate music and dance performances to particular political messages through their commentary. The camera often zooms close up on their faces and blurs the background so that focus is on their eyes and mouths, from which the important words about national identity are emanating. The remarks of the hosts, and numerous others throughout the evening, supported the legitimacy of the CCP as the necessary vanguard of China's prosperous multiethnic society. Even if one were to disagree with the idea that China is a united and harmonious place for all 56 nationalities, or that the CCP's policies on matters of ethnicity are always the best approach, the convergence of image, music and spoken language in this orthodox frame makes it difficult to miss the intended message that China is a united and prosperous multiethnic state as a result of the efforts of the Party-state.

Similar productions have continued to be broadcast in more recent years. On 7 November 2012, in the days leading up to the planned leadership change during the 18th National People's Congress of the PRC, CCTV and CNTV (promoted prominently online from the CNTV homepage) broadcast an entertainment extravaganza entitled 'Piloting China' (*Linghang Zhongguo*). The production celebrated the Chinese nation and all its achievements over the past ten years under the leadership of the CCP. It boasted of an innovative style and enterprising spirit, whereby China's youth and citizens of all nationalities were united in a single goal towards China's ongoing prosperity and development under the CCP. During the show the People's Liberation Army Choir and the 56 Nationalities Choir, dressed in a range of representative colourful ethnic costumes, joined forces to sing 'The Flag Fluttering in the Wind' (*Yingfeng piaoyang de qi*), telling audiences: 'It's you who led us on the road to revival, from victory to victory… We uphold you [because] upholding you means [we are] upholding ourselves.' As these lyrics were sung by representatives in multiethnic dress, the images presented a story of progress, beginning with the vast expanses of beautiful natural environments before shifting to man-made terraced fields and then to modern cities with skyscrapers, demonstrating the grand achievements of all Chinese under the leadership of the CCP. During the song a huge fluttering Communist Party flag emerged out of a field of flowers on a backscreen. As the camera zoomed into the flag, highlighting its importance, the music slowed to emphasize every word of the lyrics: 'We uphold you… unswervingly'. As the piece ended, the studio audience seated in representative groups as identified by their clothing – army uniforms, nurses' uniforms, multiethnic costumes and 'ordinary' people's attire – clapped together politely, demonstrating their approval of the message that China's ongoing prosperity is dependent on the unity of all workers and all nationalities in the country under the continued leadership of the CCP.

Later in the production, a mass choir of China's ethnic singers, marked by their colourful clothes, sang 'Beautiful Home' (*Meili jiayuan*) in the 'national style'. In the song, their words were accompanied by simple gestures that television viewers could follow at home. They proudly exclaimed that 'the sons and daughters of different ethnicities' are walking together 'hand in hand' (arms linking with performers on either side) with 'hearts' (heart shaped gesture with thumb and forefingers touching) 'linked' (thumbs and forefingers joining to create interlinking circles) 'to build a harmonious homeland'.

Planned and programmed by the Party leadership and its propaganda units, it is hard to image how one could have advanced a more strongly consolidated political message of a harmonious, multiethnic China. Whether audiences agreed with the message or not, there was a concerted effort to stitch language, music and visuals together into a clear message that suggested that every ethnic group in China supported the CCP, and that the future prosperity of China for all its nationalities relied on the continued leadership of the CCP.

Hand in hand, striding towards the future

Another variation of an orthodox performance involves 56 performers in colourful ethnic costumes, striding together, hand in hand. During the Opening Ceremony of the 2008 Beijing Olympic Games, audiences saw such images of 56 smiling, colourful, Chinese nationality children walking together briskly behind a huge red Chinese flag. The unity of the colourful children walking swiftly across the mass expanse of the stadium floor formed the moving part of the scene. They marched forward towards uniformed soldiers, standing erect, with a steadfast expression (suggesting the power of the nation-state), who then took the red flag and hoisted it up to its pinnacle position where it fluttered proudly in the breeze of the night sky. The forward and upward directions of the scene, following a trajectory of the red flag, suggests the unity of China's ethnic groups and a contentment with the current political status quo that will advance into the future. Parallel and encompassed within these movements was a static component, centred on the girl Lin Miaoke, who was dressed in a plain red dress, her youthful vibrancy suggesting a bright future for China. The camera swirled around Lin as she stood still, upright, and sang (lip-synched) a slow tempo version of the patriotic song 'Ode to the Motherland' (*Gechang zuguo*). While the song may have been slowed and sweetened through the voice of a young female singer to tone down the nationalist sentiment for an international audience, it also symbolically marked a sense of stability and centrality of the Party and the Chinese nation that had stood the test of time and still remained salient for today's youth.

This striding forward, hand in hand representation was also a regular feature on CCTV3's daily music video show (now on CCTV-Music), which is strongly reflective of Party-state politics. For instance, similar imagery of the colourful nationalities was used for the TV promo for the music video show during the period when the annual national decision-making meetings – the Chinese People's Political Consultative Conference and the National People's Congress – took place in Beijing in March 2008. Clearly, orthodox song and dance performances, which overtly promote a proud and modern multiethnic and unified Chinese national identity, are prominent during political events of national importance such as national political meetings, the Beijing 2008 Olympic Games and anniversaries of the Communist Party's ascendancy to power. These events and their promotion through televised music-entertainment productions are a vital component of a drive to bolster support and prove the ongoing legitimacy of the CCP. The prime goal of orthodox productions is not to highlight local difference or some 'authentic' ethnic culture, but to spread the message of multiethnic unity and support for the nation under the CCP.

While symbols of ethnicity are observable in costume, any traditional or sub-state national identity that could be expressed through musical expression or the language of lyrics has largely been erased, transformed or composed anew to fit a singular, unifying 'national' singing style. Regardless of the intention of individual singers to promote any other kind of minority nationality identification, the convergence of image, music and spoken language in orthodox performance moments points most strongly to the message of an integrated Chinese nation and patriotism to a CCP-led state.

Yuanshengtai folk songs and authentic minority culture bearers

Yuanshengtai, which roughly translates as 'original ecology' or 'primitive', has been used to refer to 'authentic' traditional ethnic arts in China in the context of the need to 'preserve' intangible cultural traditions in the face of development and social change. *Yuanshengtai* singers often sing in local folk styles. Unlike the 'national style' in which musical accompaniment is often prerecorded, *yuanshengtai* performances are usually accompanied live with traditional acoustic instrumentation made from natural materials like wood and horse hair (*matouqin*), clay (for the egg-shaped *xun*) and leaves (for leaf blowing). They most actively concern the folk music of minority nationalities, but Han Chinese performers particularly from the Northwest Shaanxi and Shanxi provinces, are also included within this genre. *Yuanshengtai* music of China's ethnic groups began to be performed regularly on CCTV in 2004 when the show *Folk Songs China* (*Min'ge Zhongguo*) began. This show claimed to be China's only television programme dedicated to *yuanshengtai* music. However, some provincial channels also run music programmes focusing on folk songs, such as *Songs From the Yellow River* (*Ge cong Huang He lai*) on Shanxi TV and *Zhaxi Show* (*Zhaxi xiu*) on Tibet Satellite Television (Tibetan style songs). In 2006, CCTV also introduced a *yuanshengtai* category in the prestigious *CCTV Youth Television Singing Competition* (*Qinggesai*).

The focus on 'authentic' folk song styles became increasingly popular on Chinese television after 2003 when Hu Jintao and Wen Jiabao took over the Chinese leadership. *Yuanshengtai* mirrored surrounding political discourse where China's leaders were reflecting on the massive social inequality, environmental degradation, and limitations of rapid economic development and globalization. The desire to promote the preservation of traditional culture and address anxieties over cultural 'loss' as a result of decades of 'processing and modification' (Rees, 2009: 48) was reflected in this style. *Yuanshengtai* performances also related to the Hu–Wen government's broader project of building a 'people-oriented' Harmonious Society (Lin in Sun and Zhao, 2009: 98–9), where local culture bearers and communities were respected for their knowledge and traditions. The *yuanshengtai* genre also emerged in the context of the Chinese government's increasing interest in promoting a positive and 'softer' image of China to its own citizens and to the world by showing that it tolerated cultural diversity within its borders, respected its minority cultures, and was meeting its obligations as a signatory to the 2003 UNESCO Convention for the Safeguarding of Intangible Cultural Heritage.

Showcasing China's ethnic and cultural diversity through *yuanshengtai* cultural programmes offered a counterpoint to commonly reported international media concerns (from both Western and overseas Chinese media) about China's abuses of minority nationality 'rights'. For instance, *China Daily* has a special website dedicated to stories on 'Transmitters of China Intangible Cultural Heritage' (see also Heng, 2008: 409). From a more cynical point of view, the references to the UN could be seen as a form of 'blue-washing', which refers to community and social responsibility campaigns that involve partnerships between organizations and the UN that are designed to showcase organizations as good global citizens who care about such things as environmental sustainability and fair labour practices and thus improve their image to consumers and clients. The *yuanshengtai* discourse also played into discourses that supported the tourism and cultural industries, helping to attract both domestic and overseas visitors to scenic spots associated with the exoticism and 'authenticity' of minority cultures. The discourse of *yuanshengtai* is therefore entangled in ongoing local and global tensions

The CCTV Youth Singing Competition

Since 2006, a *yuanshengtai* category has been included in the prestigious *CCTV Youth Singing Competition*, alongside other categories, which have included the 'national style' (*minzu changfa*), Western opera (*meisheng changfa*), pop music (*liuxing changfa*) and choral music (*hechang*). Its inclusion provides insights into mainstream perceptions of the relationship between the majority Han and China's minority nationalities. In 2008, the *yuanshengtai* category of the *CCTV Youth Singing Competition* provoked a number of discussions between contestants, hosts, judges, commentators and audiences through letters and SMS messages that were read aloud by hosts. The mainly Beijing-based musical experts gave the impression that many mainstream Chinese audiences had not had much exposure to 'local' musical cultures before, or had only begun to find this 'primitive' music worthy of appreciation and preservation. Contestants played instruments relatively unknown to the experts in the studio and sang in languages unintelligible to them and to Chinese mainstream audiences. The hosts and commentators went to great lengths to emphasize the beauty, freshness and rawness of *yuanshengtai* singing and its importance for the Chinese nation. The rawness of *yuanshengtai* contrasted with the advanced, cultured and refined 'national style' (*minzu changfa*) and 'operatic style' (*meisheng changfa*) categories. On the one hand, *yuanshengtai* was respected and appreciated. However, being a competition, performers were subject to quality judgements, although questions arose as to how such a wide variety of styles could be fairly judged against one another when the judges themselves could not possibly be experts in all the traditions.

The design of the television competition also put the professional commentators – namely military-based composer Xu Peidong (who was trained in China's conservatorium context, which draws heavily on Western norms of music education) and esteemed social commentator Yu Qiuyu – in a superior position as educators of both the contestants and television viewers. Although viewers had access to 'alternative' voices and cultural ideas rarely otherwise heard on Chinese television through the *yuanshengtai* performers, the design of the programme was biased strongly in favour of the experts having the power to lecture the contestants (and viewers) rather than on the experts and audiences learning from the *yuanshengtai* performers. While *yuanshengtai* contestants were able to perform their flair for their local traditional musical forms in full television spectacle with individual close-ups for 99 per cent of their score, they were also immediately subjected to a test of general and musical knowledge unrelated to their singing or area of expertise for the final 1 per cent of their score. After answering (generally a multiple choice question) the experts educated the contestants and audiences by elaborating on the correct answers in great depth, sometimes taking a much longer time than the original singing performance.

The topics of general knowledge questions asked during the 2008 *CCTV Youth Singing Competition* ranged from revolutionary music to folk songs, the Olympic Games, Chinese and international geography, knowledge of English, and classic performances and songs from around China and the world. The inclusion of such questions may have indicated a desire to educate audience members on items of 'common knowledge' deemed suitable for the Chinese populace. However, the contestants in the *yuanshengtai* category, who were mostly minorities, were often positioned as ignorant and uneducated as a result of their inability to answer even the most seemingly basic questions such as the location of major cities or well-known scenic spots in China. At times, the competition reinforced stereotypes of ignorant ethnic minorities from remote border regions and revealed an ongoing sense of Han chauvinism. Minority nationality contestants also seemed to have been asked more simple questions than contestants in other categories of the competition, although it was interesting that this contested point was openly raised through a letter that was read aloud during the program.

In response to an audience question about the easier questions for *yuanshengtai* performers, Yu Qiuyu remarked that he did not know the reason for sure as he did not choose the questions himself (although he knew the answer to every question in great depth). However, he suggested that it was because most *yuanshengtai* singers had their own rich cultures and languages and that it would have been impossible to test them taking into account such a diverse range of knowledge that drew on the background of every contestant. Therefore, they chose basic questions to try to create a more level playing field as best as they could. Yu acknowledged the need to respect China's minority cultures, but the sharing of non-musical multiethnic knowledge was not facilitated during this 'national' contest. The need to have such a general knowledge test at all also went unquestioned. Yet while Yu appeared to do his best to give ideologically 'correct' answers in line with the Party-state ethnic classification system, it is significant that the show encouraged him to discuss, respond to and give rationales for programme choices that were perceived by some audience members as indicating a hidden discriminatory agenda towards minority groups. This moment suggests that the tricky issue of representation of ethnic minorities was a concern of the producers.

Judging by the body language of the judges and hosts, one of the most awkward and seemingly unplanned moments during the 2008 competition was when female Tibetan-Chinese pop singer Han Hong, who appeared in an official role as a judge, struggled to translate for one Tibetan contestant who seemingly could not even speak a dialect of Mandarin Chinese, let alone the official standard, *Putonghua*. The fact that the contestant could not speak Chinese seemed to come as a surprise to hosts and the judges, and whether this moment was deliberately planned or not, it allowed for a rare moment of cross-cultural and linguistic confusion as a result of internal difference that was rarely seen on Chinese television. Some flexibility was therefore built into the competition for performers and audience members to work through some of the complex questions about Chinese identity and culture that the competition brought to light. Although the promotion of *Putonghua* has been phenomenally successful in uniting people across China, such moments also revealed unexpected fissures and limitations in the state's ability to unite and educate its massive populace across such a vast area.

One performance that I found particularly striking during the 2008 *CCTV Youth Singing Competition* for the difference it afforded to CCTV's more common representations of China's minority nationalities was that of Ah Peng (Chinese name Jiang Xuchang), a Bai nationality performer from Yunnan province, who reached the finals.[6] While many minorities dressed in exquisite, colourful costumes (presumably made for the television performance), Ah Peng occupied the stage wearing an open sleeveless coat made of animal hide, long black pants and sandals. His head was shaved, and he was short in stature compared to the imposing, tall figure of female host Dong Qing. He came across as tough and totally absorbed in his music in a style quite unlike other singers from southwest China who would sing as a collective in unison, gently and seductively turning their heads, or dancing enthusiastically while smiling for the audience. Ah Peng did not smile, not even while talking to the hosts.

While the lyrics of the song were quite subdued and sentimental – 'Seeing You and I'll Be Better' (*Jian ni bing jiu hao*) – Ah Peng's style was rough and more like a rock musician. In his performance for the formal CCTV competition, Ah Peng stood with his legs planted on the stage and wide apart, with his three-stringed *sanxian* strapped around him, which he used to accompany himself in interludes between sung verses. Indeed, as a *yuanshengtai* singer, he was privileged in being able to accompany himself with his own instrumentation, which was a rare sight among pop/rock performers on the CCTV stage at the time. He bent at his waist almost at right angles, often facing the floor, and at times wildly twisting almost as if feigning madness. The closest I saw to this performance style on other programmes was that of Hong Kong pop star Xie Tingfeng (Nicholas Tse) singing a pan-Chinese nationalistic song, 'Yellow People' (discussed further in Chapter 5). Ah Peng's voice was hoarse, and he made tremendous use of silence between lines and musical interludes to create tension. Such artistic tensions were also rarities on music-entertainment television at the time. His performance was not necessarily subversive, but the *yuanshengtai* format seemed to open up the possibility for stylistically different performances compared to the conservatory-trained voices of the 'operatic' and 'national styles', and the more commercially oriented 'popular' music styles.

Ah Peng was popular enough to make it to both the official and audience favourites' finals based on the judges' and audience votes. It may have helped that he played the game strategically when it came to answering the general questions, particularly the long monologue that he used to talk about the kindness of a visiting musician from Beijing. However, given that his performances were so engrossed and idiosyncratic and provided an image of a single 'wild' man dominating the stage and singing about a personal matter that seemingly provided little link to any notion of national unity, it would have been surprising if he had been chosen as the winner.

Indeed, the winners of the 2008 competition (a no less talented group) were comprised of the unity of two ethnicities: two Tu nationality male singers and two Miao nationality female singers from the same village, each wearing exquisite ethnic costumes. They had powerful, high-pitched voices, performed in a sweet way as they swayed gently from side to side, looking at each other lovingly. During the performance, the men carefully took the women's hands and a close-up of the 'hand in hand' image was carefully orchestrated, drawing on a common visual display of unity on Chinese television. This multiethnic group, who sang together happily and in a docile and non-threatening way, fully embodied the ideology of unity of the nationalities. CCTV happily showcased the winning group in various subsequent CCTV concerts. Despite the fact that Ah Peng did not win, it is important to acknowledge that the *yuanshengtai* category enabled the Party-state media to show itself as open to diverse representations of its multiethnic population.

It is also significant that performing in the *yuanshengtai* category of the *CCTV Youth Singing Competition* can open up doors for performers by giving them exposure to a national audience as well as a voice for further negotiating their identities in various media. Ah Peng later performed in other television competitions, making it to the top 12 in Hunan Television's *Happy Boy* (*Kuaile Nansheng*) and becoming a weekly finalist in CCTV's *Star Avenue* in 2010. Significantly, in an era where digital manipulation and cutting and pasting have become commonplace, Ah Peng also used clips from his CCTV performance in what appears to be a self-made video of a more recent song 'Difficult to Meet Each Other' (*Xiang jian nan*), which was posted to the video-sharing site Tudou. The musical backing was synthesized grunge with deep rumblings and the video depicted Ah Peng wildly waving his *sanxian*, rising into the clouds above high mountains, while standing in barren fields, and exerting heavy breathy sounds. The colour of the sky was graphically altered with harsh fluoro colours and images of fire. Rough cuts from his CCTV performances were jaggedly inserted into the video, harshly 'collapsing' into his body. This representation of himself clearly contrasts with the one on CCTV where he was just one of many ordinary minorities on a big official Chinese stage. As Peter Manuel notes in his study of cheap and easily reproduced cassette culture (cited in Harris, 2005a: 628), the online video environment opens up a space for the expression of different types of identity and its oppositional force may lie less in the content than in the means of production. This is an example of how, like elsewhere around the world, Chinese performers and consumers are engaging in the 'mash-up culture' of the digital era. In gaining access to affordable digital technologies, they can 'sample, splice and reassemble' music and visual sources and radically reinscribe these texts with new meanings beyond those intended by the 'originating powers' and thus shine light 'on their own nation's cultural projections and self-deceptions' (Coleman, 2008: 138). Ah Peng's CCTV performance, interwoven with his own production, also competes (in a small way) with CCTV's online clips for viewers in the online space.

Folk Songs China

In 2008, most of the daily episodes of *Folk Songs China* on CCTV3 featured 'authentic' (*didi daodao de*) singers from remote and rural local areas, particularly from China's southwestern provinces of Yunnan, Guangxi and Guizhou. The kind of music presented was 'untampered' with the so-called 'scientific' or 'advanced' elements of Western operatic or popular music traditions. It was usually in a local minority language, accompanied live by local instruments, and the lyrics often reflected local village concerns and folklore covering a range of emotions. Apart from putting singers on display and having hosts talk about them, there was an attempt to create a respectful dialogue with the 'culture bearers' about their music, and because the performers were afforded a 'spoken' voice as well as a musical one the programme offered a point of difference to other musical representations of China's multiethnic make-up. Ethnomusicologists were also invited to discuss the specifics of the styles of music of the different groups, and it seemed to be the only programme on Chinese television that allowed for detailed and contrasting depictions of social and performative life *within* each of the officially recognized nationality groups. Although it continued to be problematic in terms of positioning ethnic minorities as rural and their cultures as timeless and unmodern – emphasized through the programme's aim of selecting 'representative' pieces to preserve and 'box' into a recorded *Folk Songs Museum* (*Min'ge bowuguan*) collection that was to be sold to consumers – this daily programme provided an alternative voice for 'ordinary' culture bearers.

Performances involved not only songs of joy, but also (rarely, although significantly) songs of sadness. For instance, a Hani nationality folk artist named Dao Shu from Mojiang in Yunnan province, who appeared in local dress on *Folk Songs China* on 24 March 2010, explained her song in Mandarin and then in local language in a powerful teary style, while subtitles in Chinese gave a running explanation for mainstream viewers. The song was about a girl who died because of poverty and cruelty in her community. There was no moralizing at the end. The folk story was simply and powerfully told as a folkloric 'fact'. Although Dao Shu, like most other performers on the programme, continued to epitomize a stereotypical construction of minorities as rural and female, the performance was significantly different to the orthodox performances of 56 nationalities singing and dancing happily together.

Over time, however, *Folk Songs China* began to include more 'modern' elements, and ethnic minority culture was more likely to be presented as ever-modernizing and a vital part of China's rich and colourful developing cultural heritage. The studio design shifted from a simple sparse set with symbolic natural elements of a 'river', 'stars' and a 'tree' without a studio audience, towards a glitzier design that included computer graphic designs alongside brighter images of natural elements, fancier lighting, and a studio audience. It included clips of audience members in the small studio taking their own videos of the performance through their 'modern' mobile phones. Audiences in the Beijing studio were also called up on stage and audience interaction and participation was foregrounded more than an intense focus on 'the other'. The music too shifted towards more modern hybrid blends, including ethno-pop and 'national style' operatic-influenced forms, and was accompanied by more synthesized backing tracks as well as live acoustic instrumentation. There has also been a shift away from the ethnographic detailing of the performance styles of specific village cultures, particularly of elders from the smaller and less politically 'sensitive' groups in southwestern provinces like Yunnan and Guizhou, towards younger musicians and bands who see music as not just a way of life but a livelihood as well. There has also been a greater focus on the more politically 'sensitive' Tibetan, Mongolian and Uyghur nationalities – the three major ethnic groups associated with China's largest autonomous regions.

Ethno-pop stars: celebrating hybrid ethnic creativity

Blurring the boundaries with the contemporary *yuanshengtai* style is an approach to the performance of multiethnic unity that infuses minority and/or Han folk elements with Western-influenced/East Asian mass popular music (*liuxing yinyue*). By ethno-pop, I refer here to a hybrid pop style that is inspired by China's multiethnic heritage and which appeals to popular youth markets in a similar way to the 'world music' genre. Unlike the 'national style', which merges Chinese folk music with classical Western orchestral forms, the ethno-pop style mixes Chinese folk elements, such as high-pitched vocals, folk melodies and traditional musical instruments like the gourd pipe (*hulusi*) or Chinese shawm (*suona*), with elements from Western style popular music including electric keyboards and electric guitars, and mainstream pop and dance rhythms and chord structures. Unlike in *yuanshengtai*, ethno-pop performers most often wear contemporary dress, but they may also perform in creative blends of modern ethnic-inspired costumes.

Cross-fertilization between international pop and folk music and between Chinese, Western and minority nationality culture may be symbolic of a new, trendy sense of individualistic expression among cosmopolitan youth. Pop songs on Chinese television that include minority elements have been sung by Han and minority nationality pop stars alike. Contemporary ethno-pop music thus provides a platform for creatively playing with aspects of minority and Han ethnicity in a modern way, which also fits in with the Party-state's promotion of China's 'cultural modernization' and the development of its creative industries (O'Connor and Gu, 2006). Ethno-pop may also be part of an attempt to promote a unique PRC Chinese identity in a context where Chinese pop music has been dominated by artists from Taiwan and Hong Kong (see Gold, 1995: 257–60). The Northwest Wind and Tibetan Wind movements of the 1990s saw PRC artists of Han and mixed ethnic backgrounds, like Dao Lang,[7] Hang Tianqi,[8] Tian Zhen,[9] Zhu Zheqin (better known internationally as Dadawa)[10] and Sa Dingding,[11] create new music based on their inspirations from ethnic minority music and travels to minority areas.

While cosmopolitan pop culture is a creative departure from the orthodox style, and may not overtly sing the praises of the CCP or love for the country (although the state does co-opt popular music styles and incorporate popular music singers for this purpose too), popular music is not necessarily oppositional. Ethno-pop generally most effectively promotes the 'softer', outward-looking, cosmopolitan aspects of reform era state policy. Ethno-pop, like *yuanshengtai* and the orthodox 'national style', still celebrates China's multiethnic diversity *within* the official framework of the unity of the nationalities.

The state and Chinese television stations have engaged with ethnically inspired popular music artists to showcase and celebrate China's multiethnic diversity, its national traditions and contemporary cosmopolitanism. During the Beijing 2008 Olympic Games Opening and Closing Ceremonies, both orthodox and more contemporary pop styles were endorsed by officials. While the Opening Ceremony was dominated by a more serious orthodox style, ethno-pop contributed to the 'coming out' celebratory party feel of the Closing Ceremony as people performing as all 56 nationalities sang and danced together to upbeat versions of songs infused with an 'ethnic' feel, such as 'Visitors From Afar Please Stay On' (*Yuanfang de keren qing ni liu xia lai*).

The next sections examine cases of Chinese pop singers who are identified by (or whose music is identified by) their ethnicity, including Uyghur performers, chosen for being one of the ethnic groups with the most sensitive relations with the Han majority; Korean/Chaoxian, a smaller ethnic group with ethnic links to two Korean states across the border; and the majority Han, who are often the ethnically 'unmarked' group, yet whose ethnicity is still performed. These singers may not always sing ethnically inspired songs, but they nonetheless have signature pieces that help to define and create their identities and become representative of their ethnic group. The section illustrates a range of ways in which performances of ethnic pop on Chinese television contribute to visions of a vibrant multiethnic society, while on the whole upholding the state task of asserting a harmonious and unified multiethnic state. It also considers how representations of ethnic pop stars vary according to the show, the historical moment and particular television space in which they are performing.

Performing Uyghur-Chinese

The Xinjiang Uyghur Autonomous Region in China's far west is China's largest administrative area. The area borders on Mongolia, Russia, Kazakstan, Kyrgyzstan, Tajikistan, Afghanistan, Pakistan and India, and has a large population of Turkic-speaking Muslims, including more than eight million people who identify as Uyghur (also spelt Uighur) after which the region is named. Uyghur people have many similar customs to cultures and ethnicities in Central Asia. For a brief period in 1949, a separate state of East Turkestan was declared but it was officially named as part of Communist China in the same year. Since then an independence movement and separatist groups have continued to be active, particularly in the 1990s after the emergence of independent Muslim states in Central Asia following the collapse of the Soviet Union. These groups have been suppressed by Beijing and gone underground. There is widespread discontent in the area as a result of resentment over the fact that Han Chinese are infiltrating the area to the extent that they now outnumber the Uyghur population and are often given the best jobs. The state has also placed restrictions on the practice of Islam, including control over religious schools and mosques, and government departments have reportedly restricted civil servants from fasting during the holy month of Ramadan. There have been sporadic incidents of interethnic unrest in Xinjiang and outside of the region, including in Tiananmen Square in Beijing for which the authorities have blamed Xinjiang 'terrorists' (BBC News, 2014). Many Han Chinese hold negative stereotypes of Uyghurs. Music-entertainment television appears to try to offer a more positive frame of Uyghur–Han relations.

One Uyghur band to have performed on CCTV is the Xinjiang Ke'erman Band, also known as the Kerman-Dili band, named after the husband and wife duo who lead the band. They were featured for an entire *Folk Songs China* episode in December 2011. Lead singer Ke'erman introduced himself as being ethnically Uyghur, and his own website proudly marketed their Xinjiang flavour. Their style of music was not focused on the kind of 'original' or 'authentic' Xinjiang Uyghur music seen on earlier *Folk Songs China* episodes that featured *yuanshengtai* music or the *CCTV Youth Singing Competition*'s *yuanshengtai* category, which typically focused on traditional pieces and instruments. Rather, it focused on a creative hybrid of Xinjiang Uyghur melodies and rhythms and Spanish flamenco guitar styles. Host Liang Lu introduced this mix of styles as 'mysterious' (*shenqi*), suggesting it was something new that would captivate the mainstream audiences. The performers' clothing included modern styles with touches of ethnic inspiration such as in the collar designs.

As Rachel Harris (2005a: 642) explains, flamenco guitar has been an influence in Xinjiang musicians' work since the mid-1990s when the Gipsy Kings'[12] cassettes 'took Xinjiang by storm'. Harris (2005a) notes that due to the forces of politics and globalization, musicians in Xinjiang, particularly in the capital of the Xinjiang Uyghur Autonomous Region, Ürümqi, have themselves been more influenced by and open to 'outside' styles of music than forms of music associated with the Chinese nationality and state. As well as flamenco, Bollywood and Western pop stars like Madonna have also been influential in the region, much more so than in the rest of China. As such, Xinjiang performers may bring something new to mainstream Chinese audiences, which is both ethnic 'Chinese' and global/cosmopolitan/modern.[13] The fact that by 2011 flamenco blends with Chinese music still seemed to be new for mainstream Chinese audiences may relate to a more recent active promotion by the state of 'creative' hybrid East/West styles and the creative industries.

Another song performed by the Ke'erman Band on this episode included snippets from their music video 'Snow Lotus Girl' (*Xue lian guniang*), which depicts the five men in the band with their guitars, Ke'erman in a Western-style suit and sunglasses, and his wife Dili singing and dancing in ethnic-inspired costume, her long hair flowing freely as she dances in stunning scenery. A rap section of the video was included in the *Folk Songs China* broadcast. As well as helping to promote the group and Xinjiang as a beautiful tourist destination, this broadcast on CCTV helped to present the Uyghur artists as an attractive part of China's new era of modernity and resplendence.

While the focus was on hybrid blends, *Folk Songs China* hosts still requested the Ke'erman Band to discuss Uyghur traditions and play a part of the representative musical piece of the Uyghur people, the 'Twelve Muqam' suites. Host Liang Lu informed audiences that the Uyghur 'Twelve Muqam' musical suites were recognized by the global body UNESCO as an important intangible cultural heritage artefact (also see Rees, 2009: 71), thus reminding audiences about China's responsible actions and respect for the traditions of its nationalities. Ke'erman dutifully noted that the 'Twelve Muqam' were a proud part of Uyghur culture and informed audiences that they comprised 12 suites, which include dancing, singing and instrumental aspects, each requiring two hours to perform, totalling 24 hours.

Harris (2005a: 642) has discussed the complex relationship between the politics of identity and the performance of hybrid styles involving traditional and global influences in contemporary Uyghur music. She has argued that many diasporic voices in support of Uyghur national identity, distanced by changes in Xinjiang society, have blamed the Chinese (i.e., officials/Han Chinese) for 'polluting' their music, while opposition to this music from Uyghurs within Xinjiang has been more concerned with the undesirable influence of global styles that are particularly popular among youth. Many contemporary Uyghur singers and bands, however, are more concerned with making their own music out of unique blends of styles. In this instance, Ke'erman insisted that they would perform the Muqam in a new way, with Western guitars alongside the traditional Uyghur *dutars* (long-necked two-stringed lutes) – thus asserting a modern Uyghur–Chinese identity. The performance

102 *Multiethnic China*

on the national Party-state broadcaster suggested an attempt by CCTV to satisfy different positions: respect for traditional intangible cultural heritage, which may appeal more to older television viewers, and the promotion of new creative hybrid forms of musical entertainment, which may appeal more to youth and mainstream audiences.

Unlike earlier episodes of *Folk Songs China*, the musicians in the Ke'erman Band were not local rural farmers, but professional artists. Ke'erman explained on *Folk Songs China* that he and his wife had lived in Beijing, the nation's capital, for almost 14 years. When asked by the host if they ever went back to Xinjiang, Ke'erman reflected that they returned to Xinjiang about once a year to see family and learn about the new music in the area. This gave the impression that the Chinese government, via CCTV, was promoting links and learning between the capital and the sensitive region. What is interesting is the omission of details on why they left in the first place. They could have been personal, but as Nimrod Baranovitch (2007) and Rachel Harris (2005a) have explained, the state has clamped down on social and artistic life in Xinjiang since 1997, following the brutal suppression of demonstrations in the northern Xinjiang town of Ghulja (Yining in Chinese).[14] Tight censorship and oppressive political tension and ethnic discrimination continue to affect everyday life in Xinjiang. Many musicians and other artists have moved from Xinjiang to Beijing because of the unbearable restrictions in Xinjiang and deep distrust between the Uyghurs and Han Chinese there (Baranovitch, 2007; Rees, 2003: 156). As a result, Uyghur musicians have ironically found more freedom to perform in Beijing, under the noses of the central authorities, than in Xinjiang. The idea that officials in Beijing may be more open to Uyghur voices than their counterparts in Xinjiang is also illustrated by Beijing-based Uyghur singer Askar, who was banned from performing his songs live in Xinjiang, while being invited to perform to a massive nationwide television audience as part of the number one rating *CCTV Spring Festival Gala* in 2002 (Baranovitch, 2007). While CCTV's music-entertainment programmes offer spaces for Uyghur artists to perform, and allow them to showcase their unique, modern-traditional hybrid blends, they do not touch on the problems with performing in Xinjiang. Rather than being presented as internal political 'exiles' as Baranovitch contends, the general impression from CCTV is that Uyghur people have migrated to Beijing to pursue their careers in the nation's creative capital. Having bands like Ke'erman in Beijing helps to present China's capital as open, cosmopolitan, and 'civilized' (*wenming*).

Earlier I noted how the music video for 'Snow Lotus Girl' featured Dili dancing with her hair flowing freely. While this too may have been a personal choice, it is also interesting in light of the politics of ethnicity, gender and religion. Occasionally you will see Uyghur women wearing headscarves (hijabs that do not cover the face) on CCTV. Often they are older women, but sometimes younger women with headscarves will appear in a flash of ethnic diversity in a prerecorded video. However, in general there have been few representations of Muslim women in headscarves on Chinese music-entertainment television programmes.

Grose and Leibold (2015) contend that there has been a deliberate CCP policy to have female Uyghur Muslims replace their Islamic veils with colourful silk/tie-dye fabrics, embroidered doppa hats (square or round skull-caps), and braided hair, and to prescribe these as normal 'symbols of Uyghur femininity'. As part of their attempt to create new fashion standards, in 2011 officials in Xinjiang launched Project Beauty, 'a five-year, $US8 million dollar campaign aimed at developing Xinjiang's fashion and cosmetics industries', which encouraged Muslim women to 'look towards "modern" culture' by 'removing their veils'. Grose and Leibold (2015) explain how 'fashion shows, pageants, and lectures on ethnic policy, ethnic attire, and social etiquette have sought to persuade Uyghur women to "let their beautiful hair flow and show their pretty faces"'.

A popular song regularly sung on Chinese television by people of all nationalities, 'Lift Up Your Veil' (*Xianqi ni de gaitou lai*), is also widely seen to be representative of the Turkic ethnic groups in Xinjiang, including the Uyghur. While its origins are not about having Muslim women remove their veils from their culture and customs, the song could be seen as being appropriated as part of a comprehensive discourse that has emerged with this aim. The song seems to have originated in the Uzbek Republic of the former Soviet Union.[15] Well-known Soviet Armenian composer and conductor Aram Khachaturian used the melody in his Uzbek March and Dancing Song (March No. 3) composed in 1932 for the 15th anniversary of the Soviet Red Army. It soon spread westwards into China. The version that became most well-known across China was discovered and arranged in the 1930s by Wang Luobin, a renowned songwriter from Beijing who specialized in transcribing, adapting, collecting and revising the folk songs of various ethnic minorities in western China, including around 700 Xinjiang-style songs. At the end of the 1930s, Wang Luobin reportedly recorded this 'Xinjiang folk song' from a Uyghur businessman from Xinjiang in Gansu province, a province adjacent to Xinjiang.

In his musical notes, Wang explains that the upbeat song was used as a local game in the southern rural areas of Xinjiang. During the autumn harvest season while resting in the wheat fields an older man would put on a veil and a younger man would sing and dance beside him. Finally, the young man would lift up the veil only to discover not a beautiful young lady but an old white-haired man. This would be followed by laughter and then they would continue to work. Wang Luobin rearranged the song for children's performances and developed it with a more 'professional' and 'artistic' format (Baidu, n.d.). The Chinese lyrics request the lifting of the veil so that the singer can see the woman's eyebrows (which are like the curved moon), her eyes (which are bright like autumn), her face (which is round and red like a ripe apple ready to fall), and her small, red mouth (which is like a cherry in May). This song has been performed by a vast number of groups and singers. However, when female dancers in 'Xinjiang' or 'Uyghur' costumes perform on television, they invariably have long plaited hair and no veil, while those performing as Han Chinese often have bridal veils on.

On 1 February 2015, regional CCP authorities, who are dominated by the Han majority, went so far as to outlaw full-faced Islamic veils and body coverings from all public spaces in Ürümqi – a law that coincidently came into force on the same day as World Hijab Day (Grose and Leibold, 2015). Violating the prohibition came with the threat of a US$800 fine. Some local police stations began constructing a register of women who had defied the ban. A Radio Free Asia report in 2014 claimed that some local police had fired on a crowd who were protesting the detention of several women and school girls who had defied the ban. While particularly concerned for 'security' reasons by the increasing number of Uyghur women wearing the niqab, jilbab and heavy-netted veils that cover the entire head (*tor romal* in Uyghur), they have also labelled the fashionable hijab that covers the head and shoulders but not the face as abnormal. Long beards and star-and-crescent clothing have also been banned from public spaces, including public transport. While not every Uyghur woman chooses to cover her head, those who do will do so for a range of reasons including a feeling of connection to a modern, transnational Muslim community, as a fashion statement, as well as to conform to 'Islamic injunctions for female modesty'. As with the French and Belgian prohibitions, which this law closely followed, Grose and Leibold (2015) argue that the CCP's fear of the veil 'is based on a superficial and flawed premise – that dress is a reliable indicator of extremism, or even political loyalty'. They believe that de-veiling Uyghur women, and widely promoting the number and percentage of Uyghur women who have de-veiled, seeks to demonstrate to the Han community that the CCP is reducing Islamic extremism and is firmly in control and able to maintain social stability. Evidently, this extreme control is coming at a significant cost to the trust Uyghur people place in the CCP.

Interestingly, one of the most famous singers to wear a religiously inspired headscarf on Chinese music-entertainment television during the period of study was the young and dynamic Malaysian Muslim star Xila (Shila Amzah). Xila gained widespread recognition in China through her appearances on reality singing contests on provincial networks, beginning with *Asian Wave* Season 1, broadcast on Shanghai's Dragon TV in 2012, which she won. She also recorded the theme song for *Chinese Idol* (*Zhongguo Meng Zhi Sheng*) on Dragon TV in 2013, the Chinese version of the Kelly Clarkson song 'A Moment Like This'. She also appeared on the popular Hunan Satellite Television show *I am a Singer* Season 2 in 2014, was announced the most popular foreign female singer at the Chinese Golden Melody Awards in 2015, and has been listed in the top five most popular female artists in China. Through performances on globally inspired reality contests, Xila's attractive and colourful hijabs came across as uncontroversial – a trendy representation of 'foreignness'. Known for her gift for languages and ability to easily adopt Chinese as her language of communication in China as she pursued the Chinese market, her presence added to the image of China as cosmopolitan and creative and enhanced the message that it was attracting foreigners from all over the world who were coming to China to pursue their artistic dreams. I have not seen any Uyghur solo female singers appearing on stage with headscarves (although some dancers have appeared with long see-through veils hanging behind them and not covering the face).[16]

Most nationally oriented shows promote the official spoken language, *Putonghua* – but they also sometimes point to a desire to show respect for minority languages. On the *Folk Songs China* episode featuring the Ke'erman band, a brief Mandarin–Uyghur language exchange between the host and guest occurred. While host Liang Lu introduced Ke'erman's last piece using a *Putonghua* transliteration of the name of a Uyghur language song (*Wuzihaleimu*), Ke'erman corrected her language to pronounce it in the proper Uyghur way and she tried to repeat it properly, performing a degree of humbleness towards her Uyghur teacher and attempting to balance the power dynamics, however limited. On the whole, however, the show was used to promote *Putonghua*. In an attempt to be more 'interactive', the host invited young children to dance on the stage with the musicians. One little boy (presumably Uyghur), however, refused to dance. This led to the host asking him why he didn't dance, to which he responded that the others were too fast. The host jumped in and suggested that if he learnt *Putonghua* he would be able to become a host and wouldn't have to sing or dance. While taking the opportunity to educate viewers (via the child) about the benefit of speaking the proper common language, the comment also hinted at a stereotypical assumption about the limited abilities of Uyghur people to speak *Putonghua*, even children who seem to be based in Beijing, which positions the ethnic group as backward.

In theory, the government supports a bilingual approach, particularly in minority areas, and CNTV (as well as local stations) operates entire television channels in Uyghur language. However, the way the national language is pushed can appear overbearing and can position the Han Chinese as being involved in a civilizing mission aimed at raising the level of Uyghur and other ethnic peoples. In December 2012, for instance, the CNTV website featured a Xinjiang Television production entitled *'Love My China' Autonomous Regions' Third Children's Bilingual Speaking Competition.* The show featured children from Ürümqi kindergartens singing the praises of the Chinese state and their bilingual teachers. It was mainly in *Putonghua* but Uyghur and possibly other minority languages spoken in Xinjiang were sprinkled into the songs as well.[17] The performance ended with an almost exact replica of the 'orthodox' 'Love My China' (*Ai wo Zhonggua*) extravaganza detailed earlier in this chapter, but with added Uyghur lyrics alongside the original *Putonghua* verses. The imbalance in languages highlights the 'national language' as the most important unifying language.

Emphasis on the limitations of Uyghur people in terms of their limited ability to speak *Putonghua*, and the stressing of the importance of learning

Putonghua, is extended to adult performers as well. It is not only a feature of CCTV but of provincial satellite channels too. This can be seen in the representation of Uyghur rock singer Pa'erhati (Perhat Khaliq), who was a finalist in *The Voice of China* Season 3 in 2014, broadcast on Zhejiang Satellite Television. Pa'erhati had travelled from far away Ürümqi in China's Western region to China's affluent east coast to participate in the competition. Even though Pa'erhati seemed to have fluent *Putonghua*, as demonstrated in his dialogue with the coaches and fellow contestants, he explained that Chinese lyrics were not easy, adding with what appeared to be excessive modesty that 'If I didn't have [fellow contestant] Wang Zhou, I wouldn't have been able to take to the stage and sing'.

The Voice of China also depicted a brief attempt to highlight mutual linguistic and cultural exchange between two 'ethnic brothers'. In the battle round with Han contestant Wang Zhou, Wang Zhou thanked their coach, rock star Wang Feng, for putting him in the same group as Pa'erhati. Wang Zhou lowered himself by saying 'I'm just a Dongbei Yemen' (an ordinary guy from the Northeast). He explained how Pa'erhati taught him how to sing Uyghur songs and how he was preparing to create a 'Han' language (*Hanyu*) song for Pa'erhati to sing in return. At another moment Pa'erhati said 'I've studied many Uyghur songs, and I said to Wang Zhou I must translate these into Chinese for everyone to hear'. He credited Wang Zhou as his incentive for doing so, giving the impression of equal exchange across the ethnic groups.

This discussion of linguistic exchange provided the impetus for a display of interethnic camaraderie. When Wang Zhou said, 'This stage is the start for both of us. The road is long,' the two men, united through their love of rock music, each holding a guitar, gave each other a hug. Then their coach Wang Feng hugged them, calling them both 'our dream'. The hugging appears to have been adopted from the Western programme format and may be another feature that made *The Voice* seem more 'modern' than CCTV's shows. When Pa'erhati's hand was raised by the host to indicate that he was through to the next round, he tried to resist and modestly explained, 'It's definitely not fair. Really let him stay. Really if it wasn't for him I wouldn't have been able to sing this song!' Media reports explained that this kind of modesty was a Uyghur custom, but it did seem exaggerated and designed to emphasize the brotherly bond between the Uyghur and Han contestants and to create a 'feel good' mood for the majority Han audience. The theme was further extended when in the final, contestants sang the Olympic song 'Our Dream' (*Women de meng*), after which another pop star coach Wang Kun said, 'In my heart Pa'erhati is my Chinese dream'. After a wild rock music performance with coach Wang Feng, Wang Kun put her hand on Pa'erhati's shoulder and repeated 'He is the Chinese dream in my heart' (*wo xin zhong de zhongguomeng*). Excessive reiteration that this Uyghur performer was part of the Chinese collective, especially in the finals, emphasized the political status quo of multiethnic unity. In other words, while the more commercially oriented global formats on provincial satellite channels have a reputation for being more 'natural' in allowing contestants to 'express themselves' – and Pa'erhati indeed brought to the stage a non-conformist attitude and idiosyncratic rough and slightly off-key rock vocals with his work – the performances still appealed to a mainstream Han audience and fit with the discourse of multi-ethnic harmony.

In the finals of *The Voice of China*, Pa'erhati sang his version of 'Why Are the Flowers So Red?' (*Hua'er wei shenme zheyang hong?*). This folk song, attributed to the ethnic Tajik group (another ethnic Muslim group in Xinjiang), was adapted by one of the most famous 'national/ethnic music' (*minzu yinyue*) writers of the 1950s and 1960s, Lei Zhenbang, who followed in the line of work of arranger Wang Luobin. The song was used in the 1960s film *Visitors on the Iceberg* (*Bing shan shang de lai ke*) and has been widely sung across China since then. It is very typical for this Chinese-language song to be played as representative of people from Xinjiang in music-entertainment television in China, possibly because older may audiences remember the song and film from their youth. It is therefore not entirely surprising that this ethnic love song was sung by Pa'erhati in the grand finale of *The Voice of China*. The song also happens to be about the colour red – the colour of the Chinese nation and the CCP. Its lyrics link the red flower to friendship, love, freshness and the blood of youth. While Pa'erhati brought to the song a completely unique performance style with his deep wavering voice, the cutting-off of the ends of words and phrases, and passionate expression of agony, it was no doubt strategically selected to meet the expectations of audiences and to appeal to a sense of collective national feeling. The provincial channel also provided an avenue for the Uyghur artist to titillate audiences through the unusual hybrid blend of the modern, Western, rock, rough, strange and the traditional, sweet and familiar.

Pa'erhati, who was reluctant to appear on national television, has been criticized by some Uyghur musicians, who see the Han Chinese as 'colonisers intent on subsuming their culture' (*South China Morning Post*, 2015), precisely for his blends of music – particularly his rock version of Uyghur traditional classics like the 'Dolan Muqam'. But, as the *South China Morning Post* (2015) reports, 'he refuses to be shackled by either Uyghur orthodoxy or the demands of Chinese pop culture'. At the same time, Pa'erhati is respected by many for his independent spirit, tenacity to stick to his own musical style, and refusal to join government associations at a time when many other Uyghur musicians have been encouraged to do so, with the government intention of them helping to promote messages of Uyghurs as happy people who live harmoniously with Han Chinese. Although, ironically, precisely because of his original, creative and 'authentic' performances (notably he does not smile throughout the season, although he still shows warmth), which are highly respected by many mainstream Chinese, especially youth, he has become one of the most effective ambassadors for Uyghur–Han relations in recent years.

The difference between performances of Uyghur identity for national audiences and Xinjiang audiences becomes evident when *The Voice of*

China on Zhejiang Satellite Television is compared with *The Voice of the Silk Road*. The latter is an official remake of the format in Uyghur language, broadcast to a provincial audience on Xinjiang Television and available online via the CNTV website. The website, however, would have been minimally accessed by anyone who was not Uyghur given that most of the music sung by contestants on *The Voice of the Silk Road* and the conversations were in Uyghur language, while the type of music sung by most performers was unlike those on mainstream nationally oriented programs, having a strong central Asian favour that featured an 'elastic ornamentation of the vocal melodic line' (Harris, 2005b: 396). In the *Voice of the Silk Road*, all the coaches were Uyghur. While Pa'erhati was the odd one out ethnically in *The Voice of China*, Uyghurs on *The Voice of the Silk Road* 'owned' the show, while Han Chinese and those of other nationalities were the odd ones out.

Interestingly, one of the 'exotic' contestants to feature in the *Voice of the Silk Road* was Elise Anderson, an American who was living in Ürümqi at the time. Anderson made it to the fifth round, performing American jazz standards ('Orange Coloured Sky', 'Big Band Handsome Man' and 'Almost Like Being in Love') as well as a couple of Uyghur pop songs. During her chat with coaches in the first round, she shared her expertise in traditional Uyghur music, which she was researching as part of her PhD, by singing a verse from the traditional Uyghur 'Twelve Muqam'. Her fluency in the Uyghur language and ability to sing traditional Uyghur music made her an instant celebrity in the Xinjiang Uyghur Autonomous Region. She was also welcomed back to perform in the final, along with a Uyghur contestant from Kazakhstan and a Han girl from Xinjiang, who were all 'marked' as special contributors to the Uyghur Chinese family.

The above representations which highlight greater Uyghur agency over their own representations are rare on mainstream television. At highly political moments, in particular, there is considerable orthodoxy in the presentation of Uyghur people, which strongly emphasizes their identity as part of China's harmonious multiethnic collective. Prime examples include songs performed by Uyghur singers and dancers in the *CCTV Spring Festival Gala* about the good life in Xinjiang. In 1999, the lyrics of the representative Uyghur/Xinjiang song were about the happy life in Xinjiang. In 2010, after the 2009 riots in Xinjiang, the lyrics focused on the policies that had improved life in Xinjiang, including the reduction of the agricultural tax, the waving of fees for attending primary and secondary schools, the introduction of a medical insurance system, and the construction of council houses (Liu et al., 2015: 616). To emphasize the positive role of the CCP, at the end of each section of lyrics, the following words were sung repeatedly in Mandarin Chinese: 'What is *Yaxshi* [the Uyghur word for "very good", *yakexi* in Mandarin]? What is yaxshi?/The policy made by the CCP is *Yaxshi*!' Dancers and singers in traditional Uyghur costume passionately echoed the words of the main singer, 'Uncle Mehmet' (a common Uyghur name) (Liu et al., 2015: 616).

In this song as Harris (2005b: 396) notes of Sinicized Uyghur songs more generally, 'the asymmetric rhythms ... are replaced with a regular four-beat, and the complex modality ... gives way to the pentatonic scale, with the random addition of stereotypical musical markers'. As with the CCTV Spring Festival performances, the

> elastic ornamentation of the vocal melodic line, an essential marker of traditional and contemporary popular Uyghur music, is replaced in contemporary recordings by the smooth, nasalized delivery of popular [*tongsu*] Chinese singers, backed by a bouncy synthesized beat and lush orchestral breaks, plus the occasional use of a traditional Chinese instrument (often, the bamboo flute).
>
> (Harris, 2005b: 397)

While the 2009 performance of 'The Policy of the Communist Party is *Yaxshi*' (*Dang de zhengce yakexi*) started with a Uyghur-style musical introduction, it quickly transformed into a mainstream and more northwest Han-style song and dance with a few traditional musical instruments in the background giving it an 'ethnic' feel. While the dancers performed in Uyghur dress, the singers sang in Chinese, while a few interludes were spoken in local dialects of Mandarin and Uyghur. Whether intended or not, the representation exoticized the Uyghur people and made them look simple and obedient.

A CCTV report (CCTV.com, 2010) on the performance prior to the Gala focused excitedly on how the song, which 'incorporates modern music elements like rap, into an ethnic tune', was 'an instant hit with the directing team' and on how the lead singer Ahatbaker Kader, who felt honoured to perform on the *CCTV Gala*, was working hard to perfect his performance 'which manifests the solidarity of the Chinese nation'. However, as netizens got hold of the song, which was seen to be 'excessive in its praises', the performance became the impetus for a meme established to 'mock the absurdity of the state propaganda and to sardonically praise policies in the Xinjiang Uyghur Autonomous Region' (*China Digital Times*, 2015). The word '*yaxshi*', which was already well-known in the Chinese community as a Uyghur word for 'good', was turned into a mythical creature called the Yax Lizard (*Yake xi*), created through changing the last character in the Chinese transliteration of the word *yakexi* to the word for lizard, which has the same pronunciation ('xi').

Yake xi joined other mythical creatures that became widely synonymous with online critiques of the CCP in 2009. These included the 'river crab' (*he xie*), which sounds like the word for 'harmony', and was used to critique the discourse of 'Harmonious Society' widely promoted under President Hu Jintao. 'Harmonized' or 'river-crabbed' (*bei hexie*) became a euphemism for censorship. Also popular was the 'grass-mud horse' (*cao ni ma*), which sounds like 'fuck your mother'. This creature took the image of an alpaca and became a symbol of free expression and suppression of internet censorship, with 'the mother' being the Communist Party. It was also made into a cute-sounding children's song. Blogger Han Han responded to the skit by establishing a Big Yakexi Art Competition, where he invited netizens to alter the original song, apart from the words 'What is *yakexi*, what is *yakexi*, ah, The CPC Central Committee's policies are *yakexi*', with the offer of cash prizes of up to 5,000 RMB for the winner to be paid by him personally (Xiao, 2010).

While CCTV material has been actively appropriated by netizens to construct new representations and sarcastic critiques of the CCP, other netizens have uploaded Chinese television clips of Uyghur performers to video-sharing sites like YouTube to discuss ethnicity, nationality and identity politics. While the platform is banned within China, YouTube clips often spark virulent debates on ethnicity, integration and separation among people from Chinese and non-Chinese backgrounds living outside of the mainland. One example can be seen on the YouTube commentary under an unofficial post of the performance of the Uyghur dance 'Dolan Meshrep' from the 2011 *CCTV Spring Festival Gala*. 'Dolan Meshrep' is an upbeat song written and performed in the contemporary Central Asian Uyghur style by Abdulla Abdurehim (*Abudula Abudureyimu*), a well-known ethnic Uyghur singer who was also a coach on the *Voice of the Silk Road* (lyrics by Memtili Zu'nong/Maimaitili zunong). By November 2016, the video had attracted more than 320 comments, with a number of people from different countries and backgrounds engaged in heated arguments, all claiming to have the definitive history of Uyghurs or asserting the place of Uyghurs vis-à-vis Chinese. Some claimed the Uyghurs as Turkic and not Chinese, while others asserted that Uyghurs are Chinese in the sense of nationality but not ethnicity, just like African Americans are still American. In 2014, one blogger, Christopher Wu, argued that Uyghur and other ethnic groups in Xinjiang are an integral part of Chinese culture as a whole. He urged his interlocutors that if they 'only think the Chinese culture refers to Han Chinese' to visit Xinjiang and 'to read the Chinese history, which is utimately a process of ethnic fusion and national syncretism' (for a detailed discussion of online criticisms from the Uyghur diaspora, see Harris, 2012). Another blogger, Arı Duru Türkçe, strongly disagreed with this interpretation, noting:

> I don't care what it means in Chinese, Chinese in everyones [sic] minds refers to, you know, Chinese ethnicity not nationality... if you know about [the] East Turkestan national anthem there is a verse [that] says 'türktür namimiz' which means 'our name is türk'. I do not accept the definition that Uyghur, Kazakh, Uzbek, Kyrgyz and Tajik are integral culture of Chinese culture as a whole. I was against 'Uyghur Chinese' at the beginning because of this perception.

Such online debates provide perspectives on how Chinese television might be read by international as well as local audiences in ways which are both supportive and in opposition to the status quo. In the era of digital reproduction, they can also be taken out of context and used for purposes unanticipated by television producers.

As these examples of constructions of Uyghur identity on Chinese television illustrate, China's television system as a whole operates on a range of levels appealing to different political and economic imperatives at different times in shows produced for CCTV, provincial satellite television and local television channels. All channels offer both hardened, orthodox Party-political representations that put minorities squarely in their place as part of a happy multiethnic China as well as softer representations that highlight the unique contributions of talented and creative contemporary ethnic minority artists to China's vibrancy. The fact that Uyghur artists choose to appear on mainstream television suggests their attempt to seek a broader audience. Chinese television offers them a platform for generating interest in their music. This exposure may outweigh any concessions they may have to make to influences from directors and producers who may be obliged to create programmes that aim to appeal to mainstream Chinese audiences, while simultaneously supporting national messages of ethnic harmony and a modern, creative China.

Performing Korean-Chinese

Ethnically Korean-Chinese performances provide another interesting lens for examining identity politics and the framing of a multiethnic China because of the link to a 'non-Chinese' nationality outside of China. Ethnic Koreans (*Chaoxian*) are an officially recognized minority nationality of the PRC. The area of Yanbian[18] in northeast China's Jilin province, which borders on the Democratic People's Republic of Korea (North Korea) and Russia, is a designated Korean autonomous prefecture and home to about 850,000 of China's 1.9 million Korean minorities (Pease, 2006: 137) (see Chapter 6 for analysis of *chaoxianzu* and foreigners in this border area).

As with the Uyghur community, artistic performance is intimately interwoven with identity politics in China's Korean community. As Pease (2006) explains, since the resumption of diplomatic ties with South Korea in 1991, communication between Koreans in China and South Korea have dramatically increased. A large number of Chinese Koreans now travel to, work in or have emigrated to South Korea. Well-educated youth in China access South Korean satellite television, which is widely available though often illegal. They visit karaoke bars and sing South Korean music, purchase fashionable South Korean-style clothing, food, music and television dramas, and have also dyed their hair outlandish colours as part of the 'South Korean fever'.

According to Pease, the influence of South Korean culture has created a divide between older Chinese Koreans, particularly among those in rural areas with less education who prefer homegrown local PRC-based Korean 'Yanbian' culture, and younger more affluent, urban Chinese Koreans who follow the South Korean style. Culture workers including singers, dancers and radio and television hosts in Yanbian have worked hard to establish a unique Yanbian Korean culture that distinguishes between

112 *Multiethnic China*

Koreans living in China and those on the neighbouring peninsula. As many young people turned to South Korea, seeing no particular interest in a *Chinese* Korean culture, local media and cultural bodies in charge of maintaining the Chinese Korean identity began to fear the demise of their local culture. In the 1990s, Yanbian cultural workers even campaigned to restrict the foreign influences on their culture. Yet at the same time as television and radio have become reliant on advertising income for production expenses, in order to attract audiences broadcasts have reflected the shifts in taste in the area (Pease, 2006). At a 'national' level, CCTV has taken on board both the 'modern' image of South Korean-inspired Yanbian Korean culture and the more official/national/orthodox and PRC-centred Chinese-Korean styles. In addition, the traditional Korean song Arirang has played a particularly pivotal role in developing cross-cultural relations across state boundaries.

The most significant performer of cosmopolitan PRC Korean identity during the period of analysis was Jin Mei'er, who was one of three winners of the 2008 CCTV3 *Star Avenue* contest. Her success in the competition provided a solid foundation for her singing career, and she subsequently appeared in other CCTV and provincial television programmes such as *The Playlist* (*Chaoji gedan*) on Jiangxi Television. Demonstrating her versatility, she has sung, contemporary songs in Mandarin in trendy modern attire and traditional Korean songs, such as 'Bellflower Ballad' (*Jiegeng yao*), which she sang during the *Happy in China* programme in Macau, wearing a traditional Korean dress (see Chapter 6 for more on this programme). Wearing her national service cap, she also competed in the popular music (*liuxing*) category of the 2008 *CCTV Youth Singing Competition* representing the Airforce Performing Arts Troupe. Jin has also participated in big national and global celebratory events, including the 2011 *Global New Year Gala* on Beijing TV, and the *CCTV Spring Festival Gala* in 2012. During the CCTV Gala, she sang 'Flame in the Winter', well-known by audiences as a pop classic originally made famous by originally made famous by Chinese–American mixed-race star Fei Xiang (see Chapter 6) during the 1986 CCTV Gala. As such, her performance may be seen as representative of the trend towards creative mixing of ethnic and cultural symbols.[19]

In presenting these multiple identities in her television performances as a modern/Westernized Chinese woman, a representative of the army (defender of the nation) and a proud Korean Chinese, Jin helped construct the Party-state as open and cosmopolitan, and as a state that celebrates its multiethnic composition. Jin's rendition of Whitney Houston's 'I Have Nothing' in English, a sign of the modern/Western, on *Star Avenue* across 2008 was particularly significant as, even though it had become trendy to insert the occasional English word into Chinese pop songs, English songs were rarely performed on CCTV. This particular television programme offered her a chance to present a modern identity, dressed as a superstar in a golden gown, with dangling golden earrings and bubbles floating around and allowed her an opportunity to display her talents outside of the orthodox constraints in performing minority identities.

At the same time, as many other *Chaoxian* minority performers seem obliged to sing, Jin also sang the signature pan-Korean folk song, 'Arirang'. Dressed in a colourful traditional Korean-style dress, she began by singing slowly, accompanied by backup dancers also in Korean costume with large drums strung around their shoulders. However, about halfway through, the song turned upbeat and rap dancers entered the stage, giving her the chance to assert a modern ethnic Korean identity, highlighting how styles are mixed even within a single song. This cross-fertilization of styles may be used for dramatic and artistic effect, as well as to show different identity positions and satisfy different identity concerns within the Korean Chinese community.

Jin Mei'er has also performed on South Korean television, thus crossing the boundaries that divide Koreans in these different political jurisdictions. In one such show, she performed 'Arirang' as well as her rendition of Whitney Houston's 'I Have Nothing' (in English) repeating her performances that won her the *Star Avenue* title. In this appearance on South Korean television, where she wore the same traditional Korean dress, she mentioned her win on CCTV's *Star Avenue*, linking the two nations together via her television performances. According to Pease (2006: 151), in South Korea, Korean Chinese can exploit the novelty value of coming from what is considered a remote backwater and thus may attempt to capitalize on their marginalization ('otherness' and 'foreignness') in both countries in ways that fit with political and market goals.

In an example of a complex transnational flow of media, the clip of Jin Mei'er's performance on South Korean television where she conversed entirely in Korean language was subtitled into Chinese, apparently by netizens, and posted online for Chinese audiences. Between 2009 and 2012, the clip attracted more than 230 comments in Chinese praising Jin Mei'er and raising discussions about her identity and Chinese Korean cultural influence. Netizens debated about whether she was Chinese, a Chaoxian minority nationality or acting too much like a South Korean. Many comments were fixated on claiming her as a Chaoxian ethnic minority of China, and therefore the pride of the Chinese people. The trope of 56 nationalities making one flower, a line that features in the 'hardened' multiethnic song 'Love My China' (*Ai wo Zhonghua*) discussed above, also appeared in the online comments, suggesting that CCTV-style rhetoric is also adopted by ordinary Chinese people, sometimes to express nationalist sentiments in new settings.

Performing Han-Chinese

Baranovitch (2001: 375) argues that the search for pure Chineseness among Han peasants was rejected in the late 1980s after documentary television programmes like *River Elegy* (*Heshang*) expressed deep disillusionment with the primitiveness of the Han self. Minority cultures were seen as even more remote and exotic than Han peasantry, and therefore worthy of celebrating. Yet ironically the focus on the exotic, internal 'other' helped to situate mainstream Chinese Han as more modern (also see Schein, 1997). As the unmarked or non-labelled category in Chinese music-entertainment shows, the ethnic Han (officially 92 per cent of the Chinese population) has been constructed in similar ways to 'whiteness' or 'Anglo-Celtic-ness' in the West, whereby the Anglo-Celtics often remain invisible in relation to migrant communities from other backgrounds (Leibold, 2010: 10; cf. Hartley, 2004: 14). Yet the primitive 'core' Han identity has also been popularized through popular music on Chinese television, and a number of Han performers have merged traditional Han peasant culture with contemporary Western pop music in an ethno-pop fashion.

Televised representations of Han ethnic identity are often centred on music from northwest China, particularly Shaanxi and Shanxi provinces, the heartland of the Communist revolution and imagined cradle of ancient Chinese civilization. Shaanbei (the area of Yulin and Yan'an in Shaanxi province) was the location of the CCP's Central Committee and military headquarters prior to 1949 and important battles took place in the area during the anti-Japanese and civil wars. Emphasizing this region and the music from it conflates notions of Chinese civilizational longevity associated with Han customs with modern Chinese prosperity under the Communist Party. Many singers on Chinese television performing with Han influences from this region sing traditional revolutionary songs (such as 'Nanniwan', see Chapter 2).

Ah Bao, a male performer from Shanxi province, became one of the most popular singers of this Han pop style after he received a bronze award in the 2004 CCTV *Western-Area Folk Music Competition* (*Xibu Minge Dasai*) and became the winner of *Star Avenue* in 2005. He also gained notoriety after appearing on the *CCTV Spring Festival Gala* in 2006. He has also appeared numerous times on provincial television, including on Qinghai Satellite Television's New Year Gala in 2010, where he sang 'The Big Bridal Sedan Chair' (*Da hua qiao*) and on Guangdong Satellite Television's New Year Gala in 2016 where he sang 'Red Flowers Blossom' (*Shan dandan huakai hong yanyan*). Ah Bao combined high-pitched traditional and revolutionary songs with contemporary pop and dance rhythms. His ethnic costume consisted of simple peasant clothing with a cloth (*tou jin*) wrapped around his head in rural Han style, although he also appeared in modern, urban dress. His performances integrated the Han into the *minzu* system whereby the Han identity, like that of minority nationalities, was made unique by invoking rural, peasant and traditional clothing as well as CCP 'Red songs' (*hongse geyao*). The rural elements marked Ah Bao's performance as 'folk', 'exotic' and 'other', and positioned the Han identity on the same level as other minority folk cultures, presenting the Han as just one among China's unity of the nationalities.

Ah Bao's dance-style rendition of the revolutionary song 'Our Leader Mao Zedong' (*Zanmen de lingxiu Mao Zedong*) was an example of an ethno-pop Han influenced song that became popular through his CCTV performances. The song links the Han to the state and Party in a trendy, cosmopolitan way, building on the reform era Mao Zedong craze. 'Our Leader Mao Zedong' was originally developed in the northwestern Shaanxi-Gansu-Ningxia region, most likely between the Yan'an Forum in 1942 and before the founding of the New China in 1949, and spread across China, becoming an important part of China's revolutionary heritage (Qingyang City Bureau of Statistics, 2011).

Another Han star to explore traditional Han styles in an ethno-pop form was Tan Weiwei (Sitar Tan), who fist rose to fame as the runner-up of the third season of *Super Girl* (*Chaoji nüsheng*) in 2006 on Hunan Satellite Television. Tan originally became well-known for her Tibetan style singing. Having grown up in China's southwest Sichuan province, where a large population of ethnic Tibetans live, she caught the judges' attention in the 2006 *Super Girl* contest when she sang a Tibetan drinking song with high and crisp Tibetan vocal inflections. A number of her albums feature Tibetan songs and Tibetan-style singing.[20] When she participated in Season 3 of *I am a Singer* (*Wo shi geshou*) on Hunan Satellite Television in 2015, she sang in Mandarin but continued to draw on high-pitched Tibetan inflections for dramatic effect in a unique ethnic crossover style.[21]

However, in 2016 she appeared on the *CCTV Spring Festival Gala*, this time leading another unique blend which the *People's Daily* referred to as a bold fusion of rock music and the traditional folk Shaanxi/Han *Huayang laoqian* style, in a piece called '*Huayin Laoqiang* One Voice Shout' (*Huayin laoqiang yi sheng han*). The song went on for more than 15 minutes, signalling its significance, and the state-sanctioned incorporation of rock music (formerly rarely seen on Chinese television) in this hybrid Chinese-Western form. The band comprised a Western style rock band (which included one Caucasian guitarist) dressed in 'modern' black with red (Chinese) scarves at the back of the stage and a Shaanxi folk group in front who were dressed in traditional, rural, white rural costumes, also with red scarves. The performance involved a mix of rock music and the traditional *Huayin laoqiang* folk opera style music. An electric keyboard, electric guitars, drums and bass, and the rock-style vocals of Tan were combined with the grand, strong, generous, loud and sonorous singing led by Zhang Ximin, known as a legacy representative inheritor of intangible cultural heritage of the *Huayin Laoqiang* form, and a troupe of performers on traditional instruments including the *erhu* (a Chinese fiddle), *sanxian* (Chinese lute), trumpet-like *suona*, hardwood clappers and cymbals. The style of singing was rough and spirited, in a unique blend of rock and *Huayang laoqian*, while the lyrics discussed the people's hopes for a sweet life and dreams for seven rainbows.[22] Some netizens praised the song for the way it infused rock and traditional styles and noted that it helped the public to notice *Huayin laoqiang* as a kind of intangible cultural heritage.

While the song starts off quite local to the Shaanxi region, it climaxed towards the end with lyrics that could connect with any Chinese person in the reform and opening up era. The lyrics spoke of people who over thousands of years throughout the dynasties were not afraid of getting sweaty and who were dreaming of and looking forward to a happy life. Day by day, year by year and generation by generation they looked forward to the dragon turning up – which can be read as a metaphor for the rise of China as a strong, powerful and resplendent nation. The unique blend of rock music (the 'modern'/Western) and Shaanxi 'Han' folk music (Chinese traditional), which represents the strength of the nation through its tenacity to survive thousands of

116 *Multiethnic China*

years, was used to generate a sense of contemporary patriotism among Chinese audiences. This example serves to illustrate again how cultural symbols from one ethnic group, the Han included, can be transformed to represent the culture of China as a whole. Traditional elements are being infused with the modern to demonstrate the cultural dynamism of contemporary China.

Conclusion

Despite the relatively controlled nature of television programming in China, particularly of CCTV, the market era that began in 1978 has allowed for the opening of new spaces for television performers and allowed producers to draw on both folk and pop music. The styles of performance reflect various influences within the Chinese Party-state. A 'hardened' projection of multi-ethnic Party-state nationalism continues in what was described as the orthodox form, while ethno-pop performances have incorporated ethnicity in a cosmopolitan way, mixing traditional ethnic elements with contemporary pop music, reflecting the burgeoning market economy and a desire of the Party-state to present itself as open, cosmopolitan and rapidly modernizing. The use of traditional *yuanshengtai* folk music has also been used to reflect a desire to limit the kind of social inequalities, environmental degradation, rampant commercialism, and lack of respect for cultural heritage that came with the open-door policy, although its salience as a television genre appears to have waned with a preference for more 'modern' blends.

Of the three broad styles of performing multiethnic unity discussed in this chapter, the *yuanshengtai* frame, particularly in the earlier years of this research, offered the most pluralistic impression of multiethnic nationalism in China because of its focus on local difference, including language, instrumentation and musical style. Individual performers, ethnicities and styles were highlighted through singing in local languages and dialects, performing local dances, and using musical instruments unique to a specific region. *Yuanshengtai* performances offered insights into and revealed a range of subjectivities, albeit in limited ways, that were not easily observable in other televised styles. *Yuanshengtai* also opened up rare spaces in which complexities in the politics of multiethnic identity could be discussed. While CCP ideology was still reflected in *yuanshengtai* performances, it was done in a subtler way than the orthodox style, which overtly trumpets the successes of the Party-state and where differences are smoothed over to create a sense of everyone in the group as being 'the same' as shown through speaking or singing in the same national language, singing the same song in unison, and dancing the same moves.

Although many programmes involve a variety of styles, as shown in the above discussion, a decision to feature a particular style of performance (e.g., *yuanshengtai*, national/orthodox or popular) seems to depend on the purpose of a given television programme. Spectacles designed to celebrate national occasions like the anniversary of the establishment of the PRC, which have significant input from Party-state propaganda officials and which may be broadcast on multiple channels, are likely to draw more heavily on orthodox performance styles with a hardened message of multiethnic state unity. Regular programmes broadcast in the middle of the day or late at night, like *Folk Songs China*, offered the most localized of all of the performances as well as the greatest space for a more flexible interpretation of national identity.

Across all styles, the ideology of a single, unified multiethnic state remains prominent. The 56 categories of ethnicity are fixed and the official rhetoric that describes them is rather inflexible. I have only seen these internal categories challenged once on Chinese television with the appearance of Lou Jing, a contestant one *Go! Oriental Angel* (*Jiayou! Dongfang tianshi*) on Shanghai's Dragon Television in 2009. Being of mixed African-American and Chinese heritage, Lou grew up with her Chinese mother in Shanghai. Because of the colour of her skin and curly hair, the judges and audiences found her exotic and struggled to find the right terms to identify her, settling for 'Black pearl' and 'Chocolate girl'. For some she was a delight, while others saw her as a threat to the purity of the Chinese family.

Overall, the blurring and mixing of styles reflects an accommodation of different artistic, cultural, political and economic interests. All forms involve the performance of ethnic identity for the spectacle of television, and this means that even the most localized and raw performances on CCTV and provincial satellite channels alike are transformed with a national audience in mind. The more accessible programmes are to mainstream national audiences, the more attractive they will be to potential sponsors and advertisers. While the multiethnic frame is predominantly relevant in a domestic/mainland PRC context, the next chapter turns to a discussion of the range of styles used to construct a 'Greater China' family that extends beyond the borders of the PRC.

Notes

1 Jones (2001) confirms how this style drew on an earlier tradition where music was used to improve the national essence in order to mobilize the masses in the fight against Japan. Nie Er, who composed what is now China's national anthem, seems to have had significant influence on this form.
2 In many cases, folk songs have been altered significantly to fit the operatic style, or else are compositions that are designed to appear to be based on a folk song. They may simply take Chinese national themes, making it difficult to distinguish a 'national style' from the operatic style (*meisheng changfa*). Debates about the differences between these two styles abounded in the prestigious *CCTV Youth Singing Competition* in March 2008 where there were separate categories for the two styles. My distinction is based on the categories provided by the CCTV competition and in Chinese language literature.
3 According to Professor Zou Wenqin of the China Conservatory of Music (*Zhongguo Yinyue Xueyuan*) in Beijing, there are a wide variety of vocal folk genres, which include *minge, shange, xiaodiao*; local opera, and *shuochang*, a form of entertainment involving singing and comic dialogue (as discussed in Li, 2004a).
4 Two years earlier in 1988 Song Zuying also won the *CCTV Youth Singing Competition*.

5 After 2011, Song Zuying appeared irregularly on Chinese television. For instance, she appeared as a guest judge on the 2011 *Chinese Pop Music Golden Bell Awards* (*Zhongguo liuxing yinyue jin zhong jiang*) on Shenzhen TV.
6 According to Baidu, as a young boy, Ah Peng previously performed in the popular show *Dynamic Yunnan* with nationally and internationally acclaimed dancer Yang Liping. Yang travelled to remote villages of the 26 nationalities around China to find naturally talented singers and dancers to be involved in her live performances and Ah Peng was successful in his local village audition.
7 Dao Lang, called the 'Wang Luobin of the twenty-first century' (see section on Uyghur-Chinese later in this chapter) performed modern rock adaptations of a number of Wang Luobin's Western China-inspired folk songs, including 'Why are the Flowers so Red?' (*Hau'er weishenme zheyang hong?*), 'Awariguli', 'Flowers and Youth' (*Hua'er yu shaonian*), 'At a Faraway Place' (*Zai na yaoyuan de difang*), as well as 'The Grapes of Turpan are Ripe' (*Tulufan de putao shu liao*) and the famous revolutionary song 'Nanniwan'.
8 One of Hang Tianqi's representative Northwest Wind songs is 'Loess Plateau' (*Huangtu gaopo*).
9 One of Tian Zhen's representative Northwest Wind songs is 'The Hometown I Love' (*Wo re'ai de guxiang*).
10 The best known Tibetan-style piece of Han artist Zhu Zheqin (Dadawa), native to Shanghai but portrayed as a Tibetan singer, is 'Drum Sister' (*A gu jie*).
11 A popular song of Sa Dingding, who is of mixed Han and Mongolian ethnicity, is 'Alive' (which may also be translated as 'All Things'; *Wan wu sheng*), which comprises a Sinified version of a Sanskrit mantra, 'Vajrasattva Hundred Syllable Mantra'. Sa reportedly taught herself Tibetan and Sanskrit and has performed internationally at World Music events like Womadelaide in Australia, and the World of Music, Arts and Dance and Harrogate International Festivals in the UK. In 2008, she won the BBC Radio 3 Award for World Music for the Asia-Pacific region, which gave her the opportunity to perform at the Royal Albert Hall. After the Sichuan earthquake in 2008, she composed a song with Eric Mouquet of Deep Forest called 'Won't Be Long' to raise funds for disaster relief. Mouquet and Sa also collaborated on an album *Deep China*.
12 The Gypsy Kings are a Spanish-speaking group from France who became well known for bringing pop-oriented flamenco to a global audience in the 1980s.
13 During the first decade of the 2000s, for instance, a young Uyghur boy, A'erfa, was a hit on CCTV where he sang and imitated a range of foreign songs including Ricky Martin's 1998 FIFA World Cup theme song hit 'Cup of Life' (*Shengming zhi bei*), Russian/Ukrainian star Vitas' Opera No. 2 (2000) (see Chapter 7), and Justin Bieber's 'Baby' (2010).
14 A more recent serious Han–Uyghur interethnic riot occurred in July 2009 in Ürümqi, the capital of Xinjiang, resulting in 156 deaths. Some Uyghurs responded to the news of the death of two Uyghur migrant workers in a Guangdong toy factory by attacking Han businesses in Ürümqi and Hans responded by attacking Uyghur businesses. The riots fed on long-term resentments about increased Han migration to Xinjiang (Hans now outnumber the Uyghur population), major economic disparities, marginalization of the Uyghur language, disrespect for Uyghur culture, lack of religious freedom, assumption of Han superiority, racism on both sides and frustration with the Xinjiang and Central governments by both Han and Uyghur people (Clarke, 2009; Zang, 2009; Cliff, 2010).
15 Some sources say the song was formerly known as 'Aria' or 'Karakusi Um'.
16 In 'In the Arms of Our Great Motherland' (*Zai ni weida de huaibao li*), an ethnic medley at the 2016 *Spring Festival Gala*, a 'Xinjiang' dancer wore a light veil hanging behind her, while the other dancers wore braids and artistic headdresses.

17 For example, students describe the map of China as being like a chicken, with the head in the east and the tail in the west. They describe how kids salute the five-starred red flag in front of the Tianshan mountains, praise their bilingual teachers and directly declare that all kids from different nationalities are striving together hand in hand and that they love the motherland.
18 The area of Yanbian was formerly known as Kando.
19 The only other notable Chaoxian singer of late is Bian Yinghua, who won the silver award in the *yuanshengtai* category of the 2006 *CCTV Youth Singing Competition*. She sang 'Yanbian People Love Chairman Mao' (*Yanbian renmin re'ai Mao zhuxi*) on CCTV15 in 2011, dressed in traditional costume to the backdrop of a red background with yellow stars reminiscent of the Chinese and CCP flags.
20 Tan Weiwei's first album *Heart of the Highland* (*Gaoyuan zhi xin*) was in Tibetan and Mongolian style (2005). Her 2009 album *Legend* (*Chuanshuo*) was also in Tibetan style and she has done a cover of Beijing-based Tibetan pop star Han Hong's 'Sky Road' (*Tian Lu*).
21 One of the songs Tan sang on *I am a Singer* in 2015 was 'Night in Ulaanbaatar' (*Wulanbatuo de ye*). She sang in Mandarin but drew on high-pitched Tibetan inflections for dramatic effect, and was accompanied by Mongolian back-up singers dressed in traditional ethnic Mongolian costume who did throat singing and played on traditional ethnic instruments. Showcasing a Han Chinese singer mastering Tibetan style singing and fusing elements of Mongolian instrumentation and singing styles validates the treasure that these minority art forms are to the broader Chinese culture.
22 *Huayin laoqiang* is thought to have developed sometime around the 1600s in a village in Huayin Town, Shaanxi Province. It was designated as a first level national intangible cultural heritage by the State Council of the People's Republic of China and Ministry of Culture in 2006.

References

Baidu (n.d.) Xianqi ni de gaitou lai [Lift up your veil]. Available at http://baike.baidu.com/subview/3250796/13643542.htm (accessed 18 May 2017).

Baranovitch, N. (2001) Between alterity and identity: new voices of minority people in China. *Modern China* 27(3): 359–401.

Baranovitch, N. (2007) Inverted exile: Uyghur writers and artists in Beijing and the political implications of their work. *Modern China* 33: 462–504.

BBC News (2014) Why is there tension between China and the Uighurs? BBC News, 26 Sept. Available at www.bbc.com/news/world-asia-china-26414014 (accessed 18 May 2017).

CCTV.com (2010) Ethnic singers join hands at CCTV gala, 3 February. Available at http://english.cctv.com/program/cultureexpress/20100203/101271.shtml (accessed 18 May 2017).

China Digital Times (2015) Decoding the Chinese internet: a glossary of political slang. *China Digital Times*. Available at http://chinadigitaltimes.net/china-digital-times-ebooks (accessed 18 May 2017).

Clark, M. (2009) China's imperial project in Xinjiang. *Asian Currents*, The Asian Studies Association of Australia, August.

Cliff, T. (2010) The Han in Xinjiang: the view from the frontier. *Asian Currents*, The Asian Studies Association of Australia, August: 15–16.

Coleman, S. (2008) Why is the Eurovision Song Contest ridiculous? Exploring a spectacle of embarrassment, irony and identity. *Popular Communication* 6: 127–40.

Gold, T.B. (1995) Go with your feelings: Hong Kong and Taiwan popular culture in Greater China. In D Shambaugh (ed.) *Greater China: The Next Superpower?* New York: Clarendon, pp. 255–73.

Grose, T. and Leibold, J. (2015) Why China is banning Islamic veils and why it won't work. *China File*, 4 February. Available at www.chinafile.com/reporting-opinion/viewpoint/why-china-banning-islamic-veils (accessed 18 May 2017)

Harris, R. (2005a) Reggae on the Silk Road: the globalization of Uyghur pop. *The China Quarterly* 183: 627–43.

Harris, R. (2005b) Wang Luobin: folk song king of the northwest or song thief? Copyright, representation, and Chinese folk songs. *Modern China*, 31(3): 381–408.

Harris, R. (2012) Tracks: temporal shifts and transnational networks of sentiment in Uyghur song. *Ethnomusicology* 56(3): 450–75.

Hartley, J. (2004) Television, nation, and indigenous media. *Television and New Media* 5(7): 7–25.

Heng, S.H. (2008) China's cultural and intellectual rejuvenation. *Asia Europe Journal* 6(3–4): 401–12.

Jones, A.F. (2001) *Yellow Music: Media Culture and Colonial Modernity in the Chinese Jazz Age*. Durham: Duke University Press.

Lee, G. (1995) The 'East is Red' goes pop: commodification, hybridity and nationalism in Chinese popular song and its television performance. *Popular Music* 14(1): 95–110.

Leibold, J. (2010) The Beijing Olympics and China's conflicted national form. *The China Journal* 63: 1–24.

Li, X. (2004a) Minzu changfa de lu buzhi yitiao [There's not only one road towards 'national' style music]. *China Arts Journal (Zhongguo Yishu Bao)*, 6 August.

Li, X. (2004b) Minzu changfa yao duoyanghua [The 'national' style of music should be diversified]. *China Arts Journal (Zhongguo Yishu Bao)*, 13 August.

Liu, C., An, N. and Zhu, H. (2015) A geopolitical analysis of popular songs in the *CCTV Spring Festival Gala*, 1983–2013. *Geopolitics* 20(3): 606–25.

O'Connor, J. and Gu, X. (2006) A new modernity? The arrival of 'creative industries' in China. *International Journal of Cultural Studies* 9(3): 271–83.

Pease, R. (2006) Healthy, national and up-to-date: pop music in the Yanbian Korean Autonomous Prefecture, China. In K. Howard (ed.) *Korean Pop Music: Riding the Wave*. Kent: Global Oriental, pp. 137–53.

Qingyang City Bureau of Statistics/Qingyang Net (2011), Qingyang laoqu wei Gongheguo de fengxian – Longdong geyao [Qingyang old area's contribution to the PRC – Longdong folk music]. *Gansu Daily*, 29 July. http://qy.gansudaily.com.cn/system/2011/07/29/012102033.shtml (accessed 18 May 2017).

Rees, H. (2003) The age of consent: traditional music, intellectual property and changing attitudes in the People's Republic of China. *British Journal of Ethnomusicology* 12(1): 137–71.

Rees, H. (2009) Use and ownership: folk music in the People's Republic of China. In A.N. Weintraub and B. Yung (eds.) *Music and Cultural Rights*. Chicago: University of Illinois Press, pp. 42–85.

Schein, L. (1997) Gender and internal orientalism in China. *Modern China* 23(1): 69–98.

South China Morning Post (2015) Perhat Khaliq and Qetiq are bringing Uygur rock to the world – but not everyone is happy. *South China Morning Post*, 23 September. Available at www.scmp.com/lifestyle/arts-entertainment/article/1860731/perhat-khaliq-and-qetiq-are-bringing-uygur-rock-world (accessed 18 May 2017).

Sun, W. and Zhao, Y. (2009) Television culture with 'Chinese characteristics': the politics of compassion and education. In G. Turner and J. Tay (eds.) *Television Studies After TV: Understanding Television in the Post-Broadcast Era*. London: Routledge, pp. 96–104.

Xiao, Q. (2010) Yakexi: the new year's hottest internet slang? *China Digital Times*, 18 February. Available at http://chinadigitaltimes.net/2010/02/yakexi-the-new-year%E2%80%99s-hottest-internet-slang (accessed 18 May 2017).

Zang, X. (2009) Book review: *Under the Heel of the Dragon: Islam, Racism, Crime, and the Uighir in China* (Blaine Kaltman, 2007). *Asian Ethnicity* 10(1): 93–4.

5 Greater China

Global ethnic Chineseness and the re-centring of China

While the *multiethnic* sense of Chineseness has been built by the state to construct a unified *mainland* People's Republic of China (PRC) Chinese identity, the Party-state has promoted different constructions of Chineseness to connect mainland Chinese to ethnic Chinese who live outside of the mainland in Hong Kong, Macau and Taiwan (areas to which the PRC lays claim), and to ethnic Chinese who live further abroad, who are variously referred to as *huaren, huaqiao* or *huayi*.

Chapter 1 introduced the concept of Greater China. It showed how scholars like Tu Weiming (1994) were fixated on imagining that the centre of Chineseness had shifted from mainland China – where Chinese culture had originated but where traditional Chinese culture had been rejected by Communist authorities – to places on the former periphery like Taiwan and Singapore, which were emphasizing traditional Chinese values. More recently, Beng-Huat Chua (2001, 2006) has argued that there is in fact no centre, and that no essential connections between Chinese around the world exist besides a popular culture based on transient market trends. This chapter argues that Chinese music-entertainment programming is not only making stringent efforts to reconstruct for domestic and global audiences a sense of Greater China as a reality, but is also clearly attempting to re-centre mainland China within the Greater China sphere. I agree with Chua that marketable popular culture is the glue that is being used to bring diverse Chinese cultures together, and, as seen in the examples below, Chinese television channels clearly recognize the importance of popular culture and pop music (*liuxing yinyue*) in constructing a sense of solidarity.

Certain programmes are specifically intended to draw Hong Kong, Macau, Taiwanese and overseas Chinese identities into a PRC-centred Greater China family frame. The annual *CCTV Spring Festival Gala* continues to play an important role in relation to the building of the Greater China family (Zhao, 1998; Lu, 2009). Another significant show promoting Greater Chinese solidarity has been *Our Chinese Heart* (*Zhonghua Qing*), a series of large-scale concerts that has featured pop stars from Hong Kong, Taiwan and the mainland. It has been broadcast on CCTV4, CCTV's Chinese language international channel, since January 2003, and more recently on its official channel on YouTube. I have also seen episodes of this show been made available for passengers via video on demand on China Southern Airlines.

The Same Song, broadcast on CCTV3 from 1999 to 2009, is another show that attempted to harness China's 'soft power' in the context of Greater China. In its latter years, the show included tours of foreign cities where there were large numbers of Chinese residents. According to an interviewee who had worked on this show, the decision to tour abroad was partly to spice up the format that had been incredibly successful but was starting to lose audience share after many years on air.

Reality singing contests, such as *The Voice of China* on Zhejiang Satellite Television and *Sing My Song* on CCTV3, have also made concerted efforts to include overseas Chinese people through auditions in foreign countries where large numbers of Chinese people reside, including Canada, Australia, the United States, Malaysia and Thailand. Such shows have highlighted the shared dream of Chinese youth around the world, with China being presented as a place of prosperity and opportunity.

Significantly, programmes with the greatest array of Hong Kong and Taiwanese superstars have often been sponsored by commercial enterprises. For instance, CCTV's *The Same Song* had episodes sponsored by Japanese car manufacturer Toyota, the Na'aisi Group, who make household goods like toothpaste and cleaning products, and the kitchen company Oupai. Each of these shows had stellar line-ups featuring Hong Kong and Taiwanese superstars. These programmes were predominantly staged in the more affluent southern cities like Guangzhou and Shanghai, where many Taiwanese, Hong Kong and foreign businesses are based. Provincial satellite singing contests, which have also featured pop stars from Hong Kong and Taiwan, have also often been highly commercialized entities, which have attracted their own sponsors.

This chapter examines examples of performances on PRC television by pop stars and 'ordinary' people from Hong Kong, Macau, and Taiwan as well as Chinese overseas to see how they have helped to create and support PRC Party-state sanctioned visions of a stable, unified, powerful, economically developing Chinese nation. It examines nuances in performances that highlight various sensitivities that relate to the different historical, political and social relationships the PRC mainland has had with these different Chinese constituencies.

Celebrating the return of Hong Kong

The media in Hong Kong and on the mainland play an important role in reorienting citizens on both sides to what it means to be Chinese under the 'one country, two systems' framework. The Hong Kong Special Administrative Region (Hong Kong SAR), with a population of more than seven million people, borders on southeast China's Guangdong province. In the PRC Party-state imagination, the loss of the island to Britain marked the beginning of 150 years of humiliation that saw Western and Japanese aggression towards

China (Chow, 1998: 5). In 1997, Hong Kong officially become the Hong Kong SAR of the PRC after being under British administration since 1841, and enduring a period of occupation by the Japanese during the Second World War from 1941 to 1945. Ever since Hong Kong was returned to the 'motherland', it has undergone a process of 're-sinification'. The boundaries between Hong Kong and the mainland have become increasingly blurred as Hong Kong people have begun to understand their new place as part of China (Fung and Ma, 2002: 78; Ma, 2000: 177–8).

As Eric Kit-Wai Ma (2000: 175, 177) explains, since the 1990s, Hong Kong people have been exposed to new national discourses, including media celebrations of the founding of the PRC. Many Hong Kong people, not used to feeling connected to any nation-state, and holding ideas of mainland China as being backward and ridden with propaganda, at first disliked the national celebrations and symbolism espoused through such acts as raising national flags and singing national anthems. However, through multiple retellings of national stories, many Hong Kong people have started to become more sympathetic to official discourses. A focus on a shared Chinese heritage rather than politics has allowed Hong Kong people to establish a sense of unity with mainlanders. The image of one big Chinese family is acceptable to many Hong Kong people and at the same time pleases mainland officials (Ma, 1999: 56–7). Through examining musical performances and verbal discourses that have featured Hong Kong or Hong Kong performers on mainland Chinese productions, we are able to gain insights into the Party-state's attempts to draw in Hong Kong and overseas Chinese audiences as well as examine how it has framed Hong Kong in relation to the Chinese nation.

Due to financial imperatives, the Hong Kong cultural industry now increasingly depends upon mainland investment and producers, which has resulted in Hong Kong actors and directors pandering to mainland commercial and political requirements. An example is when Hong Kong action movie star Jackie Chan (Chen Long) wondered aloud during the Boao Forum for business leaders in 2009 whether Chinese people really needed democracy and suggested that too much freedom, such as in Hong Kong and Taiwan, has led to chaos. Instead, he suggested that 'we Chinese need to be controlled'. While Chan was applauded by a predominantly mainland Chinese audience of business leaders, he was sharply rebuked by Hong Kong and Taiwanese commentators (Coonan, 2009). While many Hong Kong artists have readily adapted themselves to tap into the mainland market, protests in Hong Kong in 2014, which became known as the Umbrella Movement, also underline ongoing mistrust and concerns over greater political ties with the Beijing authorities among ordinary people in Hong Kong (Brown, 2014). Cultural programming may thus be seen as part of an effort both to convince audiences of the natural place of Hong Kong in China, and to relieve fears of the PRC as a threatening force.

For many years, Hong Kong has been a trendy label for performers, making 'Hong Kong' stars attractive to the mainland market. In the 1990s, mainland audiences often regarded Cantopop (Cantonese language pop music) as superior to Mandarin songs of the mainland (Fung and Curtin, 2002). As Fung and Curtin (2002) have noted, some mainland singers even tried to remake themselves as 'Hong Kong' stars in order to break into their 'own' mainland market. One famous example is Wang Fei (Faye Wong), originally from Beijing, who was helped by Hong Kong entertainment executives to recast her image with a new name, language, and personality in the 1990s.[1] However, while Hong Kong is still known for being stylish, since the 1997 handover there has been a growing convergence between the Hong Kong and mainland popular culture industries. China has also become increasingly dominant in Asia and on the global stage, and mainland singers have become popular in the region. Yet Hong Kong and Taiwanese artists still offer something different and Chinese television channels often spice up their programmes with artists from Hong Kong and Taiwan to attract audiences and boost ratings.

From 'My Chinese Heart' to 'My Chinese Dream': Zhang Mingmin

One of the most famous performances of Greater Chinese unity on Chinese television has been the song 'My Chinese Heart' (*Wo de Zhongguo Xin*), first sung by Hong Kong singer Zhang Mingmin during the 1984 *CCTV Spring Festival Gala*. The lyrics (see also Gorfinkel, 2011) are about a man who grew up abroad and dressed like a Westerner, but who steadfastly clung to his Chinese identity, declaring that it was something he would 'never change'. He expressed an affinity with iconic symbols of the Chinese nation – the Yangtze River, the Great Wall, and Yellow Mountain – which are located in mainland China. His singing on the CCTV stage in Beijing through which the Great Wall passes represented a kind of homecoming. The lyrics suggest that long-term British influence in Hong Kong and local Hong Kong culture had minimal impact on his sense of Chineseness. Instead, they suggest that an essential, unchanging Chinese spirit ran through his blood.

Zhang, the first Hong Kong performer to appear on the *CCTV Spring Festival Gala*, appeared on PRC television in the same year that British Prime Minister Margaret Thatcher travelled to Beijing to sign a Joint Sino-British Declaration that would 'restore' Hong Kong to China in 1997. CCTV directors preparing for the 1984 show wanted a performer who could make a positive impression of Hong Kong–mainland relations following the resumption of Sino–British negotiations in 1983. The directors reportedly found Zhang by chance while listening to this song while driving in southern China near the border with Hong Kong (Da, 2005).

As a performance, the music, visual and lyrical elements pulled together in a 'hardened' way to create a clear message of ethnic Chinese solidarity. Zhang's standing at the centre of the stage in the PRC capital, Beijing, crying out his feeling of oneness with the mainland television audience, became symbolic of *all* Hong Kong people's desires to be reunited with the mainland – the 'centre' of global Chinese solidarity. His gestures invited viewers to share a heart-to-heart moment with him: as he sang he opened his jacket, repeatedly placed his hands on his heart, and reached out his arms as if sharing his heart with viewers. In the backing track, a choir echoed his words, and military-like trumpets and drums echoed the solemnness of his expression. The camera zoomed in and out, reflecting the common heartbeat of the Chinese nation as viewers connected via their TV screens at home across China and around the world.

CCTV has created a sense of nostalgia based on this performance of Hong Kong mainland solidarity through constant replays of the 1983 performance, as well as newly recorded versions. It has continued to be used to represent the bond not only with Hong Kong but also with Chinese in Taiwan, Macau and around the world. For instance, Zhang sang the same song again during the *2012 CCTV Spring Festival Gala* as part of a series of songs taking viewers down memory lane. In 2014, he appeared on the Gala again, this time shifting from 'My Chinese Heart' to a new song called 'My Chinese Dream', which reinforced Xi Jinping's slogan of the times.

Rather than focus on China's magnificent rivers and mountains and the Great Wall (although these were visually represented on a screen behind him), the lyrics for 'My Chinese Dream' were simple reflections of ordinary Chinese people's longing for a better life (Tencent Entertainment, 2014). The song was formulated as a reminder of Zhang's previous performances on CCTV and Hong Kong's return to the motherland as well as the great Chinese identity that it represented. Visually Zhang looked the same. He wore a white scarf and had his hand on his heart. With lyrics like 'My Chinese dream is forever in my heart', 'The nation's flourishing is my honour', and 'The Chinese family all have the same dream', the song aimed to give the 'Chinese sons and daughters' who are connected across 'the four seas' and 'five continents' a 'positive energy' and inspire their sense of patriotism (Souhu Music, 2014).

Like 'My Chinese Heart', the performance seamlessly linked the personal and the national with lyrics like 'When I was young my mother would often ask me/what is your dream? I lifted my head and looked up to the sky/(I) Want to give my youth to the motherland'. The song also reflected on the hard work over the years that allowed Zhang to grow and develop his 'true' identity. The lyrics were visually matched with other signs of China's economic development, such as cityscapes. The flags of the PRC, Hong Kong and Macau fluttered side by side, showcasing the growing political closeness of the greater Chinese family.

Interestingly, 'My Chinese Heart' was written in 1982 by Hong Kong songwriter James Wong (with Wang Fuling) as a protest against the Japanese Ministry of Education's distortion of the history of Japanese aggression against the Chinese people in Japanese primary and secondary textbooks. At the time, Hong Kong people also had a deep sense of ambivalence about their future with China (Ma, 2000). When Zhang became famous in the mainland for singing 'My Chinese Heart', Hong Kong residents labelled him 'patriotic', which was not considered a flattering label by Hong Kong people at the time. In any case, the song was not particularly popular in Hong Kong at a time when few people there understood Mandarin (Da, 2005). It was the PRC media, particularly CCTV, which promoted the idea that Chinese around the world, including in Hong Kong, had the same feelings as those in the mainland.

Hong Kong pop stars' co-option of Chinese nationalism

In the 1990s, as the PRC commercialized, Hong Kong pop stars deliberately began to employ nationalistic tactics to appeal to mainland consumers as well as the censors. As Anthony Fung (2003) and Yiu-Fai Chow (2007: 99) note, Hong Kong singer and film star Liu Dehua (Andy Lau) strategically reinvented his image for the mainland market in the 1990s. His patriotic 1997 release called 'Chinese People' (*Zhongguo ren*), which continues to be replayed on CCTV and performed anew on CCTV and provincial channels (including a 2016 performance by Liu on Hunan Television's International Channel, Mango TV) particularly helped with this endeavour. The song depicts Liu on the Great Wall decorated with red flags, with the Chinese characters for 'Chinese people' printed on them. Liu calls out to fellow Chinese listeners of the 'same blood' and 'same race' to 'keep our chins up, march on' and 'let the world know we are Chinese' (translation in Chow, 2007: 99). A CCTV-Music clip posted to CNTV in December 2012 included an interview with Liu in which he noted that the intention behind this song was to draw all Chinese around the world together when there was nothing other than popular music to unite them.

Xie Tingfeng (Nicholas Tse), a Hong Kong singer and actor, built on the success of Liu Dehua in the 2000s with his own nationalistic song, 'Yellow People' (*Huangzhongren*). As Chow (2007, 2009), lyricist of this song, has explained, the song as performed by Xie was designed to rev up the mainland crowds through appealing to their patriotic spirit. Lyricist Chow, however, originally wanted to challenge a dominant and essentialist reading of Chineseness (defined through collective success, an unbreakable strength and a strong bloodline) by including 'yellowness' as a vague and not necessarily flattering aspect of China's racial history[2] and alluding to other negative aspects of Chinese culture and history. However, the songwriter's control can be lost once the song is in the artist's and television producer's hands. Xie himself added into the song his own essentialist Chinese rap lyrics, which he thought would appeal to audiences. The newly added words, which spoke of the yellow faces around the world, 'marching forward' fearlessly as 'only us Chinese' (quoted in Chow 2007: 103), effectively changed the tone of the song.[3]

CCTV has welcomed Xie on-stage to sing 'Yellow People' on a number of occasions. One such case was *The Same Song* episode entitled *Entering Into Inner Mongolia – Booming Ordos* (*Zoujin Nei Menggu – Tengfei E'erduosi*) on 24 August 2007. Examination of this performance provides insights into the interplay between the Greater China and multiethnic China frames. The

128 *Greater China*

hosts explained that the aim of the *Entering Into Inner Mongolia* special was to celebrate the 60th anniversary of the establishment of the Inner Mongolia Autonomous Region – a region that borders on the separate country of Mongolia to China's north. Another aim was to celebrate the second Ordos International Culture Festival, which was drawing to a close. The 'international' event projected China as a world player with a cosmopolitan outlook. Foreign performers and Chinese from outside the mainland like Xie Tingfeng helped to present China as a nation whose vibrancy draws from its interactions with diverse people from outside of China and with colourful ethnic minorities within.

Ordos is a city in the Inner Mongolia Autonomous Region, named after its significant ethnic Mongol population. It is one of the richest areas in China, having one-sixth of China's natural resources as well as a strong textile industry. This episode was the first time *The Same Song* programme was broadcast from Ordos. It was created in partnership with the local city and prefecture governments and the Inner Mongolia provincial television station. Ironically, Ordos is also known as a ghost town, as massive investment has been put into creating a modern city with a fancy new theatre and apartments, but hardly anyone seems to be living there. Properties have been purchased for investment purposes but are too expensive for most locals to rent or purchase (Al Jazeera, 2011). The show seems to have been part of an economic drive to attract people to the city but gave no hint of the problems with Ordos' development.

In this particular episode, the two perceived goals – namely, international openness and ethnic openness – met up against each another. The 'unity of the nationalities' (*minzu tuanjie*) was implied through the co-hosting of the show by two hosts from the provincial-level Inner Mongolia TV station, one of whom spoke in Mongolian, along with the two ethnically unmarked CCTV hosts (presumably Han). Performers wore Mongolian costume and there was some linguistic exchange with the show's theme song sung in Mongolian instead of the usual Chinese, suggesting support for the maintenance of Mongolian culture. However, as Bulag (2010) notes, a great majority of Mongolians in China have lost their ability to speak Mongolian because of the active promotion of standard modern Chinese/Mandarin, or *Putonghua*. The episode was sponsored by one of China's most lucrative textile brands with the same Chinese name as the town, known as Erdos in English. Although the company itself is dominated by Han Chinese, it has accrued value by leveraging Mongolian cultural elements and symbols such as Chinggis Khan and pastoralism (Bulag, 2010: 282–3).

While a sense of Mongolian agency was emphasized in the opening scenes, this was suddenly disrupted by the appearance of Hong Kong star Xie Tingfeng and his song 'Yellow People', a performance that called for a strong, united, singular Chinese nation. In the performance, the exotic Mongolian identity that was used to attract audiences through its difference to mainstream Chineseness became overridden by an all-encompassing, and perhaps equally attractive, regional/global, 'modern' Chinese identity embodied by a Hong Kong star from the economically advanced region that stands at the gateway between the China and the West. Unlike the well-trained hosts who act as 'mouthpieces' for the Party-state, the voice and presence of a Hong Kong star may make the Party-state's propaganda more effective. Through this performance, China was shown to be opening up, reforming and deepening links between Chinese people from developed special administrative regions like Hong Kong and from less developed autonomous regions where many minorities live.

While many Mongolians in China may see themselves as part of a global 'pan-Mongolian' identity, and may feel like they have more in common with fellow Mongolians over the border in the Republic of Mongolia than with Chinese in Hong Kong, for instance, as part of a pan-Chinese identity (e.g., see Bulag, 2010), this performance did not make any reference to a 'greater Mongolian' identity that extended beyond the PRC borders. Instead, it suggested that when faced with a global perspective, Mongolian–Chinese are part of a 'greater Chinese' identity. The emphasis was on the identity of 'Inner Mongolians' (those from the PRC province of 'Inner Mongolia') – a group of Chinese people with a range of ethnicities, of which Mongols just happened to be the most numerous. A differentiated Mongolian identity – one separate to the mainstream, majority Han Chinese – was restricted to an internal, domestic multiethnic frame within mainland borders.

If one paid close attention to the lyrics of 'Yellow People' by Chow, and had read Chow's article or spoken to him about his intentions, one might have read into it a desire to challenge the status quo. But in the totality of the CCTV production there was very little evidence of such a challenge. At most, one could suggest a point of ambiguity at the end of the rap section: as the the phrase 'only us Chinese' was sustained, the music turned into a descending melody. This was matched with psychedelic swirling images on the back-screen and Xie was seen taking a few steps forwards and then backwards as if falling into an abyss. However, as the Chinese flute (the *dizi*, an emblematic 'Chinese' instrument) was heard in the musical accompaniment in a jazzy interlude, Xie stepped forward again, encouraged the audience to sing the next verse along with him, and the performance closed in the same way as it opened, with images of a massive (faceless) audience waving glow sticks in the dark – a visual sign of unity, modernity and vibrancy in the provincial Chinese city.

Overall, the sounds, visuals and lyrics tended to reinforce a brash Han-centred Chinese nationalism, with Xie's face marked by an expression of determination and anger, a feeling echoed in his body language. His feet were planted wide apart (similar to the performance of Bai nationality singer, Ah Peng, discussed in Chapter 4) and he stepped steadfastly to the beat. The rap lyrics and rhythm built to a crescendo as Xie Tingfeng walked to the end of the catwalk-like stage where he could almost touch the audience, preaching the myth of a people united by a single colour, 'yellow'. Yellow lighting and a simulated raging yellow fire on a back-screen seemed to be employed to fire up the hearts of viewers. Xie's added rap lyrics helped to clearly present 'yellow people' as a simple metaphor for the proud Chinese people.

In order to perform on CCTV, Xie's songs would have already been vetted by censors and there would have been little chance of him singing his more controversial songs, such as the drug-referencing ballad 'Without Me', which includes the English lyrics 'too much pot and heroine, too much crack and coke'.[4] It is also unlikely that CCTV would replicate such 'bad boy' images of Xie smashing a guitar on stage as he did during a May 2003 outdoor anti-SARS concert at the Hong Kong Stadium, an act that did not entirely impress all fans either judging by their comments on Chinese YouTube equivalent YouKu. It is also unlikely that CCTV would fixate on long, convoluted grunge guitar sounds, or extended singing and chatting in Cantonese, which most mainland audiences would not have been able to understand, as he has done in other concerts. Thus, while certain attractive elements of Xie's lively approach have been drawn upon (posture, stance, visual imagery), Xie has also significantly adjusted his performance for the CCTV stage.

Xie has also endeared himself to Chinese authorities by being involved in national media events such as the Beijing 2008 Olympic Games, where he sang in the closing ceremony. He also sang a Cantonese version of the Olympic song 'We Are Ready' in the lead-up to the Games. His presence effectively highlighted the Cantonese/Hong Kong people's pride in China's hosting of the major event and helped give it an international dimension, which would have helped to appeal to Chinese audiences around the world. Interestingly, the Mandarin version of 'We Are Ready' was also popularized by a fellow Hong Kong star, globally renown martial artist and comic actor turned singer Jackie Chan (Chen Long).

In 2009, Xie also sang during the highly political celebrations of the PRC's 60-year anniversary in Tiananmen Square, which also celebrated China's 'scientific development' (*kexue fazhan*). Dressed in a formal Tang jacket, he was the 'China-Hong Kong' representative, who sang the upbeat pop-like anthem 'Big China' (*Da Zhonghua*) along with a 'China-Taiwan' singer and an unmarked mainland singer. Through the lyrics he told audiences that 'We all have a family, its name is China' and asked them to look at the Great Wall that is shuttling in the clouds and the Tibetan Plateau that is wider than the sky. The three men then led the hundreds of performers who were dressed in red and dancing excitedly in the square to sing 'China – bless you. You are forever in my heart.' Such events highlight the close links between the state and popular Hong Kong stars.

The Same Song *in Hong Kong*

In other shows, apparently 'apolitical' popular music has been used to draw audiences towards more overt spoken ideological messages about unification, the success of the 'one country, two systems' policy and Chinese identity. This section provides examples from a 2007 episode of CCTV's *The Same Song*, which staged a concert in Hong Kong that celebrated ten years since the return of Hong Kong to the motherland. The concert took place on the shores of Victoria Harbour and was dubbed 'ten years since the return – ITAT night in Hong Kong'. The event's sponsor, ITAT, a Hong Kong clothing retailer based in the mainland in Shenzhen, was itself a symbol of the economic cooperation between the two sides. Signs of cooperation were also evidenced in the joint nature of the production which was produced by CCTV and Hong Kong's Television Broadcasts Limited (TVB), one of the largest commercial producers of Chinese programmes in the world. The two stations' logos appeared prominently on the stage, and two hosts from each station presented the show.

Among the performers was Wang Mingquan (Liza Wang), a well-known Hong Kong performer who was born in Shanghai and moved to Hong Kong when she was young (All-China Women's Federation, 2007).[5] Wang became popular in China after performing three songs during the *1985 CCTV Spring Festival Gala*. At the 1985 Gala, she announced that it was her first time in Beijing, and expressed her wish to one day return to her hometown Shanghai and perform in a concert there. Like Zhang Mingmin, the first Hong Kong performer on the Gala, Wang also sang about the Great Wall and the Yangtze River in addition to a song called 'Happy and Carefree' (*Huanle wuyou*), which helped set the mood for the post-socialist reform and opening up times. As she walked around 'greeting friends' and shaking hands with the studio audience, she sang about how the two sides had become so distant after all these years apart, yet there were still faint memories of a dream (to return). She urged audiences not to look back. All her songs in the 1985 performance in Beijing were in Mandarin.

In contrast, during the 2007 concert in Hong Kong, Wang sang in Cantonese, singing the sweet theme song to the popular Hong Kong television series *Journeying Over Ten Thousand Torrents and a Thousand Crags – Always Love* (also translated as *The Trials of a Long and Arduous Journey*) (*Wan shui qian shan zong shi qing*, 1982).[6] The performance in 2007 hinted at the trials and tribulations in the relationship between the two sides, but also demonstrated that the Hong Kong people were now relaxed about the relationship and were able to maintain their own identity and language while also easily fitting in with the mainland.

After the song, Wang switched to the official mainland language of Mandarin in her dialogue with the mainland host, and they discussed the progress of the 'one country, two systems' policy over the past ten years. Together, they alluded to the Hong Kong people's former doubts about the return of Hong Kong to the motherland, and to past and current difficulties. But these were quickly brushed aside as Wang emphasized that 2007 was the best year since 'the return', and even though the current situation hadn't come easily, 'everything is better' than before and 'the future [lit: tomorrow] will be even better'. The description of the successful return of Hong Kong to the motherland fit neatly with broader discourses that accentuated the positives of China's 30 years of reform and opening up.

CCTV and the Hong Kong media, which has increasingly engaged in self-censorship to access mainland markets, have played important roles in demonstrating to their audiences the successes of the 'one country, two systems' policy. They have strongly emphasized the common cultural Chinese identity that links mainland and Hong Kong people. While such programmes downplay the strong Hong Kong identity (Lo, 2008: 253–6), they add just enough hint of difference (e.g., Cantonese language songs) to satisfy viewers about the openness of the Party-state towards Hong Kong, such that even if they speak with a different 'dialect', they still belong to the same 'family'.

The show concluded on a bright note with two mainland CCTV hosts firmly connecting the 'beautiful' Hong Kong with 'our' China/'our great motherland' (*women weida zuguo*). The two Hong Kong hosts expressed their hopes for the strong relations between the two sides in a subtler way. They simply expressed their wishes for Hong Kong to be 'more beautiful', and for 'music and cultural exchanges to be more intimate in the future'. While Hong Kong singers were given plenty of airtime during the programme, the final stamp was given to a mainland singer, Cai Guoqing, who regularly sang the final theme song on *The Same Song*. In this song, 'the same song' was a metaphor for shared feelings and hopes. The lyrics painted a picture of people 'holding hands', with smiles 'engraved' on their faces, eager to share stories about their happy lives. They asserted that despite differences in location, people on both sides sing 'the same song' because they share the 'same feelings', 'same hopes' and 'same happiness'.

As this final song was sung during the 2007 Hong Kong event, the camera panned around Victoria Harbour, drawing the symbolic icon of Hong Kong into 'the same song' as that sung in every episode of the programme as it travelled across China and around the world. In the middle of the song, while sentimental instrumental music continued in the background, Cai reinforced the link between Hong Kong and 'our' China in spoken language:

> Tonight Hong Kong's colours are so beautiful, linked to *The Same Song* stage, the stars are vast. Today so many stars have gathered on *The Same Song* stage by Victoria Harbour in Hong Kong. We have gathered on a stage that is full of friendship... At this moment through *The Same Song*'s song, we will give our most beautiful wishes to spring, the beautiful Hong Kong, to our lovely China.

In a final embodied act of unity, Cai encouraged the Hong Kong audiences, along with the mainland and Hong Kong stars, to wave their hands together in the air to the beat of the song. The carefully constructed dialogues between and within acts, along with images of Hong Kong and mainlanders hand in hand, and the sound of voices singing a sentimental melody in harmony, stressed a strong message of Hong Kong's successful return to China and positive feelings for the future of this cross-border unity. The metaphor of shared happiness and friendship represented the most significant approach by the mainland singer and *The Same Song* production team to construct a non-confronting sense of shared identity with mutual benefit across the Hong Kong–mainland border. These examples show how popular songs can be used to help promote particular brands of pan-Chinese nationalism. Numerous Hong Kong stars have also featured on provincial television shows with a similar effect.

Celebrating Macau's return

Known as 'Aomen' in Mandarin, Macau is home to more than 550,000 residents and, like Hong Kong, is adjacent to mainland China's Guangdong province. The former Portuguese colony was returned to Chinese administration on 20 December 1999, and officially named the Macau Special Administrative Region (Macau SAR) of the PRC.[7] Like Hong Kong, it was incorporated into the PRC under the 'one country, two systems' policy (Lam, 2010: 660). After more than ten years of unification, Macau's politics, economy and society have been strongly integrated into the PRC system, much more so than in Hong Kong (Lo, 2008: 227).

Unlike Hong Kong, whose British history is largely underemphasized by the Chinese authorities (Lam, 2010: 656), Macau has retained a strong sense of its former colonial heritage. Its hybrid Portuguese–Chinese Macanese identity has been strongly promoted by local authorities.

A child returning to her mother

As the smallest entity in 'Greater China', Macau is often framed as a 'child' of China, largely through repetition of a well-known national song about Macau called 'The Song of Seven Lands – Aomen' (*Qizi zhi ge – Aomen*). This is in contrast to the economically stronger Hong Kong, who is depicted more as a 'brother'. The song presents Macau's connection to China as akin to a mother–child bond. It was originally written in 1925 as a poem about seven places of China (*Zhonghua*) – Macau, Hong Kong, Taiwan, Kowloon, Weihai, Guangzhou Bay, and Lüda (Lüshun and Dalian) – that had fallen into the hands of foreign imperialists (Du, 2009). In 1998, the words for the Macau verse were used for the theme song of a CCTV documentary series called *The Years of Macau* (*Aomen Suiyue*) celebrating the return of Macau. The following year the song appeared in the *CCTV Spring Festival Gala*, when a young Macau girl, Rong Yunlin, famously took the stage in Beijing. Backed by a choir of men, women and children, she shared her feelings about Macau's unity with the mainland. During one of the most socially and politically important television events of 1999 – similar to CCTV's use of the image and the voice of two young girls during the Opening Ceremony of the Beijing 2008 Olympic Games – Rong Yunlin's clear lyrical delivery, youthful image and pure, innocent child's voice signalled to audiences that Macau had a bright future as part of China.

In this 1999 performance, the song lyrics, visual performance style and musical accompaniment combined to produce a strong ('hardened') message that Macau desires to be part of, and is a natural part of, China. The tune began as a lullaby, accompanied by the tinkling of a xylophone, suggestive of childhood. A choir of more than 30 Chinese girls and boys (dressed in 'modern' Western-style dress) sang happily in unison, nodding their heads as they sang to emphasize the importance of each word. They told the studio and television audiences 'Do you know "Macau" isn't my real name?' and plainly noted that even though 'I've been away from you for so long', they (the unmentioned Portuguese colonizers) only took my 'body', not my 'soul'. In this process of appropriation, Macau was emptied of its old colonial meaning and reinvested with a new meaning: belonging to China. Its old colonial name 'Macau' was called into question and the children guided audiences towards accepting 'Aomen' as its new, appropriate, and 'real' Chinese identity.

After this verse, nine-year-old Rong Yunlin stepped out of the crowd and started to walk forward, demanding particular attention as she took a leading soloist role. To reinforce the modern, although essentially Chinese, national identity, the musical accompaniment merged modern Western instruments like the piano with Chinese musical instruments such as the Chinese zither (*guzheng*) (also see Zhang, 2010: 52). Rong repeated the first stanza as the other children followed behind, repeating particular phrases (e.g., not my real name/*bu shi wo zhen xing*, mother/*muqin*, is my body/*shi wo di routi*) as they stepped forward for emphasis. Van Leeuwen refers to this call and response style as supportive emulation, whereby the relationship of support for the leader's message is dramatized (1999: 35, 74). The image of children walking forward (like the minority nationality children walking forward with the Chinese flag during the Opening Ceremony of the Beijing 2008 Olympic Games) and the sound of many voices singing the same song en masse are commonly used in CCTV's music-entertainment programming as symbols of national unity and strength.

The performance gained momentum when a critical mass of voices could be heard as adults stepped behind the children to back up their words. This included a group of about 30 women and a separate group of around 30 men wearing 'modern' Western-style black suits and red ties. The pure voices of children and the solemn, authoritative, church-like sanctity of the choral voices of the adult men and women helped to 'eternalize' (Barthes, 1976: 124) Macau's rightful place as a member of the PRC family. As van Leeuwen has noted, this style of 'social unison' or 'monophony', where all voices sing the same notes, displays what may be seen negatively as conformity, disciplining and lack of individuality, but positively as a sense of solidarity and belonging. Drawing on Arnold, he notes that this form of singing, which developed during the Industrial Revolution in Europe (and which was readily adopted in China) uses back-up voices to 'supply chordal pillars to prop up the dominant voice' and create a 'single feeling' and exemplifies a context where no one is 'out of step' (van Leeuwen, 1999: 79, 82). In highly politicized national televised moments, the style continues to be used to symbolize national strength, national achievement, and progress.

The choice of a child to lead the collective voice of Macau has reinforced the song's lyrics in which Macau is constructed as a child of her mainland 'mother'. Metaphorically, Rong helped to establish the notion that Macau needed China just as a young child needs his or her mother. Her small stature and high pitched child's voice positioned Macau as a small but treasured part of a powerful Chinese nation. With some notes sung slightly off-key, along with her innocent-looking face on close-up, the genuineness and conviction of her message seemed clear. Singing in Mandarin, the national language, but with a local accent (e.g., '*ni kai*' instead of the national standard Beijing dialect '*li kai*' for 'depart from', '*dan si*' instead of '*dan shi*' for the word 'but', '*kui lai*' instead of '*hui lai*' for 'come back') also added to a sense of authenticity in the act of re-joining the local entity with the bigger collective nation.

The adults who echoed the child's words, and who looked ethnically indistinguishable from any other mainland Chinese citizen, indicated that they too were long-lost children of the motherland. (A similar construction of adults being long-lost relatives of mainlanders has also been used in CCTV's depiction of mainland–Taiwan relations.) In the *Spring Festival Gala*'s construction of Macau, the men, women and children unanimously told the television audience that even though they had been separated for '300 years', they never forgot who they really belonged to – the 'mother in my dreams'. They pleaded that 'us children' should be called by their pet name (i.e., Chinese name) 'Aomen', not 'Macau' (the colonial name). In increasingly authoritative tones, both children and adults called out 'Mother! Mother!' and 'I want to come back'. The performance ended with deep pulsating drums, an increasing density of instrumental backing indicating a merging of the small Macau and large China, and a final emphatic call, rising to the heroic-sounding tonic in unison: 'Mother!' (see van Leeuwen, 1999: 39, 106). Sounds of clapping from the studio audience in Beijing merged with the final resonating tones, indicating their support for the message of national solidarity.

The political relationship between Macau and its PRC 'mother' was thus made utterly clear for audiences through a combination of sound, images and clearly articulated song lyrics that mutually reinforced each other to emphasize the message of unity between Macau and its motherland, mainland China. In this case, the former colonial influence was stripped of its significance and the new Chinese identity (or mythology) constructed, emphasized and made to appear 'natural'.

Since 1998, the *CCTV Spring Festival Gala* performance of the 'The Song of Seven Lands – Macau' has been regularly replayed on various CCTV music-entertainment programmes. For example, a *China Music Television* episode called 'Songs of Memories' (*Jiyi de gesheng*) that aired in 2008 allowed audiences to recapture the nostalgic moment when Rong Yunlin and her fellow Macau compatriots expressed their yearnings to rejoin the motherland.

136   *Greater China*

Via its constant repetitions in various live and repackaged forms, the song has been used to educate mainland as well as regional and global audiences about the 'real' history of Macau, its connection to mainland China and its reintegration into the PRC.

Happy in China – Charming Macau

Another fairly hardened multimodal construction of Macau on CCTV, but one that also offered a few 'softer' moments of identity construction, was during the music-entertainment programme *Happy in China – National Day Celebration Special – Charming Macau* (*Huanle Zhongguo Xing – Guoqingjie tebie jiemu – Meili Aomen*) in October 2008. This entertainment special celebrated the 59th 'birthday' of the PRC, i.e., 59 years since Chairman Mao's declaration of the New China under the leadership of the Chinese Communist Party, and was broadcast as part of China's National Day celebrations. Unlike the previous example, this event was staged in Macau. The historical timing of the programme was soon after the end of the Olympic Games during which pride in China and the success of the Games were frequently commemorated in music-entertainment extravaganzas.

Even though Macau itself had only officially been part of the PRC since 1999, it was the number '59' that was emphasized by host Zhang Lei, who announced that 2008 was the 59th birthday of the PRC, and this represented 59 years of 'struggle/striving' and of 'pioneering' a new course for the Chinese nation. She set the national celebratory tone for the programme, explaining that 'our motherland has experienced great changes', emphasizing the importance of the Olympics, the 'great achievements of 30 years of reform and opening up' and 'feelings of pride'. While Macau was the setting, this programme firmly incorporated all of the areas and people to which the PRC laid claim or included within its Greater China worldview. Zhang called on 'all the nationalities of the whole country, Hong Kong and Macau compatriots, Taiwan compatriots and overseas Chinese to together celebrate this great day for the motherland'.

In verbal, lyrical and visual discourse, the way Macau was framed confirmed that it was a small entity within a big China. During the event, a young unknown woman from Macau was invited on stage to sing with male mainland pop star Sun Nan. The woman's spoken words emphasized her ideologically 'correct' affiliation: she said that she chose to sing 'Red Flag Fluttering' (*Hong qi piao piao*), one of Sun Nan's signature songs, in order to express her 'passion for our motherland'. The patriotic lyrics merged magnificently with this uplifting pop classic. As they sang together about the 'five-starred red flag' whose 'name is more important than my life', a camera panning across the massive audience showed male youths holding up and waving massive red PRC flags, while seated audience members waved the smaller PRC and Macau SAR flags, suggesting the strength and dominance of the motherland over the SAR. Red dominated the indoor setting: massive red lanterns hung from the ceiling, huge red drums were displayed and played, and dancers were holding red fans, reflecting their passion for the motherland. The inclusion of ordinary people – the ordinariness of the woman singing with Sun Nan was partly exemplified by her off-key singing – implied that their feelings were typical of ordinary Macanese. After the song, host Zhang Lei reiterated some of the lyrics of the song to reinforce the message of national unity. She stressed that the 'five-starred red flag flutters in *every one* of our hearts' and this is what makes 'our motherland a big strong family'.

Like the *CCTV Spring Festival Gala* discussed above, in the *Happy in China* programme, the history of Macau was also performed in ways that stressed the PRC's sovereignty. However, it also emphasized the unique 'blend' (*jiaorong*) of local Macanese and Chinese cultures. Red and green were the colour themes reflecting the respective flags of the PRC motherland and Macau SAR. The design of the huge indoor stadium also symbolically blended the Macau and PRC national cultures into 'one'. Lotus flowers, the emblematic flower of Macau, floated in pools of water below, and a huge 'lotus and five-star' design of the Macau flag (the stars adapted from the PRC flag) was seen on the ceiling, providing an artistic and political 'framing' for wide camera shots of the action on stage and the stadium at large. A group of dancers in their red and green costumes also performed in the colour scheme that reflected the merging of the motherland and Macau.

This event also emphasized to a degree Macau's unique Portuguese identity in contrast to the rest of China. Following the projection of familiar, symbolic images of Beijing, representing the heart of the motherland (Tiananmen Square, soldiers of the People's Liberation Army, Chairman Mao's portrait and the PRC flag) set to the theme of the Chinese national anthem, audiences were fed images of Macau including the remaining façade of the ruins of St Paul's cathedral – known as *dasanba paifang* in Chinese. Before 'returning' Macau to China, the Portuguese administration put substantial resources into the historical preservation of Macau's colonial history and its Mediterranean-European architecture (Lam, 2010; Edmonds, 1995: 232–4). Since 1982, historic buildings have been preserved specifically with tourism in mind (Edmonds, 1995: 232–4). Macau's hybrid culture has been a unique selling point for its tourism industry (one of its two most important industries, the other being gambling), mainly attracting Chinese tourists from Hong Kong, Taiwan and Southeast Asia.

However, in this CCTV production, rather than the colonial historical or religious significance, the buildings were imbued with new meanings more suitable to modern times. An emphatic, deep male voiceover in the official Beijing/national dialect spoke over these images of Macau to reframe Macau as a unique 'harmonious', 'peaceful' and 'beautiful land'. Introducing the clip, host Zhang Lei also emphasized the blending of cultures over the past 400 years, proudly boasting of Macau's unique buildings, which included both Chinese and foreign styles. Yet, following Barthes (1976: 117–27), the colonial associations of Macau's past were 'put at a distance and [made] almost transparent'. The facades of *dasanba paifang* are a prime example of a form that was made 'empty but present', ensuring that some features were kept (e.g., for tourism purposes, promotion of China's contemporary multicultural vitality), while others (e.g., religion) were dropped. Just as the former colonial splendour was hinted at, the colonial buildings were reappropriated to support a new message of contemporary China's openness and vitality, under a ruling Party that has demonstrated administrative competency in integrating the former colony into the fold of the PRC.

The ordering of performances in this production also revealed a greater emphasis on the Beijing-centred PRC administration-era than on Macau's former Portuguese history. In one instance, a brief reference to Macau's history under a Western power, for example, was immediately followed by a dazzling routine by an acrobatic troupe from Beijing. Such ordering may be coincidental, but overall Macau is framed in CCTV's music-entertainment programmes as firmly belonging to a revitalized PRC, rather than as a separate entity.

Celebrating cultural hybridity

Sheh and Law's (2011) comparative study of official history museums in Hong Kong and Macau helps to shed further light on differences in the ways that Hong Kong and Macau have been incorporated into the Greater China frame. They argue that the different official constructions of nationalism in the Hong Kong and Macau history museums have reflected two different faces of official PRC nationalism. Sheh and Law argue that Hong Kong's museum of history represented the narrative of national humiliation as a result of British imperialism. It completely downplayed the significance of its British colonial history and Western–Chinese cross-cultural relations, and instead emphasized Chinese patriotism through placing an emphasis on Chinese art, archaeological discoveries, maps of China and ancient Chinese inventions. The Museu de Macau, on the other hand, showcased Sino–Western cultural exchange and the blending of Eastern and Western culture, and presented Macau as a bridge between China and Europe. For instance, it included a history of trade in Eastern and Western products, displayed Western and Chinese architecture side by side, and placed significant emphasis on the culture of Macanese with mixed Portuguese–Chinese heritage, such as cross-cultural influences in Macanese cooking. Macanese culture was emphasized even though the Macanese population represented only a small minority of the current population of Macau, which is currently dominated by ethnic Chinese/Cantonese. By highlighting the peaceful co-existence between Chinese- and Portuguese-speaking peoples, Macau has been used as a cultural platform to strengthen China's strategic policy of forming new friends with countries in Europe as well as in Latin and South America where Portuguese is spoken (Lam, 2010; Sheh and Law, 2011).

Alongside the dominant focus on Macau as part of a flourishing Chinese Party-state there have also been entertainment programmes that have offered a 'softer', hybrid international outlook in their representation of Macau, similar to that of the Museu de Macau.[8] One such programme was a CCTV 'special' celebrating the tenth anniversary since the return of Macau to China in 2009 (*Qingzhu Aomen huigui zuguo shi zhounian wenyi wanhui*). While focusing on Macau as part of a great Chinese nation, featuring youth with red ribbons dancing excitedly and singing 'We will create the future of China' (*women qu chuangzao huaxia de weilai*), the programme also included elements that suggested an interest in the blending of Chinese and foreign cultures. The opening dance featured a sprinkling of Caucasian children alongside Chinese-looking children. An on-stage orchestra combined Western instruments (e.g., timpani, violins, double bass, oboe, trumpet, xylophone, European metallic flutes) and Chinese ones (e.g., *erhu*, *pipa*, Chinese wooden flutes and Chinese cymbals). Dancers in various acts wore a mixture of traditional European and Chinese costumes.

Alongside two CCTV hosts, the programme also included two other hosts, Xia Li'ao (Julio Acconci) and his twin brother Xia Jianlong (Dino Acconci). Better known in the region as a fashionable pop duo caller Soler, the image of the Macanese-born brothers' 'mixed' racial identities[9] was co-opted in a way that assisted in the performance of particular national ideologies associated with Macau and China's global outlook. At one moment during the show, in a highly scripted dialogue in Mandarin during which a few lines of a Cantonese song were inserted (Cantonese is the language spoken by most local Chinese in Macau), the twins reminisced about growing up in Macau. During the dialogue, one curiously asked the other, 'Do you think you really know Macau?' to which the other replied 'Hey? I am a Macau/Aomen person [*wo shi Aomen ren*]. Of course I understand Macau.' This dialogue seemed to address an uncertainty over whether mixed-race/Eurasian Macanese are valid Chinese, by casting doubt and then affirming their inclusion (an unofficial profile on the Chinese search engine Baidu lists the twins as being Chinese citizens). Also significant is that the identity they resolutely expressed was a 'Macau' identity not a 'Chinese' one. Their dialogue seemed to be positioned to build a message of China's friendly stance towards foreign countries rather than to promote the (uncomfortable?) reality that some Macanese may have ancestors from Western or other Asian nations. The symbolism of mixed-race Macanese appeared to be appropriated in a way that shifted the discourse away from a focus on Macau–China unity towards a China–West friendship.

The Macanese hosts emphasized that Macau has 'temples' (read: Chinese temples) as well as 'churches' (read: Western churches), and stressed that people of many nationalities live in Macau, a point reinforced via an image of the audience that included Caucasian and Asian people. They framed Macau as a socially integrated, trendy, modern city and concluded their dialogue by stating in unison that the real uniqueness of Macau was its 'blending of China and the West, [where] the old and new reflect each other' (*Zhong-Xi ronghe, gujin huiyin*). While China and the West were presented as cooperating in a friendly manner, they were still presented as separate entities, and the question of mixed identities and who is really 'Chinese' in this new era remained somewhat ambiguous.

The Macanese hosts' dialogue was immediately followed by an image of the modern city of Macau with tall buildings and neon lights, symbolic of Macau's flourishing under the Chinese administration. Portuguese music was also played but was appropriated to make Portugal seem small, simple and insignificant. The quaint sound of an accordion formed the backdrop to the performance of a Portuguese folk dance (*Putaoya tufeng wu*) performed by Caucasian and Chinese singers and dancers wearing simple, traditional Portuguese costumes, playing simple folk instruments (one Caucasian woman played the triangle, with others on an acoustic guitar and accordion), and singing a simple folk song in Portuguese.[10] The performance of the quaint Portuguese folk culture in many ways mirrored the folk performances of China's ethnic minorities on CCTV that suggested a concern with 'preserving' the intangible cultural heritage of the exotic cultures within China, which is presented in stark contrast to the professional and modern mainstream national culture. Macau was presented as part of a flourishing Chinese nation that had extended a friendly hand to its former and old-fashioned colonizers.

Highlighting the ideological significance of the event, the live performance was attended by the then Chinese president Hu Jintao, who sat in the front row of the massive audience. Hu appeared with great fanfare at the beginning of the programme, and at the end he went on stage again to extend his hand of friendship to key performers. In a scene reminiscent of the Beijing 2008 Olympic Games, President Hu was seen singing 'Ode to the Motherland' (*Gechang Zuguo*) with his compatriots, this time appearing on the stage with the chairman of the Macau SAR, as well as performers who represented various groups of the Chinese nation through their dress (minority nationality costumes, red dresses) and appearance (e.g., mixed-race Macanese). The Caucasian performers also served to suggest China's friendship with foreign countries and the attraction of foreigners to Macau and China. Clapping and singing together en masse, no less a song about the 'victorious singing voices' (*shengli gesheng*), the 'five-starred red flag' (*wuxing hongqi*) and the 'dear motherland' (*qin'ai de zuguo*), constructed a powerful message of Chinese national unity that was inclusive of China's multiethnic population and its Special Administrative Regions such as Macau. The message of unity was coupled with a strong sense of a confident nation that had an international outlook.

Provincial satellite television has also highlighted China's vibrancy, modernity and commercial savviness through the themes of hybridity, cosmopolitanism and the inclusion of Macanese performers of mixed ethnic and national backgrounds. While in general there are not many performers from Macau on mainland television, in 2016, *Sing! China* (*Zhongguo xin shengyin*, lit: China New Voice), a rebranding of *The Voice of China*, on

Zhejiang Satellite Television, featured a contestant from Macau in its number one rating show (Season 5).[11] A-rui (Ari Fabio Calangi) wowed audiences and the coaches with his musical abilities and sense of rhythm as he played the guitar and used a vocal effects pedal (*xun huan qi*) as he sang Huang Qishan's 'Come Together' (*Yiqilai*), Mark Ronson and Bruno Mars' 'Uptown Funk' and Michael Jackson's 'Beat It' with a bit of Wang Feng's 'Swing Together' (*Yiqi yaobai*) mixed in. Online reports suggested particular interest in A-rui due to his 'unusual complexion', with one calling him a 'black singer' (*hei ren*) (Mei, 2016), and another explaining that he was born to a Filipino family in Macau (Song, 2016). A voiceover in the show called him a 'Macau mixed blood' (*Aomen hun xue'er*). Song (2016) notes that A-rui considered himself a local as he spoke all four languages used in Macau (Cantonese, Portuguese, English and Mandarin). In the show, however, a voiceover made a point of explaining that he just started learning *Putonghua* the previous year, and the coaches – megastars Jay Chou and Harlem Yu from Taiwan, and Na Ying and Wang Feng from the mainland – somewhat made fun of his *Putonghua* language skills, which was part of the entertainment value of having this 'insider-outsider' identity on the show. Despite some limitations, however, he managed to converse well enough with the coaches in Mandarin, highlighting his desire to engage with the mainland. A-rui had recently returned from studying at the prestigious Berklee College of Music in the United States and had begun a career in Hong Kong. His appearance on mainland China's top ranking show seemed to help fast-track his career, leading to performance opportunities across China as well as in Thailand and the Philippines. For mainland audiences, he offered something fresh in terms of both style and looks.

In the examples presented above, the visual, linguistic and musical semiotic resources were patterned to 'naturalize' Macau's 'reintegration' into the Beijing-centred Chinese nation-state. In the first example, at the time of the handover of Macau to the PRC in 1999, visual, linguistic and musical modes strongly reinforced a single 'hardened' attitude. Even if one disagreed, it was very difficult to miss the message that Macau is to China as a child is to his or her mother. The second example, shortly after the fanfare of the Beijing Olympic Games in 2008, showed how Macau was consistently made to visually, musically and linguistically 'blend' with (and into) the greater PRC-centred Chinese national entity, while Beijing-centred China remained the central, dominant force. The presentation of foreign symbols such as colonial architecture increased the potential for diverse readings, but was constrained through CCTV's reframing and reappropriation of the symbols, which became evidence of China's unity and strength. Of the televised events discussed above, the more recent shows after the handover have offered the greatest degree of ambiguity via the greatest incorporation of foreign semiotic elements embodied in the mixed racial identities of the Acconci twins and A-rui. During this period, the programmes not only emphasized messages of national unity, but also promoted China's openness to the world, which is important for building China's international image. Through popular cultural television performances, in both 'hardened' and somewhat 'softer' moments, a unified and revitalized image of the Chinese nation-state has been established and naturalized. This has been achieved by emptying the former colonial power of its significance and subtly marking the ongoing necessity of the Beijing-centred PRC administration in order to ensure the bright future of both Macau and China as a whole.

Imagining unification/unity with Taiwan

Taiwan sits opposite Fujian province in southern China across the Taiwan Straits and has a population of around 23 million. Although the PRC claims Taiwan as an inalienable part of its territory, the island has not become a Special Administrative Region of the PRC like Hong Kong and Macau. Since 1949, it has maintained its own statehood under the name of the Republic of China (ROC). After the Qing defeat in the Sino–Japanese war and the signing of the Treaty of Shimonoseki in 1895, Taiwan was ceded to Japan who ruled the island for 50 years until 1945 (Hughes, 2000: 64).[12] After Japan's defeat in World War II, the Allied forces committed to returning Taiwan to the ROC, the name for China at the time, which was run by the Nationalist Party. However, in the years following the expulsion of Japan, the civil war in mainland China resulted in victory by the Communist Party of China (CCP) who established the PRC in 1949, while the Nationalist Party fled to Taiwan (Hughes, 2000: 64). With American intervention, the Nationalist Party made the island of Taiwan the 'last battalion' of the ROC (Kirby, 2005: 110).

During the Cold War, Taiwan became a national cause for the Communist and Nationalist parties who both claimed to represent the true 'China' (Kirby, 2005: 107). When class-based revolutionary ideology was at its peak in the PRC mainland, interest in Taiwan faded (Yahuda, 2000: 30). While the mainland was embroiled in the Cultural Revolution (1966–76), the Nationalist Party battled its own cultural war in Taiwan, arguing that it was saving the traditional Chinese culture that was being destroyed by the Communists on the mainland (Cohen, 1991: 131–2). While, like the Communist Party, it was previously 'anti-traditionalist' in outlook, Cultural Renaissance Movements were launched by the Nationalist Party government to inculcate traditional Chinese culture and Confucian teachings in order to 'restore China' and thus present the ROC to the world as the 'real' China, the 'Free China', and the centre of Chinese culture (Lee and Huang, 2002: 109; Cohen, 1991: 131–2; Chun in Huang, 2010: 17). In the reform era, the PRC has reasserted its commitment to preserving and developing traditional Chinese culture. It has attempted to re-centre the mainland as the home of Chinese culture with Taiwan as a peripheral but essential part of the Chinese nation-state.

In 1978, the new PRC constitution mentioned the 'liberation' of Taiwan, while in 1983 the updated (and most recent) constitution emphasized the 'unification' of Taiwan (Yahuda, 2000: 30).[13] Under the PRC's 'one China policy', a requisite understanding for any country wishing to develop diplomatic relations with China, Taiwan is to be considered a province of China. It is to be excluded from international organizations that require statehood for membership, and the PRC has threatened the use of force to bring about unification if Taipei makes a formal declaration of Taiwan's independence from China (Hughes, 2000: 63). The CCP has offered Taiwan to join with the mainland in the 'one country, two systems' framework like Hong Kong and Macau, and has offered significant concessions to Taiwan, such as allowing it to keep its own government and armed forces (Hughes, 2000: 79). While economic relations across the Taiwan Straits are good, a deep sense of political distrust still exists. In September 2014, President Xi Jinping again proposed to apply the 'one country, two systems' framework to Taiwan, but this was rejected by his Taiwanese counterpart, President Ma Yingjiu (Ma Ying-jeou).

Some Taiwanese believe in unification but are waiting for a time when Beijing will allow greater freedom of speech, democracy and the rule of law. But many other people in Taiwan are waiting for the CCP to take their offers a step further and are agitating for a separate 'native' Taiwanese nation and identity. While most voters in Taiwan at present do not want to be politically united with the mainland, they have also been reluctant to take the risk of declaring formal independence (Hughes, 2000: 71, 79). This political limbo has led to the emergence of a state of 'creative ambiguity', which is a strategy of developing an ambiguous stance on the political issue so that both sides can benefit from developing social and economic ties. PRC music-entertainment programming may be seen as part of an attempt to frame Taiwan as naturally and intimately connected with mainland China and to relieve fears of the PRC as a threatening force.

For the 30 years prior to the late 1970s there were virtually no media or cultural exchanges between the two sides, and the Cold War mentality meant that people on both sides could be jailed for simply listening to, watching or reading 'smuggled in' material (Hong, 1996: 91–6). Taiwanese music and media only legally entered China in the mid-1980s (Cohen, 1991: 130). Mainland culture and media were only officially allowed to enter Taiwan in the late 1980s when the Taiwanese government began to relax its anti-communist stance. Restrictions lessened in the 1990s, sparking the exchange of entertainment television programming, and great attempts have been made to separate cultural from political content, resulting in an exponential increase in media and cultural exchanges, despite occasional political setbacks (Hong, 1996: 91–6). With the PRC state's gradual retreat from the social and economic life of its citizens, popular culture from Taiwan, as with Hong Kong, began to have a strong influence on the mainland.

After the Taiwanese government lifted restrictions on doing business with the mainland in 1987 (Lee and Huang, 2002: 114), and with the rapid economic development on the mainland since the early 1990s that increased the purchasing power of mainland urbanites particularly in big coastal cities, doing business with the mainland became attractive to Taiwanese investors, including in the music, television and film sectors (Chan, 2008: 17). Since then, Taiwanese companies have exported music, movies and television programmes as well as Taiwanese stars, who have become extremely popular in the mainland (Chan, 2008: 20). As with Hong Kong culture, mainland Chinese audiences found Taiwanese culture to be fresh, exciting and mysterious due to its different production values. At the same time, people and cultural products from Taiwan were popular because of linguistic and cultural proximity to the mainland. At times, the Communist government has expressed concerns about Taiwan's influence in China, deeming much of its culture 'unhealthy' and as having too much sex and violence, but also because, in satisfying public desires for sophisticated content, it fears creating unreasonable expectations that are not in line with its political goals (Hong, 1996: 96–103).

Re-uniting separated brothers and sisters

As Taiwan's unification with the mainland is still a contested issue, CCTV's music-entertainment programmes adopt slightly different strategies to those used to highlight unity with the people of Hong Kong and Macau. The events used to celebrate the unity of the cross-Straits Chinese family have primarily been based around politically safe traditional Chinese festivals, such as the Spring Festival/Chinese New Year and the Mid-Autumn Festival, rather than events developed to celebrate PRC political achievements such as the Chinese National Day (1 October), which was discussed in the earlier section on Macau. Yet like the narratives of the separation of mother and children in relation to Macau and separated family in relation to Hong Kong, the narrative of lost brothers and sisters especially among the older generation where siblings may have been split during the civil war is utilized to reflect on the mainland's relationship with Taiwan. To illustrate these points I draw on *The Same Song – Enters Taiwan – Mid-Autumn Day Special* (*Tongyi shouge – zoujin Taiwan – Zhongqiujie tebie jiemu*) broadcast in 2008.

Musically, visually and linguistically, the *Enters Taiwan* programme attempted to create a warm family atmosphere with a small group of people sitting around circular tables symbolizing reunion (*tuanyuan*), as is part of the tradition on Mid-Autumn Day. The opening scene featured a group of hosts and a crowd of people from both sides of the Taiwan Straits (*liang'an*) congregating on the stage singing and clapping happily together, acting out a 'family reunion'. In pairs made up of one mainland Chinese and one Taiwanese, they stepped out on stage and sang a song celebrating shared traditional customs, exchanged gifts of moon cakes and looked at the moon together. The song, which seemed to be composed specifically for this programme, culminated with everyone chanting together with the lyrics relating to cross-Straits unity and the special role that the CCTV programme *The Same Song* played in bringing the two sides together. It noted that for 'nine years' the family of 'singing voices' located in the three places (mainland, Hong Kong and Macau) on the two sides of the Taiwan Straits (*liang an san di*) have been happily singing 'the same song' together on Mid-Autumn Day, as they expressed their hopes for an even brighter future (metaphorically represented through 'beautiful flowers' and 'an ever-rounder moon').

The politically neutral moon theme continued with a duet between female mainland star Na Ying and male Taiwanese star Qi Qin, who sang the Chinese classic 'The Moon Represents My Heart' (*Yueliang daibiao wode xin*). This romantic ballad was originally made famous by the sweet-voiced and elegant Taiwanese superstar Deng Lijun (Teresa Teng), hugely popular in the 1970s and 1980s among Chinese speaking communities as well as in Japan and Indonesia, where she sang in local languages. Deng's songs were originally banned in mainland China due to her official support for the Nationalist Party and the Taiwanese army as she took on the role of 'patriotic entertainer'. Her sweet songs about love and romance, which captured the imagination of the Chinese people, were also thought by the Communist Party to pervert the minds of the people and divert them from socialist ideology, while in Taiwan her songs played a special role in comforting the general population after Taiwan's succession from the United Nations in the 1970s (Tsai, 2008: 224). While officially banned, she was still hugely popular with mainland audiences who accessed her music through pirated tapes. Having the same family name as Deng Xiaoping, China's paramount leader in the 1980s (with different spelling due to Romanization conventions in Taiwan and the mainland), a popular saying circulated: 'In the daytime Deng rules, and at night Teng rules, and both Dengs rule the whole of China' (Fung, 2007: 428; 2008a: 50). Once-banned artists like Deng Lijun are now symbols of Greater China unity as well as China's opening up and reforms, which have allowed for much greater creative freedoms for its people. This scene between Na Ying and Qi Qin singing Deng's sweet love song highlights how the same nostalgic pop song can be used for multiple purposes in different socio-historical circumstances (see Tsai, 2008: 225, 242). In this performance, Na Ying and Qi Qin were shown holding hands, looking at each other sweetly, arm in arm and providing a solid symbol of close cross-Straits relations.

In another song on *The Same Song – Enters Taiwan* programme, Taiwan's Chen Mingzhen (Jennifer Chen) called on someone from the audience to sing with her, explaining that she was very happy to get closer to mainland/inland friends (*neidi de pengyou*). Clearly choreographed, yet also attempting to provide a sense of the natural affinity and desire to get closer to those on the other side of the Taiwan Straits, a man in the audience, dressed up and ready with microphone stood up casually from his seat in the front row and joined her on stage. They held hands for the entire song and looked dreamy as they sang the beautiful classic 'Pray' (*Qidao*), originally a Japanese folk song 'Lullaby of Takeda' (*Takeda no Komoriuta*).

An elderly couple and teenagers in the audience looked on sweetly, smiling and clapping along, giving their approval for the union. At the same time, to paraphrase the lyrics, the song compelled everyone to look beyond the disappointments and to hope for a world where spring lasts forever, where the sun never sets and where success is forever around us. It was a classic case of a romantic ballad being simultaneously appropriated to promote the political rhetoric of harmony and reunion.

'Hardened', orthodox CCTV music entertainment productions have also made particular use of Taiwanese residents who have family in the mainland. In the context of Taiwan, 'mainlanders' or 'outside-province people' (*waishengren*) refers to the people who left the mainland for Taiwan at around the time of civil war (1945–9), as well as their offspring. This is in contrast to the 'native' Taiwanese population (*benshengren*) who migrated from the mainland to Taiwan in earlier times. It is through these 'mainlander' Taiwanese that the family unification discourse can be most succinctly embodied. Old people in *The Same Song – Enters Taiwan* programme provided tangible family links between Taiwan and the mainland, similar to a 'lost brothers' discourse, which was used to describe the relationship between Hong Kong and the mainland at the time of its return (Pan et al., 2001). The 'aunts' and 'uncles' interviewed by hosts shared how they 'missed' the mainland because they still had family there – mothers, fathers, brothers, and sisters. Sitting around a circular table (a symbol of unity) in the 'audience', an elderly couple shared with two hosts from CCTV their happiness and warm feeling (*wenxin*) at being able to celebrate the Mid-Autumn Festival with mainland compatriots. In expressing that they felt 'just like children', they implied that Taiwan is a child of the mainland/motherland. The dialogue also emphasized connections through the trope of 'hometowns' and the shared ability to converse in local accents, suggesting a sense of intimacy and authenticity.

Yet, while the hosts were curious to know why programme guests returned to their 'homes' to visit relatives, they were never asked to comment on reasons why they left the mainland in the first place, or what life in Taiwan has been like. Instead the focus was on 'missing' and 'separation' – with a clear attempt to generate a desire to reunite. These people, who had lived for approximately 60 years of their lives in a completely different socio-political context, were presented as 'the same' as their brothers and sisters who remained on the mainland – kind people who cared about family unity. By not specifically mentioning that these people were 'mainlanders', the programme implied that *all* Taiwanese were simply lost brothers and sisters of relatives on the mainland. However, by 1985 only 5.7 per cent of the population of Taiwan were born in mainland China, making a familial link distant. Nonetheless, most Taiwanese have experienced a Mandarin education system that linguistically draws them closer (Hughes, 2000: 75).

In the dialogue between the host and an elderly couple, the personal family narrative operated as a parable for a greater geopolitical story. The story suggested that the suffering of the mother was automatically linked to her missing her child, and that once reunited all 'illnesses' would be cured, suffering would disappear, and everyone would be happy:

MALE HOST: So, since you left your home, have you been back?
OLD MAN: I've been back twice.

MALE HOST: The main reason for going back was to visit friends and relatives?
OLD MAN: To visit relatives.
MALE HOST: Why did you go back the first time?
OLD MAN: The first time my mother was seriously ill, so I went to see my mother.
MALE HOST: And the result?
OLD MAN: The result was after my mother saw me, she wasn't ill, she was better.
MALE HOST: [She] missed her son!

At the end of the dialogue, the hosts asked their elderly guests to directly give their wishes and blessings to their relatives in the mainland and Taiwan as well as to the television audiences, thus symbolically uniting *all* mainland, Taiwanese and global Chinese viewers into one Greater China frame.

While two hosts from CCTV and two from Taiwan (as identified through on-text bracketing of 'Taiwan' next to the names of those from Taiwan) ran the programme, it was clearly a 'CCTV', PRC-centred production. Unlike *The Same Song* production in Hong Kong described earlier, the *Enters Taiwan* production offered no evidence of a being a joint production with a Taiwanese broadcaster or a commercial sponsor. It thus appeared to be predominantly ideologically motivated. There was an attempt to incorporate Taiwanese hosts to give the appearance of a mutually produced programme, but the Taiwanese hosts were not identified with any particular organization, suggesting that there was minimal (if any) institutional support from the Taiwanese side. Furthermore, unlike productions of *The Same Song* in other cities and countries, no clips of outdoor scenes were shown, and the indoor location was not revealed. The entire programme was performed in a dark indoor studio and was constructed as being on Taiwanese soil – judging by the programme name *Enters Taiwan* and the rhetoric of hosts and guests. Beyond these implications, there was little evidence that the programme was in fact shot in Taiwan, suggesting sensitivities regarding performing on Taiwanese soil.

Overall, the restricted nature of the visuals and verbal discourse and the selective use of nostalgic pop music and newly created chants with overtly political lyrics served to emphasize a clear, hardened PRC mainland message that Taiwanese and the PRC mainlanders are essentially and traditionally 'the same'. The programme also provided an opportunity to imagine perfect unity and harmony between the two sides, while socio-cultural and political differences between the two sides were generally avoided. CCTV producers and directors were therefore able to use the music-entertainment genre to carefully construct a preferred image of Taiwanese people as separated family and as culturally and ethnically 'the same' as mainland citizens.

Similar messages continued to be promoted on CCTV in 2016. For instance, during the 2016 *CCTV Spring Festival Gala*, male mainland Chinese actor and singer Hu Ge and 'China Taiwan' (*Zhongguo Taiwan*) singer Xu Ruyun (Valen Hsu), known for her soft and beautiful voice, sang 'A Great Love'

(*Xiangqin xiang'ai de yi jia ren*, lit: Family Who Love Each Other). Xu was popular in the mainland and Taiwan in the 1990s, but was still familiar to many audiences through her participation in the mainland Jiangsu Satellite Television musical reality show *Masked Singer* (*Mengmian gewang*) in 2015. In the 2016 *Gala*, Hu and Xu performed on the 'Eastern provinces stage' in Quanzhou in Fujian province (on the mainland side of the Taiwan Straits). The couple sang hand in hand and looked at each other lovingly, with the shorter Taiwanese woman singer looking up to the tall handsome mainland man. Dancers in colourful minority costumes could be seen in the background completing the representation of the big Chinese family. The song, which celebrates the Chinese tradition of going home to spend festivals with family, has been popular since the mid-1990s and has been frequently used in seasonal shows such as the Spring Festival and Mid-Autumn Day. The song includes lyrics that can double as a romantic song between any couple and as a message about the desired state of the cross-Straits relations. The lyrics explain that the two sides are looking in the 'same direction'; that they have shared feelings and emotions in both good times and bad; that they have 'different ideas' but that this should not be a cause for anger; and that they also have a desire to help and console each other in times of need, 'because we are family who love each other'.

Occasionally, Minnan culture and language are used to stress a flourishing and shared cross-Straits culture (e.g., Yan, 2008). Also known as Southern Fujian in mainland China and Hokkien outside of China, this dialect and culture is associated with residents and emigres from Fujian province in China, just across the straits from Taiwan, many of whom migrated to Taiwan and consider themselves as part of the native Taiwanese population (*benshengren*). This group of people moved to Taiwan before the Mandarin-speaking 'mainlanders' (*waishengren*, lit: outsiders), who fled to Taiwan after the civil war and who have dominated Taiwanese politics since 1949. Minnan culture has been actively promoted in Taiwan, particularly by independence activists to distinguish the 'Taiwanese' from the 'Chinese'. However, Minnan culture has also been increasingly appropriated by officials, academics and media workers from the mainland as well. For instance, in 2010 the mainland's Xiamen Satellite Television Station and the Taiwanese China Television Ltd (CTV) jointly hosted the *Minnan Spring Festival Eve TV Gala*, held in Xiamen, the capital of Fujian province (English.news.cn, 2010).

Taiwan's minority nationalities who are referred to collectively in the mainland as 'high mountain people' (*Gaoshanzu*) have also had their songs performed on mainland Chinese television, or have themselves performed on it. One of the earliest and most famous songs was *The Girls of Ali Mountain* (*Alishan de guniang*), performed by Hong Kong film star Xi Xiulan (born in mainland China) during the 1984 *CCTV Spring Festival Gala*. The song refers to the beautiful girls of the Tsou (Zou) aboriginal tribe, and is one of Taiwan's most popular folk songs. Pop stars who happen to be Taiwanese aboriginals have also occasionally appeared on

Chinese television. These include Power Station (Dongli huoche, Paiwan nation), Cai Yilin (Jolin Tsai, partly Taiya nation), Fan Yichen (Van Fan, Amis nation) and Zhang Huimei (Chang Hui-mei, commonly known as A-mei, Puyuma nation).[14] The specific tribal labels appear not to be usually used on mainland television.

Taiwanese pop stars' co-option of Chinese nationalism

Like Hong Kong stars, Taiwanese stars have also used songs to promote a sense of global Chinese solidarity. As noted in Chapter 2, 'Descendants of the Dragon', originally composed and sung by Taiwanese singer Hou Dejian, has become a popular song for generating a feeling of Greater Chinese national solidarity. In more recent years, Taiwanese pop star Wang Lihong's (Wang Leehom) cover of the song, which modernizes and globalizes it further, has been welcomed by Chinese television producers. Wang's version, which became a megahit in 2000, merged heavier rock and dance elements and a rap bridge that summarized his multiple identities as a Taiwanese migrant in the USA (Jaivin, 2001: 421). Wang, an American-born Chinese singer of Taiwanese parents, rapped in English about 'a girl and a homeboy' who came 'straight from Taiwan' without work or the ability to speak English and who persevered in difficult circumstances. Wang is known for blending traditional Chinese elements, including Beijing Opera, Chinese classical orchestra and aspects from the music of minority nationalities, with hip hop and R&B. In 2004 he travelled to remote villages across China to collect sounds for his 'chinked out' album.[15] With his rapid rap lyrics including a mention of 'god', his CCTV performances have slightly shifted what is acceptable in a context where religion is rarely touched upon.

Wang has worked in various nationalistic readings of the song depending on the location of his performance in order to appeal to diverse audiences. His performances on CCTV have fit with a trend towards creating a greater sense of 'interactivity' with audienceswhile creating a sense of solidarity. As part of his style he has used the audiences' knowledge of the lyrics to fill in the blanks. The words he has passed over to the audience to articulate have all been associated with the Chinese mainland or Chineseness. A call and response tactic in one CCTV performance played out as follows:

WANG: Its name is called: 'everyone, let's sing together' [He holds out the microphone for audience members to say 'Yellow River']

...

Its name is [called] [He lets the audience sing 'China']

...

They are all: what kind of people? [He lets the audience sing 'Descendants of the Dragon'.]

Wang used similar tactics during a concert in Taipei, Taiwan, but tapped into a different, local Taiwanese identity. He similarly omitted saying all the place names in the mainland, but when it came to the part that normally reads 'Its name is the Yellow River', he instead shouted out 'What's the river called?' then answered 'Tamsui River, right?' The Tamsui is Taiwan's third largest river, which flows into the Taiwan Straits (i.e., from the opposite side to the Yellow River). In this performance, he simultaneously appealed to a common Chinese racial identity calling on 'all the black-eyed, black-haired, and yellow-skinned [people]' and marked himself out specifically as 'this ABC' (American-born Chinese).

Wang has also played with the politics of identity in relation to China's multiethnic make-up, as occurred during his performance of 'Descendants of the Dragon' in 2009 on CCTV's *The Same Song – Entering Into Ningxia, Qingxi Hui Village* (*Zoujin ningxia, qingxi hui xiang*). This was a special programme that served to celebrate 60 years of the New China and the establishment of the Ningxia Hui Autonomous Region in northern China. As with Hong Kong star Xie Tingfeng's performance in Inner Mongolia, Wang's performance of greater Chinese nationalism criss-crossed with CCTV's multi-ethnic identity frame, creating a richly entangled view of Chinese people and their place in the nation and the world.

Performing on a huge stage adorned with the dazzling neon outline of Islamic-style structures typically associated with the Hui Muslims in the area, Wang greeted the audiences as 'all the descendants of the dragon' and as 'all the Bahamut people'. Bahamut is a fish that supports the earth in Arabian mythology and subtly links to the Hui heritage. It is also a powerful dragon deity from a role-playing game called 'Dungeons and Dragons' whose exact colour is hard to specify and whose guise changes in different settings – just as Wang's does. Wang's attempt to 'localize' the dragon metaphor provided a link between the traditional Hui, the 'ordinary' Chinese people in the audience, and the contemporary 'outsider' Taiwanese–American–Chinese pop star who represents the modern Chinese identity.

After performing 'Descendants of the Dragon' as a solo with back-up dancers on *The Same Song – Entering Into Ningxia*, Wang was then asked to by the host Liang Yongbin to play the song again with Hui minority women. These women wore 'traditional' costumes and played along with their *kouxian*, a traditional 'minority' mouth-harp. A short dialogue with Wang allowed Liang to ease into a discourse that was more within the *yuanshengtai* frame. Host Liang assumed his educator voice as he introduced the exotic instrument and proudly announced that it was a 'first grade national intangible heritage [item]' (*guojia yiji feiwu wenhua yichan*). Wang positively expressed his interest in China's minority nationality instruments in response to Liang's questions.

In the performance, Wang backed the women on the *kouxian* using his Western acoustic guitar. Although it didn't really sound like 'Descendants of the Dragon' until host Liang Yongbin started singing along, visually and aurally the performance offered a unique and creative blend of instruments and an unlikely collaboration between the megastar and 'unknown' rural, minority folk. Wang's presence and his ability to attract audiences helped to highlight China's vibrancy and cosmopolitanism while subtitles along the bottom of the screen provided further details to educate audiences about the *kouxian* and Hui people. This *yuanshengtai*-pop hybrid musical performance of 'Descendants of the Dragon' enabled the unification of an array of internal and external Chinese identities. As with the performances of Xie Tingfeng, Wang Lihong had the star factor necessary to draw audiences who could then be educated on state-sanctioned ideals of Chinese national identity through dialogue inserted between songs. Wang more recently sang 'Descendants of the Dragon' during the 2012 *CCTV Spring Festival Gala* in a fiery rock version with an electric guitar shaped like a metallic dragon, highlighting CCTV's welcoming of creative ways of performing the Chinese national identity, and a new acceptance of the rock music genre that was rarely performed on CCTV in earlier years. The inclusion of entertaining and friendly Taiwanese pop stars has helped to highlight the natural interconnectedness between the mainland and Taiwan. At the same time, propaganda has also been a motive of the Taiwanese as it has strived to impress mainland Chinese audiences with Taiwan's affluence, high living standards, modern lifestyle and liberal social environment.

Embracing racial hybridity: Fei Xiang (Kris Phillips)

The first 'Taiwanese' performer to appear on the *CCTV Spring Festival Gala* was Fei Xiang (Kris Phillips). Born in Taiwan to an American father and Chinese mother, he was he was an American citizen (Culture Express, 2007). Fei became an overnight star in mainland China after his 1987 performance. Jiayang Fan (2012) in *The New Yorker* aptly described Fei as 'a statuesque six foot three' with 'chiseled features, a voluminous pompadour, and miraculous gray-blue eyes' who wore 'a shiny red single-breasted tux'. She described Fei as an 'unlikely star' who appeared at a time of considerable change 'when Taiwan was denied acknowledgement and America was still largely the model of a "capitalist roader"'. Fei, she suggested, 'offered himself as the consummate canvas onto which a generation of Chinese could imagine the forbidden glamour of the West in the familiar melody of murmured Mandarin tunes'. Chinese language sources similarly describe how seeing the 'mixed-blood Chinese–American young man' (*Zhong-Mei hunxue de xiao huozi*) was for many mainland Chinese 'just as exciting as lining up at KFC for the first time'. His handsome, tall figure and mysteriously foreign 'blue eyes' are said to have conquered the hearts of a billion 'ordinary people' (Ri, 2001: 46).

Already popular in Taiwan and Southeast Asia, Fei Xiang brought to the mainland a sense of freshness and energy in his singing and dancing style as well as through his exotic racial identity. In the latter part of the 1980s, every avenue and narrow alley was said to have been burning with Fei Xiang's upbeat 'Flame in the Winter' (*Dongtian li de yi ba huo*), a cover of the song 'Sexy Music' first made popular by Irish sisters' group the Nolans in 1980. The Nolan's rendition won the grand prize at the tenth Tokyo Music Festival in 1981 and became a number one hit in Japan. The song was covered in Chinese translation in the same year by Taiwanese singer Gao Lingfeng (Frankie Kao) as 'Flame in the Winter' (*Dongtian li de yi ba huo*), the version that Fei Xiang took to the mainland Chinese market with overnight success. He subsequently sold two million copies of his album of the single. While the original English song was not a feature of Chinese television, references to the English version started to seep into the global reality singing contests in a hybrid fashion in more recent years. For instance, *The Voice of China* Season 2 in 2012 featured ethnic Yi star Jike Junyi (Summer) singing the English version in a duo with fellow contestant Liu Haolin (Harlin Liu) who sang the Chinese version in his representative hoarse voice and original Chinese rap lyrics. The English words 'sexy music' were also inserted into the Chinese version of the song in Zhang Jingying's (Jane Zhang) performance of 'Flame in the Winter' in *I Am a Singer* Season 3.

During the 1987 *CCTV Spring Festival Gala*, Fei was seen pecking his maternal grandmother on the cheek, a gesture Fan (2012) suggests must have been completely alien to the Chinese audiences at the time. He explained how he came to the mainland to visit his grandmother who had been separated from the rest of the family and was living alone since the rift between Taiwan and the mainland in 1949. While this initial visit may have put him at some risk of being blacklisted by the Taiwanese government, he subsequently came to play a symbolic role in cross-Straits 'reunification', particularly in CCTV's constructions of his identity where he is has been marked, not as American, but as being from 'China Taiwan' (*Zhongguo Taiwan*).

While he gained stardom in China, Fei made a career for himself in both Asia and the US. After spending some time on Broadway, he 'returned' to China in 1997 (Song, 2002: 58). His return instilled a sense of nostalgia among many fans who had grown up with his songs. This nostalgia allowed audiences to reflect on their own development over this time and on China's progress as a whole. Revisiting Fei Xiang's sexy, vigorous dance moves and amorous song lines, thought to be exciting and even shocking at the time, reminded audiences of the 'beautiful' innocence of their youth (Song, 2002: 58) as well as their naivety in relation to developments outside of the Chinese mainland, thus highlighting how much they had changed and developed.

A former director of the 1987 *CCTV Spring Festival Gala* who appeared on stage during the 2008 CCTV special *Sounds of Singing Over 30 Years* (*Gesheng Piao Guo 30 Nian*) reminisced on how she had ordered the cameraman during the shooting of the show to zoom in on Fei's face to protect innocent audiences by restricting their view of his shocking dance movements – movements that seemed rather quaint by 2008 standards. A number of commentators argued that Fei Xiang returned to China in the late 1990s as a much more 'mature' artist (Ri, 2001: 47; Song,

2002: 58). But this quite possibly also reflected a self-sense of maturity of the Chinese mainlanders as well. From the way he was framed on CCTV, Fei Xiang has come to symbolize a China that was still in its early stages of 'opening up'. At the 2012 *CCTV Spring Festival Gala*, ethnically Chaoxian (Korean) Chinese pop singer Jin Mei'er (introduced in Chapter 4) enthusiastically sang and danced 'Flame in the Winter', reflecting back on Fei Xiang's classic, and highlighting a contemporary penchant for mixing ethnic influences and performance styles.

During the 1987 Gala, Fei Xiang also performed a powerful but slower song called 'Clouds of My Hometown' (*Guxiang de yun*). China's image as a rapidly developing and modernizing nation was also highlighted in Fei Xiang's subsequent video for 'Clouds of My Hometown', which was rebroadcast on CCTV3's MTV programme as late as 2008 and performed live again by Fei Xiang during the 2012 *CCTV Spring Festival Gala*. The music video 're-claims' Fei Xiang as China's 'own', a trend that Moskowitz (2010: 6) has noted more broadly of singers from outside the mainland. He is depicted in Shanghai standing on top of a skyscraper on a helipad (a sign of technology and modernization) with views of a modern city. He is also shown on an escalator, riding on the underground, walking across a large modern bridge, standing on the side of a freeway and looking up at a helicopter and up at the buildings and the sky, turning around with his arms outstretched, and admiring the development of the city with a sense of personal ownership and pride. In the lyrics, the 'wind' and the 'clouds' and the 'soil' 'call' (*huhuan*) him back to his 'hometown' and command him not to go roaming far away again (*bie zai sichu piaobo*). His homecoming was marked by his deep, resonating and 'mature' male voice. Instrumentally, he was supported by a throbbing bass drum, the uplifting call of trumpets and choral backing, and the 'open heart' sound of the panpipes – together suggesting a mounting pace and urgency to return and take in the immense changes that Shanghai (and China) has undergone. While also featuring a close-up of his 'blue eyes' and thus his 'foreignness', throughout this song and music video, Fei Xiang asserted his Chinese side by claiming the PRC mainland as his 'home'.

Like other transnationals and people of 'mixed race' backgrounds, Fei Xiang has been able to successfully 'take advantage of multiple, dynamic, and ambiguous racialized spaces' (Mahtani, 2002: 425) and has 'strategically employed' certain aspects of his identity (Mahtani, 2002: 429) to fit into the particular racially ambiguous space of Chinese television. At the same time, CCTV has also made use of Fei's racial mixture as well as his idiosyncratic dance styles, Broadway-style singing, and deep voice that were new and refreshing to Chinese audiences. While Fei Xiang has been perhaps one of the most ethnically 'exotic' performers to have represented Taiwan on mainland music-entertainment shows, numerous other Taiwanese stars have performed with a similar effect of establishing a cosmopolitan image of China that is open to cultural influences from 'the outside' and educating audiences about China's modernization.

154 *Greater China*

Performing solidarity with overseas Chinese

While Hong Kong, Macau and Taiwan are all claimed by the PRC as part of its territory through the politics of geography, Chinese who live abroad in other global jurisdictions have also been incorporated within the vision of a global Chinese collective. Having left China at different times, and dispersed and integrated into different areas around the world, overseas Chinese are far from a single monolithic group. Large numbers of Chinese settled in Southeast Asia in colonial times. Many of these people re-migrated to Western countries such as the USA, Canada and Australia in the 1970s. They were able to do so as a result of changing immigration policies in Western nations and more efficient transport and improved telecommunications technology. They were also prompted to move as a result of increased anti-Chinese discrimination in the newly constructed post-colonial Southeast Asian nations (e.g., Indonesia and Malaysia). The Southeast Asian diasporic Chinese were joined in Western nations by Chinese from Taiwan who feared the possibility of mainland military intervention, and later by (often more affluent) emigres from Hong Kong in the late 1980s and early 1990s who perceived political uncertainties with the imminent return of Hong Kong to the PRC (Ma, 2003: 1–2).

During the 1980s, as part of its open-door policy, the PRC government began to send thousands of nationals overseas on scholarships to study (mainly postgraduate degrees). Large numbers of students stayed on. Following the Tiananmen crackdown in 1989, the USA, Canada, Australia and other countries offered asylum to students after a period of strategic lobbying by students who were at the centre of anti-CCP dissident politics (Gao, 2009: 131–2; Nyíri et al., 2010: 52). Continuing economic prosperity in China, increasing ease of exit from China, and increased global business opportunities have opened the way for further waves of migration from China to Western countries, with migrants often first gaining entry on student visas and choosing to stay on.[16] Chinese students arriving in global cities in the post-Tiananmen era have come at younger ages to study at undergraduate and high school levels, and have the financial ability from their families to support themselves to study abroad rather than rely on Chinese government scholarships. Unlike the previous generation of students, many contemporary overseas Chinese students have been willing to defend China, a country that provided them with a good early education and the chance to grow up in a relatively prosperous and increasingly pluralistic society (Nyíri et al., 2010: 51).

As China's international prestige has grown alongside its economic prosperity, large numbers of Chinese migrants have returned to mainland China to invest as well as to visit their ancestral land. Vast amounts of Chinese overseas capital have flowed into China with a significant impact on the Chinese economy. Many overseas Chinese today travel frequently between China, Hong Kong or Taiwan, and their adopted countries. Many have developed cosmopolitan outlooks and multiple identities 'each with a mix of ethnic, cultural, economic and political attributes' to flexibly adapt to different contexts (Ma, 2003: 31–6).

Media reaching out to overseas Chinese is backed by organizations with competing interests. The CCP has been active in its attempts to promote its official state version of Chinese identity to overseas Chinese, with television programming playing an important role. Such programmes have had a strong impact on the continuing sense of being Chinese for many overseas Chinese peoples as they live among non-Chinese (Wu, 1991: 160, 177; Ma, 2003: 36–7; Sun, 2002, 2010). PRC media, however, increasingly clashes with such competitors such as the New York-based New Tang Dynasty Television, founded by a group of Falun Gong practitioners, which has local subsidiaries that reach in various global locations.

PRC television constructs and frames overseas Chinese in particular ways. It has tended to focus on Chinese students and entrepreneurs living overseas, often with the assumption that any Chinese person depicted in the programmes is a Chinese national who will maintain close links with the PRC state, and who will eventually return 'home' after gaining knowledge and experience overseas. Overseas Chinese are expected to support national reunification, be patriotic and love the motherland (see Guo, 2004: 44–5). Any mention of Chinese having foreign citizenship or dual allegiances is generally avoided in China's music-entertainment programmes. Rhetoric that serves to distinguish between Chinese and foreign nationals of Chinese ethnicity is also generally absent.

The Same Song *overseas*

When *The Same Song* travelled to overseas locations such as Vancouver, New York and London, it tended to focus on the 'Chinese' residents there rather than any other local group. The titles of the programmes and introductory and final acts packaged the shows as having the aim of building friendly bilateral relations through cross-cultural exchange between two countries. However, examination of the episodes as a whole revealed a much greater focus on the framing of foreign places as part of a great 'Chinese world'. That is, foreign cultural landscapes were almost always rendered 'Chinese'. By moving the 'same' CCTV stage around the world, by drawing in overseas Chinese to participate as audiences, and by intermingling with performers flown in directly from the PRC especially for the event, the productions looked almost identical to any other that took place in cities across China.

Drawing on the words of Pal Nyíri, who came to similar conclusions in a study of Chinese tourists' perceptions of Western Europe, programmes like *The Same Song* attempted to 'assert its cultural authority over foreign landscapes'. Nyíri found that written guides and people who introduce attractions to Chinese tourists 'reject, or more precisely, do not engage with, locally dominant representations of the localities' (Nyíri, 2005: 52). CCTV's roaming music-entertainment programmes likewise paid little or no attention to local representations of the foreign places they visited, but rather had their own 'master cultural narrative[s]' for enacting each foreign space in a 'standardized' way (Nyíri, 2005: 48).

As Nyíri (2005: 52) argues, the 'lack of attention' to local subjectivities 'is linguistically manifested in the wanton misnaming (or renaming) of sites'.[17] In CCTV music-entertainment productions, renaming has been conducted through the use of Chinese language in the form of voiceovers, hosts' speech and on-screen text that frames each place, as well as through choice of music and visuals. For instance, in *The Same Song – Enters England* programme in early 2008, large Chinese characters for London (*Lundun*) were stamped across the screen during the programme promo, in front of a backdrop of visual stills of historic buildings including Westminster Abbey and London Bridge, virtually the only outdoor images of England seen during the entire programme. They were accompanied by the slow 'archaic' sounds of bagpipes and a deep, authoritative voice of a Chinese-speaking male who further marked the city as 'historic'. This combination of language, image and music seemed to construct London as a relic of the past. It was starkly contrasted to the modernity of China and its lively cultural productions, marked by a sudden shift to contemporary, upbeat music and the unleashing of rapid images of the CCTV evening concert and CCTV's own cosmopolitan star performers who were actively moving around the globe. While the programme claimed to be 'revealing China–England culture and customs' and 'the hearts/minds of both sides' through 'musical communications', as well as 'transmitting the Olympic spirit' and 'praising the Olympics and the Year of China', it was really much more about the latter.

Interestingly, in *The Same Song – Enters Vancouver* (February 2007), the choice of Chinese characters used to translate the name of the city brought it directly into a family-like relationship with China. The characters for Vancouver in Chinese (*wen-ge-hua*) literally translate as 'warm-brother-Chinese'. Like the *Enters England* programme, the vast number of Vancouver faces in the programme, including practically the entire indoor audience as well as performers, were Chinese-looking. There was only a sprinkling of Caucasian or 'foreign' faces in the audience and very few non-Chinese performers. Even though ethnic Chinese are a significant minority in Vancouver,[18] the programme re-created a scene where the on-screen audiences looked exactly like the audiences who appeared on shows produced in China. The scattering of Caucasian Canadians were like the 'foreigners' who appear in the audiences of many mainland-based programmes, while the majority of Vancouver's people appeared to be 'just like us'. Just as in films, television dramas and fiction, CCTV's global roaming music-entertainment programmes clearly went to great efforts to produce a sense of 'familiarity' for its viewers by turning global cities of the West into 'national sites' (Nyíri, 2005: 46; also see Sun, 2002: 67–111).

Ethnic Chinese people living abroad who participated in *The Same Song* were given few opportunities to perform 'foreign' or 'hybrid' identities no matter how long they had lived abroad, although in some instances they tried. For instance, in the *Enters England* production, one young female, presumably a student, when asked her name in an entirely Chinese-speaking production gave her English name, noting that she had been living in England for six years. However, similar to the case with 'mainlanders' in Taiwan, hosts never dwelt on the multiple influences on their identities, and no questions were ever asked about the process of adjusting to British culture, why emigres departed China or whether they intended to return. The length of time away was simply linked to the amount of time they had been separated from the motherland. The hosts equated living in England for six years with missing home for six years. This gave the impression that all Chinese people overseas are fully committed to their Chinese cultural backgrounds and to China no matter where they are or how long they have been outside China.

Like the programmes staged in Western countries, *The Same Song* in Japan in 2007 highlighted 'friendly' bilateral relations between the two countries in the programme's promotional rhetoric. As in other programmes, *The Same Song* itself was credited for the special role it played in bringing the 'two sides' together. While the 'two sides' seemingly refers to Chinese and Japanese nationals, the show was much more about bringing together overseas Chinese in Japan with compatriots in the PRC. In an attempt to solidify the spirit of a Greater Chinese national identity, a Chinese national 'entrepreneur' who presumably lived in Japan exemplified this collective feeling when he went on stage to say he was 'very happy that *The Same Song* had come to Japan and that this was a big celebration for the overseas Chinese community [*huaren shehui*]'.

The link between Chinese people in Japan and in China was also extended to incorporate on-screen audience members in the production, a technique used across CCTV music-entertainment programmes to give the impression that 'ordinary' audience members at each international location are united with their Chinese brothers and sisters in mainland China. One host walked into the audience with his microphone and questioned a man about his origins. When the man told the host he was from Beijing, the host emphasized their hometown connections, rather over-enthusiastically remarking 'as soon as I heard [you] I knew you must have been a *laoxiang* [a person from the same town]'. He shook the man's hand, who smiled cautiously, then asked him how long he had been in Japan. The man responded 'over ten years'. The hosts did not ask about how he had negotiated cross-cultural relations or changed as a result of moving to Japan. Instead, he moved on to enquire about his family (drawing on the family metaphor), and had a discussion in Mandarin Chinese with the man's daughter who was sitting beside her father:

HOST: How old are you?
GIRL: This year I'm nine years old.
HOST: How many years have you been in Japan?

GIRL: Nine years [laughter from audience].
HOST: What song do you like?
GIRL: I want to hear 'My Motherland' (*Wo de zuguo*).
HOST: Oh, can you sing it?
GIRL: Yes.
HOST: Can you sing it for us?

While standing in front of her seat in the audience, the girl then took the microphone and sang the first stanza of the song perfectly. The first stanza's lyrics detail a naturally idyllic life beside a wide river. Yet the song was frequently performed on CCTV with strong force, often by distinguished female Party singer Guo Lanying and younger 'national style' stars such as Song Zuying, Zhang Ye and Peng Liyuan (President Xi Jinping's wife), as well as by other state-affiliated popular music artists such as Han Hong. Regular CCTV audiences were likely to know that the rest of the lyrics were aimed at celebrating a 'beautiful', 'heroic' and 'strong motherland' – 'the place where I grew up'. The dynamics at this moment are significant for understanding the way in which Chinese families abroad have been constructed in carefully structured CCTV programming for a mainland and greater Chinese television audience. This girl had apparently spent her whole life thus far in Japan, but at nine years old demonstrated her Chinese identity through her perfect Mandarin and perfect rendition of one of the most patriotic Chinese songs. One could speculate that the audience laughter highlighted recognition of an apparently incongruous situation of appearing to be so patriotic to China but potentially never having lived in China. However, the performance seemed to suggest that even if one isn't physically living in the mainland, one's Chinese heart is there – just as in the case of the Chinese heart that lasted for more than 300 years under Portuguese rule in Macau, and under British rule in Hong Kong, as suggested by Zhang Mingmin in his song 'My Chinese Heart' performed at the 1983 *CCTV Spring Festival Gala*.

Indeed, it is no coincidence then that that next song was 'My Chinese Heart', sung by the Chinese hosts, Chinese PhD students studying in Japan and Chinese entrepreneurs working in Japan who had gathered on the stage together. This song was constructed to look like an impromptu feature. Without instrumental backing, they sang together out of tune (the out of tune nature helped to give the impression of being an unstudied and impromptu act of unity), arms over each other's shoulders and swaying from side to side in an obvious attempt to construct an image of national camaraderie. Even if the performers seemed somewhat uncomfortable on stage, the attempt to provide a message of transnational Chinese unity was made abundantly clear.

Along with entrepreneurs, students were a key feature of overseas Chinese productions on *The Same Song*. Reducing the possible reasons why Chinese wished to leave the mainland to their desire to expand their knowledge enabled students to be held up as a kind of model for viewers and linked them to China's development and integration with the world at the highest level. The emphasis on studying carried with it an assumption that one can learn knowledge that does not interfere with a stable, fixed cultural background. This aligned perfectly with the design of the programme which itself 'travelled' abroad, but culturally barely changed. In *The Same Song – Enters England* programme, around 30 representative Chinese students came onto the stage, many wearing sweaters with 'London' or the name of a prestigious British university, tapping into the pride and prestige of studying at some of the most elite universities in the world. Yet what individual student representatives emphasized was not their life in England, but the fact that 'even though we aren't in the motherland', 'our hearts are joined together', and that they would 'study hard' (implying that they would make the motherland proud).

Songs and the image of singing together have been used to demonstrate a patriotic and united identity. In the *Enters England* programme, the students together with male singer Guo Feng, who gained significant exposure on CCTV prior to the Olympic Games for solidarity-building songs, sung 'Fill the World with Love' (*Rang shijie chongman ai*). This song, which was frequently heard on television music-entertainment programmes in the wake of the massive Sichuan earthquake (12 May 2008) which killed at least 69,000 people, provided a strong link between the overseas students and their compatriots back home. The image and feeling of global Chinese solidarity was reinforced visually with students singing together, arm in arm, hand in hand, swaying together from side to side as a collective, along with members of the audience who also sang along, smiling happily and waving glow sticks together in the dark.

In the context of overseas student lives, the lyrics 'you will never be alone again' seemed to imply that living in England must be a lonely experience, and that any Chinese student who goes there must be making a sacrifice to be away from one's family and homeland. This relates to Yang's (2002: 200) observation of urban Chinese 'going to alien lands where they must struggle to survive through their own labour and wits' as being comparable to 'the image of city people in the Cultural Revolution going down to the harsh life of physical labour on a production brigade in the countryside'. Given such 'hardships' they need to be reminded through CCTV's presence and through the lyrics that there is a support group, that fellow villagers and countrymen and women are always standing by, holding their hand, wiping their tears, sharing the same happiness, the same burdens and the same hopes, and going through the same ups and downs. The 'warmth that will never change', encased in the touching sentimentality of the sweet melody, emphasized a preferred reading of the naturalness of this united feeling. While popular television dramas in the 1990s like *A Beijinger in New York* (*Beijing ren zai Niuyue*) dispelled myths that one could rely on relatives overseas (Yang, 2002: 202; Sun, 2002), contemporary CCTV music-entertainment programmes like *The Same Song* have tried hard to reconstruct this myth by suggesting that all Chinese people, no matter where in the world they live, are part of one big Chinese family who are there to support them as they support the development of China.

The imagination of patriotic Chinese overseas who continue to show a desire to identify with the motherland suggests the existence of a 'global Chinese village' that achieves cohesion through shared support for the Chinese nation (Sun, 2002: 192). This sense of patriotism in turn increases political legitimacy for the Chinese government (Sun, 2002: 190). In stressing a strong cultural unity between Chinese in foreign lands and those 'at home', the Chinese state (via the media) have also tapped into Chinese fears 'of being corrupted by alien outside forces' and of losing their 'self and identity' (Yang, 2002: 202–3). The 'world' of the song 'Fill the World with Love' and the world created by *The Same Song* programme also reflected a global Chinese village that shared characteristics with the multiethnic frame. While in the multiethnic frame the imagined Han centre is surrounded by colourful minorities dotted around its boundaries, in the global view the dominating 'Chinese' group is surrounded by a sprinkling of white and black foreigners.

As Sun (2002: 213) suggests, many homesick and nostalgic overseas Chinese like to reconnect with their 'homeland' and maintain links with China through such television productions. This suggests that Chinese music-entertainment programmes play particularly important roles for Chinese migrants who have departed the mainland. However, the programmes themselves are not necessarily designed to actually encourage these overseas Chinese to return home. The issue of return to China has been cautiously side-stepped in the productions. According to an International Organization for Migration study of Chinese students studying in Europe in the early 2000s – mainly in the UK, Germany and France – only 30 per cent of them returned home (Omelaniuk, 2005: 194). In fact, since 1949 the PRC government has had a fairly passive policy towards the return of overseas Chinese, and has had a policy of supporting and encouraging them to freely settle in host countries, to assume the nationality of host countries and live in harmony with their people. Returning overseas Chinese have added to social problems as their re-integration has not always been a smooth process. Some have had difficulty finding work, particularly as a result of high salary expectations, and others have placed a heavy burden on the state given its preferential policies for returned overseas students. If unsatisfied back in China the fear is they may return to the foreign country, escalating the financial cost and damaging China's global reputation. On the other hand, since the 1990s, overseas Chinese who are often highly skilled are welcomed back to China for investments and expertise (Omelaniuk, 2005; Liu, 2005). Thus, maintaining positive family links with overseas students and entrepreneurs, encouraging them not to 'forget' China, is in China's interest in relation to its ongoing economic and scientific development.

Overall, the focus of *The Same Song* programmes shot in locations outside the mainland was on creating a sense of greater Chineseness that extended beyond the borders of China. The orthodox moments described here on CCTV and *The Same Song* in particular clearly attempted to establish the PRC mainland as the political centre for all Chinese, and was invested with having the power to bring Chinese people from all regions of Greater China and around the world harmoniously together.

With some differences reflecting different political situations and sensitivities, Chineseness appears to have been defined in similar ways in CCTV music-entertainment programmes shot in Hong Kong, Macau, Taiwan and abroad in Vancouver, London and Japan. In the hardened, orthodox moments discussed above, there was no evidence of any particular desire to engage directly with differences within the Greater Chinese population or to inform mainstream PRC audiences about them, let alone the cultures and histories of non-Chinese populations from foreign countries. Unlike the multiethnic frame, internal difference within the global Chinese community has been strongly downplayed in preference for the image of a single, global Chinese family.

Overseas Chinese and the China Dream

Reality television shows have promoted the image of greater Chinese solidarity in a slightly different way. They have been particularly adept at showing overseas Chinese returning to China to pursue their singing dreams, which has helped to frame China as a vibrant cosmopolitan country that is full of opportunity and potential. The stories of overseas Chinese contestants have also been used to highlight that although they may have some cultural differences to mainlanders, the overseas Chinese have maintained an essential Chineseness or dedication to China regardless of how long their families had been abroad. Their stories have also been used as opportunities to promote the global spread of Chinese language and culture. Producers for shows like *The Voice of China* on Zhejiang Satellite Television and *Sing My Song* on CCTV3 have actively recruited overseas Chinese contestants through auditions in foreign countries such as the United States, Canada, Singapore, Malaysia and Australia.

Chen Yongxin (Melody Tan), a 21-year-old Malaysian Chinese descendant (*huayi*), for instance, competed in the third season of *The Voice of China* in 2014. During her performances she explained that 'ever since I was young my dad always hoped I would study Chinese well. I also like to sing Chinese songs.' She thanked her coach, mainland singer Yang Kun, for 'leading me into this big family' (*dai wo jinru zheme da de jiating*) and noted that 'after the broadcast, I received much support from overseas Chinese [*haiwai huaren*]'. Audiences were shown images of Malaysian newspaper reports that featured her success on the stage in China. In her battle round with Liu Ke from Nanchang in Jiangxi province, the young overseas Chinese girl and the mainland Chinese boy held hands, looked and smiled at each other nervously, sang a sweet love song in harmony, and later shared a sweet exchange with tears in their eyes, hugging each other as cameras swirled around them. Singing and speaking predominantly in Mandarin, such interactions framed overseas Chinese as being committed to the project of Greater Chinese unity which is centred in China.

Sixteen-year-old Langgalamu (Vanatsaya Viseskul) from Thailand who also competed on the *Voice of China* Season 4, 2015, provided another entry point into a collective Chinese identity. This Thai Chinese descendant had an unlikely obsession with Deng Lijun (Teresa Teng) (introduced above), the popular Taiwanese singer who had died 20 years earlier. Dubbed by some as the Thai Teresa Teng, Langgalamu's performances would no doubt have served as a point of memory and nostalgia for the older generation who grew up with Deng's beautiful soft ballads. In a documentary about Langgalamu on Beijing Television after her appearance on *The Voice of China*, audiences were given a glimpse into her life in Thailand and interest in Chinese language and China, made possible through her love for the Chinese pop star. The programme followed Langgalamu as she returned home to Thailand after a year in China where she went to study and sing. Langgalamu explained that until she was seven she only sang Thai songs, but her parents brought her a disk of Deng Lijun after travelling to Hong Kong and the songs immediately felt familiar to her. She was able to sing the songs after listening to them just two or three times even though she had never studied Chinese before. Then her father employed a friend from China to teach her Mandarin to improve her pronunciation. In the documentary she could be seen travelling with her Chinese teacher to the Imperial Mae Ping Hotel room in Chiang Mai, one of Deng's favourite places, where she had died 20 years earlier at 42 years of age from a severe asthma attack. The room had been kept as a memorial to Deng. Langgalamu expressed a great degree of emotion and sense of nostalgia in the place. With tears in her eyes, she explained how she felt a real connection to Deng, and missed her. Langgalamu explained that as soon as she heard Deng's songs when she was seven she wanted to study in China. At the time, Chinese lessons weren't available at schools in Thailand. However, the documentary made a point of showing how all primary school children in Thailand now learn English and Mandarin, with scenes of Langgalamu singing one of Deng Lijun's classic songs 'Sweetness' (*Tian mimi*) with students in her old primary school. Langgalamu was shown to be a great ambassador for spreading Chinese language and culture in her country.

Qin Yuzi, who appeared on *The Voice of China* Season 3 in 2014, was also an interesting example. Not only was she an overseas Chinese from the USA, but she also made a point about being ethnically Zhuang, one of China's recognized ethnic minorities. This was in a context where overseas Chinese were rarely identified as minorities. In her blind audition she sang the English song 'I Love Rock 'n Roll' (originally recorded and released by the London-based band The Arrows in 1975). In this performance she inserted a high-pitched Guangxi folk song as well as an original Chinese rap verse, through which she explained her ethnic make-up:

> *[In Putonghua]*
> I've roamed around and come from Zhuang blood
> I am a Chinese descendant returning from across the Pacific
> My musical style has a personality that's a little naughty
> From beautiful folk songs to mad rock music, everyone calls me UZ
> [UZ is a nickname based on her given name Yuzi]

Since I was young I have pursued my singing dream
In non-stop pursuit of my own musical palace
Now I reach the stage that most suits me
Cry out UZ
Crossing the eras
[In Zhuang language, Chinese translation appears on screen]
Zhuang nationality, beautiful scenery
Bright sunny March

In chatting with the coaches after her initial performance, Qin introduced herself as an American national and overseas Chinese, whose hometown was Nanning city, Guangxi province. Mentor Yang Kun then asked, since she had American citizenship, why she didn't participate in America's *The Voice*. This gave her another opportunity to assert her Chineseness as well as her ethnic Zhuang identity: 'China is my roots. I was born and grew up here and I'm proud to be a Zhuang person.' Her family also dressed in colourful minority clothes as they cheered her on, while she wore a minority-inspired modern dress in some performances. During the show, audiences were also shown a clip of the modern Qin going back to the countryside to experience life with local minority famers (presumably from where she was born), travelling on an old cart amid sugar cane fields, and singing with them in local dress.

Her performance of 'Are You Ready' later in the season also presented Qin as an example of the ongoing modernization of people from rural and ethnic minority areas, who, despite their modernity, would never let go of their roots. The performance began with a young girl on stage wearing a colourful ethnic costume singing a folk song. It then dramatically shifted to Qin's modern rock mix in Chinese and English. Wearing a red dress and high heels, with Chinese and Caucasian male dancers skimpily clad in black leather, Qin engaged in a somewhat unlikely dynamic interplay between a modern, sexy English-language (international) song and a folk song (*shange*). In the middle of the song, she inserted a folk song verse sung in an ethnic language (presumably Zhuang). As her coach Qi Qin said: 'She has both ethnic elements and an international style.' Fellow coach Yang Kun praised her for her 'world music feel'. Qin was thus able to showcase blends of her 'internal' and 'external' otherness to full advantage to attract curiosity and attention.

Qin's performances on other television shows also allowed her to showcase different aspects of her multifaceted identity. For instance, on CCTV3's *Star Avenue* she introduced herself initially as being a Zhuang person from Guangxi province. Her American identity was subsequently revealed when host Bi Fujian asked why her *Putonghua* wasn't quite up to scratch, to which she explained that she migrated with her family to the United States when she was 13. Qin quickly added, 'But I really love my motherland'. She thus came across as a model for overseas Chinese people who maintained continued commitment to China.

Conclusion

PRC music-entertainment programmes have allowed for a range of both ideologically constrained and cosmopolitan moments related to expressions of a Greater Chinese identity. Stars from Greater China have been used to attract older audiences through a sense of nostalgic connection to songs that were popular across the Chinese speaking world as well as to attract youth through the singing of contemporary pop songs which are both 'national' and 'global' in feel.

The selected examples highlight how the greater Chinese and multiethnic frames often intersected when overseas Chinese, Taiwanese and Hong Kong singers performed in concerts that celebrated particular minority nationalities, such as when *The Same Song* travelled to the Inner Mongolia Autonomous Region and the Ningxia Hui Autonomous Region. They also showed, in rare instances, hybrid identities like Qin Yuzi, who claimed both an overseas Chinese and minority nationality identity. In such cases, overseas Chinese, Hong Kong and Taiwanese performers have tended to come across as economically superior, more modern, trendy and cosmopolitan by comparison with mainlanders and minorities, and have helped to raise the level of China's international positioning.

Overall, the impression given is that Chineseness has been conceptualized as a single ethnicity when the frame encompasses Chinese outside of the mainland, while minority nationalities (especially those from sensitive groups like Mongolians, Tibetans and Uyghurs, who are identified with independence movements or who have strong cultural links to neighbouring countries) tend only to be differentiated *within* China. This has implications for Mongolian-Chinese or Tibetan-Chinese, for instance, who are slotted in with a pan-Chinese rather than a pan-Mongolian identity at a global level. Representing an overseas Chinese as Zhuang or a smaller minority group which is more generally accepting of CCP-rule is less of an issue.

Language has played a particularly key role in defining Greater China on China's terms. It is often through verbal interactions between hosts and singers between songs, or even within songs, that key politically sanctioned messages about China's development and modernization and more ideological messages about China, the motherland and unification have been presented. Hong Kong, Macau and Taiwanese Chinese have been marked by Chinese television as different *and* as securely belonging to PRC China through the ubiquitous on-screen text that identifies performers as being from *Zhongguo Xianggang* (China Hong Kong), *Zhongguo Aomen* (China Macau) or *Zhongguo Taiwan* (China Taiwan). Hardened expressions of identity, in terms of belonging to 'China', have been reinforced in the verbal introductions of guests by hosts. Generally, the only unmarked group has been the mainland Han, who have been constructed as the default position to which all others are compared. This serves to centre the mainland PRC within the Greater China frame.

Hybridity has also been expressed linguistically through the use of Mandarin and English (such as in the songs of Wang Lihong); it may be visually embodied (such as through performers like Fei Xiang); or it may be expressed musically, for instance, by combining R&B and hip hop with Chinese flute in a contemporary style that may appeal particularly to youth, or through experimenting with hybrid operatic–popular music forms. These expressions of difference can be attractive to Chinese television producers and audiences in that they can provide something fresh for audiences and may entice them to watch, which increases ratings and draws advertising and sponsorship revenue. Being able to attract audiences may also satisfy conservatives who wish to share the message of sameness, unity and unification.

Popular music has clearly played a particularly significant role in making the Greater Chinese identity a reality. Old pop songs have been used for new political purposes and new songs have been composed with certain Party-state sanctioned themes. Messages of unification have been stressed during the orthodox, ideologically hardened moments, while a sense of greater Chinese nationalism has been stressed during the more cosmopolitan and softer moments. Both frames have highlighted the success of China's opening up and reform policies. China's music-entertainment programmes described in this chapter have worked hard to emphasize the dynamism of contemporary China, how Greater Chinese singers can be part of the China Dream, and the important role the PRC plays in bringing Chinese from around the world together. The next chapter moves from the construction of an ethnic Chinese global identity centred in the PRC mainland to consider the attraction of non-Chinese foreigners to China and the implications this has had for Chinese national identity construction.

Notes

1 Chen Sitong (Vivi/Vivienna Chen) is a more recent example of a mainland singer who has tried to repackage herself as a 'Hong Kong' singer. She believed this identity would have a better chance of market success than the identity of a 'Yunnan girl', which failed to make inroads (according to Eva Leung, personal communication, 2010).
2 For critical discussions on 'yellowness' as a 'racial' term introduced during the colonial era by the West to assert 'white' superiority over Chinese, and adopted by Chinese to assert their own superiority over 'blacks', see Dikötter (1992: 161) and Teng (2006: 149). Also see Jones (2001) for a discussion of 'yellow music', the so-called lewd, low-class music of the folk, influenced by the 'black' idiom of jazz, popular in China in the 1920s.
3 Taiwanese singers such as Zhou Jielun (Jay Chou) (see Fung, 2008b), and mainland singers including Gao Feng, famous for the 1994 hit 'Big China' (*Da Zhongguo*), and other performers from the mainland and beyond (see Baranovitch 2003: 234) have also successfully used the tactic of singing nationalistic songs and fitting in with the mainland's political and cultural agenda of celebrating traditional Chinese values, which has given them airtime on CCTV and access to a massive audience.
4 This song was used for the soundtrack of the 2001 Hong Kong film titled *2002*.
5 According to the article, Wang 'still regards herself as a mainland citizen' and has had a political career having been nominated by representatives of Guangdong Province to represent the Hong Kong People's Congress (in those days, people of Hong Kong did not make the selections) (All-China Women's Federation, 2007).

6 Wang Mingquan later sang 'Journeying Over Ten Thousand Torrents and a Thousand Crags' on *The Same Song – Tomorrow Will Be Even Better (Mingtian hui geng hao)* concert in 2009.
7 The Portuguese had used Macau as an entrepot for foreign trade since the 1550s. Portugal and China signed a secret pre-agreement in 1979 during which both sides agreed that Macau was Chinese territory under Portuguese administration. In 1987, China and Portugal signed an agreement on the process for handing over Macau to Chinese administration (Lam, 2010: 660).
8 Lam (2010: 672–3) notes that Macau has been used as an economic and symbolic platform to try and build strategic trade relationships with Portugal and African and Latin-American states that were former colonies of Portugal, including countries such as Brazil, Angola, Mozambique, Cape Verde, Guinea Bissau and East Timor (also see Sheh and Law, 2011; Zhou, 2010).
9 According to Wikipedia (https://en.wikipedia.org/wiki/Soler_(band)), the brothers were born to an Italian father and Karen mother and raised as Roman Catholics in Macau where they attended a local Chinese school. As adults they moved to Italy to pursue their music and returned to Macau in 1999 before achieving success as performers in Hong Kong. They received the Commercial Radio Hong Kong Music Awards 2005 Best Group Newcomer Gold Award and have released popular albums in Cantonese and Mandarin.
10 Translated lyrics appeared in Chinese subtitles at the bottom of the screen explaining that the song was about a boy in the north of Portugal who could not sing and dance. But the girls didn't care about his money or whether he wrote them letters as long as he would dance with them.
11 As part of the rebranding, the show design has been slightly altered so that instead of the chairs swiveling around to face the contestant when a coach presses the button to choose the voice they like, the chair zooms forward down a ramp closer towards the singer at such a speed that you can see the wind go through the coach's hair.
12 In earlier history, Taiwan was ruled by various regimes including the Dutch (1624–62) and the rebellious army of Cheng Cheng-kung (1662–83). It formally came under the control of China's Manchu government/Qing Dynasty (1683–1895) in 1684.
13 Chiang Kai-Shek also did not claim Taiwan in earlier draft constitutions in 1925, 1934 and 1936 (Yahuda, 2000: 30).
14 A-mei has been popular in Greater China including the PRC mainland since the mid- to late 1990s. In 2000, she was banned in China after performing the National Anthem of the Republic of China at the first presidential inauguration of Chen Shui-bian. When she was able to return to the mainland, she faced protests from ultra-nationalists at her concerts who accused her of supporting Taiwanese independence, while in Taiwan her patriotism was questioned when she tried to apologise and make amends with the mainland media. An advertisement for Sprite which featured A-mei and her song was also pulled from China at the time. A-mei has since redeemed herself by emphasizing her intentions are about peace and not politics. She was a coach on *The Voice of China* in Season 2 and an adviser in Season 4.
15 Interestingly, Wang Lihong's uncle Li Jianfu, also a singer who later became the CEO of Yahoo! Asia, profited the most from singing and recording 'Descendants of the Dragon' when it was first released in 1980. Hou had sold the rights for the song to a record company for US$150, which he thought was a good deal at the time, while Li Jianfu's recording sold millions of copies (Jaivin, 2001: 10, 421).
16 According to research by the International Organization for Migration, only 30 per cent of students from China studying in Europe ever return home (Omelaniuk, 2005: 190, 194).

17 Nyíri's comment is in relation to the overwriting of Tibetan village names with Chinese names for scenic spots.
18 Vancouver has had a strong Chinese presence. Ma (2003: 27) notes that 50 per cent of all immigrants to Vancouver from 1991 to 1996 were Chinese. This includes a large number of migrants from Hong Kong who were apprehensive about their political future prior to 1997. From 1984 they were able to migrate to Canada under the Entrepreneur Immigrant Program.

References

Al Jazeera (2011) China's empty city of Ordos, 9 September. Available at www.youtube.com/watch?v=0brcZTVde-I (accessed 18 May 2017).
All-China Women's Federation (2007) Wang Mingquan: 'Big Sister' in Hong Kong entertainment circle, 6 February. Available at www.womenofchina.cn/womenofchina/html1/news/celebrity/8/2865-1.htm (accessed 18 May 2017).
Baranovitch, N. (2003) *China's New Voices: Popular Music, Ethnicity, Gender and Politics, 1978–1997*. Berkeley: University of California Press.
Barthes, R. [trans. S. Heath] (1976) Rhetoric of the image. In *Image, Music, Text*. New York: Hill and Wang.
Brown, K. (2014) End of innocence for Hong Kong. *Asian Currents*, 6 October. Available at http://asaablog.tumblr.com/post/99311274001/end-of-innocence-for-hong-kong (accessed 18 May 2017).
Bulag, U.E. (2010) Alter/native Mongolian identity: from nationality to ethnic group. In E.J. Perry and M. Selden (eds.) *Chinese Society: Change, Conflict and Resistance* (3rd edn). Abingdon: Routledge Curzon, pp. 261–87.
Chan, J.M. (2008) Toward television regionalization in Greater China and beyond. In Y. Zhu and C. Berry (eds.) *TV China*. Bloomington: Indiana University Press, pp. 15–39.
Chow, R. (1998) Introduction: on Chineseness as a theoretical problem. *boundary 2* 25(3): 1–24.
Chow, Y.F. (2007) Descendants of the dragon, sing! In E. Jurriëns and J. de Kloet (eds.) *Cosmopatriots: On Distant Belongings and Close Encounters*. New Amsterdam: Rodopi, pp. 95–104.
Chow, Y.F. (2009) Me and the dragon: a lyrical engagement with the politics of Chineseness. *Inter-Asia Cultural Studies* 10(4): 544–64.
Chua, B.H. (2001) Pop culture China. *Singapore Journal of Tropical Geography* 22(2): 113–21.
Chua, B.H. (2006) Gossip about stars: newspapers and pop culture in China. In W. Sun (ed.) *Media and the Chinese Diaspora: Community, Communications and Commerce*. London: Routledge, pp. 75–90.
Cohen, M.L. (1991) Being Chinese: the peripheralization of traditional identity. *Daedelus* 120(2): 113–34.
Coonan, C. (2009) Chinese shouldn't get more freedom, says Jackie Chan. *Independent*, 20 April. Available at www.independent.co.uk/news/world/asia/chinese-shouldnt-get-more-freedom-says-jackie-chan-1671337.html (accessed 18 May 2017).
Culture Express (2007) Kris Phillips/Fei Xiang, CCTV9, uploaded 17 March. Available at www.youtube.com/watch?v=h91OJFNNTFE&feature=related (accessed 18 May 2017).

Da, Y. (2005) Zhang Mingmin de rensheng lu [Zhang Mingmin's life journey]. *Beijing Radio and Television Journal – People Weekly (Beijing Guangbo Dianshi Bao Renwu Zhoukan)*, 27 January. Available at www.gmw.cn/content/2005-01/27/content_160612.htm (accessed 18 May 2017).

Dikötter, F. (1992) *The Discourse of Race in Modern China*. Oxford: Oxford University Press.

Du, J. (2009) Cong 'Wu zi zhi ge' dao 'Qi zi zhi ge' [From 'The Song of Five Lands' to 'The Song of Seven Lands']. *Dahe Daily (Dahe Bao)*, 9 June. Available online at http://cathay.ce.cn/history/200906/09/t20090609_19276579.shtml (accessed 18 May 2017).

Edmonds, R.L. (1995) Macau and Greater China. In D. Shambaugh (ed.) *Greater China: The Next Superpower?* New York: Clarendon, pp. 226–54.

English.news.cn (2010) *2010 Minnan Dialect Spring Festival Eve TV Gala*. English.news.cn, 15 January. Available at http://big5.xinhuanet.com/gate/big5/news.xinhuanet.com/english2010/photo/2010-01/15/c_13137008.htm (accessed 18 May 2017).

Fan, J. (2012) The most handsome Chinese man I've ever seen. *The New Yorker*, 30 January. Available at www.newyorker.com/culture/culture-desk/the-most-handsome-chinese-man-ive-ever-seen (accessed 18 May 2017).

Fung, A. (2003) Marketing popular culture in China: Andy Lau as a pan-Chinese icon. In C.C. Lee (ed.) *Chinese Media, Global Contexts*. London: Routledge Curzon, pp. 257–69.

Fung, A. (2007) The emerging (national) popular music culture in China. *Inter-Asia Cultural Studies* 8(3): 425–37.

Fung, A. (2008a) *Global Capital, Local Culture: Transnational Media Corporations in China*. New York: Peter Lang.

Fung, A. (2008b) Western style, Chinese pop: Jay Chou's rap and hip-hop in China. *Asian Music* 39(1): 69–80.

Fung, A. and Curtin, M. (2002) The anomalies of being Faye (Wong): gender politics in Chinese popular music. *International Journal of Cultural Studies* 5: 263–90.

Fung, A. and Ma, E. (2002) 'Satellite modernity': four modes of televisual imagination in the disjunctive socio-mediascape of Guangzhou. In S.H. Donald, M. Keane and H. Yin (eds.) *Media in China: Consumption, Content and Crisis*. London: Routledge Curzon, pp. 67–79.

Gao, J. (2009) Lobbying to stay: the Chinese students' campaign to stay in Australia. *International Migration* 47(2): 127–54.

Gorfinkel, L. (2011) Ideology and the performance of Chineseness: Hong Kong singers on the CCTV stage. *Perfect Beat: The Pacific Journal of Research into Contemporary Music and Popular Culture*, 12(2): 107–28.

Guo, Y. (2004) *Cultural Nationalism in Contemporary China*. London: Routledge Curzon.

Hong, J. (1996) Cultural relations of China and Taiwan: an examination of three stages of policy change. *Intercultural Communication Studies* 1(1): 89–109.

Huang, S.L. (2010) *Re-Mediating Identities in the Imagined Homeland: Taiwanese Migrants in China*. PhD Dissertation, University of Maryland, College Park. Available at http://drum.lib.umd.edu/bitstream/handle/1903/10381/Huang_umd_0117E_11225.pdf;jsessionid=070530BE6D82CAFA61A9BFE27E0CB5E1?sequence=1 (accessed 18 May 2017).

Hughes, C. (2000) Post-nationalist Taiwan. In M. Leifer (ed.) *Asian Nationalism*. London: Routledge, pp. 63–81.

Jaivin, L. (2001) *The Monkey and the Dragon: A True Story about Friendship, Music, Politics and Life on the Edge*. Melbourne: Text Publishing.

Jones, A. (2001) *Yellow Music: Media Culture and Colonial Modernity in the Chinese Jazz Age*. Durham: Duke University Press.

Kirby, W.C. (2005) When did China become China? Thoughts on the twentieth century. In J.A. Fogel (ed.) *The Teleology of the Modern Nation-State: Japan and China*. Philadelphia: University of Pennsylvania Press, pp. 105–14.

Lam, W.M. (2010) Promoting hybridity: the politics of the new Macau identity. *The China Quarterly*, 203: 656–74.

Lee, T.D. and Huang, Y. (2002) 'We are Chinese' – music and identity in 'cultural China'. In S.H. Donald, M. Keane and H. Yin (eds.) *Media in China: Consumption, Content and Crisis*. London: Routledge Curzon, pp. 105–15.

Liu, H. (2005) New migrants and the revival of overseas Chinese nationalism. *Journal of Contemporary China*, 14(43): 291–316.

Lo, S.S.H. (2008) *The Dynamics of Beijing-Hong Kong Relations: A Model for Taiwan?* Hong Kong: Hong Kong University Press.

Lu, X. (2009) Ritual, television, and state ideology: rereading CCTV's 2006 *Spring Festival Gala*. In Y. Zhu and C. Berry (eds.) *TV China*. Indianapolis: Indiana University Press, pp. 111–25.

Ma, E. (1999) *Culture, Politics, and Television in Hong Kong*. London: Routledge.

Ma, E. (2000) Renationalization and me: my Hong Kong story after 1997. *Inter-Asia Cultural Studies* 1(1): 173–9.

Ma, L.J.C. (2003) Space, place, and transnationalism in the Chinese diaspora. In L.J.C. Ma and C. Cartier (eds.) *The Chinese Diaspora: Space, Place, Mobility, and Identity*. Lanham, MA: Rowman and Littlefield, pp. 1–49.

Mahtani, M. (2002) Tricking the border guards: performing race. *Environment and Planning D: Society and Space* 20(4): 425–40.

Mei, Z. (2016) Zhongguo xin gesheng heiren A-rui Ge ren ziliao puguang zan Halin wei Zhongguo ban MJ – A-rui jianjie [Sing! China black guy A-rui's personal profile – Halin exposes China's MJ (Michael Jackson)]. laonanren.com, 31 July. Available at www.laonanren.com/news/2016-07/120867.htm (accessed 18 May 2017).

Moskowitz, M.L. (2010) *Cries of Joy, Songs of Sorrow: Chinese Pop Music and Its Cultural Connotations*. Honolulu: University of Hawai'i Press.

Nyíri, P. (2005) Scenic spot Europe: Chinese travelers on the Western periphery. In B. Gransow, P. Nyíri and S.C. Fong (eds.) *China: New Faces of Ethnography*. Münster: Transaction Publishers.

Nyíri, P. and Zhang, J. with Varrall, M. (2010) China's cosmopolitan nationalists: 'heroes' and 'traitors' of the 2008 Olympics. *The China Journal* 63: 25–55.

Omelaniuk, I. (2005) Best practices to manage migration: China (notes and commentary). *International Migration* 43(5): 189–206.

Pan, Z., Lee, C.C., Chan, J.M. and So, C.K.Y. (2001) Orchestrating the family-nation chorus: Chinese media and nationalism in the Hong Kong handover. *Mass Communication and Society* 4(3): 331–47.

Ri, L. (2001) Guanyu Fei Xiang de yixie shi yixie qing [A few things about Fei Xiang and his loves]. *China New Times* (*Zhongguo Xin Shidai*) 2: 46–8.

Sheh, W. and Law, K. (2011) *Contrasting the Political Re-Presentation in Hong Kong and Macau History Museums after the Handover to China: Two Faces of Nationalism during the Rise of China*. Unpublished paper presented at the Symposium on China's Appeal and its Discontents, Hong Kong Shue Yan University, 22 June.

Song, K. (2002) Fei Xiang yi zhu shengmingli wangsheng de yehua [Fei Xiang, a vibrant wildflower]. *International Music Exchange* (*Guoji Yinyue Jiaoliu*) 8: 58–59.

Song, W. (2016) The Voice of Macau: Local Macau singer wows in the hit reality TV show *Sing! China*. Macau Closer Living and Arts Magazine, October. Available at http://macaucloser.com/en/magazine/voice-macau (accessed 18 May 2017).

Souhu Music (2014) Zhang Mingmin Chunwan gandong Zhongguo 'Wo de Zhongguo Meng' you Cui Shu chuangzuo [Zhang Mingmin moves China at the Spring Festival with 'My China Dream' composed by Cui Shu], 8 February. Available at http://music.yule.sohu.com/20140208/n394610331.shtml (accessed 18 May 2017).

Sun, W. (2002) *Leaving China: Media, Migration, and Transnational Imagination.* Lanham: Rowman and Littlefield.

Sun, W. (2010) Motherland calling: China's rise and diasporic responses. *Cinema Journal* 49(3): 126–30.

Tencent Entertainment (2014) Zhang Mingmin deng Chunwan xian chang zuguo 'Zhongguo xin' bian 'Zhongguo meng' [Zhang Mingmin changes 'China Heart' to 'China Dream' in his offering to the motherland at the *Spring Festival Gala*], 30 January. Available at http://ent.qq.com/a/20140130/008039.htm (accessed 18 May 2017).

Teng, E. (2006) Eurasian hybridity in Chinese utopian visions: From *One World* to *A Society Based on Beauty* and beyond. *Positions: East Asia Cultures Critiques* 14(1): 131–63.

Tsai, E. (2008) Existing in the age of innocence: pop stars, publics, and politics in Asia. In B.H. Chua and K. Iwabuchi (eds.) *East Asian Pop Culture: Analysing the Korean Wave*. Hong Kong: Hong Kong University Press, pp. 217–42.

Tu, W. (1994) Cultural China: the periphery as the centre. In W. Tu (ed.) *The Living Tree: The Changing Meaning of Being Chinese Today*. Stanford: Stanford University Press, pp. 1–34.

van Leeuwen, T. (1999) *Speech, Music, Sound*. London: Macmillan.

Wu, D.Y. (1991) The construction of Chinese and non-Chinese identities. *Daedalus* 120(2): 159–79.

Yahuda, M. (2000) The changing faces of Chinese nationalism: the dimensions of statehood. In M. Leifer (ed.) *Asian Nationalism*. London: Routledge, pp. 21–37.

Yan, J. (2008) Haixia liang'an Minnan wenhua jiaoliu xianxing xianshi yanjiu [On antecedence and fortaste of Minnan cultural communication on both sides of the Straits] [original English title]. *Journal of Fujian Administration Institute*, April. Available at http://en.cnki.com.cn/Article_en/CJFDTOTAL-FZFZ200804020.htm (accessed 18 May 2017).

Yang, M.M. (2002) Mass media and transnational subjectivity in Shanghai: notes on (re)cosmopolitanism in a Chinese metropolis. In F.D. Ginsburg, L. Abu-Lughold and B. Larkin (eds.) *Media Worlds: Anthropology on New Terrain*. Berkeley: University of California Press, pp. 189–210.

Zhang, Y. (2010) *Zhongguo dalu liuxing wenhua yu dang guo yishi* [Mainland China's Popular Culture and Party State Consciousness]. Taipei, Taiwan: Showwe Information Co.

Zhao, B. (1998) Popular family television and party ideology: the Spring Festival Eve happy gathering. *Media, Culture and Society* 20(1): 43–58.

Zhou, Z. (ed.) (2010) 2007 nian Zhongyang dianshitai tong gang, ao ji Taiwan jiaoliu yu hezuo jishi [2007 Chronicle of CCTV's Exchange and Cooperation with Hong Kong, Macau and Taiwan]. Provided by the editing department of CCTV's overseas program centre, cctv.com, 19 January. Available at http://cctvenchiridion.cctv.com/special/C20624/20100119/103282.shtml (accessed 18 May 2017).

6 Foreign identities

This chapter will show that performances of foreigners are less about teaching Chinese about foreign cultures, and more about presenting to Chinese audiences an image of a revitalized China at the centre of world civilization. China is constructed as a place that attracts foreigners and allows them to realize their dreams. By delving into the performances of artists from such countries as the USA, UK, Nigeria, Sierra Leone, Russia, South Korea and Japan, it also considers how particular historical relationships and tensions underlie individual performers' CCTV performances.

Sinophiliac and foreigners' obsessions with China

From 2002 to 2009, one regular music-entertainment programme called *Sinophiliac* (*Tongle wuzhou*, lit: Same Happiness Five Continents) specialized in showcasing the performances of foreigners (CCTV.com, 2002). Broadcast on CCTV3 (the domestic-oriented variety channel) and later on CCTV4 (the Chinese language international channel), the show celebrated foreigners' attraction to Chinese culture. The weekly show was shot in China, mostly indoors in the CCTV studios in Beijing, and occasionally outdoors in different locations around China, particularly in minority nationality areas. The location of the programmes demonstrated foreigners' physical presence in China, and tapped into foreign and Chinese viewers' assumed interest in China's mainstream traditional and colourful minority cultures.

Chapter 5 explained how the show *The Same Song* focused on building mainland relations with overseas Chinese and Chinese in Taiwan, Hong Kong and Macau, while Chapter 4 emphasised how *Folk Songs China* has focused on building an understanding of China's minority nationalities. In an interesting parallel with these, *Sinophiliac* stressed cross-cultural exchange between the Chinese people and foreign nationals of different cultures. (At least one episode of *Sinophiliac* in 2009 was, however, shot overseas with a format aimed at attracting overseas Chinese as opposed to foreigners of other ethnicities in Sydney, Australia, who may have been 'missing home' during the Spring Festival (CCTV4, 2009).) *Sinophiliac* emphasized China–Western relations, framed as two concrete and opposing extremes, with the aim of reaching a relaxed and harmonious 'unity of opposites' (*dui li tong yi*). The element of

172 *Foreign identities*

exchange was suggested by pairing up a Chinese host (usually Ji Xiaojun or Bing Xian) with a Caucasian foreign host (usually Aihua/Charlotte MacInnis from the USA or Da Niu/Niu Hansheng/Daniel Newham from the UK).

Typically, the hosts stressed singing as a metaphor for happiness, friendship and the creation of a small world unified through music. For instance, in an episode entitled 'Happy Singing Voices', broadcast in March 2009, performers from different countries stood happily together singing a song entitled 'Everlasting Friendship' (*Youyi dijiutianchang*). This song blended Chinese lyrics with the globally well-known 'Auld Lang Syne', a Scottish folk melody and poem by Robert Burns, traditionally sung in Scotland and English-speaking countries on New Year's Eve.

However, the emphasis on foreigners' attraction to China far outweighed any sense of mutual influence of cultures, possibly because *Sinophiliac* had a somewhat conflicting aim of showing foreigners and Western culture 'entering into' China's culture (*Sinophiliac* website, 2010). Most acts emphasized the attraction of Chinese culture and civilization to foreigners. The English title *Sinophiliac* itself pointed to the notion that there is a global 'craze' or 'obsession' for Chinese language and culture. The CCTV stage and rich Chinese culture were presented as the spaces and contact zones that had the power to attract people from around the world into a harmonious unity.

The Five Continents Singing Group (*Wu zhou changxiang yuetuan*), which was visually rendered multicultural by their different skin colours ('white', 'black' and 'yellow'), epitomizes the framing of global harmony based on foreigners' and the Chinese people's shared obsession with Chinese culture and China. During the 'Happy Singing Voices' (*kuaile gesheng*) episode of *Sinophiliac* in March 2009, for instance, the multinational group were dressed in modernized black Chinese-style robes. While the foreigners danced excitedly and followed along, Chinese performers drove the performance: one Chinese-looking male performer stood at the centre of the group, metaphorically representing the central role of China within this microcosm of world relations.

The Five Continents Singing Group did not just demonstrate the members' interest in Chinese culture, but sang songs with lyrics that actively declared their support for China. One song was called 'Sing Towards China' (*Changxiang Zhongguo*) and included the lyrics 'We want to ensure that the more we sing the brighter Great China will be', demonstrating their support for China's cultural and political status quo in a similar way to performances by Chinese people on CCTV. Without making direct mention of the CCP, these lyrics were happily sung in Chinese by foreigners from around the world, in unison with Chinese people on the CCTV stage, while wearing Chinese-style clothes and accompanied by Chinese instruments (e.g., the *erhu*). This provided a fairly easy to read and thus 'hardened' multimodal message of foreigners' attraction to an already prosperous China, a sense of harmonious global solidarity facilitated by China, and a projection of a brighter future as long as things continued on the same stable path.

The Chinese names of foreigners play an important role in creating a positive impression of their dedication to China. A prime example is Aihua

(Charlotte MacInnis), a Caucasian American host of *Sinophiliac* whose stage name literally translates as 'Love China'. Aihua moved from the United States to China with her family in 1988 when she was seven years old. According to Butchy (2002), her family already had links to China with her father born there to parents of Scottish and Norwegian descent. CCTV's description of MacInnis in an online report titled 'Charlotte MacInnis (Ai Hua): a white-faced Chinese', highlights the significance of her name as she has attempted to integrate into Chinese society:

> Charlotte MacInnis, an American girl who has embraced and adopted Chinese culture and tradition as her own. Meanwhile, she is beloved by the Chinese people, and they have accepted her as a Chinese, not a foreigner ... 'Ai Hua', meaning Love China, is her Chinese name. And the name proves very appropriate, for not only does she love the Chinese, but the Chinese love her as well.
>
> (CCTV.com, 2011)

Despite embracing Chinese language and culture as her own, MacInnis has spoken of the difficulties of assimilating, given her racial difference. In an interview on China Radio International (CRI) she reportedly said: 'No matter how Chinese I feel or how perfect the Chinese I speak, people look at me and will say you are not Chinese. It's difficult for me.' The CRI reporter tried to make sense of people like MacInnis who are in such an 'in-between position', and referred to foreign children like her growing up in China as an 'egg' – 'white on the outside, and yellow on the inside', 'similar to Chinese brought up in Western cultures who are dubbed "bananas"'.

Aihua's name was a focal point in her performances as a host on *Sinophiliac* and was used as a pivot from which to negotiate the boundaries between the foreign other and the Chinese self. When Aihua was introduced to audiences in a *Sinophiliac* programme in March 2008, her fellow host, Chinese male performer Jiang Kun, told audiences that she had a perfectly genuine Chinese name (*Zhongguo mingzi*, literally 'name of China') and repeated her name 'Aihua, Aihua' several times for the audience to fully grasp its significance. Speaking in perfect Mandarin just as a Chinese host would, Aihua referred to '*our*' ancestors in China attempting to further the bond and make it seem that she not only loved China but was fully assimilated. However, Aihua could not truly be acknowledged as 'Chinese' given her racial/ethnic differences. After playfully toying with her identity, host Jiang then directly dismissed Aihua's credentials as a Chinese person and announced to audiences that 'no matter how you look at her, she doesn't look Chinese'. He referred to her by saying 'you Americans', and Aihua then shifted her identity to 'us Americans'. The performance of foreigners as Chinese is rarely long-lasting and is often treated as a kind of 'joke' accompanied by laughter. Foreigners' attraction to, rather than assimilation into, China and Chinese culture are the focal point of these acts.

Another example from the same programme involves a man called Tang Aiguo (lit: 'Love the country'). He joked with Aihua that if you put Aihua ('Love China') and Aiguo ('Love the country') together 'then we are cousins'. This comment seemed to bring the China-loving foreigners into the greater China family tree, once removed from the brother–sister relationship between the 56 nationalities. However, this 'family relationship' comment was also taken as a joke, evidenced by visual and aural displays of laughter from the performers on stage and the audience, and it was not expressed in the serious manner in which the 56 nationalities are said to be related. Nonetheless, these jokes point out an ambiguity in the official line between foreigners and Chinese, and a lack of clarity about how close China should stand with the rest of the world.

In another episode of *Sinophiliac*, staged outdoors in Guizhou, Aihua had a slightly different subjective starting point, which connected her with China's minority nationalities. As a result of effective place-based marketing in reform-era China, mention of Guizhou province immediately gives rise to an image of colourful and happy minority nationalities. Pre-introduction song and dance acts highlighted the 'colourful' flavour of the programme. For this programme, Aihua wore a pink, embroidered 'minority nationality' dress, which the male Chinese host, dressed in a modern, Western-style black suit, made a special point of highlighting. He chivalrously held Aihua's hand as if about to introduce something special, and as he let it go, gesturing at Aihua, he said to the audience, 'Everyone, what do you say? [Is she] beautiful? [Does she] look good?' Aihua laughed exuberantly, and murmured cheers could be heard in the soundtrack, before she expressed how much she liked the dress, suggesting it was a novelty and something exotic. The male host then asked the audience whether Aihua, in wearing Yi clothing, really looked like a Yi girl. Aihua modelled the dress and called out 'So do I look like [a Yi girl]?' The male host jumped in to answer, 'Don't kid me. To me she doesn't look like (a Yi girl). No matter how you look at her she is still an American.' Aihua acted rejected and disappointed, although still with a smile on her face suggesting she too was just playing. At the same time, the male host put his arm on her back as if to comfort her, and left it there as he told her not to worry 'because up next we'll see what *real* Yi girls look like'. So, while there was some to-and-fro-ing between Aihua's identity as a Chinese, a minority or a foreigner based on her dress, speech and acting as a Chinese host, the line between Chineseness and foreignness based on her racial appearance and country of origin was finally sharply drawn in the declaration of the authoritative male Chinese host.

Sinophiliac also promoted China's unique civilization through foreigners shown to be learning, appreciating, acquiring skills in and performing Han Chinese traditional arts. In 2008, there was an episode specifically devoted to *quyi*. *Quyi* refers to Chinese folk art forms that include ballad singing, storytelling, comic dialogues, clapper talks and crosstalk (*xiangsheng*). The programme emphasized foreigners' engagement with 'China's folk arts'

Foreign identities 175

(*Zhongguo quyi*) or 'our Chinese [China] folk arts' (*women Zhongguo quyi*). The majority of folk arts featured in this episode were presumably 'Han' traditions given that they were otherwise 'unmarked'. In other words, Han Chinese are presented as the norm by not having any particular labels assigned to them, whereas non-Han people and cultural traditions are specifically labelled by hosts or through on-screen text as belonging to a particular minority (or foreign) culture which marks them as unusual, exotic or different. Yet, as well as stressing accomplishments in standard Mandarin, *Quyi* is interesting because there is an emphasis on the use and mastery of *local* Mandarin dialects and not just *Putonghua*. Performances in 'original' local dialects can be considered akin to the multiethnic performances in the *yuanshengtai* frame (see Chapter 4). However, rather than being rendered exotic, these traditions were reified in a discourse of civilization. This was often done through older, distinguished master teachers coming on stage to perform with their foreign students who had apparently taken the endeavour seriously and spent long hours mastering traditional musical skills.

This production seemed to redress an imbalance whereby the traditions of 'exotic' minorities have been marketed much more consistently than local Han folk traditions in the name of China's contemporary vibrancy and openness. As Helen Rees (2009: 72) argues, a 'wealth of distinctive but little-known regional folk traditions belonging to citizens classified as Han' are often ignored. *Sinophiliac* was possibly one of the few television spaces in which local Han musical traditions were emphasized in the face of competition for television airspace from Western-influenced and 'exotic' minority nationality arts.

Comparable to *Folk Songs China* (Chapter 4), which placed minority nationalities in the past by aiming to create a museum of their living traditions, *Sinophiliac* showcased foreigners enacting the Chinese past by featuring them performing traditional and nostalgic Chinese cultural acts. Foreigners' attraction to Chinese culture through traditional arts were exaggerated, with Aihua remarking that '*all* foreign friends' come to China to appreciate Chinese folk arts (*Quyi*) and to sing a couple of lines. As foreigners demonstrated their curiosity and desire to learn Chinese art forms (modern and traditional) they became objects of the Chinese gaze. Through the novelty of seeing foreigners obsessed with learning Chinese cultural traditions and wanting to better 'understand China', the show could achieve its aim of educating Chinese audiences on their 'own' cultural traditions so they could better understand themselves.

As noted above, while people from 'the five continents' may perform happiness together, the kind of diplomacy offered in *Sinophiliac* was not often focused on mutual cultural exchange. Foreigners on the programme often demonstrated a willingness to adopt various elements of Chinese culture, thus highlighting their attraction to China. They often dressed in traditional Chinese clothes, whether Han- or minority nationality-style, spoke the official standard (often Beijing-inflected) dialect of Mandarin, and showed their

176 *Foreign identities*

skills in various Chinese art forms like crosstalk and Beijing Opera as well as contemporary Chinese popular music. With the occasional exception, audiences were given few glimpses of foreign art forms, and Chinese performers rarely performed acts marked as 'foreign'. Chinese people, on the other hand, were shown to maintain their Chinese identities. In this way, the strength of traditional and modern Chinese culture was highlighted. This can be compared to the way that the Chineseness of Chinese students and residents living overseas was emphasized in *The Same Song* (Chapter 5), where any degree of assimilation into the cultures present in the countries where they were living was downplayed.

Pride in the Chinese language has also been embedded into highly commercial pop songs, which are then covered on Chinese television by foreign performers. Most prominent in the People's Republic of China (PRC) around 2007–8[1] was the Taiwanese girl group S.H.E.'s song entitled 'Chinese Language' (*Zhongguohua*).[2] This song, which included complex rap lyrics made up of Chinese tongue twisters, also featured a chorus that explained a global craze for the language. It told audiences that the 'whole world' (*quan shijie*) is learning to speak, and is speaking, Chinese, that 'Confucian thought is becoming increasingly international' (*Kongfuzi de hua yuelaiyue guojihua*) and that the whole world will listen to 'us' and whatever we have to say (*women shuo de hua, rang shijie dou renzhen tinghua*). The rap lyrics describe the intense influence of Chinese culture in the world with a girl named Marilyn buying a cheongsam (*qipao*) for her mother in London, Fuski falling in love with Chinese beef noodles in Moscow, Susanna opening a Chinese lounge bar in New York, and Wolfgang pairing an *erhu* with his electric guitar in Berlin.

The reworking of the Taiwanese stars' pop song 'Chinese Language' on the CCTV stage by foreign performers during the *My Chinese Life Awards Gala* (the show on which I participated and which was affiliated with *Sinophiliac*) worked to conflate such commercially based nationalism with the projection of China's soft power. Host Wang Yige welcomed friends from China, the USA, and the West African nation of Gabon to show their passion for Chinese language by singing about their 'Chinese Language'. As these foreigners sang, with Chinese dancers in the background, they presented an image of the Chinese language as trendy and achievable, breezing through the tongue twister lyrics and in many ways breaking the common stereotype that Chinese is inherently too sophisticated for most foreigners to learn well. Foreigners performing the song further validated S.H.E.'s message that Chinese is taking off around the world and that Chinese people should feel proud of their superior and attractive culture and language.

The lyrics of 'Chinese Language' directly alert to racial differences, noting that people of 'different skin colours' (*ge zhong yanse de pifu*) and 'different hair colours' (*ge zhong yanse de toufa*) are attempting to roll their tongues and speak the increasingly popular Chinese language. They also indicate a need to correct an imbalance in power relations between English and Chinese learning. In the song, the lyrics directly refer to the struggle that 'we' had in learning English pronunciation and grammar (*duoshao nian women kulian yingwen fayin he wenfa*). Chinese, on the other hand, is advertised as being a sophisticated and 'elegant' language, developed by and belonging to the 'clever Chinese people' (*hao congming de Zhongguo ren, hao youmei de Zhongguohua*). This catchy song was actually remarkably popular with foreigners learning Chinese, and a number of foreigners recorded their own versions and uploaded them to video sharing websites, highlighting how highly catchy nationalistic songs can be appropriated by a range of people for different purposes.

Theme songs for China's international events

During China's Olympic year (2008) there were variations on the theme of presenting foreigners from around the world happily together on Chinese soil, with several 'softer' depictions of foreigners' attraction to China. The English version of the official theme song for the 2008 Beijing Olympic Games Torch Relay, 'Light the Passion, Share the Dream', for instance, featured a choir of global contestants from the 2007 Miss World beauty competition (*Mykiru*, 2007) singing in unison in English 'forever as one'. The music video featured the foreign women dynamically singing atop the Great Wall and in front of the Olympic Stadium, known as the Bird's Nest, in Beijing. Beijing was foregrounded visually alongside the lyrics as the 'place where we join in harmony'. While the use of such captivating landmarks may seem like a logical choice for a theme song for an Olympic city, it remains significant that depicting people with different skin colours singing 'in harmony' about global harmony on Chinese soil was consistent with larger patterns in the framing of foreigners' attraction to China on Chinese television. It depicted the foreign women as colourful and happy, coming in from the periphery and gathering together in Beijing, much like the depiction of minorities who come to perform in Beijing from China's border regions (see Leibold, 2010: 3) (see Chapter 4).

'Light the Passion, Share the Dream' was written by East Asian composer, arranger, and performer Chris Babida, who was born in Hong Kong and studied jazz at Berklee College of Music in Boston. Babida noted that he wrote it while sitting in his recording studio (apparently in Taiwan) imagining the scene 'looking far out in[to] China Mainland, then looking up the sky and imagining the Olympic Stadium in front of me'. Like Zhang Mingmin's 'My Chinese Heart' and Hou Dejian's and Wang Lihong's 'Descendants of the Dragon', the outsider-insider's perspective seems to offer validation of the magnificence of China. Babida also alluded to 'duties' he had in writing the song in that it 'had to have a "Grandness" with a lot of Depth and Width' as well as warmth, power and an appealing ' "Chorus Section" so as to let people remember the song easily'. While he referred to this as 'a commercial touch' (Chris Babida blog, n.d.), given that the Olympics is also a highly political event, the song also tapped into the politics of the time. The mass montage of women of different skin colours, matched by their sweet, harmonious voices, presented a 'soft' construction of boundaries between the foreigner and the Chinese self. This blurring of boundaries also reflected the notions of a Harmonious Society and Harmonious World that were key tenets of the Party-political discourse under the leadership of President Hu Jintao and Premier Wen Jiabao (2002–12).

Significantly, however, 'Light the Passion, Share the Dream' was one of the few Olympic-related music-entertainment television clips featuring foreigners at all on CCTV in the lead-up to the Olympic Games (notwithstanding the few foreigners who appeared on *Sinophiliac*). Most music videos and on-stage performances that related to the Olympics focused on images of Chinese people and on generating a sense of national Chinese pride. Many other music videos broadcast on CCTV at the time featured red flags, Chinese gold-medal-winning athletes, geographic and cultural symbols like the Great Wall, and signs of economic development and modernization like freeways and airplanes. This particular officially sanctioned video was unique in its global, cosmopolitan appeal, and this difference likely reflects the purpose of the video, which was intended to be viewed by international as well as domestic audiences in the lead-up to and throughout the Games.

A similar performance that featured global unity was seen during a countdown event prior to the Shanghai Expo in 2010 where the international stars Vitas (from Russia), Rain (from South Korea), Laura Fygi (from the Netherlands, of Egyptian and Dutch heritage, who grew up in Uruguay), Fei Xiang/Kris Phillips (of Caucasian American and Chinese heritage, who grew up in Taiwan), Li Wen/Coco Lee (American Chinese pop singer, originally from Hong Kong), and mainland Chinese pop star Sun Nan sang the Michael Jackson classic 'We Are the World' (*Tian xia yi jia*) in English. The on-stage performance began with a series of spliced self-recorded clips of 'ordinary' foreigners from Malaysia, the USA, Australia, the UK and China singing lines of the same song. The feeling was one of global unity, with the Chinese performers being embedded within – rather than overpowering or guiding – the global conversation.

The Shanghai World Expo official theme song video '2010 Awaits You', sung by Hong Kong stars Chen Long (Jackie Chan) and Liu Dehua (Andy Lau) as well as actress and singer Li Bingbing, who graduated from the Shanghai Theatre Academy, and Shanghai TV host Yang Lan, also included images of foreigners of different races and colours such as youth, businessmen and a woman in an African costume embracing Chinese and smiling and waving at the camera. However, the depiction of foreigners only started three minutes into the video, and the song was entirely in Chinese, highlighting that it was directed at domestic audiences. The video presented Shanghai as sophisticated, with new and impressive architectural structures, which were juxtaposed with traditional performances of martial arts, tea ceremonies, drumming, fan dancing and Chinese opera, thus reinforcing the message of the Chinese people's ability to modernize and retain their unique culture and heritage and be proud of both at the same time. The video also depicted images of grand doors of famous buildings opening as a sign of 'welcoming', also symbolic of the reform and opening-up policy that has led to this 'magic era'. This music video thus positioned foreign guests as witnesses to China's impressive development and cultural prowess. In other words, the gaze of the foreigner could be said to reinforce the success of China's policies to domestic audiences.

The music video of the theme song of the 16th Asian Games in Guangzhou 2010, 'Reunion', sung by pop stars Sun Nan and Mao Amin, was interesting from the perspective that it was one of the few times where an Asian identity was asserted on Chinese television. It constructed a scene of Asia as ethnically diverse, with people of 'black eyes and blue', with 'dark and light skin'. The video depicted people of different ethnicities walking towards each other with big smiles and embracing each other. A particular focus was placed on an 'exotic' charming young man in a white Muslim robe of the kind typically seen in the Middle East. There was also a clip of a female sprinter from a Middle Eastern background wearing a sporty headscarf. Images of black athletes and Caucasian spectators were also included, highlighting the 'global' nature of this event, and again using the white person's gaze to reinforce the significance of the event.

While there were images of famous traditional buildings, including temples and mosques across Asia, scenes of 'modernity' dominated the 'Reunion' video with images of developed cities with skyscrapers and stadiums, which appeared at the same time as the line of the song, 'Here [Asia] is the most beautiful'. The climax of the song was also matched with a sustained focus on the Guangzhou/Canton Tower that was built especially for the Games, and which was for a moment the tallest tower in the world. The video thus effectively mapped Asia onto the typical domestic image of China as a rapidly developing nation that has managed to retain its own unique culture. The trope of children being the future of the nation, commonly used in a domestic context, was also applied to Asia as a whole, with images of happy children from different Asian ethnicities appearing to support the lyrics 'Here [Asia] is most bright'.

Significantly, the music video for 'Reunion' made use of three languages, including a snippet of spoken Cantonese at the beginning, a dialect spoken in and around the city of Guangzhou and by most people in Hong Kong and Macao, which are located just across the border from Guangdong Province in which Guangzhou is situated (Deng, 2010). The song itself alternated between Mandarin (the language of most viewers) and English (the lingua franca of the region, athletes, officials and other visitors from abroad). The token use of Cantonese was significant in light of the controversy surrounding a proposal put forth by the city committee of the Chinese People's Political Consultative Conference in the months prior to the Games advising Guangzhou TV 'to broadcast its news programmes more in Mandarin or launch a new Mandarin channel'. This was in a context where:

TV stations in China are required to use Mandarin. But since Guangdong is adjacent to Hong Kong and Macao where Cantonese is widely used, Guangzhou TV was approved by the State Administration of Radio, Film and Television in the 1980s to use Cantonese in order to attract viewers from the two regions.

(Deng, 2010)

The proposed new ruling led to local Cantonese speakers expressing their fears that Cantonese and related local culture would become extinct, while others suggested that the two Chinese 'dialects' could continue to co-exist (Deng, 2010). The 'Reunion' music video revealed interesting insights into the issue of linguistic and cultural representation when attempting to appeal simultaneously to international, Greater Chinese and domestic audiences.

Rediscovering exotic China

Chinese television shows have also emphasized foreigners' attraction to exotic, minority nationality cultures and ethnic minority areas of China. For instance, on the regular show *Sinophiliac*, Chinese hosts (presumably Han, as they are usually unmarked) often acted as mediators between 'foreigners' and 'minorities' – that is, between the global and local 'other' (see Tan, 2001: 17). For instance, when *Sinophiliac* travelled to the minority nationality areas of Guizhou and Changbai in 2008, female on-the-scene reporter, Le Le (lit: happy happy – 'le' also the same character that appears in the word for music, although with a different pronunciation) guided her foreign guests around. In the introductions and clips, foreigners often exaggerated their surprise and excitement in experiencing China's colourful diversity. In the episode on Changbai Ethnic Chaoxian (Korean) Autonomous prefecture in Yanbian Korean Autonomous County, the foreigners exaggerated their sense of excitement at seeing the exotic local minority peoples – people who were framed as objects of both the Chinese and foreigners' gaze. At the same time, the calm and collected (civilized) Chinese host used the opportunity to educate audiences about China's multiethnic splendours.

The exoticism of the natural beauty of minority nationality and border areas is often emphasized through Han Chinese exploring the areas with fun-loving 'foreign friends' who are equally fascinated by China's diversity. There is thus a kind of *double exoticism* of seeing minorities and foreigners together on television. This may be designed to attract mainstream Chinese audiences by encouraging them to rediscover 'their' colourful national heritage, the worth of which can only be fully appreciated when foreigners are shown to be interested in them as well.

In the episode based in the Changbai Korean nationality autonomous county, which borders on the Democratic People's Republic of Korea (North Korea), hosts emphasized the special fascination of the border town that 'attracted the whole world'. The foreigners performed bizarre acts of falling in love with the natural scenery of the area. Male actor Jie Gai (Francis Tchiegue) from Cameroon, who had been studying with Ding Guangquan, famous for teaching crosstalk to foreigners (Wei, 2006), stopped at a waterfall, lifted his hand up and in a dramatized voice, in a perfectly staged slow speech of the *langdu* reading-out-aloud style, called out 'Ah Changbai, so beautiful'. Following suit was British actor Da Niu (Daniel Newham), an occasional host of *Sinophiliac*. His foreign identity was emblazoned on his T-shirt with the image of the British flag. He gestured to the waterfall and dramatically repeated his amazement at its beauty in Chinese. While the two men were pointing up to the waterfall, Maliya (Maria/Mariatu Kargbo), from Sierra Leone (depicted on the cover of this book),[3] entered the scene adding to the drama: 'Jie Gai, Da Niu, what's wrong with you?' The men turned around and in unison called out 'Changbai, I love you'. When reporter Le Le came calmly into the picture to find out what was going on, the two foreign men shouted out 'We're not leaving' because 'this place is too beautiful' (Jie Gai) and because 'I've decided I want to be a Changbai person' (Da Niu). The two men then engaged in a mock argument about who should stay and who should go as if it were a competition while the reporter Le Le was calmly seen talking directly to viewers about the magnificent, green scenery. The suggestion is that the scenery of China was so spectacular it had turned the foreigners crazy – crazy enough to want to 'become' locals. While this was presented as a joke, it was also a way of emphasizing to Chinese audiences a sense of pride in their country and the beauty of its natural scenery and minority cultures.

This episode revealed a curious interplay between 'internal orientalism' (Schein, 1997: 70) with respect to Han/mainstream portrayals of minorities and the way that 'othering' operates in relation to the presentation of foreigners, wherein foreigners and minorities are both exotic spectacles for mainstream Han Chinese television audiences. The Changbai episode also depicted a series of stereotypical links to food, clothing, singing and dancing. The two foreign men were seen curiously watching men and women who wore traditional Korean dress pound rice with a hammer. Women in traditional Korean dress were also seen feeding Jie Gai, putting food directly into his mouth. This follows a stereotype described by Schein (1997: 70) as being widespread in the 1980s, particularly in relation to minority nationality women catering to the needs of urban Han men with disposable incomes travelling to rural minority nationality areas for pleasure. Viewing foreigners engaged in 'strange' acts with minorities presents a scene that is doubly exotic.

Argentinean Nati/Nadi, like Sierra Leonean Maliya, is a long-term resident of China and had established a television and online presence in China (both were contestants on *Star Avenue*). In another episode, these two foreign women, Nati/Nadi and Maliya, were seen rather shockingly, although in jest, pinching another foreigner's nose and forcing him to drink spirits (symbolic of minority groups) after being knocked out of a singing contest game. To anthropologist Eileen Walsh (2001: 111), such scenes seem designed to gratify the pleasure of the viewing 'tourists' (in this case Chinese television viewers) who are seeking a '"primitive" and happier past, a more "natural" existence where people are less distracted by the cares of an advanced society'. At the same time, the audience is given a moment to laugh at the foreigner and gain a sense of superiority (Song, 2015: 116).

This 'double exoticism' also appeared to be used in ways that supported the political status quo. In the 'Changbai' episode, we saw not just the Chaoxian/Korean Chinese people singing and dancing on the stage, but foreigners singing and dancing with them in a mixed minority nationality–foreigner performance. The medley design where foreigners performed one after another, and then together, was similar to the pattern noted for minority nationalities in Chapter 4, suggesting that 'othered' subjects perform on CCTV's music-entertainment programmes in similar ways. The song in which minorities and foreigners joined together in unison was a sweet and uplifting 'Red classic' (*hongse jingdian*), 'The Red Sun Shines on the Border Regions' (*Hong taiyang zhao bianjiang*). This revolutionary song, which has its origins in 1966, celebrates the beauty of Changbai and achievements in farming, mining and building dams, as well as the local people's will to fight, their unity with the army and the Communist victory.

It seems almost incongruous to see a young Caucasian British man, host Da Niu, singing the praises of Chairman Mao as he 'leads *us* towards victory' more than 30 years after Mao's death. However, the scene offers a sense of proof that the struggle towards the goal of national strength and prosperity has been achieved thanks to the guiding role of the Communist Party, with friendly foreigners supporting its ongoing legitimacy. The scene of foreigners *and* minority nationalities singing a revolutionary classic about border regions happily together on the CCTV stage in the reform era promotes the image that China's internal and external 'others' are willingly supportive, not just of China, but of the Party's ongoing role.

Foreigners have also directly sung the praises of the CCP in other CCTV programmes in relation to the now exotic revolutionary Han culture. For instance, during the 90th anniversary of the founding of the CCP in 2011, CCTV English ran a special on British expat Iain Inglis' passion for Chinese revolutionary songs. Inglis, who moved to Sanya in Hainan province after falling in love with his Chinese wife, explained that he first learnt to sing 'Socialism is Great' in 2004. As the only non-Chinese contestant, Inglis gained fifth place at the China National Red Song competition held in Nanchang, Jiangxi province, surpassing thousands of professional contestants. The reporter talks about how hard he worked to practice his singing and dancing, dressing with a white *tou jin* cloth wrapped around his head and sheepskin vest, and dancing in a Northern Shaanxi *yangge* style to 'appear like a Shaanxi farmer'. Inglis himself downplayed the politics of singing red songs, saying that they were just an opportunity to sing for his 'second hometown', and the reporter explained that 'love can overcome bias and cultural differences'. However, while the political meaning and intention behind red classics has changed, CCTV's use of the songs remains politically significant in the context of the CCP's ongoing claim to legitimacy.

Inglis gained significant fame in China after competing in 2011 *China's Got Talent* Season 3 on Shanghai Oriental Television. During the performance he sang a series of revolutionary songs including 'Learn From the Great Model Lei Feng' (*Xuexi Lei Fang hao bang yang*), 'Socialism is Great' (*Shehui zhuyi hao*), 'Shining Red Star' (*Shanshan de hong xing*), 'I Love Reading Chairman Mao's Books Most' (*Mao zhuxi de shu wo zui ai du/Du Mao zhuxi de shu*) and 'Yangge Supporting the Liberation Army' (*Yong Jun Yangge*). 'I Love Reading Chairman Mao's Books Most' is a song that was rarely performed on Chinese television at the time, yet it appears to have been a well-known song. As Inglis explained through the song's lyrics that he 'deeply comprehended the profound truth embedded in the book', which warmed his 'heart and head', this song received great applause and laughter from the audience.

As part of the act, Inglis progressively stripped off clothing to reveal a couple of Red Army uniforms, ending with a sheepskin vest and long red ribbons for his *yangge* dance. He also sang a snippet from 'Sing a Folk Song for the Party' (*Chang zhi shange gei dang ting*), while kneeling down and stretching out his arm to his mother-in-law, with his wife looking on, showing devotion and respect to his Chinese parents/mother, as well as to the 'motherland' and Party. He also explained that his (Chinese) dream was to sing red songs across China. According to the UK's *Daily Mail* (Gye, 2013), Inglis made it to the semifinals, but was barred from progressing further. He is quoted as saying:

> As far as I knew I was through to the final round. But the day before I was due to perform I got a phone call saying the Bureau of Broadcasting said I wasn't able to go on. There was no real reason given – perhaps they weren't very keen on having a foreigner singing songs about Communism. I was very disappointed, but that's just how it is.

Inglis has since made himself available for hire at concerts and private parties. Inglis' case provides insights into how foreigners' performances of Chinese culture can be both exotic fodder for commercial television audiences and commercially lucrative for the performer. The performances show them pursuing their 'China dreams', which highlight the attractiveness of contemporary China. The example also highlights the interconnections between CCTV and provincial channels as they draw on content – often with popular reality singing contests on provincial channels initially generating broad public interest across the nation and CCTV carrying on with work aimed at clarifying the significance of the performance for the nation. Inglis' case also demonstrates the unclear boundaries between what is and isn't politically acceptable for television performance. Revolutionary songs from the Cultural

Revolution era, such as the one about the Red Books, were rarely seen on China's music entertainment shows at the time. Having a foreigner sing them may have made the performance seem more acceptable to producers. Yet, as Inglis' experience suggests, the closer one gets to the finals, the stricter the political oversight seems to be. Given the variety of political and cultural underpinnings of this song, it is unclear why the song attracted the reactions it did. As Jones (2014: 56) notes, drawing on Jacques Derrida and Alexei Yurchak, song meanings shift according to the time and space of performance, and are subject to 'semantic promiscuity', whereby original meanings may lose significance in certain contexts.

Marrying China

Transnational marriage can be seen as a symbol of China's opening up and modernization, with a cosmopolitan lifestyle and cosmopolitan family being representative of a rising middle class and China's growing strength (Song, 2015: 109–10). At the same time, transnational marriage is a sensitive issue as it can seem to threaten or weaken an essentialized Chinese identity. On Chinese music-entertainment television, the issue is generally tackled in a way that stresses a sense of fun and exoticism. It tends to stress foreigners falling in love with China and Chinese people as the reason for such liaisons, rather than the other way round. In this way, foreigners falling in love with and marrying Chinese people becomes another way of demonstrating foreigners' love for China and Chinese culture. As I noted at the beginning of this book, in my own performance on CCTV I was introduced to the viewing audience as a 'wife of China', stressing my connection to the Chinese nation as a result of my marriage through the joke that I should get an award for this accomplishment.

Sierra Leonean Maliya became quite well-known for her performances of the catchy uplifting pop song 'Marry a Chinese Man' (*Jia gei Zhongguo ren*, lit: marry a person from China). The lyrics explain: 'I am a girl from Africa whose heart has turned towards the mysterious East', and go on to describe a girl carrying her travel bags to find her dreams. It describes Chinese people as being honest, simple and kind-hearted, always smiling, and China's young men as elegant, natural and loving girls most dearly. This is how she has found the man she loves, who makes her feel 'like flowers opening in her heart'. Chinese men are constructed as ideal husbands for foreign women, as 'to marry a Chinese man, is to become a happy bride'. The final phrases describe a traditional Chinese marriage scene where a foreigner adopts Chinese customs, wears an embroidered wedding dress, gets into the bridal sedan chair, sings opera and looks on shyly 'with sweetness/happiness in her heart'.

The lyrics depict the foreigner behaving in Chinese ways and experiencing joy in marrying a Chinese man. They do not focus on Chinese people's interest in foreign cultures. The fact that this song is sung by an African woman may highlight to Chinese audiences how far the reach of

China's attractiveness has extended, given that for many ordinary Chinese people, Africa is a very distant place. In this sense, China is represented as a 'Land of Opportunities' for foreigners and as a place for fulfilling their dreams.[4]

At the same time, embedded within the sounds and visuals are a mix of styles and cultures. In an article published in *The Global Times* on 30 September 2009, Maliya described her 'dream to bring the cultural heritage of Africa and China together to improve social harmony'.[5] Her video clip of 'Marry a Chinese Man' – available on RenRen (a Chinese equivalent to Facebook) and on Maliya's Chinese blog, and which has also been shown on CCTV4 – stresses a degree of cultural mixing. The clip begins with Maliya drawing a line from Africa to China on a map. In the various scenes, Maliya is dressed in African-inspired fashions (she was the Miss World Talent and Best World Dress Designer winner in 2004) as she tours Beijing, and in a traditional Chinese marriage costume. Foreign women with a range of skin colours are also shown singing together, dressed in African, Chinese and Western-style clothing, in front of young, fashionably dressed Chinese men who are wearing Western-style clothes and rapping. At the same time, in a typical format where China's modernization is promoted alongside its cultural traditions, we see images of a freeway juxtaposed with a statue of Confucius, a rickshaw and the Forbidden Palace. The 'cool' combination of foreign and Chinese singers celebrating a contemporary hybridization of the new and traditional China helps to showcase China's cosmopolitanism and modernization.

The saga of Maliya's search for a Chinese husband was the subject of a documentary on CCTV News (CCTV13) posted to CNTV on 6 November 2012 entitled *Celebrating the 18th National People's Congress – Into the Grassroots – My 10 years here – Maliya: Thank You China* (*Xinying shiba da – Wo zhe shinian Maliya: Xiexie Zhongguo*). The host introduced Maliya as someone who deeply loves China. The report showed a snippet of Maliya's video 'Marry a Chinese Man' and documented her search for a Chinese husband, including her call for suitors on Weibo, a Chinese microblogging platform. It also introduceed her new song, 'Thank You China' (*Xiexie Zhongguo*), which mixed African music with Chinese and instruments. In one report she explained how the song celebrates how China changed her life. After a tough childhood in Sierra Leone, she found herself with appendicitis when she came to China. A Chinese woman sent her to hospital, looked after her for two weeks and showed her motherly affection she said she had never felt before. The song also explained her particular love for her friends in Sichuan, survivors of the Sichuan earthquake ("'Black Pearl' finds oyster in China', 2012).

Maliya herself has described China as her fate and the place where she got an opportunity to change her life to the point where many people say she is Chinese. In helping to turn Maliya into a celebrity by featuring her performances and making documentaries about her, CCTV was able to highlight to its viewers China's global interactions, the celebration of international person-to-person relations, and the benefits of having friendly foreigners – potential wives of China – who love China and who can spread positive messages about China around the world.

The performance of 'husbands', or at least 'grooms', of China is also evident in CCTV's music-entertainment programming. Such acts also stress foreigners' attraction to China. In the final scene in the *Sinophiliac* outdoor special in Changbai Korean nationality autonomous county, a mock wedding took place in what looked like a tourism 'nationality village', a phenomenon that has become ubiquitous across China. Cameroon actor Jie Gai was seen talking to the camera, saying, 'I am today's groom', while a heart appeared on the screen as a transition to the next shot as was typical of wedding videos. Both Jie Gai and UK actor Da Niu, who both expressed their undying 'love' for the local place 'Changbai' and threatened never to leave, were seen carrying roses towards women whose heads were covered and whose faces the audience could not see. As the men walked down towards the two brides, the expectation was that they were marrying beautiful Changbai Chaoxian/Korean minority nationality women, the women of the *place* they 'loved'. It was then revealed that one of the people they were 'marrying' was Maliya, singer of 'Marry a Chinese man'. Everyone pretended to be shocked, before collapsing into a fit of laughter. The final shot was a happy global 'family' picture made up of Chinese, minority nationalities and black and white foreigners, with all the actors and other Changbai people together shouting out the programme slogan: 'The same five continents, five continents the same happiness!' (*Tongle wuzhou, wuzhou tongle*). The picture expanded out to a happy 'global' family with separately identified nationalities, though not (yet) messily intertwined through intermarriage. Despite being presented as a bit of fun, the scene suggests a degree of uncertainty about how much China should accept the foreign 'other', as well as possibilities for ongoing and deeper relationships.

The image of foreigners engaging with and integrating into Chinese life fits with what Farrer (2008: 23) identified in an ethnographic study of intermarriage in Shanghai.[6] Farrer found that foreign spouses were expected to 'make some accommodations to a Chinese lifestyle' and were 'most admired when they mastered elements of Chinese culture and language'. While Chinese spouses using marriage as a ticket out of China is suggestive of an abandonment of a weak China (an angle that has not been the focus of any Chinese music-entertainment show I have encountered), the reverse trend towards foreigners choosing to live in China with their spouses and adapting to Chinese ways of life highlights the attractiveness of China for foreigners and presents a reason for feeling greater pride in a strong nation.

Internationalizing China with stars from abroad

Many foreigners who develop a performing career as singers or musicians in China are popular singers of ethnic Chinese backgrounds from Singapore (e.g., Sun Yanzi/Stephanie Sun and Cai Jianya/Tanya Chua – a mentor on the 2014 CCTV3 hit *Sing My Song*) and Malaysia (e.g., Cai Jingru/Fish Leong and J.J.

Lin). Such singers who can easily blend into the local market, however, are best categorized as overseas Chinese. In this section, I focus on foreign singers from a non-ethnic Chinese background who performed frequently on Chinese television.

Notably, there have been few performances of globally renown pop stars from outside of China, and when they have performed on CCTV, they have tended to do so in partnership with Chinese stars, emphasizing an equal bilateral relationship between the two nations, with China as host. For instance, pop star Celine Dion from Canada appeared on the *CCTV Spring Festival Gala* in 2013 in a duet with China's 'national style' 'diva' Song Zuying. British singer Sarah Brightman, who sang the theme song for the 1992 Barcelona Olympic Games, was invited to sing the theme song of the 2008 Beijing Olympic Games, *You and Me*, in a duet with China's Liu Huan (one of the most well-known singers in mainland China) during the Opening Ceremony.

A smattering of foreigner stars from non-Asian countries have appeared on Chinese reality shows on provincial channels. One example, *Sing For China* (*Wei Zhongguo ge chang*) run by Guizhou provincial satellite television and China Radio International and sponsored by the cosmetics brand Wenbiquan (Wetherm), was a one-off contest staged in Beijing on the eve of the New Year going into 2014. In this reality singing competition, four foreign stars competed against four Chinese stars with the requirement that they all had to sing Chinese songs.

The foreign contestants were Luola Feiqi/Laura Fygi, a globally renown Dutch singer of Egyptian and Dutch heritage, who recorded a Chinese song 'Rose, Rose, I Love You' (*Meigui meigui wo ai ni*); Xila/Shilah Amzah, a young Malaysian Muslim singer who had made inroads into the Chinese market through her prior performances on *Asian Wave*, *Chinese Idol* and *I am a Singer* (see Chapter 5); Hao Ge/Uwechue Emmanuel, born in Liberia, with Nigerian nationality, who was introduced by the host as 'China's black horse star', and who gained fame as a finalist in CCTV's *Star Avenue* in 2006 (see further details later in this chapter); and Cai Yan, from South Korea, labelled by the host as 'Korea's Beyoncé'. The Chinese stars were Mongolian-Chinese Teng Ge'er (introduced as being 'from the grasslands'), Qi Yu from 'China Taiwan', China's 'first female rock star' Luo Qi, and Fan Yichen/Van Fan from 'China Taiwan', with ancestry from the Taiwanese Amis tribe, who first became popular in China in 2002 with his Chinese version of the theme song ('I Believe') from the popular South Korean film *My Sassy Girl*. All performers were exotic in their own way in terms of their mixed cultural backgrounds and/or global musical influences. They all chose to sing Chinese pop songs from various eras.

After all the contestants had sung their song, the 500 members of the live audience cast their votes for their favourite singer on the day. Despite great efforts spent explaining the fair process of the votes, the selection of a Chinese star, Qiyu, to win, with Laura Fygi as runner up, reinforced the superiority of the Chinese singers over foreign ones. During the show, the question of whether this contest was fair in terms of asking a foreigner to compete with

Chinese singers in the singing of Chinese songs was raised with contestants. The Chinese singers said it was not fair, but two of the foreign singers spoke of this in a positive light: Hao Ge said it was not fair but it was an opportunity to learn, while Laura Fygi said 'I think it's a good think because… it's not about the singer, it's the song'. Foreigners' interest in learning Chinese songs – especially foreign pop stars – helped to cement the significance of Chinese culture in the world. A point was made about the particular effort that Laura Fygi, who did not speak Chinese, went to transliterate the lyrics. They showed audiences the unusual transcription that Fygi had written out and referred to during her performance.

The show had all the elements of the global reality singing contests. It emphasized the star factor by having the celebrities arrive in a luxury car and step out onto a red carpet as they walked into the studio building. It emphasized the artists 'real selves', such as through setting up conflicts behind the scenes, allowing audiences to see their 'true' natures. For instance, audiences saw glimpses of Laura Fygi flustered and frustrated by constantly being followed by cameras as she prepared for the show. They also showed her confused by the inclusion of a trumpet in the back-up band for her song during rehearsals, which she didn't like. By including some conflict, this made the overall positive cross-cultural relations between Chinese and foreigners, and among the cosmopolitan group themselves, seem 'genuine' too. There was also an interesting mix of languages used, with Xila speaking a mixture of English and Chinese, and Cai Yan speaking a mixture of Chinese and Korean with a translator explaining Korean sections for Chinese viewers. Allowing the contestants to flip between their mother tongue and Chinese helped to present performers as more 'naturally' choosing to learn and incorporate Chinese into their lives, and was a style that was much less commonly found on CCTV where foreigners were more likely to be seen speaking entirely in Chinese. During the show, host Sa Beining spoke of the show as being an 'international style music programme'. Explaining the slogan for the show, he noted that while 'Chinese voices are seeking resonance around the world, the world's voices are singing for China' (*Zhongguo shengyin, shi jie gongming*), highlighting the programme's attempt to demonstrate to Chinese viewers the success of its global cultural outreach.

Pop singer Adam Lambert, who became widely known after appearing on the eighth season of *American Idol* in 2009, where he was runner up, was another global star to appear on Chinese television. He appeared on *Chinese Idol*, the official show of the same *Idol* franchise on Shanghai Oriental/Dongfang Satellite Television in 2013. The openly gay artist is known for showcasing his individuality through theatrical performance styles and unique fashion. During this show, he was a guest judge during the auditions round, along with resident judges who included American-Chinese pop star Li Wen (Coco Lee) and mainland Tibetan-Chinese pop star Han Hong. Significantly, in another example of the 'blending of opposites' and 'double exoticism' Lambert was invited to judge a minority nationality female contestant named Yang Jima, of Menba/Monpa ethnicity, a little-known ethnic group from Tibet.

Yang Jima's audition song 'The Timeless Beauty of Prayer' (*Qidao yongheng de meili*) was in the *yuanshengtai* style, a Menba ethnic song, which she learnt from her grandmother. She emphasized the traditional nature of the song, saying 'In the future I will continue singing it to my children, and hope they will continue singing it', while the audience was shown images of her strolling through beautiful 'untouched' mountains and beside a lake (presumably in her hometown). She wore a traditionally inspired free-flowing dress, no shoes, and sang with her eyes closed and sitting cross-legged on the floor, while accompanying herself with tiny cymbals. Lambert acted as the fascinated foreigner. Conversing in English he said, 'I like your outfit. It's so beautiful. It's traditional yeah?' to which Yang Jima replied 'Half' (in English), thus suggesting her links to both tradition and modernity/globality.

There was a concerted effort to construct her music as 'international'. The producer asked Yang Jima, 'Do you think your performance can reach the international hall?' to which she replied, 'I believe ethnic things forever belong to the world'. As she began singing, Lambert looked intently with a smile emerging on his face, while Tibetan Han Hong closed her eyes, totally engrossed in the moment. After the performance, Lambert told her, 'It was beautiful. It was just so angelic. You were just so grounded in your energy and focused. It was beautiful. I loved it.' Han Hong added 'You are the pride of our people. Your music is infectious and international.' Yang Jima went on to become the runner-up of the national competition, singing pop songs inspired by Tibetan/Menba ethnic traditions. Bringing a peaceful and ephemeral tone to the songs, with a hint of sadness, along with her elegant posture and free-flowing ethnic-inspired dresses, the graduate of the Communications University of China in Beijing was labelled as a 'goddess' (*nüshen*) by the judges throughout the show.

Lambert's own performance on the big stage was of the song 'Mad World', originally sung by the pop/rock band Tears for Fears in 1982, which is about people going about their daily business and going nowhere. He spoke about the lyrics being important because they are about 'being an outsider feeling like you don't fit in, being an alien almost', which he explained he had felt 'in many parts of my life'. However, drawing on the power of music and musical fans, he suggested that 'together we can pretend like that never happened'. Despite very different backgrounds and aesthetics, Lambert's song reflected a similar tone and feeling to Yang Jima's performances in their desire to express a genuineness marked by a slight sense of despair possibly as a result of their ethnic or sexual differences to mainstream culture.

This example serves to highlight that double exoticism occurs in provincial reality shows as well as on CCTV through the pairing of an internal ethnic 'other' with an external foreign 'other'. However, the provincial television shows have allowed for the performances of more flamboyant international stars, stressed the significance of each artist's individuality, and allowed each international artist to sing on their own and assert their own identities, and were not necessarily always constrained through 'bilateral' duets between foreign and Chinese performers.

190 *Foreign identities*

Another CCTV channel, CCTV Guide, has also aired ad hoc prerecorded concerts of foreign stars with footage likely coming from transnational music or television companies. The Guide seemed to be intended to lure audiences towards CCTV's premium pay TV channels, where more international concerts may be accessed. In 2008, I saw prerecorded concerts of Australia's Kylie Minogue, Canada's Celine Dion and various Japanese and British stars, which suggests that different CCTV channels are taking different approaches to the kinds of foreignness that mainland audiences can access.

Red and Black: African Star Hao Ge

Apart from Maliya from Sierra Leone, another African singer to have established himself as a celebrity in China is Liberian/Nigerian singer Hao Ge (Uwechue Emmanuel). Hao Ge, whose name most appropriately is a homophone for the Chinese words for both 'good brother' and 'good song', came to fame after becoming the runner-up in the yearly finals of *Star Avenue* on CCTV3 in 2006. He stood out for his talent and unique style that mixed gospel-R&B with popular, sentimental and revolutionary Chinese songs. His album title *R&B*, which stands for Red and Black, summarizes the blend between the racial, artistic and political references in his work. With his rhythm and blues musical influence, Hao Ge brought a new style to the Chinese television stage and his performances helped to present a cosmopolitan view of the Chinese state and its national culture. His fresh take on revolutionary songs can be seen as a parallel to performers like Ah Bao (discussed in Chapter 4), who helped to revitalize CCP classics through the combination of Shaanbei style and a Western dance beat to appeal to a younger audience, appealing at once to commercial goals and satisfying the authorities' desire to spread messages about the key ongoing role of the CCP in Chinese society.

One of Hao Ge's most captivating performances on CCTV was of the song 'In Memory of the Brother in Arms' (*Huainian zhanyou*) during the *Star Avenue* finals. The song, a masterpiece of celebrated Chinese film music composer Lei Zhenbang, was featured in the classic 1963 revolutionary film called *Visitors to the Icy Mountain* (*Bing shan shang de lai ke*), which was about the Communist Army's liberation of Xinjiang, China's Western province. The lyrics are written from the point of view of a soldier whose close comrade had frozen to death in the icy border-region mountains, still tightly clasping his rifle. The music mournfully draws on the Tajik flavour of one of the ethnic groups in the area.

According to one report, Hao Ge watched the film in detail numerous times before the performance (Very CD, n.d.). As well as the original film version, he was able to draw on a large number of contemporary male singers who have performed the nostalgic song in their own signature styles. They include noted pop star Liu Huan (Hao Ge's mentor), Daolang (a Han pop star who became famous singing 'Xinjiang' style music), Teng Ge'er (China's most famous ethnic Mongolian male pop singer) and Dai Yuqiang (an operatic/'national style' military singer). Hao Ge thus joins a list of strong Chinese male luminaries from different ethnic backgrounds who have performed this classic song of national salvation, solidarity and compassion for one's countrymen.

This performance was highly choreographed. With a short piano introduction that built up the tension, Hao Ge stepped out of the blackness through a huge star (representing both contemporary celebrity culture and the Party-state) and walked towards the studio audience in the spotlight. Dressed in white, a symbolic offering of peace, audiences then saw him close-up and heard his powerful gospel-inspired voice belt out the famous opening line in Chinese, 'Tianshan [in the Xinjiang Uyghur Autonomous region] is my beautiful hometown'.

Savouring each word, the lines connected this man from faraway Africa to the furthest reaches of the Chinese nation, Xinjiang – both exotic areas to most Han Chinese who live in the coastal and central regions. The music also connected him to the CCP's Red Army, which liberated and united the nation. Before the first line was finished the audience was cheering and applauding. By line three, Hao Ge had put his hand on his heart as a sign of respect and offering. As the audience began to clap along, the camera panned across the stage so that audiences could see actors in old Red Army uniforms posing on both sides of Hao Ge like statues, shifting their stances from upright and kneeling, to looking ahead, to steadfastly holding their rifles, replicating scenes from the movie. To back up his words was a large choir of men and women who stood up piously, singing from black books with lyrics, much in the style of those early Christian hymns first adopted for secular uses during the Taiping Revolution (see Chapter 2), stressing the solemn importance of the moment.

As the tension resolved with the slowing tempo at the end of the chorus, a sublime moment of emotional solidarity was established between the foreign black soloist, Chinese accompanying singers, dancers and instrumentalists, and the on-screen audience. Hao Ge closed his eyes and put his hand on his heart again, as he sang of the dear soldier who 'will never hear me play the piano again, [or] hear me sing'. Audiences were seen clapping and nodding, then a mournful trumpet solo (imitating a soldier's bugle) was heard, with images of the conductor and the whole audience waving glow sticks in unison. For verse two, the camera panned around the whole studio, which was lit with warm red lights, giving an impression of a closed and safe space, interspersed with close-ups of Hao Ge, still absorbed until the end when he bowed, which was followed by more cheers from the audience.

This performance was one of the rare moments I have seen on Chinese television where a foreigner has commanded the centre of attention and been the driving force of such a significant construction of national emotion. Hao Ge did not simply imitate Chinese artists, but brought to the song his powerful voice and unique R&B rendition of the revolutionary Chinese classic. While this choice of repertoire highlighted his respect for Chinese culture, language and politics, his differences in voice and looks

192 *Foreign identities*

brought a fresh look and sound for Chinese audiences, and may have helped to reignite their interest in classic red songs that emphasize the CCP's important role in unifying China.

Success on *Star Avenue*, given his popularity with audiences and positive adjudication by authorities, opened the doors for Hao Ge to appear on multiple programmes, including the *CCTV Spring Festival Gala*. In the 2007 Gala, he appeared alongside Beijing-based Tibetan pop star Han Hong, singing 'The Place Far Away' (*Zai nar yaoyuan de difang*). Co-starring with a successful minority nationality pop star helped to further promote a cosmopolitan image of China where both internal and external 'otherness', exoticism and colour is celebrated. The merging of Africa, a foreign place which Hao Ge embodies, and the distant Western regions of China, which he sings about can also be seen as a kind of 'double exoticism'. At the same time, Beijing was constructed as the central meeting place for all the world's people, including minority nationalities and foreigners.

Hao Ge's performances also exemplified the theme of foreigners' love for and attraction to China – not only in his choice of songs but also in his spoken dialogue and in the media discourse about him. Like Maliya, CCTV also produced a documentary on Hao Ge that emphasized that he came to China to pursue his dreams. It said he had long wanted to be a professional singer and had travelled the world looking for an opening without luck until he came to China. Hao Ge, like Maliya, showed gratitude towards China in his interviews on CCTV to the point where he said he hoped he could be accepted as Chinese. After performing a Beijing Opera piece on *Star Avenue* in 2006, dressed in traditional costume with a long beard (that was partly coming undone!), Hao Ge was asked by host Bi Fujian why he wanted to learn Beijing Opera. His response was:

> I like China. I like Chinese culture, and what I want to say is, I've been to many countries and the feeling China has given me is very warm [he puts his hand on his heart] and safe. I have many friends here and many friends that like my music. I hope one day I can become a Chinese person. I love [*re'ai*] China.

During the *'My Chinese Life' Global Chinese Storytelling Competition* (the show on which I appeared, see the Preface), Hao Ge appeared as a special guest to sing 'A Question Asked Ten Million Times' (*Qianwan ci de wen*), the theme song from the television drama series *A Beijing Native in New York* (*Beijing ren zai Niuyue*), popular in the 1990s (see Barmé, 1999; Sun, 2002: 68–85,101; Yang, 2002: 201–2). The song was originally made famous by his mentor Liu Huan, who sang the 2008 Beijing Olympic Games theme song with Sarah Brightman, and who wrote the lyrics for the theme to *A Beijinger in New York*. The song conjures up images of the protagonist Wang Qiming struggling to survive in his new life in New York, eventually emerging stronger and transformed (Sun, 2002: 81). In Hao Ge's rendition, this song became emblematic of a foreigner who has struggled to survive around the world, but finally developed self-awareness and gained success through transformation in Beijing. How times have changed!

It is also interesting to note that the performances of Hao Ge and Maliya came at a time when there was an increase in African economic migration to China, particularly since the 1990s (Li, 2008). A large number of Africans have studied at universities in Beijing since the 1960s, when Chairman Mao welcomed students in the name of Third World solidarity and helped train African students in development-oriented subjects like engineering, medicine and science. There has also been a significant degree of anti-African discrimination among Chinese that emerged from colonialist racial discourses in the late nineteenth and twentieth centuries whereby 'white' and 'yellow' races were placed above 'blacks'. Residual stereotypes of black people have made living in China difficult for them. Showcasing talented African performers who love China may be part of an attempt to address sensitivities and reverse negative stereotypes of African people in China.

Hao Ge's celebrity status has also inspired other Africans in China, some of whom have copied his performance style. For instance, an African blogger calling himself Red Song Prince, Hao Di (lit: good little brother – a play on the name 'Hao Ge', which sounds like 'good older brother'), uploaded a video of himself on YouTube in 2011 marching, dancing and singing red classics like 'If There Was No CCP, There'd Be No New China' (*Meiyou gongchangdang jiu mei you xin Zhongguo*) and 'Chairman Mao's Words Remembered by Heart' (*Mao Zhuxi de hua'er ji xin shang*). Hao Di stood in what looked like a dorm room (in the vein of China's YouTube sensation the 'Back Dorm Boys'), in front of a poster of Chairman Mao and a Chinese flag, dressed in a green army T-shirt and cap with a red star, and Red Book in hand. In one scene in typical official discourse, on the occasion of the CCP's 90th birthday, he expressed his wish that Chinese and Africans be good brothers forever. This online performance came across as a spoof, as he rather ironically picked up a gun and casually brandished it while singing (or lip-synching) the original lyrics of the Red classics: 'No matter how fierce and aggressive the enemy, put down the dragnet, take those bandit jackals and wolves, and bury them all.' While Chinese television provides fodder for, and has to compete against, irony, mocking and sarcasm online, the fact that such spoofs exist suggests that the original programmes are also attracting some attention.

Overall, Hao Ge's performances appear to have been a win-win situation for him, the Chinese state and music-entertainment market. He has had a major platform from which to perform and to gain exposure to a massive audience. At the same time, he has helped to attract audiences to Party-state messages of a revitalized Chinese state that is open to cross-cultural influence through the blending of his 'foreign' R&B singing style and 'racially other' appearance with revolutionary classics of the CCP and nostalgic and popular Chinese songs.

Red and White: Russian star Vitas

Russian-Ukrainian singer Vitas (*Weitasi* in Chinese, born in the Ukraine as Vitaliy Vladasovich Grachyov) became a star in Russia in 2000 with his hit song, 'Opera No. 2' (*Geju 2*), which makes use of his incredibly high-pitched voice and energetic use of falsetto (somewhat like Ah Bao, see Chapter 4). His popularity soon spread to other parts of the world, including China. But it wasn't until June 2006 that he began to become well-known in China after being invited by CCTV to participate in 'The Year of Russia in China' festivities. Vitas was one of few Caucasian foreign superstars I have seen on China's regular music-entertainment programmes. While China and Russia have had fraught relations over time, since 1991 they have generally been cordial. Vitas was the representative Russian singer to have gained a notable presence on Chinese television aimed at mainstream mainland Chinese audiences at the time of research for this book.

Vitas' artistic style was unique, and he often performed in spectacular, self-branded costumes with the letter 'V' on one sleeve. In performing his most famous song 'Opera No. 2' on the CCTV stage for *The Same Song* in 2006, he stood rigidly in a highly choreographed way, occasionally raising his arm slowly as he built towards a climax to reveal the 'V' label on his sleeve. This was a unique form of self-promotion that I had not seen any other stars on the Chinese television stage – Chinese or foreign – use in such an explicit way. The closest would be the branding of People's Liberation Army performing arts troupes who perform in uniform and in a sense 'advertise' the Chinese army. Even when Vitas performed for a 2009 self-promotional production for Shanghai Dongfang Satellite Television, entitled *The Wind Comes from the East* (*Feng Cong Dongfang Lai*), he still had his personal 'V' brand on his sleeve. For this performance, Vitas was paired with popular Chinese female pop star Wei Wei to sing the theme song of the same name. While Wei Wei sang live on set, Vitas appeared prerecorded on a screen on the stage. While the logo for Shanghai Television was a white star on a red background, in the video Vitas was the 'white (Caucasian) star' on a red background.

While most other foreign stars on Chinese television (e.g., Hao Ge) have made their mark in China by singing in Chinese and displaying their accomplishments in aspects of Chinese culture and civilization, Vitas is one of the few foreign performers I saw on China's popular music-entertainment programmes at the time who entered the Chinese television market displaying little knowledge of Chinese language and culture. He frequently sang in Russian, commanded the stage with his own songs, and foregrounded his own unique vocal style, clothing designs and on-stage movements. Although he made an effort to master a few greetings to audiences in Chinese (e.g., 'I love you', 'Thank you', 'Dear friends'), the pronunciation suggested that these words were likely the extent of his Chinese abilities. Most of his on-stage conversations with hosts and the audience was conducted in Russian through a translator – a rarity when most foreigners on CCTV were shown to speak fluent Chinese.

As time went on and his knowledge of Chinese language and culture deepened, Vitas engaged in more nuanced cross-cultural linguistic and musical exchanges. For instance, during the 2010 *Beijing Television Online Spring Festival Gala*, Vitas sang the Chinese classic 'Great Sea Ah, Hometown' (*Da hai a, guxiang*), although in a Russian translation. This came after a senior citizen showed off her musical and linguistic skills by singing his 'Opera No. 2' in the Russian original. To wrap up the set, famous Chinese female impersonator Li Yugang offered his rendition of the Chinese version of 'Moscow Nights' (*Mosike jiaowai de wanshang*), the Russian song most familiar to Chinese audiences, originally composed for the 1956 Soviet documentary film *In the Days of the Big Movement* (*Zai yundong dahui de rizi li*) and translated into Chinese in 1957. Li intermixed Vitas-style vocal inflections into his performance. The combined acts were labelled on the show in the host's discourse as a mapping or image of China and Russia on one another. During the same event, Vitas also displayed his growing skills in Chinese, demonstrating his desire to adapt to the Chinese market when he sang the high-pitched song 'Qinghai-Tibetan Plateau' (*Qingzang Gaoyuan*) in a duo with highly polished Chinese female soprano Tang Can.

During the *CCTV New Year's Eve Gala* on 1 January 2016, Vitas again sang 'Opera No. 2', which merged into a Chinese opera performance by Li Yugang before Vitas re-entered the stage and the two performers mixed an unlikely combination of Western pop opera and traditional Chinese operatic styles. The feature of all these performances was creative cultural exchange based on the Russian and Chinese singers' shared ability to sing in a high pitch as well as a blending of differences in language and their trademark singing styles. In adapting to the Chinese context, Vitas' presence in China helped to support the image of foreigners, even superstars in their own countries, coming to China to advance their careers and pursue their dreams, thus highlighting the modernization, cosmopolitanism and creativity of contemporary China.

Vitas' performances have also helped to tell the story of China's modernization in relation to its multiethnicity. In 2006, he performed on *The Same Song* on CCTV staged in western China's Ningxia Hui Autonomous Region – the same region where he was participating in the filming for the feature film *Mulan*.[7] Similar to Hao Ge and Greater China pop stars Xie Tingfeng (Nicholas Tse) and Wang Lihong (Wang Leehom), Vitas' 'foreign' performance on the CCTV stage (in the same episode as Wang Lihong, described in Chapter 5), was juxtaposed with the performances of China's 'internal others', emphasizing China's 'colour' and vitality in a domestic and global context. Commanding the huge outdoor stage with a Hui/Muslim building design, outlined by flashing neon lights, Vitas metaphorically linked the outside world to the minority nationality area. The spectacular 'international' performance transformed the stage and Ningxia into a 'transnational' space, and the high feeling associated with Vitas' performance intermeshed with subsequent acts that emphasized an internationalized, modern multiethnic Chinese culture.

Vitas' own music video for 'Opera No. 2', which I have not seen on Chinese television, and which in late 2012 had 3.9 million views on YouTube and more than 19,000 on YouKu, was extremely eccentric. He acted as a lonely man who kept fish in glass jars (mimicking a woman he had a crush on) and performed as part-fish himself with fish-gills on his neck. Netizens from around the world clearly had fun trying to work out the weird metaphors embedded into the clip: Why the fish (fish out of water?)? How could his high-pitched sounds break the glass fish jars and even blow up a glass telephone box? Was he playing on the legend of mermaids (in this case mermen) who are believed to have voices that can hypnotize human hearts? Both the video and the stage performance were hypnotic, and Vitas' allure even led to Chinese netizens creating their own amusing mash-ups, combining the song with elements from Chinese movies with Vitas' singing. While this particular video may not have appeared on Chinese television (and very few original music videos with foreign artists have been available on mainstream PRC television, as opposed to, say, MTV China which requires has required a subscription and has had restrictions on access), it is significant that Vitas was admired by Chinese netizens and by television producers who invited him to perform in China for his creativity and talent at a time when China too was promoting its creative industries.

While China has had strong historical and political links with Russia and the former Soviet Union, Vitas' appearances seemed more geared towards generating interest among youth rather than opening a space for reminiscing about bonds or overcoming difficult diplomatic moments in the past. Nostalgia for a Soviet past, however, has occasionally appeared through Chinese and Russian language renditions of the popular Russian love song 'The Kalina/Raspberry Flowers are in Bloom' (*Hong mei hua'er kai/Oy Cvetet Kalina*), composed by Jewish Soviet composer and People's Artist of Russia Isaak Osipovich Dunayevsky for the 1949 film *Cossacks of the Kuban*.[8]

Overall, Vitas, as a foreign pop star, has been able to strategically market himself in China by connecting with the Chinese national discourse. His own website proudly highlighted among his achievements an invitation to perform in festivities celebrating the Beijing 2008 Olympic Games.[9] Vitas was declared part of the 'gold team of superstars of world culture' who cooperated in presenting a magnificent Olympics in Beijing (Vitas Official Website, 2010). He also performed at the 2010 Shanghai Expo and supported the commemoration and survivors of the Sichuan earthquake that hit China on 12 May 2008 by performing in a benefit concert a year later and releasing a song (in Russian) called 'Mommy and Son' in late October 2009 in remembrance of the earthquake victims.[10]

Learning from the Korean Wave

The flow of culture between the Republic of Korea (South Korea) and China has been significantly in South Korea's favour (Shin, 2009: 106–8; Chua, 2008: 89). The ties between the two nations began to strengthen after 1992, when South Korea became the last Asian country to switch allegiances and recognize the PRC rather than the Republic of China on Taiwan. The volume of cultural exchange increased when the South Korean government began to actively promote its popular cultural exports and cultural industry after the 1997 East Asian financial crisis, and after the PRC liberalized its film and television industries and allowed greater collaborations (Chua and Iwabuchi, 2008: 3–4; Chua, 2008: 73). In what has become known as the Korean Wave (*Hanliu* in Chinese, *Hallyu* in Korean), popular culture from South Korea, or K-pop, featuring stars with 'good looks, amazing dance moves, and catchy tunes' (Visit Korea, n.d.) has been the most popular foreign popular music culture in China and around in the Asian region the since the late-1990s (Chua and Iwabuchi, 2008: 2).

CCTV was the first Chinese broadcaster to air a Korean drama in 1993 (*Jealousy, Jidu*) (Leung, 2008: 59), but over time local and provincial stations such as Hunan Satellite Television became particularly known for broadcasting popular dubbed or translated Korean language dramas (Leung, 2008: 54). Over time, a feeling of familiarity with Koreans emerged based on a shared 'East Asian pop culture' (Chua and Iwabuchi, 2008: 2). Korean formats including *Where Are We Going, Dad?* (*Baba qu nar?*) and the singing show *I am a Singer* (*Wo shi geshou*), which both started in 2013 on Hunan Satellite Television, have become hugely popular in China.

Chinese music-entertainment television's own formats have also stressed the close economic ties between South Korea and China as a result of cultural exchange. While the flow has been unbalanced in the direction of South Korea into China (Chua and Iwabuchi, 2008: 3), CCTV in particular has attempted to at least give an impression of an equal and opposite flow of PRC Chinese culture into Korea. One such programme was *The Same Song – China-ROK Friendship Concert/The Same Song in Korea* (*Zhong-Han youhao daxing gehui*), sponsored by the South Korean–Japanese food and shopping enterprise Lotte (*Le Tian*) on 16 January 2009. In December 2007, *The Same Song* also broadcast an *Enters the Republic of Korea (Hanguo)* special. This programme was entitled the *4th China-ROK Pop Fest* (*Zhong-Han Gehui*) and was a joint production by the Korean Broadcasting Station (KBS) and CCTV. Four hosts, two from each station, compered the show. The production consistently stressed the close relations between the two countries and a level of familiarity with each other's cultures. Given the joint nature of the production, it had a good basis for constructing a relationship based on a feeling of equality in cultural exchange. The programme stressed the dynamic relations in a contemporary context through a significant proportion of the programme dedicated to uplifting contemporary pop music and idols from both sides.

The close relationship in a dynamic period of cultural exchange was directly stressed in the hosts' explanations. In the opening remarks, each of the four hosts emphasized the large number of people from Korea who travel to China for leisure and business and vice versa, as well as the close political and economic ties. Chinese host Liang Yongbin emphasized the important role of music-entertainment in bringing the two sides together, drawing on the CCTV programme name *The Same Song* to stress its function as a unifying force:

> We use songs to enhance cross-cultural exchange, as singing *the* same song/s and dancing the same dance/s strengthens understanding on both sides and gives people on both sides a good impression.

Like the Greater China frame, contemporary popular East Asian cultural products – songs, films and television programmes – were the links on which mutual familiarity was based (Chua, 2001; 2006; Chua and Iwabuchi, 2008: 2). Hosts stressed that many famous Korean artists were known to Chinese people, while a few Chinese artists were known to Koreans. They also mentioned the popularity of South Korean TV dramas and actors in China. When asked by a South Korean host whether he could sing any Korean songs, CCTV host Liang Yongbin expressed his familiarity with Korean songs, saying he had known the pan-Korean classic 'Arirang' (*Alilang*) since he was young. 'Arirang' is a popular representative Korean song both in South Korea and among the Chaoxian-Korean nationality in the PRC, and thus creates a smooth link between the 'two' peoples. Liang also said he knew the 1988 Seoul Olympic Games theme song 'Hand in Hand' (*Shou la shou*), providing a bond between the two nations who had entered the club of countries who had hosted this prestigious international event. In return, Korean female host Huang Xiudong also showed familiarity with the Chinese classic pop song 'Sweetness' (*Tianmimi*), originally sung by popular Taiwanese singer Deng Lijun in 1979 – one of the most popular songs in China as it began its reform and opening-up process. The host was, however, only familiar with the tune and not the lyrics.

Overall, more seemed to be known about Korean culture by Chinese than vice versa, but the show offered a concerted effort to present the cross-cultural exchange as mutual through alternating praise for each other's cultures by hosts, and through alternating Korean and Chinese on-stage singing performances. It is also significant to note that the sense of bonding between the Chinese and Koreans did not appear to go any deeper than these pop culture connections. Even a quick quiz between hosts on traditional foods from the respective cultures revealed a lack of deeper knowledge.

A suggestion of mutual exchange and understanding between the two countries was also highlighted through mixed-language conversations among the hosts. They conversed as if they understood what the other said, each in turn responding in their respective languages without the use of interpreters. It was made to seem entirely natural, even though it is unlikely that the hosts understood each other's languages. They acted as if they fully understood each other by nodding at each other's comments, saying 'Yes, that's right' etc. in their own languages at the appropriate moments. CCTV audiences could see what was being said in Chinese subtitles for the dialogue in Korean. Singers too sang in each other's languages, using prepared notes – showing more familiarity with the most well-known musical tunes than each other's languages.

The closest and most touching moment of the programme came at the end with the suggestion of Chinese–Korean brotherly love when two major stars, China's Sun Nan and South Korea's Shen Chenxun (Shin Seung-hun), sang the song 'I believe'. This song, which was originally sung by Shen as the theme song for a Korean movie *My Sassy Girl*, became popular across Asia when the movie was released in 2001. The song was translated into other languages and Sun Nan is well-known in China for his Mandarin rendition. However, in this CCTV-KBS programme Sun did his best to sing in Korean with Shen, reading the lyrics using prepared notes. The two 'trendy' men, both famous for the same song, clearly had fun singing together. For a brief moment, Sun Nan switched to Chinese and Shen quickly pulled out his piece of paper pretending to follow in Chinese for a moment before reverting back to the original Korean. This act was clearly designed to be a crowd-pleasing grand finale. As the song drew to a close, the two men sang with their arms around each other, with playful smiles on their faces. The performance drew many cheers from the crowd. As the hosts wrapped up the programme, they re-emphasized how touching it was to see these two singers 'like brothers'. This moment was the closest the programme got to including Chinese and South Koreans together in a family metaphor. Despite the somewhat forced construction of mutual exchange in this instance, it is important to consider the role that pop stars can play in making cross-cultural connections and bilateral relations feel 'real'.

There has also been a clear attempt to establish mutual commercial benefits for Korean artists and CCTV. CCTV has promoted certain Korean pop stars on particular programmes apparently with the aim of attracting Chinese youth to CCTV. For instance, in 2012 Korean pop stars were heavily promoted in CCTV's pay TV music channel Phoenix Music, with particular programmes devoted to K-pop. In 2012, Big Bang, a K-pop boyband, was also promoted in reports on the CCTV-Music Weekend Music Talk (*Zhoumo yuetan*) show, which introduced their first concerts in China as part of their Big Bang Alive 'Galaxy' Tour, sponsored by the Samsung Galaxy smartphone. Korean stars were also linked to CCTV programme branding and product advertising on CCTV, such as when megastar Rain (Jung Ji-hoon) appeared in a shampoo advertisement in every advertisement break during the 'Longliqi' 2008 *CCTV Youth Singing Competition*. Longliqi is a brand that manufactures shampoo and was the official sponsor of the three-week CCTV television event.

Chinese television also jumped on popular global crazes emerging out of Korea with new renditions of Korean artist Psy's amusing 'Gangnam Style' song and dance music video, which went viral in 2012. 'Gangnam Style' appeared several times on CCTV in late 2012 including on the CCTV-Music National Musical Instrument (*Minzu qiyue*) Competition 'innovation' category, where a woman dressed in a Chinese cheongsam (*qipao*) played the song on the *guzheng*, a traditional Chinese stringed instrument, alongside a man who made sound effects into a microphone. CCTV-Music programmes reported on the global craze of this online hit emerging from Asia, and on the famous stars from Western countries who have copied this music and dance in a tone suggesting an emerging reversal of global flows of popular culture from the West to Asia (CNTV, 2012a). In a new programme that began on CCTV-Music in late 2012 called *Culture Noon* (*Wenhua Zhengwu*) with the tagline 'culture is strength, feeling, influence and warmth – disseminate culture, affect China' (*Chuanbo wenhua, yingxiang Zhongguo*), a discussion was held on why 'Gangnam Style' was so hot around the world, with one host expressing her wish that a Chinese song would also catch on around the world (CNTV, 2012b). 'Gangnam Style' was the first YouTube video to reach one billion views (Gruger, 2012). Thus, 'Gangnam Style' epitomized for Korea the type of global interest in the country that China so desired for itself. The Korean cultural and creative industries were set up as examples for Chinese creatives to follow.

The CCTV versions have not been the only or most popular Chinese renditions of 'Gangnam Style'. The song was also performed on provincial satellite channels, including a 2016 version with a rock feel by Taiwanese singer Su Jianxin, also known as Shin, on the Korean format *I am a Singer* on Hunan Provincial Satellite Television. There have also been numerous amusing online renditions including a Chinese Red Army version, made up of mashups from a socialist-era film, a version by Chinese dissident Ai Weiwei, who is celebrated in the West, and a version by foreign students in China.

American Fulbright scholar Jesse Appell, for example, released a self-made music video on YouTube called 'Laowai Style' in 2012. While the original 'Gangnam Style' song 'pokes fun at the luxurious lifestyle of the South Korean elite' (Arons, 2012), Appell's version featured Chinese language rap lyrics that tried to deflect some of the stereotypes of rich foreigners in the Sanlitun area of Beijing, famous for its foreign bars, and international stores. The lyrics canvass the stereotypes of foreigners who drive flashy cars use expensive phones, fail to integrate into Chinese society as they eat at KFC, use Western-style utensils, don't make Chinese friends and are ignorant of and uninterested in Chinese language and culture. They also explain how such foreigners are thought to typically get ripped off at the markets and are overly concerned about traffic laws. Appell constructs himself as a foreigner who is none of these things, but rather as one who drives a second-hand electric bike, not a BMW, who knows Beijing well enough to avoid the north third ring road at rush hour, and who researches Chinese culture at the prestigious Tsinghua University. Rather than separate themselves from 'real' Chinese society, the video features himself and his foreign friends doing 'ordinary' things in Beijing, such as using the outdoor gym equipment, dancing with Chinese locals in public parks and riding on the subway (Appell, 2012).

The success of his parody of the Korean song was used as a basis for a feature on Appell on the CCTV.com website. The site asked foreigners to express their 'China Dream' and gave them a platform for sharing their fascination with life in China. Appell studied *xiangsheng*, a traditional form of Chinese stand-up comedy, under Ding Guangquan (Dashan's master teacher) 20 years earlier with a US State Department-funded Fulbright fellowship. He noted in the documentary that he wanted to show that while foreigners may do silly things Chinese people might not normally do, they also know about how people in China live. It was part of his attempt to 'find ways to bring China and the West together through humour' (China Dream, 2014; Laugh Beijing, 2016). The use of parodies (as opposed to remakes with individual artists bringing their fresh new style to an existing piece) was an uncommon practice on Chinese television, especially CCTV at the time. Yet this 'Korean' parody appeared to open up a space for different kinds of discussions on intercultural relations.

In 2015, CCTV introduced a new show called *Bite, Cough, Throat, Boom, Choke*, a rough translation of the show's onomatopoeic name *Ding Ge Long Dong Qiang*, that features acting and singing stars from South Korea performing with mainland Chinese stars. Billed as an entertainment feast, the new 'variety reality show' (*zongyi zhenrenxiu*) aimed to break ground stylistically by combining behind the scenes and intimate 'chats' with young stars, fast-paced editing of concert clips, sound effects, on-screen text that popped up around the screen like bubbles rather than conventional subtitles, and fashion. The general message, however, reflected that of earlier shows involving foreigners. The show featured Korean stars coming to China and studying traditional forms of opera in Beijing, Zhejiang and Sichuan with a Chinese teacher. While accommodating, and acknowledging a fascination with Korean culture among Chinese youth, the overall programme turned the focus back onto China by showcasing China's vitality and attractiveness to Korean stars.

Korean stars on satellite provincial channels seem to have had more of a chance to 'be themselves' by singing Korean pop classics alongside Chinese classics than stars from other countries. For instance, Huang Zhilie (Hwang Chi Yeul), who participated and gained third place on *I am a Singer* Season 4 in 2016, gained great acclaim as he sang a mixture of Chinese and Korean love songs and upbeat pop songs. When he first appeared singing in Chinese, the production made a point of emphasizing the sense of happy surprise in seeing the talented Korean sing in Chinese. During his performance there was a cutaway to another contestant who stated that he was 'Singing in our national language!' (*chang Guoyu*), followed by a cutaway of another contestant's exaggerated facial expression of keen surprise. Through his performances on *I am a Singer*, Huang rose from relative obscurity in China (he reportedly had one fan to greet him when he first arrived at Changsha airport for the recording of the show) to becoming a highly acclaimed pop star over the course of the show. It was only around a year earlier that he broke out as a pop star in his home market after been requested to compete on Mnet Korea's reality show *I Can See Your Voice*. In March 2016, Huang won the prize for Most Powerful Singer of the Year at the KU Music Asian Music Awards (*Ku yinyue yazhou shengdian*) in Guangzhou. He was also named the Overseas

Multitalented Entertainer (*Haiwai quanneng yiren*) and the Overseas Most Popular Singer (*Haiwai zui shou huanying geshou*) at the Music Radio: China's Top Music Awards (Music Radio *Zhongguo TOP yinyue shengdian*) in Beijing in May 2016.

In recognition of the important social role of pop stars, in March 2016, he was also appointed as an honorary goodwill ambassador for Korea–China cultural exchange by the Korean Cultural Centre in Shanghai. The 12-month appointment aimed to promote cultural exchanges between South Korea and China and foster friendships between people from both countries. Huang noted that he was 'honored to be appointed the position of working as a messenger between the two cultures' and he would try his best to 'promote Korean culture to many Chinese people and help them understand Korea better' (Lee, 2016). In the same year, he was invited to be a regular member of CCTV3's *Bite, Cough, Throat, Boom, Choke* Season 2, starting in September – a show that aimed to enhance China's soft power.

Similar to other foreign artists who have used China as a base for enhancing their musical careers, in Huang's introduction video for *I am a Singer*, he spoke of his singing dreams and what he hoped for in front of Chinese audiences, highlighting the role that Chinese television could play in fulfilling foreign artists' dreams of having their music and singing talents recognized:

> I moved up to Seoul from my hometown 10 years ago to make my dream come true. I worked as a vocal coach for a living and have never let go of music. I went through a tough patch and so many times I thought about giving up, but I always kept my small dream of becoming a singer in my heart and I hoped that I would be singing in front of many people someday. Now I want to let many people hear my voice. I am Hwang Chi Yeul.
> (Mango TV, 2016)[11]

Cautious nostalgia with Japan

Unlike South Korea whose cultural relations with China appear to be thriving, Japan's image suffers from 'a troubled history' and 'unresolved legacy' of colonization in China and across the Asian region. It is an image that is difficult to forget 'even when focusing on contemporary cultural processes' (Shin, 2009: 103). Even Japanese popular culture (which includes J-pop, or new forms of music in Japan inspired by Western pop), which was popular across the East Asian region including in China in the 1990s and has been a model for Korean, Cantonese and Mandarin popular cultural activities, has not been able to totally erase the taste of Japan's colonial past (Monty, 2010: 127). In addition, since the 2000s, J-pop has re-focused back on the Japanese market[12] and has not had as significant a presence on Chinese television as Korean popular culture in the 2000s. Yet, China's music-entertainment programmes have still engaged with Japan and Japanese artists in a friendly, neighbourly manner.

Foreign identities 203

Some Japanese stars, like singer Qiao Shanzhong (Joe Yamanaka), have played important roles in making CCTV cosmopolitan in similar ways as described for Korean pop stars, Vitas and Hao Ge. Qiao appeared on at least two occasions on CCTV's *The Same Song* in about 2007–8 in both Japan and China. He was introduced as a famous Japanese singer on *The Same Song – Enters Japan* (*Tongyi shouge zoujin Riben*) held on 14 December 2007, appearing directly after the theme song. Born to a Japanese mother and black American father, he was striking for his 'black mixed blood' (*heiren de hunxue*)[13] appearance, his dreadlocked hair, hoarse and versatile voice, and reggae-inspired singing style, otherwise rarely seen at the time on Chinese television. His visual and aural points of difference were likely attractive to audiences and highlighted CCTV's openness to otherness, although it is interesting that few other Japanese stars featured on Chinese television at the time. One of the other few stars with Japanese heritage to appear on Chinese television in this era was mixed Taiwanese and Japanese singer and actor was Jin Chengwu (Takeshi Kaneshiro). Yet, as Jin grew up in Taiwan, he wasn't labelled as a Japanese star and Chinese people mainly thought of him as Taiwanese. Popular in the 1990s, he acted in many Hong Kong and Taiwanese movies. Compared with Korean stars, Japanese stars have not had the same exposure on Chinese music-entertainment television. One other exception was Fushan Yazhi (Fukuyama Masaharu) who occasionally performed on Shanghai's Dragon TV.[14]

As with the *Enters Korea* programme and with the 'Greater China' frame, nostalgic use of popular culture was taken as the point for drawing the two sides closer together. Each time Qiao appeared on CCTV he sang the same song – 'Straw Hat Song' (*Cao mao ge*), which was the theme song of the Japanese movie *Witness* (*Renzheng*, 1977). Interestingly, the chosen song was in English rather than Japanese, which somewhat further played down his Japaneseness. Such choices in repertoire may be conscious or unconscious decisions as a result of Japanese culture still having a strong sense of negative 'cultural odour' (Iwabuchi, 2002: 27). Although there have been various Chinese renditions of the classic song, Qiao's original version was in English, a language not commonly used on CCTV's music-entertainment programmes, but which was well-known as a regional and international language. The movie, which was popular regionally in the 1980s, also had a transnational theme and a story that spanned the boundaries of the East and West. It was about a boy, played by Qiao, who like Qiao was born to a Japanese mother and black American father. After the character's parents separated, his father sent him to Japan to find his mother who eventually killed him to protect her own reputation and that of another son born to another father. The other son was later shot dead in the US as a result of crime and the mother killed herself after learning the news. The lyrics of the theme song were about a straw hat his mother gave him. It was the 'only one [he] really loved', but the hat was blown away by the wind. This hat was compared to the life his mother gave him. The strains in Qiao's voice and the simple tune were emphatic and touching. His attraction seems to have come from his talent, individual style and a common cultural point of transnational interest in negotiating a modern life between Asia and the West.

Apart from focusing on shared popular culture, CCTV's music-entertainment programmes in relation to Japan appear to have attempted to soften tensions between the two nations through spoken language. The Chinese Party-state has been in a difficult position vis-à-vis Japan. On the one hand, the Party-state bases its ongoing legitimacy on a 'victim narrative', which focuses on the suffering of the Chinese people during a 'century of humiliation' (Gries, 2005: 847), including under colonial Japanese rule in the 1940s, and as such must show a degree of tacit support for anti-Japanese sentiment in China. At the same time, it must attempt to change Chinese public opinion on Japan in order to meet its economic goal, which likewise affects its legitimacy. China has benefited immensely from investment and technology as a result of strong economic ties with Japan (Sun, 1995: 203; Gries, 2005: 848).

Given that the CCTV music-entertainment genre is a non-confrontational genre that aims at providing happy entertainment, I am not surprised that I have never seen the victim narrative brought up directly in any of these programmes. However, the CCTV stage has occasionally been used to present messages that stress the need to overcome tensions in China–Japan relations with messages of hope for the future. While the exact nature of the tensions is not mentioned, they may be hinted at. For instance, on CCTV, at the end of *The Same Song – Enters Japan* concert, a recorded interview with noted Japanese singer Gucun Xinsi (Tanimura Shinji), who performed at the Opening Ceremony of the Shanghai Expo in 2010, was shown. Speaking in Japanese with Chinese subtitles, he spoke directly of the important role music can play in overcoming political difficulties, as well as of his particular interest in using music to set up a bridge between China and Japan. Gucun Xinsi's comment thus hinted at the sensitive relations between the two countries without threatening the spirit of friendship that has been the focus of China's music-entertainment programmes.

On-screen text and voiceover promos for the *Enters Japan* programme worked together in a more stilted way than the upbeat joint production with Korean television. The Japan episode stressed Japanese and Chinese singers coming together politely in friendship in the spirit of honest communications. Many of the same techniques as the *Enters Korea* programme focusing on popular culture were used to highlight mutual exchange. Japanese singers greeted the audience in Chinese, while Chinese singers greeted in Japanese. Chinese male singer Cai Guoqing, well-known for singing *The Same Song* theme song, dressed in Japanese clothes and sang the classic Chinese romantic song 'The Moon Represents My Heart' (*Yueliang daibiao wode xin*) with a female Japanese singer dressed in a Chinese *qipao*. The camera made a point of ensuring a close up of their interlocking hands. However, although pop stars from both sides performed, the spirit of the programme seemed more constrained than the dynamic contemporary popular culture programming in the South Korean episodes. Most significantly, unlike the production in South Korea, the focus of the *Enters Japan* programme was on Chinese living in Japan (described in Chapter 5) and not a celebration of a flurry of transnational cultural exchange.

There has been a little more interaction with contemporary Japanese pop music on provincial satellite television. For instance, in 2012, Shanghai Dragon TV bought the copyright of the Japanese broadcaster NHK's *Red and White Singing Contest* (*Kohaku uta gassen*) for its *New Year's Gala* and arranged a sub-venue in Tokyo showing the performance by AKB48, a successful Japanese girl group with its own theatre, which also has a Shanghai franchise or 'sister group'. Japanese male pop star Shanxia Jiuzhi (Yamashita Tomohisa) also came to Shanghai to perform on Dragon TV. During both performances, the young Japanese pop stars sang in Japanese, while Yamashita Tomohisa managed to say a couple of phrases in Chinese to appeal to Chinese audiences.

Conclusion

This chapter has focused on the construction of Chineseness in terms of foreigners' attraction to and assimilation into Chinese culture and civilization. It began with a focus on *Sinophiliac*, the programme that specializes in showcasing foreigners 'entering into' China, as well as star performers on other programmes. On these shows foreigners have been labelled as outsiders – as Australian, Japanese etc. – and have appeared exotic by virtue of their racial appearance, a feature that is likely to assist with audience interest and ratings. But at the same time, many foreigners have been depicted trying to 'become' Chinese through their performances.

At the hardened extreme, the various modes could be seen working together to provide strong messages of foreigners' attraction to China and Chinese culture: they speak Chinese, sing in Chinese, wear Chinese clothes, learn traditional Chinese arts and adopt Chinese names. Foreigners' attraction to Chinese culture links to Chinese nationalism and efforts to revive ideas of the Middle Kingdom where China is imagined as being the centre of the civilized world. At the cosmopolitan extreme, however, there have been more points of difference. Foreign artists have brought their own individually unique singing, dress and dance styles, and at times have been able to showcase their own languages. The more cosmopolitan moments appear to have offered a freer celebration of China's openness and modernity, often making strong use of popular music. While *Sinophiliac* may have had a greater concentration of the more overtly political 'hardened' moments than the other programmes described, many shows have offered a spectrum of hard and soft moments, which reveals an ambivalence as to where to place foreigners in relation to the Chinese nation, and which may depend on the relationship China has had with the performer's country of origin.

As time has passed, no longer are there just a few 'China experts' or *Zhongguo tong*, but rather, the majority of foreign performers, especially on

CCTV, have been shown to be 'expert' in elements of Chinese culture. The *Zhongguo tong* who loves Chinese culture and China has become the new 'authentic' foreigner. Along with China's rising confidence, China's media is increasingly asserting its pride in the fact that foreigners are fluently speaking their Chinese language and learning Chinese arts. It is in China's interest to highlight for the common Chinese viewer that the average foreigner, not just the odd 'expert', is attracted to, engaged with and loves China.

The 'double exoticism' of internal and external 'otherness' in simultaneous performances of minority nationalities and foreigners has been another feature of music-entertainment programming in China. This approach has offered audiences an attractive way to draw attention to the 'fact' of China's harmonious multiethnic society, and to learn about the multiethnic 'us' at the same time as being exposed to the foreign 'other'. Whether consciously designed or not, audiences have been educated on a degree of Han ethnocentricity, given that Hans remain the only unmarked or 'normal' group in interactions. In exploring minority nationality areas, foreigners have often been guided by the unmarked Chinese who has stood between the 'internal' and 'external' others. As foreigners show how captivated they are by the exotic minority nationality cultures when the programme travels to border regions, an opportunity is provided to educate audiences on China's diverse multiethnic culture, as well as on how the diverse groups are unified within China's geographic boundaries. Foreign and Han Chinese interest in minorities is used to draw attention to the Party-state's 'multiethnic' definition of Chineseness. Han ethnocentricity is also suggested through foreigners' use of spoken Chinese, which, just as for most Chinese and minority nationalities on Chinese television, is almost always *Putonghua*. Rarely do foreigners speak minority languages or even their native languages, although they may occasionally dabble in local Han Chinese languages or dialects as appropriate to local performing art forms. A rare exception is American Elise Anderson, who communicated in Uyghur language as a contestant on Xinjiang Television's *The Voice of the Silk Road* (see Chapter 4).

Foreigners on Chinese television during the period of analysis were overwhelmingly shown to perform on the PRC mainland and not in their 'own' or 'other' countries. This is significant, given that CCTV programmes that travelled abroad tended to focus on overseas Chinese rather than non-ethnic Chinese locals from those countries (see Chapter 5). One advantage of having foreigners perform in China is that it is much easier to construct them as trying to adjust to Chinese culture in a way that cannot be done when the television organization itself is a guest in a foreign country. It may also be much more practical for the television producers to use foreign talents in China. But more than anything, depicting foreigners in China allows both the state and cultural nationalists to highlight the significance and attractiveness of the Chinese civilization to the world and its rightful place among the world's top nations. By blurring the boundaries between Chinese national culture and the Chinese Party-state, the PRC state itself is highlighted as legitimate and worthy among the world's leading political entities.

Foreigners expressing their desire to act Chinese, and even 'become Chinese', may also offer a dramatized depiction of a reverse image of a much bigger trend of emigration from China where Western developed countries in particular have been seen as attractive destinations for Chinese migrants. Since China has opened up, large numbers of Chinese have moved overseas or maintained transnational lives (e.g., Sun, 2002; Lull, 1991; Nyíri, 2003). In this context, Chinese programmes may be attempting to offer the perception of an equal and opposite flow in a way that highlights the attractiveness of contemporary China to foreigners as well.

Foreigners have also worked within the context of the Chinese television business for their own purposes, and positioned themselves in various ways in relation to Chinese people. For some professional performers like Hao Ge and Vitas, and hosts like Da Niu, performances on Chinese television may have been a lucrative source of income as well as opportunity to develop their artistic careers in a place where they could stand out more easily than in their home countries. The same may be said of 'foreign monkeys' who accept commercial gigs offered to them by virtue of their appearance. Like the 'Greater China' stars, foreigners have strategically adjusted their acts to meet the requirements of state and cultural politics as well as the market, thereby increasing their potential for further exposure and contracts. Exposure on national television can open the doors to many new opportunities.

Compared with provincial networks, CCTV shows like *Star Avenue* seem to have more actively showcased foreigners coming into China from a wider range of countries and backgrounds, and have paid special attention to ensuring that 'black people' (*heiren*) are included. One interviewee who worked on *Star Avenue* noted that this helped present China's media as globalized and open to diversity and show that China as a whole is an open country. Interviewees who had worked for provincial satellite music-entertainment programmes seemed to remember few foreigners on their shows, unless they were popular singers from surrounding Asian countries like Korea and Japan or overseas Chinese from countries like Malaysia and Singapore. Indeed, provincial TV reality singing contests like *The Voice of China* tended to only invite foreigners who were overseas Chinese. The global nature of these shows have been demonstrated instead through the use of foreign formats with foreign designs, the inclusion of overseas Chinese contestants, and through Chinese contestants singing popular songs in English.

It is significant that when foreigners have been seen performing - on CCTV in particular – they have most frequently been seen speaking and singing in Chinese. Indeed, as interviewees working for CCTV shows noted, there is a very practical reason for the need to speak and sing in Chinese, which is to better connect with Chinese audiences. Most foreigners on the reality singing contest, *Star Avenue*, like their Chinese counterparts, were not originally well-known singers. These foreigners spoke good Chinese, having lived in China for a long time. Their Chinese language ability was also a requirement, as contestants often spent considerable time chatting and joking with the host.

Speaking in Chinese meant that audiences would understand them, but audiences also liked it when foreigners sang Chinese songs like 'I Love You China' (*Wo ai ni Zhongguo*). While the interviewees did not say why audiences like seeing foreigners perform patriotic Chinese songs, it could be assumed that the scene of a non-Chinese looking person singing about their love for China would appeal to a sense of novelty as well as a sense of patriotism and pride in Chinese culture. The fact that foreigners are making the effort to learn Chinese, enjoy Chinese culture and live in China, speaks to the revitalization and attractiveness of contemporary China and also fits with broader political goals of presenting China as strong and rejuvenated.

Other CCTV shows like *The Same Song* and the *CCTV Spring Festival Gala* have invited popular and well-known singers. While some foreigners have sung in English, which may appeal to a global identity, and have used simple Chinese to greet audiences to appeal to a national spirit, there is a pragmatic risk in inviting too many foreigners who sing in foreign languages as this could result in many audiences switching off or switching channels. As an interviewee who had worked on the *CCTV Gala* noted:

> It should be highlighted that the foreigners performing in the *Spring Festival Gala* are usually extraordinary worldwide. If some audiences know them or are fans of them, these audiences will enjoy their performance very much. However, if some audiences do not know them and have never heard of them, they may have no interest in watching foreigners' performances.

A few programmes, such as *Asian Wave* on Oriental TV, which recruited Chinese singers from Asia, have featured singers singing in their local language. However, in general foreign languages (apart from English) have not played a significant role in Chinese music-entertainment programming. All of China's music-entertainment shows have focused on themes of harmony, and foreigners have been presented as 'friends' who are welcome in an open, cosmopolitan, modern and rejuvenated China.

Notes

1. I often heard the song blaring from accessory, clothing and other shops popular with youth in Kunming in 2008.
2. S.H.E. is a successful girl group from Taiwan, whose name is based on the first letter of the three singers' English names Selina, Hebe and Ella – names created to fit the title of the group. Apart from S.H.E.'s own performances of their song on CCTV, they also had their own MTV clip that featured the three singers in a bamboo forest, Chinese kungfu artists, as well as black and white foreigners breakdancing and foreigners asking the way in Chinese in Shanghai.
3. Maliya was Miss Sierra Leone in 2009.
4. The China Dream metaphor applies to entertainers and entrepreneurs, as exemplified in a 2012 series named *China: Land of Opportunities* on CCTV-News and

CNTV. Available at http://cctv.cntv.cn/lm/bizasia/series/Chinalandofoppotunities/index.shtml (accessed 18 May 2017).
5 The article 'Model Behaviour' from *The Global Times* (30 September 2009) is available on Maliya's blog at http://blog.sina.com.cn/s/blog_674864f00100jvap.html (accessed 18 May 2017).
6 Based on interviews with spouses and an analysis of a Shanghai television program *OK! New World* (*OK! Xintiandi*) from 1999 to 2006, which featured interviews with couples.
7 As Vitas' Chinese developed, he also starred in the Chinese film *Mulan* (2009) about the life of legendary patriotic heroine Hua Mulan, and recorded music for the film's soundtrack (in English) (Vitas Official Website, 2010).
8 In 2016, CCTV's Russian language international channel (in operation since 2009) featured a 30-part TV drama series by the same name, originally made in 2009. The series was about a group of young Chinese who went on exchange to the Soviet Union in 1956 to study aircraft design. It followed their work and love lives over 30 years and featured a marriage between a Chinese man and a Russian girl. The film was in Chinese and primarily intended at Chinese audiences, but also contained Russian subtitles for the CCTV-Russian broadcast and online versions.
9 The *Centenary Dream – Welcome to the Olympics – 2008* show held in Beijing on July 29 was, in the words on Vitas' website, 'organized by China's Ministry of Propaganda, the national Gym chief Bureau, Beijing Olympic Committee, the Government of Beijing and CCTV.' A note uploaded to his website thanked 'Mr Vitas' for his participation in the event designed to 'declare [the] 'countdown' to the Opening Olympic Games', which was to be watched by 'millions of people all over the world'. His website also explained that he was invited by the Organizing Committee of the Beijing 2008 Olympic Games to take part in the Opening Ceremony of the Olympic Sailing Games event in the seaside city of Qingdao on 9 August 2008.
10 Interestingly, other foreign singers also aimed to connect with the Chinese people through this tragedy. American singer Michael Maley and his group SIRUS released an original tribute song on 12 May 2009 called 'God Bless Sichuan' (*Shangtian zhufu Sichuan*). According to one blogger, it become popular in Mainland China and was covered by mainland media outlets. SIRUS may have been the first foreign group to have released an original Chinese language album (in 1997).
11 Huang Zhilie sang 'I Have You on the Way' (*Yi lu shang you ni*) in Chinese during the 2016 *Hunan TV Spring Festival Gala*. He then performed an upbeat Korean dance song called 'Lie' (*Huangyan*), originally performed by Korean boy band, Big Bang with a few English words intermixed. He ended his appearance by chatting with the hosts in Chinese: 'I like China', 'Wish you all a happy new year, *gongxifacai*, give me a red envelope!' He had a translator standing behind him to help if needed. Other popular South Korean stars to have appeared on Chinese television include Rain, who was well-known in China as an actor, singer and model. Rain sang 'Hip Song' during the 2016 *Dragon TV Spring Festival Gala*. Another star Kangta (Ahn Chil-hyun/An Qixuan) sang the song *Ding ge long dong qiang*, the theme song to the CCTV show of the same name with Chinese female model Xiong Dailin. The song was mostly in Chinese, but Kangta added some Korean in the latter part of the song. They also sang the song during the 2016 *CCTV Spring Festival Gala* along with a black foreigner. Kangta was a member of a boyband called HOT, who were popular in China in the 1990s.
12 Unlike Korean popular culture, which is supported by the Korean government, J-pop was largely promoted through its cultural hardware industry through brands such as Sony and Panasonic (Monty, 2010: 123).

210 *Foreign identities*

13 As described on the CCTV *Film Legends* (*Dianying Chuanqi*) programme on the background to the film *Witness* ('*Renzheng*' *zhi mama*, 'The Mother in 'Proof'') on 19 Nov 2007.
14 For example, Fukuyama Masaharu sang 'Favourite' (*Zui ai*) in Japanese at the 18th Shanghai TV Festival Michelia Alba Awards Ceremony in 2012, and spoke a few sentences in Chinese by way of introduction.

References

Appell, J. (2012) Laowai style! Foreigner in Beijing's Gangnam Style parody! 11 October. Available at www.youtube.com/watch?v=7Dp5X5WOf2Q (accessed 18 May 2017).
Arons, R. (2012) Ai Weiwei's 'Gangnam Style' knockoff. *The New Yorker*, 26 October. Available at www.newyorker.com/culture/culture-desk/ai-weiweis-gangnam-style-knockoff (accessed 18 May 2017).
Barmé, G.R. (1999) *In the Red: On Contemporary Chinese Culture*. New York: Columbia University Press.
'Black Pearl' finds oyster in China: Sierra Leonean star Mariatu Kargbo talks about her new home (2012), 25 December. Available at http://tieba.baidu.com/p/2065530369 (accessed 18 May 2017).
Butchy, L. (2002) Cross-cultural exchange. *Columbia College Today*, March. Available at www.college.columbia.edu/cct_archive/mar02/mar02_feature_macinnis.html (accessed 18 May 2017)
CCTV.com (2002) Zhongyang dianshitai si tao, jiu tao jiemu quanmian gaiban [Comprehensive changes to programming on CCTV4 and CCTV9], 21 August. Available at www.cctv.com/news/entertainment/20020821/196.html (accessed 18 May 2017).
CCTV.com (2011) Charlotte MacInnis (Ai Hua): a white-faced Chinese, 16 March. Available at http://english.cntv.cn/program/learnchinese/20110316/109205.shtml (accessed 18 May 2017).
CCTV4 (2009) *Happy Five Continents* special program in Sydney, uploaded 7 October. Available at www.youtube.com/watch?v=IEHwRHMnFPQ (accessed 18 May 2017).
China Dream (2014) Available at http://english.cntv.cn/chinadream (accessed 18 May 2017).
Chris Babida blog (n.d.). Available at www.chrisbabida.com/news.asp?menuid=1&ln=en (accessed 18 May 2017).
Chua, B.H. (2001) Pop culture China. *Singapore Journal of Tropical Geography* 22(2): 113–21.
Chua, B.H. (2008) Structure of identification in watching East Asian television drama. In B.H. Chua and K. Iwabuchi (eds.) *East Asian Pop Culture: Analysing the Korean Wave*. Hong Kong: Hong Kong University Press, pp. 73–90.
Chua, B.H. and Iwabuchi, K. (2008) Introduction – East Asian TV dramas: identification, sentiments and effects. In B.H. Chua and K. Iwabuchi (eds.) *East Asian Pop Culture: Analysing the Korean Wave*. Hong Kong: Hong Kong University Press, pp. 1–12.
CNTV (2012a) 'Jiangnan Style' fengmi quanqiu yinfa mofang dachao [Gangnam Style global fashion leads to tide of imitations], 11 December. Available at

http://music.cntv.cn/2012/12/11/VIDE1355163329130678.shtml (accessed 18 May 2017).
CNTV (2012b) Jiangnan style wei shenme zheyang hong [Why is Gangnam Style so hot?]. *Culture Noon* (*Wenhua Zhengwu*), 18 December. Available at http://tv.cntv.cn/video/C39311/400bdcbd3174480cb3df62c9de408d66 (accessed 18 May 2017).
Deng, S. (ed.) (2010) Proposal for news in Mandarin angers Guangzhou citizens. *English.news.cn*, 9 July. Available at http://news.xinhuanet.com/english2010/china/2010-07/09/c_13392543.htm (accessed 18 May 2017).
Farrer, J. (2008) From 'passports' to 'joint ventures': intermarriage between Chinese nationals and Western expatriates residing in Shanghai. *Asian Studies Review* 32: 7–29.
Gries, P.H. (2005) China's 'new thinking' on Japan. *The China Quarterly*, 184: 831–50.
Gruger, W. (2012) Psy's 'Gangnam Style' video hits 1 billion views, unprecedented milestone. *Billboard*, 21 December. Available at www.billboard.com/biz/articles/news/1483733/psys-gangnam-style-video-hits-1-billion-views-unprecedented-milestone (accessed 18 May 2017).
Gye, H. (2013) British expat who became overnight celebrity in China by singing revolutionary songs on *China's Got Talent*. *Daily Mail Australia*, 26 March. Available at www.dailymail.co.uk/news/article-2298861/Iain-Inglis-British-expat-overnight-celebrity-China-singing-revolutionary-songs-Chinas-Got-Talent.html (accessed 18 May 2017).
Iwabuchi, K. (2002) *Recentering Globalization: Popular Culture and Japanese Transnationalism*. Durham and London. Duke University Press.
Jones, A.F. (2014) Quotation songs: portable media and the Maoist pop song. In A. Cook (ed.) *Mao's Little Red Book: A Global History*. Cambridge: Cambridge University Press, pp. 43–60.
Laugh Beijing (2016) Available at www.laughbeijing.com/the-comedian (accessed 18 May 2017).
Lee, H.J. (2016) Singer Hwang Chi Yeol appointed honorary ambassador for Korea China culture exchange. Koogle TV website, 28 March. Available at www.koogle.tv/media/news/singer-hwang-chi-yeol-appointed-honorary-ambassador-for-korea-china-culture-exchange (accessed 18 May 2017).
Leibold, J. (2010) The Beijing Olympics and China's conflicted national form. *The China Journal* 63: 1–24.
Leung, L. (2008) Mediating nationalism and modernity: the transnationalization of Korean dramas on Chinese (satellite) TV. In B.H. Chua and K. Iwabuchi (eds.) *East Asian Pop Culture: Analysing the Korean Wave*. Hong Kong: Hong Kong University Press, pp. 53–69.
Li, Z. (2008) Ethnic congregation in a globalizing city: the case of Guangzhou, China. *Cities* 25(6): 383–95.
Lull, J. (1991) *China Turned On: TV Reform and Resistance*. London: Routledge.
Mango TV (2016) Promo for Hwang Chi Yuel. Available at http://m.mgtv.com/#/play/2946396 (accessed 18 May 2017).
Monty, A. (2010) Micro: global music made in J-pop? *Inter-Asia Cultural Studies* 11(1): 123–8.
Mykiru (2007) 'Light the Passion, Share the Dream' – the 2008 Olympic song, 21 Nov. Available at www.mykiru.ph/2007/11/light-passion-share-dream-2008-olympic.html (accessed 18 May 2017).
Nyíri, P. (2003) Chinese migration to Eastern Europe. *International Migration* 41(3): 239–65.

Rees, H. (2009) Use and ownership: folk music in the People's Republic of China. In A.N. Weintraub and B. Yung (eds.) *Music and Cultural Rights*. Chicago: University of Illinois Press, pp. 42–85.

Schein, L. (1997) Gender and internal orientalism in China. *Modern China* 23(1): 69–98.

Shin, H. (2009) Reconsidering transnational cultural flows of popular music in East Asia: transbordering musicians in Japan and Korea searching for 'Asia'. *Korean Studies* 33: 101–23.

Sinophiliac website (2010). Available at www.cctv.com/program/tlwz/01/index.shtml (accessed 18 May 2017).

Song, G. (2015) Imagining the other: foreigners on the Chinese TV screen. In R. Bai and G. Song (eds.) *Chinese Television in the Twenty-First Century: Entertaining the Nation*. London: Routledge, pp. 107–20.

Sun, W. (1995) *People's Daily*, China and Japan: a narrative analysis. *International Communication Gazette* 54(3): 195–207.

Sun, W. (2002) *Leaving China: Media, Migration, and Transnational Imagination*. Lanham: Rowman and Littlefield.

Tan, C.B. (2001) Tourism and the anthropology of China. In C.B. Tan, S.C.H. Cheung and H. Yang (eds.) *Tourism, Anthropology and China*. Bangkok: White Lotus Press, pp. 1–26.

Very CD (n.d.) Hao Ge 'Hong yu hei dangdai R&B' [Hao Ge 'Red and Black Contemporary R&B']. Available at www.verycd.com/topics/160636/ (accessed 18 May 2017).

Visit Korea (n.d.). Singers. Available at http://english.visitkorea.or.kr/enu/CU/CU_EN_8_7_1.jsp (accessed 18 May 2017).

Vitas Official Website (2010) Available at www.vitas.com.ru/pressa_eng.php (accessed 18 May 2017).

Walsh, E.R. (2001) Living with the myth of matriarchy: the Mosuo and tourism. In C.B. Tan, S.C.H. Cheun and H. Yang (eds.) *Tourism, Anthropology and China*. Bangkok: White Lotus Press, pp. 93–124.

Wei, T. (2006) A Cameroonian learning Chinese. *Crosstalk in China*, 26 November. Available at http://english.cri.cn/3178/2006/11/14/61@162579.htm (accessed 18 May 2017).

Yang, M.M. (2002) Mass media and transnational subjectivity in Shanghai: notes on (re)cosmopolitanism in a Chinese metropolis. In F.D. Ginsburg, L. Abu-Lughold and B. Larkin (eds.) *Media Worlds: Anthropology on New Terrain*. Berkeley: University of California Press, pp. 189–210.

7 Conclusion

China's music-entertainment programmes highlight the ongoing strategic use of music and culture for political purposes, including for building a sense of national consciousness. While the Communist Party of China (CCP) focused on using art to persuade the masses on the benefits of socialism in earlier years, the key political messages since the 1990s have been about nation-building and creating a sense of solidarity based on national unity. The use of entertaining and engaging programming with national themes helps to create a sense of contentment with the political status quo, which is key to maintaining legitimacy in a context where 'communism', the underlying basis of the CCP, is no longer the focus.

Music plays an important role as a symbol of harmony, unity (e.g., through singing the same song together with one voice), modernity (e.g., through Western musical instruments, orchestral, choral, operatic and pop music), and Chineseness (e.g., through Chinese folk music and musical instruments). Key political themes and achievements (e.g., Harmonious Society and the China Dream) have been embedded in lyrics or in dialogue between songs. By constantly replaying old songs and performances, audiences can reflect on the development and modernization of China over time, thus highlighting the successes of the CCP, particularly over the past 30 to 40 years. Familiarity with classic songs and remakes of old songs can also ensure an ongoing sense of shared memories across the generations. The vast number of songs about the Chinese nation and the Party thus form a repertoire for the collective consciousness. At the same time songs about the nation are 'tuned' to fit the present climate (Chambers, 1986: 13) and document ongoing cultural and political trends as well as visions for China's future. As such China's music-entertainment television programmes are often 'Janus-faced' – like the Roman statue, they look to the past and future simultaneously (cf. McFarlane-Alvarez, 2007).

This book has examined such questions as: How is Chinese identity constructed? What are the roles of words, images and music that make up the music-entertainment shows in creating a sense of the Chinese nation? Who counts as Chinese? How are cultural and ethnic 'others' marked? To do so, it canvassed many examples of music-entertainment television performances of minority nationalities, Han people, people from Hong Kong, Macau and

Taiwan, overseas Chinese, and foreigners who have appeared on CCTV and mainland China's provincial satellite music-entertainment programmes. It also examined the role of hybrid identities, such as American-Chinese, Uyghur-Chinese, and foreigners living in China, and what their television representations signify culturally and politically for the Chinese state.

It identified are a variety of ways in which each of these identities have been portrayed, from relatively 'hardened', 'orthodox' and controlled constructions in which key Party-state messages have been carefully constructed, to 'softer', less dogmatic constructions, which have celebrated diversity, difference and cosmopolitanism. At the hardened extreme, linguistic, visual and musical modes reinforce each other to create relatively easy to read and fixed Party-state ideological messages of unity, unification and the importance of China in a new world order. Even if one were to disagree, the tight combination of reinforcing symbols makes the messages clear. A relatively fixed, rigid and stable identity is often constructed around such symbols of nationalism as the Chinese flag, the colour red, the Yellow River, the Great Wall and sometimes the direct mention of the CCP.

In the multiethnic frame, 'orthodox' performances overtly stress the unity and happiness of the 56 nationalities. Performers in colourful minority costumes are seen holding hands, dancing together or marching forward in a visual sign of unity. One singer, often dressed in red (the colour of China), provides the central focal point and singular voice that represents the entire group, while a 'national style' song in Mandarin waxes lyrical about the unity of the 56 nationalities.

In the Greater China frame, 'orthodox' moments include those where music, visuals and language work together to produce a clear message of a successful unification between the mainland and Hong Kong or Macau since their 'return' to the motherland, as well as a sense of national connection and desire for unification between the mainland and Taiwan on both sides. It also refers to performances that clearly show overseas Chinese as being firmly linked to their ancestral homeland in mainland China. Foreigners in the orthodox frame are also shown to be engrossed by Chinese culture as they come to China, adopt Chinese names, speak Chinese, sing Chinese songs, play Chinese musical instruments, wear traditional Chinese clothes, demonstrate their love for China and even sing songs in praise of the CCP. Such hardened moments are more common in the lead-up to and during important political and commemorative events. However, they are not restricted to these events as they are interwoven into many music-entertainment shows. While CCTV is particularly known for offering more overtly ideological constructions, they can be found across provincial satellite channels as well.

Softer expressions of Chineseness have been created where the linguistic, musical and visual modes pull in different directions, and where points of difference are highlighted. These moments celebrate abundance, colour, diversity and dynamism in an increasingly globally connected China. In this frame, hybridity and mixed identities are celebrated: Uyghur-Chinese, Chinese-Americans, overseas Chinese who are also ethnic minorities and Caucasian-Chinese mixed-race stars. In the softer constructions, differences are marked through the 'blending of opposites', through dabbling in and dropping words in different dialects and languages (particularly minority languages, Cantonese, English), through different styles of dress and creative body movements, and through the blending of different types of music and musical instruments (e.g., Chinese gongs and Western-style drum kits). Internal 'others' (minority nationalities), external 'others' (foreigners) and mainstream Han are brought together in a 'unity of opposites', and boundaries between these identities are blurred. In television design, this kind of hybridity is seen in local programmes and adaptations of global formats, which may be seen as 'glocal' cultural productions (Robertson, 2012). The focus on difference allows for more ambiguity in the meaning of such multimodal content, although these moments nonetheless serve to promote state messages of China's openness. At the very least, programmes that celebrate diversity appear to attract mainstream audiences, which is important for both political and commercial reasons.

The focus on mixed cultural elements suggests that Chinese music-entertainment television programmes, as in other global contexts, can be conceptualized as a manifestation of the complex forces of globalization. They represent a meeting place between modernization/Westernization and re-localization (Gentles, 2012). As in other countries, it is the very project of modernity that 'systematically produces hybrid cultural forms', yet the sense of modernity created is still specific to the particular historical, political and cultural context (Kraidy, 2008: 50–1). Thus, while some shows like *The Voice* may have a global feel, and modern blends demonstrate the 'interpenetration' of cultures (Shim, 2006), a strong assertion of Chinese national identity remains a key theme across the genre. While there are differences in the ways the three frames are performed, all performances help to support a number of key Party-state messages: that China is strong, modern and globally oriented as well as attractive, united, harmonious, creative, confident and proud as a result of treasuring its traditions. Multiethnic Chinese, Greater Chinese and foreigners are all shown to love, support and respect this modern, revitalized China.

Different genres of televised music have been shown to connect to different national and political aims. Popular music plays a particularly important role in the construction of Greater China through bringing together pop stars from Taiwan, Hong Kong, Malaysia and Singapore, mainly on mainland soil, and occasionally in roaming concerts outside the mainland. The 'national style' of singing emphasizes messages of a strong nation and Party through lyrics and modern operatic tunes that align with national and Party themes – although other genres of music, including pop and rock, are employed to do this as well. *Yuanshengtai*, made up largely of a body of 'unknown' works of minorities and rural Shaanbei Han, reflects concerns about the need to 'preserve' China's national culture within a global framework of sustainable development, and inclusion of this genre serves to highlight China as a responsible world leader. Ethno-pop and *yuanshengtai* also relate to the changing circumstances of increased consumption and the tourism industry.

In what appears to be a re-emerging emphasis on the notion of China as the Middle Kingdom, the People's Republic of China (PRC) mainland is constructed in its music-entertainment shows as being at the centre of the Chinese-speaking world. This is created through strong images of flows from the outside (Hong Kong, Macau, Taiwan, overseas Chinese, foreigners) into mainland China, much more than the other way round. There are also strong images of flows towards the nation's capital, Beijing, especially on CCTV. Showcasing so many overseas Chinese 'returning' to the motherland and foreigners flocking to China to fulfil their dreams effectively demonstrates to Chinese audiences how attractive China is to the world, and thus attempts to entice them to be proud of their own nation and culture.

CCTV is well known for its more ideological programming given its close connection with the central levels of the Party-state. Provincial channels, in contrast, seem at first glance to be more globalized, attractive, commercial and less ideological. This is especially true of channels that have bought the rights to re-produce foreign reality formats like *The Voice* and *Idol*. Such shows have offered different models for creative performance on television that were uncommon, at least on CCTV, in earlier years. For instance, more singers could be seen accompanying themselves with their own instruments (especially guitars), and greater attention was placed on live pop bands on stage, which were previously hidden from view. Overall, the focus of global reality television shows has tended to be more on showcasing contestants' individual personalities and talents, rather than a collective spirit. The focus has often been on telling stories that draw out contestants' 'genuine' natures and their personal journeys towards self-development and self-fulfilment. While CCTV has emphasized the 'ordinary person' (*laobaixing*), this has been done in quite a different and much more dogmatic way than on reality TV shows. It has been less to represent individual personalities and more about showcasing the individuals as token nurses, farmers, street sellers, etc. who are happy with their lives despite hardships.

Yet closer examination also reveals that the key national themes, including pride for China, national solidarity, and overseas Chinese people's desire to reconnect with their ancestral land are replicated in global reality shows on provincial channels as well. Provincial channels also have their share of more dogmatic music-entertainment programming, and weave in nation-building and Party-political messages at key moments or in specifically created programmes. Like leading provincial satellite channels, CCTV has tried to follow global and Chinese trends and produce programming that is equally enticing to young people. Music-entertainment programming across CCTV and provincial satellite channels which address a national audience promote a shared national identity as part of their appeal, and do so in a way that supports a consistent message of China as dynamic, creative, strong, and united. Thus, while there is competition between the stations, they all work together in a collaborative television system under the supervision of the Party-state and promote key Party-state messages. While the differences between the channels are notable and important, I have argued that they may not be as extensive as earlier scholarship has implied.

The choice to focus on national culture is also practical. Television programmes with cultural proximity are most likely to attract audiences, so those that are as close to viewers as possible in language, ethnic appearance, dress, style, humour, historical reference and shared topical knowledge tend to touch the right cultural chords (Shim, 2006: 37). They also allow audiences to feel the 'pleasure of recognition' (Ang cited in Shim, 2006: 39). At the same time, the shows reflect certain longstanding political and post-colonial influences, including the desire to modernize and develop by learning from the West whilst maintaining a strong national identity, which is necessary for promoting national solidarity and avoiding disintegration.

The shows may be seen as spaces of negotiation, subversion and resistance from the point of view of standing up to the dominant and former imperial West (cf. Bhabha cited in Gentles, 2012). Former colonial countries and cultures such as England and Portugal are barely represented, but when they are, they come across as quaint and historic – quite unlike the proud and culturally rich Chinese nation. Although there is often a token gesture to the discourse of cultural exchange, Chinese programmes that provide glimpses into Western countries typically render the foreign landscapes just like China – thus erasing any sense of autonomy of the West. The programmes are not negative about foreign people or countries, but they barely highlight anything about foreign cultural differences unless they are incorporated in a hybrid way with Chinese cultural cues that represent China's modernity. As far as foreign people are concerned, they focus on showing foreigners' active interest in a rejuvenated, revitalized and cosmopolitan China, with their gaze on China. They feature foreigners flocking to China, absorbing Chinese culture, loving China and, ultimately, as long-term China commentator Bill Bishop (2015) notes, 'respecting' China, which satisfies the national psyche and reflects a period of national confidence.

While the shows stand up to the West from the point of view of being domestically produced with messages of national pride, there is little space for resistance and subversion in terms of domestic politics. There are no ironic songs or performances critical of the ruling Party. One needs to go online to find such content. China's music-entertainment television programmes are all about maintaining the political status quo through presenting constructions of a stable, united and happy multiethnic population. Overall, music and singing are used to spread happiness and harmony and to help PRC citizens to take their minds off their busy and stressful lives and celebrate being part of a proud, confident and creative nation.

Chinese music-entertainment television deals with 'otherness' in a number of ways. As Kraidy (2008: 51) has noted of reality television in other global contexts, China's music-entertainment programmes can represent minorities in stereotypical ways as rural, backward and primitive, with a focus on minorities in China's Western regions. The result is not only exotic and entertaining but also raises the feeling of modernity for the 'ordinary Chinese' (*laobaixing*) – typically a Han Chinese residing in cities on the east coast. At other times, there are efforts to showcase 'modern' minorities, such as singers who inflect pop and rock music with minority themes and vocal inflections or who may wear ethnically inspired contemporary dress. From this positive point of view, it may be said that the song and dance shows provide spaces where minorities can negotiate their own representations and 'struggle' over what kind of modernity they would like to represent for themselves and their ethnic group (cf. Kraidy, 2008: 50–1). There are many ways in which this can be done as long as they still frame themselves as an essential part of the Chinese nation as a whole, and are not agitating for independence or separation.

This book has surveyed music-entertainment shows from 2008 to 2016, including four years under the leadership of President Hu Jintao and four under President Xi Jinping. The main differences in programming between the times of these two presidents has been an emphasis on themes of a 'Harmonious Society' and 'Harmonious World' under Hu, and an emphasis on 'China Dream' themes under Xi. The period under Xi saw global formats like *The Voice*, *Idol*, *X Factor* and *I am a Singer* officially enter China, which gave Chinese television a more global feel. The greater sanctioning of rock music with acceptable themes, 'world music' blends, and live bands accompanying singers as well as self-accompaniment (e.g., with acoustic guitars) has also been much more evident during this latter period. There has also been an intensified focus on creative blends of styles, reflecting an increased emphasis on the creative industries. We have also seen a receding interest in the *yuanshengtai* style that featured original folk songs in minority languages without modern accompaniment or embellishments and that reflected reflecting a greater concern for grassroots practices and the preservation of intangible cultural heritage – themes that were more prominent in the Hu era. In accordance with earlier scholarship, across the period of analysis it appears that commerce and politics in the culture and entertainment realm have remained in a cosy working relationship with each other. In the PRC context, the music-entertainment genre has been relatively uncontroversial and it has been easy for the more commercially oriented shows to wind in key Party-state themes when they need to, while simultaneously creating trendy shows that appeal to mainstream audiences, including youth.

This study provides a baseline for comparing the uses of musical performance for nation-building and national identity construction with other time periods and in other media contexts, including city and township television channels. It also provides a basis for comparison with nation-building content on Chinese radio and podcasts, and in various online contexts. Future research may also investigate differences in media constructions of Chinese identity between music-entertainment programmes produced by PRC and non-PRC Chinese producers for Hong Kong, Macau and Taiwanese audiences, as well as for overseas Chinese, such as by New Tang Dynasty Television. Ethnographic studies and further interviews with professionals in the television industry as well as performers may shed further insights on what drives programme choices, the inclusion of certain lyrics and themes, and the personal meanings given to particular songs. While the sheer number of music-entertainment programmes during the period of analysis and high ratings for a number of shows in the genre suggests they have had considerable audience appeal, further research could also delve into ethnographies of audiences who watch music-entertainment programmes to examine more specifically how (and whether) such programmes influence their own views of their identity and perceptions of China in the world.

This study has considered China's online and mobile television dimensions. Technology is constantly changing and it is worth examining further how Chinese television is adapting to the digital era – and what that means for nation-building. Further analysis of what Chinese television is doing with its mobile online media platforms and the particular role that music-entertainment plays in attracting China's tech-savvy domestic and overseas audiences to Party-state messages (or not) is required. This would help to answer the question: Does the Chinese nation still matter in the digital and mobile era, or are Chinese people (especially millennials) switching off from these themes?

While this book has focused on national and ethnic aspects of Chinese identity, future studies of CCTV music-entertainment television could also tackle constructions of different types of identities, including those associated with gender, class, geography (e.g., rural/urban) age and disability. The important role of the performing arts troupes as well as army, navy and air force performers and how these interact with national/ethnic identities could also be further examined.

There is also considerable scope for a global comparative perspective, and for situating Chinese music-entertainment television within a broader international context. Comparisons could be made with music-entertainment television programmes on national broadcasters in other countries to assess the extent to which the PRC mainland's mix of local and global forms, and the types of performances of national identity embedded in the programmes, is unique to China.

To conclude, like de Kloet et al. (2011: 131) and many other scholars, I have shown how the idea of the 'state-driven ideal of an imagined community' is one that is actually comprised of 'different, contested articulations of "China" and "Chineseness" ... [of] what China stands for and what it means to be Chinese'. Chinese television reflects the idea that Chinese identity comes in a multiplicity of forms. While it offers 'hardened', monolithic, static, orthodox framings of Chineseness, it also attempts to take into account a changing society and accommodate 'softer' expressions of Chineseness coming from both within and outside of the mainland PRC, even if it remains restricted by Party-state ideology.

Like all identities, Chineseness is never fixed. Producers, propagandists, intellectuals and marketers are constantly engaged in imagining who 'we' are. They do so through finding ways to position 'us' besides 'others' with whom we come into contact in a constantly changing world. It is through various forms of human communication that our perception of ourselves and our world is both formed and complicated. We draw boundaries around ourselves, renegotiate those boundaries, and attempt to define differences and similarities with others through the use of words, images, and sounds. While the desire to fix identities forms part of a need to retain the status quo as well as a sense of stability and solidarity, the complexity and multiplicity of identities represented in Chinese music-entertainment productions reflects efforts to adapt and make sense of a constantly changing society. The past 30 years have seen rapid changes in Chinese society and in its relations with the world as a result of economic and political reforms. At the same time, the CCP has tried hard to maintain stability and legitimacy in difficult circumstances. It seems only understandable that in this context its television system, and music-entertainment programming in particular, reflect both the desire to control its image through 'harder' and more constrained constructions, and softer, blurred and shifting boundaries of a more globally engaged China.

References

Bishop, B. (2015) China and the world: what to expect in 2016, *The China-Africa Project*, 23 December. Available at www.chinaafricaproject.com/podcast-china-foreign-policy-africa-bill-bishop (accessed 18 May 2017).

Chambers, I. (1986) *Popular Culture: The Metropolitan Experience*. London: Routledge.

de Kloet, J., Chong, G.P.L. and Landsberger, S. (2011) National image management begins at home: imagining the new Olympic citizen. In J. Wang (ed.) *Soft Power in China*. New York: Palgrave Macmillan, pp. 117–33.

Gentles, K. (2012) *West Indian Women, Cultural Hybridity and Television*. Paper presented at the annual meeting of the International Communication Association, Dresden International Congress Centre, Germany, 25 June.

Kraidy, M. (2008) Reality TV and multiple Arab modernities: a theoretical exploration. *Middle East Journal of Culture and Communication* 1: 49–59.

McFarlane-Alvarez, S.L. (2007) Trinidad and Tobago television advertising as third space: hybridity as resistance in the Caribbean mediascape. *Howard Journal of Communications* 18(1): 39–55.

Robertson, R. (2012) Globalisation or glocalisation? *The Journal of International Communication* 18(2): 191–208.

Shim, D. (2006) Hybridity and the rise of Korean popular culture in Asia, *Media, Culture and Society* 28(1): 25–44.

8 Glossary

Chapter 1 – Introduction

People
Chen Kaige	陈凯歌
Dashan (Mark Rowswell)	大山
Gao Xingjian	高行健
Han Shaogong	韩少功
Mao Zedong	毛泽东
Tu Weiming	杜维明
Zhang Yimou	张艺谋

Places
Gansu	甘肃
Guangxi	广西
Lishui	丽水
Ningxia	宁夏
Shaanxi	陕西
Xinjiang	新疆
Xizang (Tibet)	西藏

Ethnic groups/classifications
Africans (Feizhou ren)	非洲人
Asians (Yazhou ren)	亚洲人
Audience friends in front of television sets (dianshiji qian de guangzhong pengyoumen)	电视机前的观众朋友们
Black people (heiren)	黑人
China expert/old China hand (Zhongguo tong)	中国通
Chinese nationality (Zhonghua minzu)	中华民族
Compatriots (tongbao)	同胞
Foreign devil (yang guizi)	洋鬼子
Foreign friends (waiguo pengyou)	外国朋友
Foreigners (waiguo ren, laowai)	外国人, 老外
Han majority (Hanzu)	汉族
Japanese devil (Riben guizi)	日本鬼子
Minority nationalities (shaoshu minzu)	少数民族
Overseas Chinese (huaren, huaqiao)	华人, 华侨
Overseas Chinese friends (huaren pengyoumen)	华人朋友们
Pan-Chinese nation (Zhonghua minzu)	中华民族
People of China / Chinese people (Zhongguo ren)	中国人
Tiny Japanese (xiao Riben)	小日本

222 *Glossary*

True friend (zhengyou) 诤友
White person (bairen) 白人

Other
A Beijinger in New York (Beijing ren zai Niu Yue) 北京人在纽约
A unitary 'multiethnic' (or 'multi-national') state 统一的多民族国家
  (tongyi de duo minzu guojia)
Blending of ethnicities (minzu jiaorong) 民族交融
Cheongsam (qipao) 旗袍
China Dream (Zhongguo meng) 中国梦
Confucius Institutes (Kongzi xueyuan) 孔子学院
Crosstalk (xiangsheng) 相声
Four identifications (Si ge rentong) 四个认同
Friendship (youyi) 友谊
Global village (diqiu cun) 地球村
Innate talents in singing and dancing (neng ge shan wu) 能歌善舞
National identity (minzu) 民族
National language (Putonghua) 普通话
Nationalist Party (Guomindang/Kuomintang) 国民党
Open-minded (kaifang) 开放
River Elergy (He Shang) 河殇
Root-seeking (xungen) 寻根
The Central Nationalities Song and Dance Troupe 中央民族歌舞团
  (Zhongyang minzu gewu tuan)
The Northwest Wind (Xibei feng) 西北风

Chapter 2

People
Bao Wei'er 包威尔
Black Duck Trio (Hei yazi zuhe) 黑鸭子组合
Bo Xilai 薄熙来
Chang Sisi 常思思
Chen Lin 陈琳
Cheng Fangyuan 成方圆
Cheng Long (Jacky Chan) 成龙
Dai Yuqiang 戴玉强
Deng Lijun 邓丽君
Deng Xiaoping 邓小平
Dong Wenhua 董文华
Guang Weiran 光未然
Guo Jingjing 郭晶晶
Guo Lanying 郭兰英
Han Hong 韩红
Hong Xiuquan 洪秀全
Hou Dejian 侯德健
Hu Jintao 胡锦涛
Huang Xiaoman 黄小曼
Hukou Waterfall 壶口瀑布
Jiang Qing 江青
Jiang Zemin 江泽民

Jin Tielin	金铁霖
Li Guangxi	李光曦
Li Guyi	李谷一
Li Jianfu	李建复
Li Lanqing	李岚清
Li Wen	李玟
Liu Bin	刘斌
Liu Dehua	刘德华
Liu Huan	刘欢
Mao Zedong	毛泽东
Nie'er	聂耳
Peng Liyuan	彭丽媛
Ping An	平安
Qiao Jun	乔军
Qu Qiubai	瞿秋白
Shaanxi	陕西
Shi Guangnan	施光南
Song Zhigang	宋志刚
Song Zuying	宋祖英
Sun Nan	孙楠
Tang Can	汤灿
Tang Jianping	唐建平
Wang Hongwen	王洪文
Wang Li	王莉
Wang Zining	王紫凝
Wen Jiabao	温家宝
Xi Jinping	习近平
Xu An	徐铵
Xue Haoyin	薛皓垠
Yan Weiwen	阎维文
Yao Ming	姚明
Yao Wenyuan	姚文元
Yi ming wu bai (Artists Five Hundred group)	艺名五百
Yu Runze	余润泽
Zhang Chunqiao	张春桥
Zhang Ye	张也
Zhang Yimou	张艺谋
Zhang Yingxi	张英席
Zhou Enlai	周恩来
Zhou Huajian	周华健
Zu Hai	祖海

Places

Harbin	哈尔滨
Liangjiahe	梁家河
Yan'an	延安

Organizations

August First Film Studio (Ba yi dianying zhipian chang)	八一电影制片厂
Beijing Film Studio (Beijing dianying zhipian chang)	北京电影制片厂
Central Newsreel and Documentary Film Studio (Zhongyang xinwen jilu dianying zhipian chang)	中央新闻纪录电影制片厂

224 *Glossary*

China Central People's Broadcasting Station/China National Radio (Zhongyang renmin guangbo diantai)	中央人民广播电台
China Society of Ethnic Minority Vocal Music (Zhongguo shaoshu minzu shengyue xuehui)	中国少数民族声乐学会
Chinese Musicians' Association (Zhongguo yinyuejia xiehui)	中国音乐家协会
Chinese National Vocal Music Art Research Association (Zhongguo minzu shengyue yishu yanjiuhui)	中国民族声乐艺术研究会
Chinese People's Political Consultative Conference (Zhongguo renmin zhengzhi xieshang huiyi)	中国人民政治协商会议
Nationalist Party	国民党
Opera Troupe of the Political Department of the Central Military Commission (Junwei zhengzhibu gongzuo geju tuan)	军委政治部工作歌剧团
Second Artillery Song and Dance Troupe of the Chinese People's Liberation Army (Zhongguo renmin jiefangjun di'er paobing zhengzhibu wengong tuan)	中国人民解放军第二炮兵政治部文工团
Song and Dance Troupe of the Political Department of the Chinese People's Liberation Army Airforce (Zhongguo renmin jiefangjun kongzheng wengong tuan)	中国人民解放军空政文工团

Song titles

A Small Umbrella (Yi zhi xiao yusan)	一只小雨伞
Anti-Japanese Military University Song (Kang ri junzheng daxue xiaoge)	抗日军政大学校歌
Anyuan Minors Club Song (Anyuan lukuang gongren julebu zhi ge)	安源路矿工人俱乐部之歌
Beijing Welcomes You (Beijing huanyin ni)	北京欢迎你
Big Dreams, Small Dreams (Da mengxiang, xiao mengxiang)	大梦想小梦想
Big Xi Loves Mama Peng (Xi dada aizhe Peng mama)	习大大爱着彭麻麻
Celebration Drinking Song (Zhu jiu ge)	祝酒歌
Chairman Mao's Brilliance (Mao Zhuxi de guanghui)	毛主席的光辉
Cheers to Life (Wei shengming hecai)	为生命喝彩
China Dream, Our Dream (Zhongguo meng, women de meng)	中国梦，我们的梦
Descendants of the Dragon (Long de chuanren)	龙的传人
Everyone has a China Dream (Mei ge ren dou you yi ge Zhongguo meng)	每个人都有一个中国梦
Fight Tyrants and Divide the Land (Da tuhao fen tiandi)	打土豪分田地
Forever Blessings for the Motherland (Zuguo yongyuan zhufu ni)	祖国永远祝福你
Forever Friends (Yongyuan de pengyou)	永远的朋友
Friends of Agriculture Song (Nong you ge)	农友歌
Full Moon (Shiwu de yueliang)	十五的月亮
Good Days (Hao rizi)	好日子
Great Holiday (Weida de jieri)	伟大的节日
Harmonious Society Cultivates a New Wind (Hexie shehui shu xin feng)	和谐社会树新风

I Love My Motherland (Wo ai wo de zuguo)	我爱我的祖国
I Love You China (Wo ai ni Zhongguo)	我爱你中国
In the Fields of Hope (Zai xiwang de tianye shang)	在希望的田野上
Into a New Era (Zoujin xin shidai)	走进新时代
Little Sister Finds Brother With Tears Flowing (Meimei zhao ge lei hua liu)	妹妹找哥泪花流
Lovebird (Aiqing niao)	爱情鸟
Love My China (Ai wo Zhonghua)	爱我中华
March of the Volunteers (Yingxiong jinxing qu)	义勇军进行曲
Martyrdom Song (Jiuyi ge)	就义歌
Misery Era (Ku'nan de niandai)	苦难的年代
Motherland is Forever My Home (Zuguo shi wo yongyuan de jia)	祖国是我永远的家
My Chinese Heart (Wo de Zhongguo xin)	我的中国心
My Motherland (Wo de zuguo)	我的祖国
Nanniwan	南泥湾
National Anthem of the PRC (Zhonghua renmin gongheguo guoge) / National Anthem (Guo ge)	中华人民共和国国歌/国歌
Ode of the Dragon River (Long jiang song)	长江颂
Ode to the Motherland (Ge chang zuguo)	歌唱祖国
On the Dock (Hai gang)	海港
Peaceful China (Ping'an Zhongguo)	平安中国
People's Liberation Army March (Zhongguorenmin jiefangjun jinxingqu)	中国人民解放军进行曲
People's Liberation Army Occupies Nanjing (Renmin jiefangjun zhanling Nanjing)	人民解放军占领南京
Qilü Long March (Qilü changzheng)	七律长征
Raid on the White Tiger Regiment (Qi xi bai hu tuan)	奇袭白虎团
Rely on You, Me, Him/Her (Yao kao ni wo ta)	要靠你我他
Sailing the Seas Depends on the Helmsman (Dahai hangxing kao duoshou)	大海航行靠舵手
Shajiabang	沙家浜
Soldier Man (Dang bing de ren)	当兵的人
Spring Returns to the Great Land (Chun hui dadi)	春回大地
Story of Spring (Chuntian de gushi)	春天的故事
Taking Tiger Mountain by Strategy (Zhi qu wei hu shan)	智取威虎山
Taking Up Arms to Rebel (Naqi wuqi nao geming)	拿起武器闹革命
The East is Red (Dongfang hong)	东方红
The Internationale (Guojige)	国际歌
The Legend of the Red Lantern (Hong deng ji)	红灯记
The Road to Prosperity and Strength (Fuqiang zhi lu)	富强之路
The Three Represents and One Flag (San ge daibiao yi mian qi)	三个代表一面旗
Tomorrow Will Be Better (Mingtian hui geng hao)	明天会更好
Unity is Strength (Tuanjie jiushi liliang)	团结就是力量
Wish You Peace (Zhu ni ping'an)	祝你平安
Without the Communist Party There Would Be No New China (Meiyou Gongchandang jiu meiyou xin Zhongguo)	没有共产党就没有新中国
Workers, Famers, Soldiers Unite (Gong nong bing lianhe qilai)	工农兵联合起来
Yellow River Cantata (Huanghe dahechang)	黄河大合唱

You and Me (Wo he ni)	我和你
Dance titles	
Dai Garland Dance (Daizu huahuanwu)	傣族花环舞
Korean Long Drum Dance (Chaoxianzu changguwu)	朝鲜族长鼓舞
Li Grass Dance (Lizu caoliwu)	黎族草笠舞
Miao Lusheng Dance (Miaozu lushengwu)	苗族芦笙舞
Red Detachment of Women (Hongse niangzi jun)	红色娘子军
The White-Haired Girl (Baimao nv)	白毛女
Xinjiang Dance (Xinjiang wu)	新疆舞
Programme titles	
Build the China Dream – New 'China Dream' Theme Song Gala' (Gongzhu Zhongguo meng – 'Zhongguo meng' zhuti xin chuangzuo gequ yanchanhui)	共筑中国梦 –'中国梦'主题新创作歌曲演唱会
Song Voices Float Over 30 years – 100 Golden Songs Gala series (Gesheng piaoguo 30 nian bai shou jinqu yanchanghui)	歌声飘过三十年百首金曲演唱会
Organizations	
Suning Electronics (Suning Dianqi)	苏宁电器
Other	
10, 000 cups and still not drunk! (Qian bei wan zhan ye bu zui!)	千杯万盏也不醉！
2008 Beijing Olympic Games (2008 nian Beijing aoyunhui dashi jinqu mingdan)	2008年北京奥运会大使金曲名单
Children of the Storm (Fengyun ernü)	风云儿女
China is heading to wealth and power (Zhongguo zhengzai zouxiang fuqiang)	正在走向富强
Country (guojia)	国家
Eight model operas (bage yangbanxi)	八个样板戏
Erhu (Chinese fiddle)	二胡
Gang of Four (siren bang)	四人帮
Harmonious China (hexie Zhongguo)	和谐中国
Harmonious Society (hexie shehui)	和谐社会
Harmonious World (hexie shijie)	和谐世界
Hundred Songs in Praise of China (Baige song Zhonghua)	百歌颂中华
Listeners' Favourite Broadcast Songs (Tingzhong xi'ai de guangbo gequ)	听众喜爱的广播歌曲
Literature and Artwork Forum (Wenyi gongzuo zuotan hui)	文艺工作座谈会
Love the nation (ai guo)	爱国
Mao Zedong quotations (Mao zhuxi yulu)	毛主席语录
National style (minzu changfa)	民族唱法
New Culture Movement (Xinwenhua Yundong)	新文化运动
One China principle (yi ge Zhongguo zhengce)	一个中国政策
Only if China is strong can the peoples' happiness be guaranteed (Zuguo qiangda renmin de xingfu baozhang)	祖国强大人民的幸福保障
Pipa (Chinese lute)	琵琶
Positive energy songs (Zhengnengliang gequ)	正能量
Red songs (hongse geyao)	红色歌谣

Glossary 227

Remarks on Suggestions to the Central Conservatory of Music (Dui zhongyang yinyue xueyuan yijian de pishi)	对中央音乐学院意见的批示
Respect their careers (jingye)	敬业
Resplendence (huihuang)	辉煌
Revolutionary model operas (geming jingju)	革命京剧
Sing for China (Chang xiang Zhongguo)	唱响中国
Song and dance troupes (gewu tuan)	歌舞团
Songs (gequ)	歌曲
To use the old to create the new and use the foreign to create a Chinese national art (gu wei jin yong, Yang wei Zhong yong)	古为今用，洋为中用
Yangge	秧歌

Chapter 3

People

Bi Fujian (Lao Bi)	毕福剑（老毕）
Bian Xiaozhen	卞小贞
Dong Qing	董卿
Duan Linxi	段林希
Han Lei	韩磊
Huang He	黄鹤
Jike Junyi	吉克隽逸
Li Yuchun	李宇春
Liu Zhongde	刘忠德
Qu Bo	曲波
Wu Yimin	邬毅敏
Xu Guangchun	徐光春
Zhang Liangying	张靓颖
Zhang Wei	张玮
Zhu Zhenming	朱振铭

Organizations

China Radio, Film and Television Group (Guangbo yingshi jituan)	广播影视集团
Guangdong Agency for Cultural Affairs (Guangdong sheng wenhua ting)	广东省文化厅
Guangdong Musicians' Association (Guangdong sheng yinyuejia xiehui)	广东省音乐家协会
Guangdong Provincial Party Committee Propaganda Department (Zhonggong Guangdong sheng wei xuanchuan bu)	中国广东省委宣传部
Guangdong Radio, Film and Television Bureau (Guangdong sheng guangbo dianying dianshi ju)	广东省广播电影电视局
Star China (Canxing)	灿星
State Administration of Radio, Film and Television (SARFT, Guojia guangbo dianying dianshi zongju)	国家广播电影电视总局

Song titles

China Dream (Zhongguo zhi meng)	中国之梦
Descendants of the Dragon (Long de chuanren)	龙的传人
I Love You China (Wo ai ni Zhongguo)	我爱你中国
Me and My Motherland (Wo he wo de zuguo)	我和我的祖国
Ode To Yan'an (Yan'an song)	延安颂
Party, Beloved Mother (Dang a, qin'ai de mama)	党啊，亲爱的妈妈
Red Flag Fluttering (Hongqi piaopiao)	红旗飘飘
Sing a Folk Song/Mountain Song for the Party (Chang zhi shange gei dang ting)	唱支山歌给党听
Spring has Come (Chuntian laile)	春天来了
The Sun is the Reddest, Chairman Mao is the Closest (Taiyang zui hong, Mao zhuxi zui qin)	太阳最红，毛主席最亲

Programme titles

China Idol (Zhongguo ouxiang)	中国偶像
China is Listening (Zhongguo zhengzai ting)	中华正在听
China Love Big Gala (Zhongguo ai da ge hui)	中国爱大歌会
China Music Television (Zhongguo yinyue dianshi)	中国音乐电视
China Red Songs Gala (Zhongguo hong ge hui)	中国红歌会
China Star Strength (Zhongguo xing liliang)	中国星力量
China Tibetan Songs Gala (Zhongguo Zang ge hui)	中国藏歌会
China's Got Talent (Zhongguo darenxiu)	中国达人秀
China Dream Show (Zhongguo menxiang xiu)	中国梦想秀
Chinese Idol (Zhongguo meng zhi sheng)	中国梦之声
Dream China (Mengxiang Zhongguo)	梦想中国
Feichang 6+1	非常6+1
Folk Songs China (Min'ge Zhongguo)	民歌中国
Freely Classic (Zongheng jingdian)	纵横经典
Frontline Music (Yinyue qianxian)	音乐前线
Happy Blue Sky (Kuaile lantian xia)	快乐蓝天下
Happy Boy (Kuaile Nansheng)	快乐男声
Happy Camp (Kuaile Dabenying)	快乐大本营
Happy in China (Huanle Zhongguo xing)	欢乐中国行
I am a Singer (Wo shi geshou)	我是歌手
I Want to Enter the Spring Festival – Direct to the Spring Festival Gala (Zhitong Chunwan)	我要上春晚 – 直通春晚
Live House (Xingguang xianchang)	星光现场
Mid-Autumn Festival Gala (Zhongqiu wanhui)	中秋晚会
MTV Style Gala (Chaoji shengdian)	超级盛典
Music Gala (Yinyue shengdian)	音乐盛典
Music Masterclass (Yinyue da shike)	音乐大师课
National Day Gala (Guoqing wanhui)	国庆晚会
Open the Door to Luck (Kaimen daji)	开门大吉
Our Chinese Heart (Zhonghua qing)	中华情
Passionate Square (Jiqing guangchang)	激情广场
Progress Every Day (Tiantian xiang shang)	天天向上
Sing for China (Wei Zhongguo ge chang)	为中国歌唱
Sing My Song (Zhongguo hao gequ)	中国好歌曲
Sing Towards the China Dream (Bai ge song Zhonghua)	百歌颂中华
Singing China (Changyou Zhongguo)	唱游中国
Songs From the Yellow River (Ge cong Huanghe lai)	歌从黄河来

Spring Festival Big Gala (Chunjie da lian huan)	春节大联欢
Star Avenue (Xingguang dadao)	星光大道
Super Diva (Mama miya)	妈妈咪呀
Super Girl (Chaoji nvsheng)	超级女声
Super Idol (Chaoji Ouxiang)	超级偶像
The Playlist (Chaoji gedan)	超级歌单
The Same Song (Tongyi shou ge)	同一首歌
The Voice Hong Kong (Chaoji Jusheng, lit: Super Giant Voice)	超级巨声
The Voice of China (Zhongguo hao shengyin)	中国好声音
Welcoming the New Spring Arts and Entertainment Gala (Ying xin chun wenyi wanhui)	迎新春文艺晚会
Wind-Cloud Music (Yunfeng yinyue)	风云音乐
X Factor (Zhongguo zui qiang yin)	中国最强音
Youth Television Singing Competition (Qingnian geshou dianshi dajiangsai)	青年歌手电视大奖赛
Zhashi Show (Zhaxi xiu)	扎西秀

Organizations

Enlight Media (Guangxian chuanmei)	光线传媒
Jiaduobao	加多宝
Longliqi	隆力奇
Mongolian Cow Yoghurt (Meng niu suan suan ru)	蒙牛酸酸乳
Oupai	欧派

Regulations

Notice on How to Apply the 2014 Television Variety Channel and Programmes Arrangement and Record (Guanyu zuohao 2014 nian dianshi shang xing zonghe pindao jiemu bianpai he bei'an gongzuo de tongzhu)	关于做好2014年电视上星综合频道节目编排和备案工作的通知
Some Provisional Regulations Concerning Local Foreign Affairs Work in Radio and Television (Guangbo yingshi xitong difang waishi gongzuo guanli guiding)	广播影视系统地方外事工作管理规定
Suggestions for Further Strengthening the Programme Management of Comprehensive Arts/Variety Programming on Satellite Television (Guanyu jinyibu jiaqiang dianshi shangxing zonghe shipin jiemu guanli de yijian)	关于进一步加强电视上星综合频道节目管理的意见

Other

Ai Xiyou	爱西柚
Chang'an	长安
Choral singing (hechang)	合唱
Comprehensive arts and entertainment / variety (zongyi)	综艺
Dongfang Weishi (Shanghai Dragon Television)	东方卫视
Have a home, have love – and have Oupai (You jia you ai you Oupai)	有家有爱有欧派
Lantern Festival (Yuanxiao jie)	元宵节
Limit Entertainment Order (Xian yu ling)	限娱令
Main melody (Zhu xuanlv)	主旋律
Motherland/ancestral land (Zuguo)	祖国

230 *Glossary*

National style (minzu changfa)	民族唱法
One Click, One World (Shiting Zhongguo, Hudong shijie)	视听中国，互动世界
Popular music (liuxing changfa)	流行唱法
Pouring Love on Guangzhou (Qingqing yangcheng)	情倾羊城
Specials (tebie jiemu)	特别节目
Taking Tiger Mountain by Strategy (Zhiqu wei hu shan)	智取威虎山
Throat and tongue (hou she)	喉舌
Tracks in the Snowy Forest (Lin hai xue yuan)	林海雪原
Two meetings (Lianghui)	两会
Western operatic/bel canto style (meisheng changfa)	美声唱法
Yuanshengtai (original ecology folk songs)	原生态

Chapter 4

People

A'erfa	阿尔法
Abdulla Abdurehim (Abudula Abudureyimu)	阿卜杜拉·阿卜杜热伊木
Ah Bao	阿宝
Ah Peng (Jiang Xuchang)	阿鹏（姜续昌）
Bai Yansong	白岩松
Bian Yinghua	卞英花
Dao Lang	刀郎
Dao Shu	刀舒
Dong Qing	董卿
Fei Xiang (Kris Phillips)	费翔
Han Han	韩寒
Han Hong	韩红
Hang Tianqi	杭天琪
Hu Jintao	胡锦涛
Jin Mei'er	金美儿
Ke'erman Band	克尔曼乐队
Lei Zhenbang	雷振邦
Liang Lu	梁璐
Lin Miaoke	林妙可
Maimaitili zunong (Memtili Zu'nong)	买买提力·祖农
Mao Zedong	毛泽东
Nie Er	聂耳
Pa'erhati (Perhat Khaliq)	帕尔哈提
Sa Beining	撒贝宁
Sa Dingding	萨顶顶
Song Zuying	宋祖英
Tan Weiwei (Sitar Tan)	谭维维
Tian Zhen	田震
Wang Feng	汪峰
Wang Luobin	王洛宾
Wang Xiaoya	王小丫
Wang Zhou	王卓
Wen Jiabao	温家宝
Xie Tingfeng (Nicholas Tse)	谢霆锋

Xila (Shila Amzah)	茜拉
Xu Peidong	徐沛东
Yang Liping	杨丽萍
Yu Qiuyu	余秋雨
Zhang Wei	张玮
Zhang Ximin	张喜民
Zhu Zheqin (Dadawa)	朱哲琴
Zou Wenqin	邹文琴

Nationalities/ethnic groups

Bai nationality	白族
Ethnic Koreans (Chaoxian zu)	朝鲜族
Han nationality	汉族
Hani nationality	哈尼族
Miao nationality	苗族

Places

Beijing	北京
Gansu	甘肃
Guangxi	广西
Guizhou	贵州
Hunan	湖南
Mojiang	墨江
Ningxia	宁夏
Qingyang	庆阳
Shaanbei	陕北
Shaanxi	陕西
Shanxi	山西
Tianshan mountains	天山
Xinjiang	新疆
Yan'an	延安
Yanbian	延边
Yining (also known as Ghulja)	伊宁
Yulin	榆林
Yunnan	云南

Song titles

Alive (Wan wu sheng)	万物生
Arirang	阿里郎
Beautiful Home (Meili jiayuan)	美丽家园
Bellflower Ballad (Jiegeng yao)	桔梗谣
Cup of Life (Shengming zhi bei)	生命之杯
Difficult to Meet Each Other (Xiang jian nan)	相见难
Drum Sister (A gu jie)	阿鼓姐
Grass-Mud Horse Song (Cao ni ma zhi ge)	草泥马之歌
Huayin Laoqiang One Voice Shout (Huayin laoqiang yi sheng han)	华阴老腔一声喊
In the Arms of Our Great Motherland (Zai ni weida de huaibao li)	在你伟大的怀抱里
Lift up your veil (Xianqi ni de gaitou lai)	掀起你的盖头来
Loess Plateau (Huangtu gaopo)	黄土高坡
Love My China (Ai wo Zhonghua)	爱我中华
Night in Ulaanbaatar (Wulanbatuo de ye)	乌兰巴托的夜
Ode to the Motherland (Gechang zuguo)	歌唱祖国

Our Dream (Women de meng)	我们的梦
Our Leader Mao Zedong (Zanmen de lingxiu Mao Zedong)	我们的领袖毛泽东
Red Flowers Blossom (Shan dandan huakai hong yanyan)	山丹丹花开红艳艳
Seeing You and I'll be Better (Jian ni bing jiu hao)	见你病就好
Snow Lotus Girl (Xue lian guniang)	雪莲姑娘
The Big Bridal Sedan Chair (Da hua qiao)	大花轿
The East is Red (Dongfang hong)	东方红
The Flag Fluttering in the Wind (Yingfeng piaoyang de qi)	迎风飘扬的旗
The Hometown I Love (Wo re'ai de guxiang)	我热爱的故乡
The Policy of the Communist Party is Yakexi (Dang de zhengce yakexi)	党的政策亚克西
The Red Sun Shines on the Border Regions (Hong taiyang zhao bianjiang)	红太阳照边疆
Visitors From Afar Please Stay On (Yuanfang de keren qing ni liu xia lai)	远方的客人请你留下来
Why are the Flowers So Red? (Hua'er wei shenme zheyang hong?)	花儿为什么这样红？
Yanbian People Love Chairman Mao (Yanbian renmin re'ai Mao zhuxi)	延边人民热爱毛主席

Programme titles

CCTV Concert Hall (Yinyue ting)	CCTV音乐厅
Chinese Idol (Zhongguo meng zhi sheng)	中国梦之声
Chinese Pop Music Golden Bell Awards (Zhongguo liuxing yinyue jin zhong jiang)	中国流行音乐金钟奖
Folk Songs China (Min'ge Zhongguo)	民歌中国
Folk Songs Museum (Min'ge bowuguan)	民歌博物馆
Go! Oriental Angel (Jiayou! Dongfang tianshi)	加油！东方天使
Happy Boy (Kuaile Nansheng)	快乐男声
I am a Singer (Wo shi geshou)	我是歌手
Love My China: Nationalities' United Special Evening of Entertainment (Ai wo Zhonghua: Minzu tuanjie zhuanti wanhui)	爱我中华：民族团结专题晚会
Love My China' Autonomous Regions' Third Children's Bilingual Speaking Competition (Ai wo Zhonghua zizhiqu di er shao'er shuangyu kouyu dasai)	爱我中华 自治区第三届少儿双语口语大赛
Master of Music (Yinyue dashi ke)	音乐大师课
Piloting China (Linghang Zhongguo)	领航中国
River Elergy (Heshang)	河殇
Songs From the Yellow River (Ge cong Huang He lai)	歌从黄河来
Super Girl (Chaoji nüsheng)	超级女声
Western-Area Folk Music Competition (Xibu Minge Dasai)	西部民歌大赛
Youth Television Singing Competition (Qinggesai)	青歌赛
Zhaxi Show (Zhaxi xiu)	扎西秀

Musical instruments and styles

Choral music (hechang)	合唱
Erhu (Chinese fiddle)	二胡
Folk song (minge, shange)	民歌,山歌

Gourd pipe (hulusi)	葫芦丝
Matouqin (bowed stringed instrument)	马头琴
Mouth organ (kou xian)	口弦
National style (minzu changfa)	民族唱法
National/ethnic music (minzu yinyue)	民族音乐
Pop music singing style (liuxing changfa)	流行唱法
Popular music (liuxing yinyue, tongsu yinyue)	流行音乐, 通俗音乐
Red songs (hongse geyao)	红色歌谣
Sanxian (Chinese lute)	三弦
Shuochang	说唱
Suona (Chinese shawm)	唢呐
Western opera/ Operatic style (meisheng changfa)	美声唱法
Xiaodiao (folkmusic genre)	小调
Xun (egg shaped musical instrument)	勋
Yuanshengtai (original ecology folk songs)	原生态

Organizations

China Conservatory of Music (Zhongguo yinyue xueyuan)	中国音乐学院
Propaganda Department of the CCP Central Committee (Zhongyang xuanchuan bu)	中央宣传部
State Ethnic Affairs Commission of the PRC (Guojia minzu shiwu weiyuanhui)	国家民族事务委员会
United Front Work Department of the CCP Central Committee (Zhongyang tongzhan bu)	中央统战部

Other

Authentic (didi daodao de)	地地道道的
Civilized (wenming)	文明
Dongbei Yemen (an ordinary guy from the Northeast)	东北爷们
Grass-mud horse (Cao ni ma)	草泥马
Han language (Hanyu)	汉语
He is the Chinese dream in my heart (Wo xin zhong de zhongguomeng).	我心中的中国梦
Heart of the Highland (Gaoyuan zhi xin)	高原之心
Legend (Chuanshuo)	传说
Mandarin (Putonghua)	普通话
Modernization (xiandaihua)	现代化
Mysterious (shenqi)	神奇
River crab (he xie) (homonym for 'harmony')	河蟹/和谐
River-crabbed (bei hexie)	被河蟹/被和谐
Scientific (kexue)	科学
State development (guojia fazhan)	国家发展
Tang-style suit (Tang zhuang)	唐装
The CCP leads us towards victory, towards the future (Gongchang dang lingdao women shengli xiang qian fang)	共产党领导我们胜利向前方
Tou jin (cloth head covering)	土巾
Visitors on the Iceberg (Bing shan shang de lai ke)	冰山上的来客
Yax Lizard (a play on the word Yakexi, meaning 'good' in Uyghur)	亚克蜥 (a play on 亚克西)

Chapter 5

People

A-rui (Ari Fabio Calangi)	阿瑞
Cai Guoqing	蔡国庆
Cai Yilin (Jolin Tsai)	蔡依林
Chen Mingzhen (Jennifer Chen)	陈明真
Chen Sitong	陈思彤
Chen Yongxin (Melody Chen)	陈永馨
Cui Shu	崔恕
Deng Lijun (Teresa Teng)	邓丽君
Deng Xiaoping	邓小平
Fan Yichen (Van Fan)	范逸臣
Fei Xiang (Kris Phillips)	费翔
Gao Feng	高枫
Gao Lingfeng (Frankie Kao)	高凌风
Guo Lanying	郭兰英
Han Hong	韩红
Hu Ge	胡歌
Huang Jiajia	黄佳佳
Huang Qishan	黄绮珊
Jackie Chan (Chen Long)	成龙
Jike Junyi (Summer)	吉克隽逸
Jin Mei'er	金美儿
Langgalamu (Vanatsaya Viseskul)	朗嘎拉姆
Li Jianfu	李建复
Liang Yongbin	梁永斌
Liang Yongqi (Gigi Leung)	梁咏琪
Lin Xinru (Ruby Lin)	林心如
Liu Dehua (Andy Lau)	刘德华
Liu Haolin (Harlin Liu)	刘昊霖
Liu Ke	刘珂
Liu Tao	刘涛
Ma Yingjiu (Ma Ying-jeou)	马英九
Na Ying	那英
Peng Liyuan	彭丽媛
Power Station (Dongli huoche) (band)	动力火车
Qi Qin	齐秦
Qin Yuzi	秦宇子
Rong Yunlin	容韵琳
Song Zuying	宋祖英
Sun Nan	孙楠
Wang Fei (Faye Wong)	王菲
Wang Feng	汪峰
Wang Fuling (James Wong)	王福龄
Wang Lihong (Wang Leehom)	王力宏
Wang Mingquan (Liza Wang)	汪明荃
Weng Bingrong	翁炳荣
Weng Qianyu (Judy Ongg)	翁倩玉
Xi Jinping	习近平
Xi Xiulan	奚秀兰
Xie Tingfeng (Nicholas Tse)	谢霆锋
Xu Ruyun (Valen Hsu)	许茹芸
Zhang Huimei (Chang Hui-mei, A-mei)	张惠妹 (阿妹)
Zhang Jingying (Jane Zhang)	张靓颖

Glossary 235

Zhang Lei	张蕾
Zhang Mingmin	张明敏
Zhang Ye	张也
Zhou Jielun (Jay Chou)	周杰伦

Ethnic groups / classifications

Chinese community (Huaren shehui)	华人社区
Chinese descendant (*huayi*)	华裔
Ethnic minorities (in Taiwan) (Gaoshanzu lit: high mountain people)	高山族
Laoxiang (a person from the same town)	老乡
Macau mixed blood (Aomen hun xue'er)	澳门混血儿
Mainland/inland friends (neidi de pengyou)	内地的朋友
Minnan	闽南
Mixed-blood Chinese-American young man (Zhong-Mei hunxue de xiao huozi)	中美混血的小伙子
Native Taiwanese population (benshengren)	本省人
Outside-province people (Waishengren)	外省人
Overseas Chinese (Haiwai huaren, huaqiao)	海外华人华侨

Places

China (Zhonghua)	中华
China Taiwan (Zhongguo Taiwan)	中国台湾
Dalian	大连
Fujian	福建
Guangxi	广西
Guangzhou	广州
Hong Kong, China (Zhongguo Xianggang)	中国香港
Jiangxi	江西
London	伦敦
Lüshun	旅顺
Macau, China (Zhongguo Aomen)	中国澳门
Nanchang	南昌
Shenzhen	深圳
Taipei	台北
Taiwan Straits (liang'an)	两岸
Taiwan, China (Zhongguo Taiwan)	中国台湾
The ruins of St. Paul's cathedral (Dasanba paifang)	大三巴牌坊
The three places (mainland, Hong Kong and Macau) on the two sides of the Taiwan Straits (Liang an san di)	两岸三地
Vancouver	温哥华
Weihai	威海

Song titles

A Great Love (Xiangqin xiang'ai de yi jia ren, lit: Family Who Love Each Other)	相亲相爱的一家人
A Spray of Plum Blossoms (Yi jian mei)	一剪梅
A Thousand Words (Qianyan wanyu)	千言万语
Big China (Da Zhongguo)	大中国
Chinese people (Zhongguo ren)	中国人
Clouds of My Hometown' (Guxiang de yun)	故乡的云
Come Together (Yiqilai)	一起来
Fill the World with Love (Rang shijie chongman ai)	让世界充满爱
Flame in the Winter (Dongtian li de yi ba huo)	冬天里的一把火

236 *Glossary*

Happy and Carefree (Huanle wuyou)	欢乐无忧
If the Clouds Knew (Ruguo yun zhidao)	如果云知道
Lover (Airen)	爱人
My Chinese Heart (Wo de Zhongguo xin)	我的中国心
My Motherland (Wo de zuguo)	我的祖国
Ode to the Motherland (Gechang Zuguo)	歌唱祖国
Pray (Qidao)	祈祷
Red Flag Fluttering (Hong qi piao piao)	红旗飘飘
Swing Together (Yiqi yaobai)	一起摇摆
The Girls of Ali Mountain (Alishan de guniang)	阿里山的姑娘
The Moon Represents My Heart (Yueliang daibiao wode xin)	月亮代表我的心
The Song of Seven Lands – Aomen (Qizi zhi ge – Aomen)	七子之歌-澳门
Victorious singing voices (Shengli gesheng)	胜利歌声
Yellow People (Huangzhongren)	黄种人

Programme titles

A Beijing Native in New York (Beijing ren zai Niuyue)	北京人在纽约
Entering Into Inner Mongolia—Booming Ordos (Zoujin Nei Menggu—tengfei E'erduosi)	走进内蒙古-腾飞鄂尔多斯
Entering Into Ningxia—Qingxi Hui village (Zoujin Ningxia, qingxi hui xiang)	走进宁夏，情系回乡
Happy in China – National Day Celebration Special – Charming Macau (Huanle Zhongguo Xing – Guoqingjie tebie jiemu – Meili Aomen)	欢乐中国行-国庆节特别节目-美丽澳门
Journeying over ten thousand torrents and a thousand crags – always love (also translated to as The trials of a long and arduous journey) (Wan shui qian shan zong shi qing)	万水千山总是情
Masked Singer (Mengmian gewang)	蒙面歌王
Our Chinese Heart (Zhonghua Qing)	中华情
Overseas Chinese Star Avenue (Huaren Xingguang Dadao)	华人星光大道
Sing! China (Zhongguo xin shengyin, lit: China New Voice)	中国新声音
Songs of Memories (Jiyi de gesheng)	记忆的歌声
Sounds of Singing Over 30 Years (Gesheng Piao Guo 30 Nian)	歌声飘过30年
Special celebrating the tenth anniversary since the return of Macau to China (Qingzhu Aomen huigui zuguo shi zhounian wenyi wanhui).	庆祝澳门回归祖国十周年文艺晚会
The Same Song – enters Taiwan – Mid-Autumn Day special (Tongyi shouge – zoujin Taiwan – Zhongqiujie tebie jiemu)	同一首歌-走进台湾-中秋特别节目
The Years of Macau (Aomen Suiyue)	澳门岁月

Musical instruments and styles

Dizi (Chinese flute)	笛子
Erhu (Chinese fiddle)	二胡
Folk song/mountain song (shange)	山歌
Guzheng (Chinese zither)	古筝

Kouxian (mouth harp) 口弦
Pipa (Chinese lute) 琵琶
Pop music (Liuxing yinyue) 流行音乐
Portuguese folk dance (Putaoya tufeng wu) 葡萄牙土风舞
Yuanshengtai (original ecology folk songs) 原生态

Organizations
Oupai (Kitchens) 欧派

Other
Blend (jiaorong) 交融
Blending of China and the West, [where] the old and new reflect each other (Zhong-Xi ronghe, gujin huiyin) 中西融合，古今辉映
Call (huhuan) 呼唤
Dear motherland (qin'ai de zuguo) 亲爱的祖国
Five-starred red flag (wuxing hongqi) 五星红旗
Leading me into this big family (Dai wo jinru zheme da de jiating) 带我进入这么大的家庭
Na'aisi 纳爱斯
Not my real name (bu shi wo zhen xing), mother (muqin), is my body (shi wo di routi) 不是我真姓，母亲，是我的肉体
Not to go roaming far away again (Bie zai sichu piaobo) 别再四处漂泊
Our China/Our great motherland (Women weida zuguo) 我们伟大祖国
Putonghua 普通话
Reunion (tuanyuan) 团员
Scientific development (kexue fazhan) 科学发展
Unity of the nationalities (minzu tuanjie) 民族团结
Warm feeling (wenxin) 温馨
We will create the future of China (Women qu chuangzao huaxia de weilai) 我们去创造华夏的未来

Chapter 6

People
Ah Bao 阿宝
Ai Hua (Charlotte MacInnis) 爱华
Bing Xian 冰娴
Cai Yan 蔡妍
Chen Long (Jacky Chan) 成龙
Da Niu (Niu Hansheng/Daniel Newham) 大牛
Dashan (Mark Rowswell) 大山
Dai Yuqiang 戴玉强
Deng Lijun (Teresa Teng) 邓丽君
Ding Guangquan 丁广泉
Fan Yichen 范逸臣
Fei Xiang (Kris Phillips) 费翔
Five Continents Singing group (Wu zhou changxiang yuetuan) 五洲唱响乐团
Fushan yazhi (Fukuyama Masaharu) 福山雅治

Hao Ge (Uwechue Emmanuel) 郝歌
Hou Dejian 侯德健
Hu Jintao 胡锦涛
Huang Zhilie (Hwang Chi Yeul) 黄致列
Ji Xiaojun 季小军
Jiang Kun 姜昆
Jin Chengwu (Takeshi Kaneshiro) 金城武
Kangta (Ahn Chil-hyun) 安七炫
Le Le 乐乐
Lei Zhenbang 雷振邦
Li Bingbing 李冰冰
Li Wen (Coco Lee) 李玟
Li Yugang 李玉刚
Liang Yongbin 梁永斌
Liu Dehua (Andy Lau) 刘德华
Liu Huan 刘欢
Luo Qi 罗琦
Qi Yu 齐豫
Qiao Shanzhong (Joe Yamanaka) 乔山中
Sa Beining 撒贝宁
Shanxia Jiuzhi (Yamashita Tomohisa) 山下久智
Shen Chenxun (Shin Seung-hun) 申承勋
Su Jianxin (Shin) 苏见信
Sun Nan 孙楠
Tang Aiguo 唐爱国
Teng Ge'er 腾格尔
Wang Lihong (Wang Leehom) 王力宏
Wang Qiming 王起明
Wei Wei 韦唯
Weitasi (Vitas) 维塔斯
Wen Jiabao 温家宝
Xie Tingfeng (Nicholas Tse) 谢霆锋
Xila 茜拉
Xiong Dailin 熊黛林
Yang Jima 央吉玛
Yang Lan 杨澜

Ethnic groups/classifications
Black mixed blood (Heiren de hunxue) 黑人的混血
Black people (Heiren) 黑人
Changbai Korean (Chaoxian) 朝鲜
Yi family girls (Yijia meizi) 彝家妹子
Zhongguo tong 中国通

Places
Beijing 北京
Guangzhou 广州
Guizhou 贵州
Sichuan 四川
South Korea (Hanguo) 韩国
Tianshan 天山
Xinjiang 新疆
Xizang (Tibet) 西藏
Zhejiang 浙江

Song titles

A Question Asked Ten Million Times (Qianwan ci de wen)	千万次的问
Arirang (Alilang)	阿里郎
Chairman's Words Remembered by Heart (Mao Zhuxi de hua'er ji xin shang).	毛主席的话儿记心上
Chinese Language (Zhongguohua)	中国话
Everlasting Friendship (Youyi dijiutianchang)	友谊地久天长
Great Sea Ah, Hometown (Da hai a, guxiang)	大海啊故乡
Hand in Hand (Shou la shou)	手拉手
I Have You on the Way (Yi lu shang you ni)	一路上有你
I Love Reading Chairman Mao's Books Most (Mao zhuxi de shu wo zui ai du/Du Mao zhuxi de shu)	毛主席的书我最爱读
I Love You China (Wo ai ni Zhongguo)	我爱你中国
If There Was No CCP, There'd Be No New China (Meiyou gongchangdang jiu mei you xin Zhongguo)	没有共产党就没有新中国
In Memory of the Brother in Arms (Huainian zhanyou)	怀念战友
Learn From the Great Model Lei Feng (Xuexi Lei Fang hao bang yang)	学习雷锋好榜样
Lie (Huangyan)	谎言
Marry a Chinese Man (Jia gei Zhongguo ren)	嫁给中国人
Missing (Sinian)	思念
Moscow Nights (Mosike jiaowai de wanshang)	莫斯科郊外的晚上
Opera No.2 (Geju 2)	歌剧2
Qinghai-Tibetan Plateau (Qingzang Gaoyuan)	青藏高原
Rose, Rose, I Love You (Meigui, meigui, wo ai ni)	玫瑰玫瑰我爱你
Shining Red Star (Shanshan de hong xing)	闪闪的红星
Sing a Folk Song for the Party (Chang zhi shange gei dang ting)	唱支山歌给党听
Socialism is Great (Shehui zhuyi hao)	社会主义好
Straw Hat Song (Cao mao ge)	草帽歌
Sweetness (Tianmimi)	甜蜜蜜
The Kalina/Raspberry Flowers are in Bloom (Hong mei hua'er kai)	红莓花儿开
The Moon Represents My Heart (Yueliang daibiao wode xin)	月亮代表我的心
The Place Far Away (Zai nar yaoyuan de difang)	在那遥远的地方
The Red Sun Shines on the Border Regions (Hong taiyang zhao bianjiang)	红太阳照边疆
The Timeless Beauty of Prayer (Qidao yongheng de meili)	祈祷永恒的美丽
The Wind Comes from the East (Feng Cong Dongfang Lai)	风从东方来
We are the World (Tian xia yi jia)	天下一家
Yangge Supporting the Liberation Army (Yong Jun Yangge)	拥军秧歌

Programme titles

4th China-ROK Pop Fest (Zhong-Han Gehui)	中韩歌会

Celebrating the 18th National People's Congress – Into the Grassroots – My 10 years here – Maliya: Thank You China (Xinying shiba da – Wo zhe shinian Maliya: Xiexie Zhongguo).	喜迎十八大·我这十年玛利亚：谢谢你中国
Culture Noon (Wenhua Zhengwu)	文化正午
Ding ge long dong qiang (lit: Bite, Cough, Throat, Boom, Choke)	叮咯咙咚呛
KU Music Asian Music Awards (Ku yinyue yazhou shengdian)	酷音乐亚洲盛典
Music Radio: China's Top Music Awards (Music Radio 中国zhongguo TOP 音乐盛典yinyue shengdian)	Music Radio 中国 TOP 音乐盛典
National Musical Instrument (Minzu qiyue) (competition)	民族器乐
Sing For China (Wei Zhongguo ge chang)	为中国歌唱
Sing Towards China (Changxiang Zhongguo)	唱响中国
Sinophiliac (Tongle wuzhou)	同乐五洲
The Same Song – China-ROK Friendship Concert / The Same Song in Korea (Zhong-Han youhao daxing gehui)	中韩友好大型歌会
The Same Song – Enters Japan (Tongyi shouge zoujin Riben)	同一首歌走进日本
Weekend Music Talk (Zhoumo yuetan)	周末乐坛

Musical instruments and styles

China's folk arts (Zhongguo quyi)	中国曲艺
Guzheng (Chinese zither)	古筝
Quyi (a folk art form)	曲艺
Red classic (Hongse jingdian)	红色经典
Yuanshengtai (original ecology folk songs)	原生态

Organizations

Longliqi	隆力奇
Lotte (Le Tian)	乐天
Wenbiquan (Wetherm)	温碧泉

Other

A Beijing Native in New York (Beijing ren zai Niuyue)	北京人在纽约
Cheongsam (qipao)	旗袍
Chinese name (Zhongguo mingzi)	中国名字
Chinese voices are seeking resonance around the world, the world's voices are singing for China (Zhongguo shengyin, shijie gongming)	中国声音，世界共鸣
Clever Chinese people (Hao congming de Zhongguo ren, hao youmei de Zhongguohua)	好聪明的中国人，好优美的中国话
Confucian thought is becoming increasingly international (Kongfuzi de hua yuelaiyue guojihua)	孔夫子的话越来越国际化
Crosstalk (xiangsheng)	相声
Culture is strength, feeling, influence and warmth – Disseminate Culture, Affect China' (Chuanbo wenhua, yingxiang Zhongguo)	传播文化，影响中国
Different hair colours (Ge zhong yanse de toufa)	各种颜色的头发
Different skin colours (Ge zhong yanse de pifu)	各种颜色的皮肤

Goddess (nüshen)	女神
Happy Singing Voices (Kuaile gesheng)	快乐歌声
In the days of the big movement (Zai yundong dahui de rizi li)	在运动大会的日子里
Mandarin (Putonghua)	普通话
Our Chinese/China folk arts (Women Zhongguo quyi)	我们中国曲艺
Overseas most popular singer (Haiwai zui shou huanying geshou)	海外最受欢迎歌手
Overseas Multitalented Entertainer (Haiwai quanneng yiren)	海外全能艺人
Singing in our national language (Chang Guoyu)	唱国语
The many years we spent struggling to learn English pronunciation and grammar (Duoshao nian women kulian yingwen fayin he wenfa)	多少年我们苦练英文发音和文法
The Same Five Continents, Five Continents The Same Happiness! (Tongle wuzhou, wuzhou tongle).	同乐五洲，五洲同乐！
The whole world will listen to 'us' and whatever we have to say (women shuo de hua, rang shijie dou renzhen tinghua)	我们说的话，让世界都认真听话
Tou jin (cloth head covering)	头巾
Unity of opposites (Dui li tong yi)	对立统一
Variety reality show (zongyi zhenrenxiu)	综艺真人秀
Visitors to the Icy Mountain (Bing shan shang de lai ke)	冰山上的来客
Whole world (quan shijie)	全世界
Witness (Renzheng)	认证

Index

A Beijinger in New York 20, 159, 192
Abdurehim, Abdulla 110, 115
accordion 32
Adele 63–4
Advertising 19, 51–3, 59, 63, 112, 117, 165–6, 194, 199; *see also* sponsorship
A'erfa 118
Africans 15; African music 185; migration to China 193; *see also* African Americans, Hao Di, Hao Ge, Maliya
African Americans 15, 110, 117; *see also* Lou Jing, Qiao Shanzhong (Joe Yamanaka)
Ah Bao 114, 190, 194
Ah Peng 95–7, 118
Ai Weiwei 200
Aihua (Charlotte MacInnis) 172–4
AKB48 205
A-mei (Zhang Huimei/Chang Hui-mei) 148, 166
America *see* USA
Shilah Amzah *see* Xila
Anderson, Benedict 1–2, 5
Anderson, Elise 108, 206
Andy Liu *see* Liu Dehua
Appell, Jesse 200–1
Arabic 69
Arirang 113, 198
A-rui (Ari Fabio Calangi) 141
Asia-Pacific Economic Cooperation (APEC) 45
Asian: people 15; identity 179–80; *see also* East Asian pop culture, Japan, Korea (South)
Asian Games 59, 179
Asian Wave 104, 187, 208
Askar 102
audiences: appeal to 50, 117, 152, 182; and applause 135, 140, 145, 183, 191; and complaints 59, 71; fragmentation of 2; indoctrination of 54; and laughter 158, 173–4, 183; on-screen 139–40, 145–6, 156–8, 191; participation/interaction 68, 98, 105, 149, 174; and pop charts 32; as producers of content 96–7; and re-appropriation of content 110, 113, 177, 196, 200; *see also* online content, ratings, voting
Australia 35, 123, 154, 161, 171, 178; *see also* Minogue, Kylie
Austria 39

Babida, Chris 177
Back Dorm Boys 193
Bai nationality 7; *see also* Ah Peng
Bai, Ruoyun 66, 74
Bai Yansong 89
Baranovitch, Nimrod 102, 113
Barmé, Geremie 15
the Beatles 32
Beethoven 32
Beijing: as a creative capital 102, 138, 195; and foreigners 200; as a global city 177, 192–3, 216; opera 176, 192; television 50, 54–5, 66, 195; *see also* *A Beijinger in New York*
bel canto *see* operatic music
Berklee College of Music 141, 177
Berlin 176; *see also* Germany
Beyoncé 63
Bi Fujian 72, 163, 192
Bieber, Justin 118
Big Bang 199
Bing Xian 172
Black Duck Trio 40
blends of Chinese and Western music/art 164–5, 215, 217; and Chinese modernity 28, 46; in socialist era 30;

Index   243

during Cultural Revolution 32; in television xi, 64–5; and duets between Chinese and Western singers 187; and pairing of hosts from China and the West 172; *see also* blends of traditional and modern elements, ethno-pop, flamenco, Hao Ge, Jin Mei'er, mixed race, national style, Portugal rock music, Tan Weiwei (Sitar Tan), Vitas
blends of traditional and modern elements 11, 61, 64–5, 112, 137; *see also* clothing
Bo Xilai 42
Bollywood 101
Brady, Anne-Marie 15
Brightman, Sarah 187
Britain xii, 60–1, 157, 159–60, 178, 182–3; and colonialism 14, 138, 217; *see also* the Beatles, Brightman, Sarah, Da Niu, Hong Kong, Iain Inglis, the Nolans, Thatcher, Margaret
Broadway 152

Cai Guoqing 132, 204
Cai Jianya (Tanya Chua) 186
Cai Yilin (Jolin Tsai) 148
Cameroon 181, 186
Canada 123, 154, 156, 161, 167; *see also* Dashan, Dion, Celine, Rowswell, Mark
Cantonese 130–1, 138–9, 141, 179–80
CCP (Chinese Communist Party) xi; and Chinese culture 11; and 'four identifications' 9; and legitimacy 75, 89, 91, 213; and leadership 44; and national identity 3, 213; and power struggles 19, 50; and prosperity xii, 89–90; songs in praise of 4, 27, 30–1, 42, 46, 64, 183, 190; and supervision of art and culture 8, 26–7, 34, 43, 75–6; and support for 90, 182
CCP Central Committee 53
CCTV Guide 190
CCTV (China Central Television): history and overview of 50, 53–62, 67–8; and Chinese outside of the mainland 57; parodies of 201; political role of 183, 214, 216
CCTV Spring Festival Gala see Spring Festival Gala
CCTV Youth Singing Competition see Youth Singing Competition
cello 32
censorship 75–6, 102, 109, 132; and market 66, 75–6; self-censorship 74

century of humiliation 14, 123, 138, 204
Changbai 180–1, 186
Chang Sisi 36
Chang'an Ford 63
Chaoxian nationality 30, 99, 111–13, 119, 153, 180–2, 186, 198; *see also* Arirang, Changbai, Jin Mei'er, Yanbian
Chen Kaige 10
Chen Sitong (Vivi/Vivienna Chen) 165
Chen, Xiaomei 19
Chen Yongxin (Melody Tan) 161
Cheng Long (Jacky Chan) 40–1, 124, 130, 178
children 20, 45, 56–7, 90, 103, 105, 109, 133–5, 139, 146, 162, 173, 179
China Central Television *see* CCTV
China Dream xi, 9, 42–3, 106, 208, 213, 218; and foreigners 16, 183, 185, 195, 200–2, 216; and Greater China 126; and overseas Chinese 161–3, 165; shows 44; songs 44, 65; *see also* Olympic Dream
China expert *see* Zhongguo tong
China Network Television *see* CNTV
China Southern Airlines 57
China's Got Talent 62, 183
Chinese Communist Party *see* CCP
Chinese Communist Party Propaganda Department 52
Chinese Idol 62–3, 104, 187–8
Chinese language: 2, 29, 70, 87; dialects 132, 137, 175, 179, 206, 215; and minority nationalities 97, 105, 128; and foreigners 20, 172, 175–7, 194–5, 205–8; in Japan 204; local accents 135, 146; in Macau 139, 141; and overseas Chinese 157, 161–3; promotion of 105–6, 161; and Taiwan 146; *see also* Love My China
Chinese Language (*Zhongguohua*) (song) 176
Chinese overseas *see* overseas Chinese
Chinese People's Political Consultative Conference *see* CPPCC
Chineseness 1; shared popular culture 12, 122, 127; *see also* Cultural China
choir *see* choral music
Chongqing 41–2
choral music: 27, 43, 57, 59, 65, 93, 177, 213; and singing in harmony 4, 116; *see also* Fei Xiang (Kris Phillips), Hao Ge, Macau, My Chinese Heart, Zhang Mingmin
Chou, Jay *see* Zhou Jielun

Index

Chow Yiu-Fai 127
Chua, Beng-Huat 12, 122
Civilizational China xi, 14
class consciousness 5, 11
clothing: and foreigners 172, 174–5, 184–5, 205, 214; and modern/traditional blends 88, 98, 100, 111, 112, 114–5, 134, 189; *see also* colourful minorities
CNTV (China Network Television): 69–70, 89, 105, 108, 127
Cold War 50, 142–3
collaboration: between CCTV and provincial satellite broadcasters xi, 216–7
colonialism: and Britain 14, 138; and France 14; and Germany 14, 27; and Japan 14, 27, 123–4, 126; and Portugal 135, 140; and United States 14
comic sketches 53, *see also* jokes
commerce: and politics 58, 59, 183
compatriots 5, 135–6, 140, 146, 157, 159
competition: between broadcast and online content 70, 110; between CCTV and provincial satellite broadcasters xi, 68
Confucianism: and Confucius statue 185; and global interest in 176; as point of unity between Chinese people globally 11–12; and national identity 12; rejection of 11; revival of 3, 11–12, 142; and suffocation of Han culture 10; and Taiwan 142; and weakness of China 27; *see also* Confucius Institutes
Confucius Institutes 12, 20
conservatories of music 36, 38, 117
Constitution 8, 28, 142
cooperation: between CCTV and provincial networks 68; between CCTV and TVB 131
corruption 12, 34, 39, 42, 54
cosmopolitanism: celebration of 10, 128; and television 52; and global formats 63, 140–1, 207, 218; and multiethnicity 85, 98–9, 101–2, 112; and foreigners 178, 195, 205–6; and Chinese/Taiwanese 150, 153–4, 161, 164; *see also* cross-cultural marriage, ethno-pop
CPPCC 36, 57, 75, 91
creative industries 59, 99, 101, 196, 200, 218
cross-cultural marriage 9, 20, 184–6
cross-Straits relations 34; *see also* Hou Dejian
Cultural China: history of 11; and re-centring of the PRC 12, 164
cultural imperialism 32
cultural industries 85, 92, 124, 197
cultural pluralism 10
cultural proximity 217
Cultural Revolution 5, 8, 28, 31–3, 35, 42, 46, 50, 87, 142, 159; *see also* eight model operas

Da Niu (Niu Hansheng/Daniel Newham) 172, 181–2, 186, 207
Dadawa *see* Zhu Zheqin
Dai Yuqiang 36, 190
Dao Lang 99, 118, 190
Dashan 17–18, 201; *see also* Rowswell, Mark
Deep Forest 118
democracy 34–5, 39, 124, 143; *see also* voting
Deng Lijun (Teresa Teng) 34, 145, 161–2, 198
Deng Xiaoping 33, 35, 37, 51, 145
depoliticization 68
Descendants of the Dragon 34–5, 149–51, 166, 177
Ding Guangquan 181, 201
Dion, Celine 187, 190
disco 34, 36
Dong Qing 58, 88, 95
Dong Wenhua 37
double exoticism 180, 182, 188–9, 192, 206
dragon: as symbol of China 34, 115, 150–1, *see also* Descendants of the Dragon, Dragon TV
Dragon TV 62, 104, 117, 203, 205, 207, 209
drums 4, 18, 30,113, 115, 126, 135, 137, 153, 178, 215

East Asian pop culture 197
The East is Red 28, 29–30, 42, 87, 50
economic development xii, 9, 58; and environmental degradation 39, 92; and ghost towns 128; *see also* economic reforms, scientific development
economic reforms: 8, 14, 32–3, 50, 131, 136, 165, 179; *see also* market economy
education: on common knowledge 94–5; about enemies in war 15, 27,

126; about identity xi, 3, 26, 65, 151, 153, 206; and ideology 28–9, 37, 39, 55; about music 61, 93, 151; overseas 20, 154; patriotic 9; programmes 71; and singing 36, 42; through entertainment 54; and traditional culture 175, 180; *see also* Chinese language, hosts
eight model operas 31, 50, 72
England *see* Britain
English: language 69, 141, 162, 176–7, 188–9, 209; names 157; songs 39, 112, 149, 152, 162–3, 177, 179, 203, 207–8
Enlight Media 60
entertainment industry 35; development of 51
entertainment television: in socialist era 50; and cultural identity 26; and foreign style shows 52; and ideology 26, 74–5; language learning shows 52; popularity of 53; quiz shows 52
Erdos 128
erhu (two-stringed fiddle) 32, 115, 139, 172, 176
ethnic minorities *see* minority nationalities, colourful minorities
ethnic pluralism xi
ethno-pop xii, 85, 98–9, 114–6, 216
exchanges: between ethnicities 106; with Japan 204–5; between mainland and Hong Kong 132; with other nations 38, 138, 171, 175, 185, 197–8, 202, 217

Falun Gong 35, 155
family: and foreigners 186; and Han Chinese 10; and Hong Kong people 124; and Macau 134; and mainland Chinese 19; and multiethnicity 10, 88; and overseas Chinese 16, 157, 161; as a political symbol 16, 36, 56, 88, 124, 130, 134, 144, 148, 157, 161, 186; and role of television 2; and Taiwan 144; *see also* Greater China, Spring Festival Gala
Fei Xiang (Kris Phillips) 112, 151–3, 165, 178
Five Continents Singing Group 172
flags 126, 136, 181
flamenco 100–1
flows: of popular culture 13, 196–7, 200, 216; of television shows 60, 113
flutes 109, 129, 139, 165

Folk Songs China 57, 61, 92, 97–8, 100–2, 117, 175
foreign: cities 123: imperialists 6; influences 112; languages 58; occupations and humiliation 27, 138; pop stars 73; *see also* colonialism, foreign friends, foreigners
foreign friends 15, 31, 38, 138–40, 185, 208
foreigners x, 5; and Chinese names 172–3, 205; and English teaching 18; as foreign monkeys 18, 207; on television 16, 171–220; gaze of 19, 179, 217; historical relationship with 14; love for/attraction to China xii, 19–20, 173–7, 184–6, 192, 205–8, 214, 216; and relationship to minority nationalities 174, 180; as objects of Chinese gaze 175; orthodox representation of 160, 205; and skin colour 172, 176–8, 185; stereotypes of 14–15, 19, 193, 200; *see also* clothing, foreign, foreign friends, hijabs, Inglis, Iain, jokes, Olympic Games
France: and colonialism 14; and French songs 38; and overseas Chinese 160
friends *see* foreign friends
Fujian 148
Fung, Anthony 54, 127
Fygi, Laura 178, 187–8

Gang of Four 33, 46
Gangnam Style 199–201, 209
Gansu 10
Germany 39, 160; *see also* Berlin
global: brands 59; centre xii, 160, 216; competition 58, 68; stage 19, 60; harmony 172; image 141; integration 158; interactions 185; investment 65, 160; knowledge 94; outlook 139; performance 195; player 128, 188; positioning 164; recognition xi, 154, 189; reputation 160; stars 187; style 163; *see also* global formats, globalization, Olympic Games
global formats 53, 59, 60, 64, 71, 197
globalization x, 215; and international trade 60; and touring shows 61; *see also* CNTV, cross-cultural marriage, *yuanshengtai*
gospel 190–3
Grammy Awards 37
Great Hall of the People 29, 31, 44

246 Index

Great Leap Forward 8
Great Wall 125–7, 130–1, 177–8, 214
Greater China xi, xii, 4–5, 122; and centring of the PRC 13; orthodox representations of 165, 214
Guangdong 65–6, 114, 118, 123; *see also* Guangzhou
Guangxi 6, 97, 162–3
Guangzhou 58, 58, 123, 201; *see also* Asian Games
Gucun Xinsi (Tanimura Shinji) 204
guitar 98, 130, 141, 151
Guizhou 65, 97–8, 174, 180, 187
Guo Feng 159, 165
guzheng 199
Gypsy Kings 118

Hainan 182
Han Chinese: xii, 4, 5; as ethnically 'unmarked' 99, 113–4, 164, 175, 180, 206; folk arts 175; and mainstream culture 10; music, 113–16; and occidentalism 19; and patronizing attitude towards minorities 10, 94, 113, 206, 218; and Shaanxi/Shanxi 92, 114; and superior culture vis a vis foreigners 20; *see also* Confucianism
Han Hong 40, 94, 119, 158, 192
Han Shaogong 10
Hani nationality 97
Hao Di 193
Hao Ge (Uwechue Emmanuel) 187–8, 190–5, 207
Happy Boys 62, 96
Happy Camp 62
Happy Five Continents xiv
Happy in China 112; in Guangzhou 58; in Macau 112, 136–8; and mimicking of format 66; and mix of styles 57; and naming rights 58; *see also* National Day
Harbin 36, 66
'hardened' ideological messages x, 214; and foreigners xii; and Macau 134, 141; and Taiwan 146
Harmonious China 33, 90
harmonious city 58
Harmonious Society xi, 16, 39, 213, 218; and television regulations 71; and Hong Kong 132; and multiethnic China 89, 107; and 'river crab' 109; songs 39, 45, 178
Harmonious World xi, 16, 39, 218; *see also* Olympic Games
Harris, Rachel 4, 100–1

Heilongjiang 10
hijabs (veil/headscarf) 102–5, 118, 150, 179
hip hop 165
Hong Kong xii; music 34, 125; and celebration of return to China 40, 123–33; and fear of return 154; and TV shows 57, 60; and joint ventures with the mainland 13; and 'one country, two systems' 123, 131–2; and reconfiguration of products for mainland audiences 13; and repackaging of mainland performers 165; and re-sinification of 124; *see also* Cheng Long (Jacky Chan), Liu Dehua (Andy Lau), MTV, Wang Mingquan (Liza Wang), Xie Tingfeng (Nicholas Tse), Zhang Mingmin
hosts (television): on CCTV 88–9, 100, 105, 136–7, 139, 166, 188; and conversations with guests 131; and the drawing of lines between ethnicities 174–5; as Party members 89; political role of 89, 129, 136, 157–8, 164
Hou Dejian 34–5, 149, 166
Houston, Whitney 112–3
Hu Jintao xi, 9, 34, 39, 92, 109, 140, 178, 218
Huang Zhilie (Hwang Chi Yeul) 201–2, 209
Huayin Laoqiang 115, 119
Hui nationality 150–1, 195
hulusi (gourd pipe) 98
human rights 17–18, 35, 218
Hunan: television 46, 60, 62, 127, 197, 209; *see also I am a Singer*, *Super Girl*
Hu-Wen era 16, 34, 40, 92
hybridity *see* blends of Chinese and Western music/art, mixed identities

I am a Singer 62, 104, 115, 119, 152, 187, 197, 200–2, 218
I Love You China (song) 41; *see also* Liang Bo, Ping An, Wang Feng
I Want to Enter the Spring Festival Gala 59, 68–9
ideology: and CCTV 57; and directors 19; and entertainment 26; and news 26
Imagined Communities 1
Inglis, Iain 183, 214
Inner Mongolia 6, 128–9, 164; *see also* Mongolia, Ordos, Teng Ge'er
intangible cultural heritage xii, 92, 102, 115, 119, 150–1

Index   247

internal orientalism 10, 181
international *see* global
The Internationale 28, 30
the Internet x, 45, 61, 69, 110, 113; *see also* online content, YouTube
interviews: with television practitioners xii, 61, 63–4, 123, 207–8, 219
Islam *see* Muslims
Israel 59
Italian operas 38
ITAT 131
ITV Studios Global Entertainment 60–1

J-pop 67, 202, 209
Jackson, Michael 63, 141, 178
Jacky Chan *see* Cheng Long
Jaivin, Linda 34
Japan xii: and colonialism/imperialism 14, 27, 123–4, 126, 202, 204; and 'cultural odour' 203; and derogative terms 15; economic ties with 204; folk song 145; invasion of 5; relations with 28; and Taiwan 142; and tensions with 204; and trade in television shows 61; troubled history 202; *see also* Deng Lijun, J-pop, Jin Chengwu (Takeshi Kaneshiro), Qiao Shanzhong (Joe Yamanaka), The Same Song, Shaanxi, Sino-Japanese Wars, Toyota
jazz 108, 129
Ji Xiaojun 172
Jiaduobao herbal tea 63, 75
Jiang Kun 173
Jiang Qing 31, 46
Jiang Zemin: and the 'Three Represents' 37–8; and '45 World Famous Songs' 37
Jiangsu satellite television 60, 148
Jiangxi: and red Song competition 182; province 161; television 64, 65, 69, 112
Jie Gai 181, 186
Jike Junyi (Summer) 152
Jilin 111
Jin Chengwu (Takeshi Kaneshiro) 203
Jin Mei'er 112–3
Jin Tielin 36
joint ventures: between television producers from the PRC and Hong Kong and Taiwan 13
jokes 181–2, 184, 186, 207; *see also* audiences

K-pop 67, 196–202
karaoke 36

Kazakhstan 108
Kerman-Dili band 100–102
Keshet International 59
keyboard 98
Khachaturian 103
Korea (North/Democratic People's Republic of Korea) 180
Korea (South/Republic of) xii, 61, 111–13, 187, 201; and mixed-language conversations 198; *see also* Big Bang, Chaoxian nationality, Gangnam Style, K-pop, Psy, Rain, Shen Chenxun (Shin Seung-hun)
kouxian (mouth harp) 150–1
Korean wave *see* K-pop, Korea (South/Republic of)

Lambert, Adam 77, 188–9
langdu 181
Langgalamu (Vanatsaya Visekul) 161–2
Lao Bi *see* Bi Fujian
Laowai Style 200–1
Law on Regional National Autonomy 8
Le Le 180
Lee, Coco *see* Li Wen
Li Guangxi 32
Li Guyi ix, 36
Li Jianfu 35, 166
Li Lanqing 37, 38
Li Wen (Coco Lee) 40, 178, 188
Li Yugang 195
Liang Bo 64
Liang Lu 100, 105
Liang Yongbin 150–1, 197–8
lianghui (two meetings) 57
liberated zones 38, 73
Liberia *see* Hao Ge
Lin Junjie (JJ Lin) 58
Liu Dehua (Andy Liu) 40, 127, 178
Liu Huan 187, 190
London 61, 161, 176; *see also* Britain, Royal Albert Hall
Long March 54
Longliqi 58, 199
Lotte 197
Lou Jing 117
Love My China 37, 87, 105, 113
love: for China 16, 39, 43; as a political symbol 36; *see also* foreigners, Spring Festival Gala, Xi Jinping

Ma, Eric Kit-Wai 124
Macau, xii, 40, 55, 57, 133–44, 166
Madonna 101

Malaysia 11, 123, 161, 178, 186
Maley, Michael 209
Maliya (Maria/Mariatu Kargbo) 181, 184–6, 192–3, 208–9
Manchu nationality 27, 36
Mandarin Chinese *see* Chinese language
Mao Zedong: and class 5; and folk songs 29; and foreigners 182, 193; on friends and foes 15; and mass participation 28, 30; ridicule of 72–3; and self-determination for non-Han 6; songs about 30, 114, 183, 193; *see also* Bo Xilai, the East is Red, Mao Zedong Craze, Mao Zedong Thought, Nanniwan, Xi Jinping, Yan'an Talks
Mao Zedong Craze 36; and little red book 31
Mao Zedong Thought 31, 36, 50
March of the Volunteers 28
marriage *see* cross-cultural marriage
Mars, Bruno 141
Martin, Ricky 118
Marxism 36, 74
mass songs 27, 41
May Fourth Movement 27
Menba/Monpa nationality 188–9
merging of styles *see* blends of Chinese and Western music/art
Miao nationality 30, 96
Mid-Autumn Festival 56, 66, 144–6
Middle Kingdom Mentality 19; *see also* Cultural China
Midea 59
military 18, 35, 43, 57; *see also* Red Army
Ministry of Radio, Film and Television *see* SAPPRFT
Minnan culture 148
Minogue, Kylie 190
minority nationalities: xii, 4; categorization of 6–7, 8; discrimination of 94, 102; and ethnic colour 9, 11, 95, 148; foreigners' interest in 171, 174; and freedom of representation 9; and Han superiority 10, 94; history of 5, 9; and modernization 10; orthodox representations of xii, 88–90, 110, 112, 160, 214; and overseas Chinese 163; and persecution 8; and self-determination 6; and skin colour 9; stereotypes of 9–11, 94, 97, 100, 105, 181, 218; in Taiwan 148; *see also*
double exoticism, Han Chinese, multiethnic China, Olympic Games, *yuanshengtai*
MIPTV (Marché International des Programmes de Télévision) 60
Mittler, Barbara 31–2
mixed identities 7, 214–5; and foreigners 173; and overseas Chinese 154–7, 164–5
mixed race 20, 139–41, 151–3, 203, 215: *see also* A-rui (Ari Fabio Calangi), Fei Xiang (Kris Phillips), Jin Chengwu (Takeshi Kaneshiro), mixed identities, Qiao Shanzhong (Joe Yamanaka)
mixing of styles *see* blends of Chinese and Western music/art
mobile phones 58, 60, 70, 72, 98
modernization xii: and advanced culture 38, 46, 65, 97; and Chinese essence 178; and foreigners 19; of folk songs 29, 84–5, 116; and minority nationalities 112, 218; and overseas Chinese 164; and skyscrapers 90, 153; 179 and technology 53, 70; and television design 98; *see also* economic development, globalization, cross-cultural marriage, mobile phones, the West
Mongolia (Republic of): 100, 119; *see also* Inner Mongolia
Mongolian Cow Yoghurt 63
moral corruption 32, 99; *see also* spiritual pollution
Moscow 176; *see also* Russia
Moscow Nights 39, 195
motherland xii; and foreigners 18, 183; and hosts' discourse 136; and overseas Chinese 157–8, 163; songs in praise of 41, 126, 140, 158; *see also* Ode to the Motherland
Mozart 32
MTV 67, 196
multiethnic China: xi, xii, 10; frame 4; and Greater China interactions 150; history in China 5; and 'orthodox'/ 'hardened' styles of representation 84–91, 110, 112, 116, 214
music videos x; on CCTV 57, 61, 91, 101, 135, 153; and international events 40, 177, 179–80; on the internet 44, 61, 70, 96, 193, 200, 208; *see also* MTV, *Tudou*, *YouTube*, *YouKu*

Muslims 100, 179; *see also* hijabs, Hui nationality, Uyghur nationality, Xinjiang
My Chinese Heart (song) 41, 125–7, 158, 177

Na Ying 141, 145
Na'aisi Group 123
Nanniwan (song) 30, 45, 114
Nati (Nadi) 181
national anthem 28, 30, 41, 87, 110, 117, 124, 137, 166
National Day 56, 58, 66, 136, 144
National People's Congress *see* NPC
national style (music) 36–7, 44, 59, 85–91, 93, 158, 190, 214–5; compared with other styles 91, 95, 98–9, 117; *see also* blends of Chinese and Western music/art
nationalism: definition of 3; and colonialism 138; and creative blends 150, 165; and multiethnicity 116; and pan-Chinese identity 129, 133; and soft power 176, 205; symbols of 214; *see also* 'hardened' ideological messages
Nationalist Party 5, 29, 27, 38, 50, 54; *see also* Deng Lijun, Taiwan
Naxi nationality 7
New Culture Movement 27
New Tang Dynasty Television *see* NTDTV
New York 61, 176; *see also A Beijinger in New York*, USA
New Zealand 35
news 26, 45, 50, 53, 73–4
Nie'er 28
Nicholas Tse *see* Xie Tingfeng
Nigeria *see* Hao Ge
Ningxia 6, 150, 195
the Nolans 151
Northwest Wind 10, 99, 118
nostalgia 126, 152, 162, 196, 202–3, 213
NPC (National People's Congress) 6, 57, 89, 91
NTDTV (New Tang Dynasty Television) 35, 155
Nyíri, Pal 154–6, 167, 207

Occidentalism 19
Ode to the Motherland 30, 41–2, 84–6, 91, 140
Olympic Dream 34, 60; songs 40, 41, 41

Olympic Games (Beijing): and children 133–4; and foreigners 177–8, 196, 209; knowledge about 94; and minority nationalities 40; ongoing celebrations of ix, 136; and orthodox style 90–1; songs 99, 106, 130, 159; stadium 35; theme song 187; *see also* Song Zuying
One China policy 142–3
One China principle 40
one country, two systems policy 123, 130–3, 143
online content 58, 60–1, 97, 193; and mash-up culture 96; and political irony 74, 193, 217; *see also* CNTV, the Internet
operatic music 50; and advanced culture 97; Chinese opera 184, 201; Western opera (*meisheng changfa*) 36, 59, 93, 95; *see also* blends of Chinese and Western music/art
Ordos 127–30, 164
Oupai (Oppein) 58–9, 123
Opium Wars 14
orchestral music 4, 28–9, 44, 84, 213; *see also* national style
orientalism 19
Our Chinese Heart 57, 122
overseas Chinese xii, 5, 154–63, 171; entrepreneurs 158, 160; students 158, 166, 176

Pa'erhati (Perhat Khaliq) 106–7
Paralympics 40
Passionate Square 56, 66
patriotism: 43; and 'main melody' 55; patriotic spirit 54; and provincial satellite reality singing contests 64; songs 66, 158; *see also* Xi Jinping
Pavarotti, Luciano 38
pay TV 61
peaceful rise 39
peasants 27
Peng Liyuan 36–7, 44, 158
People's Daily 43
People's Liberation Army *see* PLA
Phillips, Kris *see* Fei Xiang
Philippines 141
Phoenix television 45
piano ix, 32, 134, 191
Ping An 44, 64
pipa (Chinese lute) 32, 139
PLA (People's Liberation Army): choir 89–90; performing arts troupes 43, 112; songs in praise of 31, 183

250   *Index*

Political Department of the Chinese People's Liberation Army Airforce 43
Pop Idol 56, 62
popular music (*liuxing changfa*) ix, 59, 93, 122, 213; and advanced culture 97, 152; and 'big' English songs 63, 112; and bilateral relations 197, 199, 204; and Greater Chinese 165, 215; and ideological messages 130, 146–7, 159, 165
Portugal 217; and Portuguese language 141; *see also* Macau
PRC mainland: as a global centre 164, 171
preservation: of traditions 3, 93; *see also yuanshengtai*
Procter and Gamble 59
propaganda x; and Hong Kong 124, 129; and market exploitation 36; and national identity 5; and Taiwan 151; and television in the reform era 51, 55, 65; and television in the socialist era 50; and use of arts/music 28–9, 45, 76; and *yaxshi* 108–9; *see also* indoctrination
Propaganda Department 52, 55, 87
Psy 199
public service advertisement 59
Putonghua (standard Chinese) *see* Chinese language

Qi Qin 145, 163
Qiao Shanzhong (Joe Yamanaka) 203
Qin Yuzi 162–3
Qing Dynasty 5, 27
Qinghai 114
qipao (cheongsam) 204
Qu Qiubai 28

R&B 149, 165, 190
radio ix–x, 33, 40, 53
Rain 178, 199, 209
rap music 45, 113, 129, 149, 162, 176, 185, 200
ratings 52, 165, 205
reality singing contests x, 53–4, 59, 64, 74, 189, 216; *see also* China Dream, Ping An, Xila (Shila Amzah)
red: as symbolic colour 42, 86–7, 107, 130, 136–7, 139, 214
Red Army 28, 54, 103, 183, 190–3
red flag 90, 127, 178; songs about 136, 140, 214
Red Guards 31

red songs 30–1; competition 182; and foreigners 182–3, 193; and karaoke 36; in reform era 35–6, 41–2, 114
Red Sun 36
Rees, Helen 175
reform and opening up *see* economic reforms
reggae 203
regulations 64, 70–5
revolutionary art and culture 66, 28, 38; in reform era 35–6, 94, 182–4, 190–3; *see also* red songs
Rising Star 59
River Elegy 19, 113
rock music: 106–7, 115, 149, 151, 162–3, 218; and reality singing contests 64; *see also* Ah Peng, spiritual pollution, Tan Weiwei, Wang Feng, Wham!
root-seeking movement 10
Royal Albert Hall 37, 118
Rowswell, Mark 17–18; *see also* Dashan
Rudd, Kevin 17
rural areas: and minority nationalities 97; and increased prosperity 51; and Han 114; and overseas Chinese 163
Russia/Russian xii; language 69, 194–6; music 28; songs 39, 196; tv drama 209; and 'The Year of Russia in China' 194; *see also* Vitas

Sa Beining 88, 188
Sa Dingding 118
Said, Edward 19
Samsung 199
sanxian 95–6, 115
SAPPRFT (State Administration of Press, Publication, Radio, Film and Television) xi, 52–3, 67, 70–5
SARFT *see* SAPPRFT
satellite television: history of 51; and transnational flow of Chinese culture 13
saxophone 32
Schein, Louisa 10, 181
scientific development 130, 160
Shaanxi 10, 30, 92, 114–5, 119, 182; *see also* Han Chinese, *Huayin laoqiang*, Nanniwan, Northwest Wind, red songs, *yuanshengtai*
Shanghai Expo 17, 178–9, 196, 204
Shanghai television 66, 123, 178, 183, 188, 194, 202–3, 205, 209; *see also* AKB48, Dragon TV, Fei Xiang (Kris Phillips), S.H.E., Wang Mingquan (Liza Wang)

Shanxi 65, 92, 114; *see also* Yellow River
S.H.E. 176, 208
Shen Chenxun (Shin Seung-hun) 199
Shi Guangnan 33
Sichuan: earthquake 34, 115, 118, 159, 185, 196, 209; television 65
Sierra Leone *see* Maliya
Sing! China see The Voice of China
Sing For China 187
Sing My Song 60, 123, 161, 186
Singapore 11, 161; *see also* Cai Jianya (Tanya Chua), Sun Yanzi (Stephanie Sun)
singing: by children 134–5; in harmony 161, 213, 217; off-key 135–6, 158; in unison 134–5, 140, 144, 172, 177, 182, 213; *see also* choral music
Sino-Japanese wars 15, 27, 29, 114, 117, 142
Sinophilliac 171–7, 186, 205
social media 45, 69, 185
social stability 57, 86, 88, 91, 104
socialist core values 57
socialist market economy *see* market economy
soft entertainment x, xii, 26
soft power 20, 123, 176, 202
song and dance troupes 8, 29, 32, 43, 77, 86, 112, 115, 138, 194, 219
Song Zuying 36–7, 87–8, 117–8, 158, 187
songs: and politics 36; *see also* mass songs, orchestral music, red songs, revolutionary songs
Soviet Union: and *agitprop* 27, 29; and establishment of Chinese television stations 50; *see also* Khachaturian
Spanish: songs 39; language television 69
Specials 56–7, 89, 116, 136, 139, 150
spiritual pollution campaigns 8, 34, 75
sponsorship: and audiences 117, 165; by Chinese companies 41, 58–9, 63, 75, 123, 128, 131, 187; on city and county television 66; by foreign companies 123, 197, 199; and naming rights 58; by state propaganda departments 44, 85; *see also* CCTV
Spring Festival Gala 55–6, 87–8, 108, 110, 112, 118, 122; internal event 33, 75; performances 17, 44, 102, 114, 125–7, 131, 133–5, 147–9, 151–3, 158, 187, 192; *see also* Hong Kong, *I Want to Enter the Spring Festival Gala*, Macau, Taiwan, Zhang Mingmin

Stalin, Joseph 6
Star Avenue 44, 69, 112–4; and foreigners 181, 187, 190–3, 207, 209; and Han Chinese 114; and mixed styles 57, 59; host 72; and minority nationalities 96; and overseas Chinese 163
Star China (*Canxing*) 60–1
State Administration of Press, Publication, Radio, Film and Television *see* SAPPRFT
State Administration of Radio, Film and Television *see* SAPPRFT
Su Jianxin (Shin) 200
Sun Nan 40, 136, 178, 179, 199
Sun Yanzi (Stephanie Sun) 186
Suning electronics 41
suona (Chinese shawm) 98, 115
Super Girl 56, 62–4, 71–2, 75, 115
Sydney 37, 61

Taiwan xii, 144–9; and cultural trade/exchange 60, 142–3; and decadent music 34; history of 166; independence 142–3, 148, 166; and joint ventures 13; and minority nationalities 148; pop stars 123, 149–53; and travel to mainland 34; and unification with mainland xii, 31, 142–3, 146, 152; *see also* Cultural China, Fei Xiang (Kris Phillips), Hou Dejian, MTV, One China policy, One China principle, Our Chinese Heart, S.H.E., Wang Lihong (Wang Leehom), Zhou Jielun (Jay Chou)
Tajik nationality 107, 190
Tan Weiwei (Sitar Tan) 115, 119
Tang Can 36, 195
technology 53, 50
television: access to 51–2; dramas 53, 54; foreign owned Chinese language channels 66; and history of in China 50–2; as an ideological weapon 50; and leisure time 51; and link to national identity 2; number of channels 66; and overseas Chinese 160; political supervision of 52, 54; tiers of 51, 66
Teng Ge'er 187, 190
Thailand 123, 141, 161–2
Thatcher, Margaret 125
The Same Song: enters England 157, 159; enters Japan 157–9, 203–5; enters Ningxia 164, 194–5; enters Ordos

127–30, 164; *enters Taiwan* 144–7; *enters Vancouver* 21, 156; as a global touring show 61, 155, 161; and Greater China 123; in Guangzhou 123; in Hong Kong 131–3; and international sponsors 59; in Korea 197–8; and mixed styles 57; and overseas Chinese 155–61, 176; in Sydney 61; and *Tomorrow Will Be Even Better* concert 166

the Three Tenors 38

Tian Han 28

Tiananmen Square: and interethnic unrest 100; performances in 130; protests/crackdown 3, 19, 34–5, 154

Tibet/Tibetans 6; and Han singers 115, 118–9; and independence movement 75; as part of China 65; persecution of 8; and resistance to Han rule 7; as source of Chinese culture 10; and television programmes 65, 69, 92, 94, 98; *see also* Menba/Monpa nationality

Tibetan Plateau 130

Tibetan Wind 99

tourism: and leisure time 51; and minority nationalities 8–9, 101, 186; and Western Europe 155; *see also yuanshengtai*

Toyota 123

trade of television programs *see* CCTV Guide, ITV Studios Global Entertainment, global formats, Keshet International MIPTV (Marché International des Programmes de Télévision), pay TV, Star China (*Canxing*), Universal Music Group

transnational marriage *see* cross-cultural marriage

trumpets 126, 153, 191

Tse, Nicolas *see* Xie Tingfeng

Tu nationality 7, 96

Tu Weiming 11, 122

Tudou 69, 96

TVB 69, 131

Twelve Muqam 101, 108

UNESCO 92

United Kingdom (UK) *see* Britain

Universal Music Group 60

urban culture xii, 10, 51

USA xii, 11, 123, 178; and American hosts 172–4; and American songs 38–9, 67; and colonialism 14; exports to 58; and joint ventures 63; and television programmes 52, 62; tours of 87; and overseas Chinese xi, 149–54, 161–3; and support for Taiwan 50, 142; *see also* African Americans, Aihua (Charlotte MacInnis), Anderson, Elise, Appell, Jesse, Beyoncé, cross-cultural marriage, Fei Xiang (Kris Phillips), Houston, Whitney, Jackson, Michael, Lambert, Adam, Li Wen (Coco Li), Lou Jing, Madonna, Maley, Michael, Mars, Bruno, Qiao Shanzhong (Joe Yamanaka), Qin Yuzi, Wang Lihong (Wang Leehom)

Uyghur nationality: as Chinese xi; independence movement 100; and interethnic unrest 100, 118; and language 69, 105, 108, 206; and long beards 104; music 108–9; musicians 100–2, 107; performances 62, 98, 108, 110, 118; persecution of 8; and relationship to Han Chinese 99; and resistance to Han rule 7, 107; stereotypes of 100, 105; *see also Folk Songs China* hijabs, Pa'erhati, Twelve Muqam, *The Voice of the Silk Road*, *Spring Festival Gala*, Xinjiang

van Leeuwen, Theo 4, 134

Vancouver 167; *see also The Same Song*

veil (Islamic) *see* hijabs, Uyghur nationality

Vienna Golden Hall 37

Vietnam 60

Vitas 118, 178, 194–6, 207, 209

The Voice of China xii, 44, 60, 62–4, 68–9, 75; and 'big' English songs 63; and Chinese songs 63; and Macau 141; and minority nationalities 106, 152, 166; and overseas Chinese 123, 161–3, 207

The Voice of the Silk Road 62, 108, 206

voting 33, 60, 67–8

Wang Fei (Faye Wong) 125

Wang Feng 64, 106, 141

Wang Lihong (Wang Leehom) 149–51, 165–6, 195

Wang Luobin 103, 107, 118

Wang Mingquan (Liza Wang) 131, 165–6

Wang Xiaoya 88

Wang Yige 176
Wang Zhou 106
War of Resistance Against Japan *see* Sino-Japanese wars
Wei Wei 194
Wen Jiabao 34, 39, 42, 92, 178; *see also* Hu-Wen era
Wenbiquan (Wetherm) 187
the West: catching up with 59; flows to and from 200; glamour and idealization of 19, 151; interaction with 171; taking the best from/learning from 27, 32, 217; Sinification of 156
Western influences 14, 34, 46, 125
Wham! 34
white monkey 18; *see also* foreign monkey
Why Are the Flowers So Red? (song) 107, 118
world music 118, 163; *see also* blends of Chinese and Western music/art
World Trade Organization (WTO) 53, 60
world *see* global

X Factor 61–2
Xi Jinping xi, 9, 32, 43–5; *see also* China Dream
Xia Jianlong (Dino Acconci) 139–40, 166
Xia Li'ao (Julio Acconci) 139–40, 166
xiangsheng (cross-talk) 17, 201
Xie Tingfeng (Nicolas Tse) 95, 127–30, 150, 195
Xila (Shilah Amzah) 104, 187
Xinjiang: music and songs 6, 30, 33, 100–3, 190–3; television 105, 108, 206; *see also* Northwest Wind Uyghur nationality, The Voice of the Silk Road
Xu Peidong 93

Yan Weiwen 36, 37
Yan'an 29–30, 114
Yan'an Forum 114
Yan'an Talks 29
Yanbian 111–12, 119, 180
Yang Jima 188–9
Yang Kun 161, 163

Yang Lan 178
yangge 29, 182–3
Yangtze River 125, 131
yaxshi 108–9
Yellow River 28–9, 92, 149–50
Yellow River Cantata 28–9
Yellow People 95, 127–30
Yellow Mountain 125
yellow: music 165; as a racial term 3, 165, 193
Yi nationality ix, 152, 174
YouKu 69, 130, 196
youth: appeal towards xii, 60, 63, 85, 98, 102, 164–5, 196, 199, 218; corruption of 34, 75; culture 2, 33, 98, 101, 107, 111, 201; dreams of 123; education of 32; songs about 36; spirit of 89, 91, 136, 139
Youth Singing Competition 58–9, 92–7, 100, 112, 117, 119
YouTube 56, 69, 110, 123, 130, 193, 196, 200–1
Yu Chengqing (Harlem Yu) 141
Yu Qiuyu 93–4
Yu Quan 40
Yu Runze 45
Yuanshengtai xii, 59, 91–8, 150, 175, 189, 215, 218; definition 84–5, 91–2; and ethnic pluralism 116
yueqin (moon zither) 32
Yunnan 6, 97–8, 118, 208

Zhang Jingying (Jane Zhang) 152
Zhang Lei 136–7
Zhang Mingmin 125–7, 158, 177
Zhang Ye 36, 158
Zhang Yimou 10, 41
Zhao Baole ix
Zhejiang Satellite Television 62, 108, 141, 161
Zhongguo tong (China expert) 16–17, 205–6
Zhou Enlai 29–30, 33
Zhou Jielun (Jay Chou) 165
Zhu Zheqin (Dadawa) 99, 118
Zhu, Ying 54, 58
Zhuang nationality 162–3
Zu Hai 36, 39–40

Taylor & Francis eBooks

Helping you to choose the right eBooks for your Library

Add Routledge titles to your library's digital collection today. Taylor and Francis ebooks contains over 50,000 titles in the Humanities, Social Sciences, Behavioural Sciences, Built Environment and Law.

Choose from a range of subject packages or create your own!

Benefits for you

- Free MARC records
- COUNTER-compliant usage statistics
- Flexible purchase and pricing options
- All titles DRM-free.

Benefits for your user

- Off-site, anytime access via Athens or referring URL
- Print or copy pages or chapters
- Full content search
- Bookmark, highlight and annotate text
- Access to thousands of pages of quality research at the click of a button.

REQUEST YOUR FREE INSTITUTIONAL TRIAL TODAY

Free Trials Available
We offer free trials to qualifying academic, corporate and government customers.

eCollections – Choose from over 30 subject eCollections, including:

Archaeology	Language Learning
Architecture	Law
Asian Studies	Literature
Business & Management	Media & Communication
Classical Studies	Middle East Studies
Construction	Music
Creative & Media Arts	Philosophy
Criminology & Criminal Justice	Planning
Economics	Politics
Education	Psychology & Mental Health
Energy	Religion
Engineering	Security
English Language & Linguistics	Social Work
Environment & Sustainability	Sociology
Geography	Sport
Health Studies	Theatre & Performance
History	Tourism, Hospitality & Events

For more information, pricing enquiries or to order a free trial, please contact your local sales team:
www.tandfebooks.com/page/sales

Routledge — Taylor & Francis Group | The home of Routledge books

www.tandfebooks.com